W9-AQC-992

CONTENTS

Chapter 2

APPLYING PUBLIC INFORMATION AND PERSUASIVE COMMUNICATION THEORIES

STRATEGIC COMMUNICATIONS

FOR PR, SOCIAL MEDIA AND MARKETING

8TH EDITION

LAURIE J. WILSON, APR, FELLOW PRSA
Brigham Young University

JOSEPH D. OGDEN
JDO Communications Strategists

CHRISTOPHER E. WILSON
Brigham Young University

Kendall Hunt
publishing company

Cover images used under license from Shutterstock, Inc.

Kendall Hunt
publishing company

www.kendallhunt.com
Send all inquiries to:
4050 Westmark Drive
Dubuque, IA 52004-1840

Chapter 5

SETTING GOALS AND OBJECTIVES   99

Chapter 10

CALENDARING AND BUDGETING

PREFACE

As the pace of change in communications and marketing continues to accelerate, new careers are popping up everywhere. The opportunities for work are vast and diverse. Some will continue to work with mainstream media while others will live in an entirely owned digital world. The segmentation of jobs is now as prevalent as the segmentation of publics.

The growth is all around us. We live in a hyperconnected world of communications channels with a multiplicity of voices. We used to measure social media users in the millions, now we count them in the billions. Social and digital media have changed the way we live. They have altered what we eat, how we shop, who we date, how we express ourselves, and where we go to stay informed.

Millennials, once the darlings of every marketing campaign, are now "old." They have been replaced by Gen Zs. And we are already observing the unique behaviors and character traits of Gen Alpha, the first group to be born entirely in the 21st century.

The metamorphosis of communications and marketing have presented opportunities for extreme segmentation of publics and of the channels to reach those publics. Sadly it has also led, in many cases, to the polarization of publics and the explosion of disinformation, sometimes called "fake news."

Luckily there is new hope. As you will read in Chapter 1 more and more people around the globe are looking to businesses as catalysts for social change and stability. That's where you come in. Every business, nonprofit and government entity needs solid communicators. And as diverse as the careers in our industry have become, one constant remains — the necessity of strategy!

The need for research-driven analysis, strategic planning and implementation has never been greater. Mastering these skills will be a lifelong pursuit, but one that will bring satisfaction, success and intrinsic validation. Being able to think strategically is more important than any other aspect of communication.

This book is dedicated to strategic communication for marketing and public relations professionals. The "matrix approach" was developed over 30 years ago as a tool to learn strategic thinking and strategic planning for communications. It continues to evolve with the times — keeping with current trends, practices and tools in the field. It has further evolved in this 8th edition of "Strategic Communications Planning" as we have fine tuned the planning sequence in the Strategic Communications Matrix:

- Key publics are selected before the big idea.
- Primary messages are designed as key publics are identified.
- Secondary messages are fleshed out in the implementation/tactics creation step through the use of the strategy briefs.

We have made several other noteworthy changes as well including:

- More concise descriptions of each step of the matrix.
- New and refreshed examples, figures and tables throughout the book.
- An entirely rewritten social and digital media chapter with the most current information available.
- A renewed and narrowed focus on strategic planning.
- New and updated Mini Cases.
- New and updated Tips from the Pros.
- Short Application Cases replacing chapter exercises — encouraging students to immediately apply matrix concepts learned in each chapter.
- Updated and expanded discussion of strategies and tactics
  - Adding more guidance on how to be strategic in channel and tactic selection;
  - Updating the interactivity and personalization grid; and
  - Including the PESO model as a strategic selection tool.
- A new appendix with a complete matrix case example.

Although much of the content for this edition is new, we believe we have kept the elements that have made it a go-to guide for strategic communications. The "matrix approach" continues to be refined, but remains the core of the text.

We're excited to share the 8th edition of "Strategic Communications Planning for PR, Social Media and Marketing." We recognize that we all share in the responsibility to train and grow new generations of professionals to shape our world.

Joseph Ogden
Los Angeles, California
March 2023

ACKNOWLEDGMENTS

I begin by acknowledging my personal mentors and colleagues whose support led me to develop the initial Strategic Program Planning Matrix and write a text based on that for use in our senior capstone campaigns class at Brigham Young University over 30 years ago. In the early 1990s, lacking an analytical tool for students to use in solving public relations problems within the RACE model, those early BYU PR faculty members provided invaluable insight and assistance into the development of a process that specifically outlined the type of research needed and how that research and its subsequent analysis should direct the planning and communications steps. Supplementing my early work to develop the matrix were Bruce Olsen, Ray Beckham, Brad Hainsworth, Larry Macfarlane, and JoAnn Valenti.

That senior campaigns class was unlike any other in the nation, and we needed a text to help the students with their research and campaign planning for a real client. It fell to me to write it. Because of our students' success with this planning process the book began to be picked up by other universities, and I was unexpectedly launched into revisions and new editions to keep the text current. Through the fast paced shifts and changes in our industry, "the matrix" as it has come to be known by students and practitioners across the country has endured as a cohesive and useful tool for planning and implementation of communications efforts. Now evolved to the Strategic Communications Matrix, the foundation of research and planning for effective implementation remains.

The addition of Joseph Ogden as a co-author in 2004 was a wise decision, as he brought currency not only to the content, but to the design of the text and its use of mini cases and tips from professionals. His extensive experience and ongoing work as a consultant to clients worldwide provide tremendous insight into the latest practices and trends in communications, especially in digital and social media. For the last edition, we added a third author, Dr. Chris Wilson, a rising young star in public relations and communication education who will help us maintain currency with his knowledge and grasp of continuing research on theory and practice. I gratefully acknowledge his hard work and diligence in every facet of this new edition.

Today, the matrix is used by more than 200 universities and colleges around the world to train budding professionals in the art and science of strategic communications. It provides a structure for effective communication that inherently teaches analytical skills that are too often missing from education today.

Additionally, we are grateful for the thousands of graduates, practitioners and professors across the country who have learned, applied and helped shape the matrix into its current form. We welcome your continued feedback as the matrix advances to remain relevant in a rapidly changing communications landscape.

We also would like to gratefully acknowledge the contributions of practitioners from across the globe whose advice, counsel and examples are found in every chapter.

We appreciate these professionals for taking the time and effort to share their experience and wisdom. We also acknowledge PRSA's collection of Silver Anvil winners from which we have drawn several cases and examples. And we thank our exceptional graphic designer, Jon Woidka, for his work keeping the design of the book current and appealing to today's students.

We recognize and appreciate the assistance of Angela Willenbring at Kendall Hunt who has patiently steered us through the process, responding to requests for material and permissions and shepherding the project to completion. And lastly, we acknowledge our unfailingly supportive families and friends whose patience has been endless.

As the Strategic Communications Matrix continues to evolve and moves into a new era of strategic communications, marketing, and digital and social media, I salute all who have had a hand in shaping the process and in spreading its use, from those who first had the vision to help create it years ago, to those who have contributed to keep it current.

Laurie J. Wilson
Sandy, Utah
March 2023

ABOUT THE AUTHORS

Laurie J. Wilson

An award-winning emeritus professor of communication at Brigham Young University, Laurie was recognized in 1990 as the Public Relations Student Society of America Outstanding Faculty Adviser and subsequently served four years as the national faculty adviser. In 2001, she was named the Outstanding Educator by PRSA and is a member of the PRSA College of Fellows. She received a Utah Golden Spike award as Professional of the Year in 2010. Laurie has also received the prestigious Karl G. Maeser Teaching Award and three Student Alumni Association Excellence in Teaching Awards from BYU.

After working in public relations and marketing for several years, Laurie earned her Ph.D. at American University in Washington, D.C. She joined the BYU faculty in 1989 where she served two terms as chair of the communication department and for several years directing the public relations program. She also served six years as the university's faculty director of internships. At the same time, Laurie co-chaired a national PRSA task force on internships, which created the first-ever standards for quality public relations internships. She has served as national chair for several education initiatives and task forces in PRSA, has served in the public relations division of the Association for Education in Journalism and Mass Communication, and has served on the diversity task force of the Association of Schools of Journalism and Mass Communication. She represented PRSA on the Joint Commission on Public Relations Education, chairing the undergraduate curriculum committee. She has served on site teams accrediting communications programs for the Accrediting Council for Education in Journalism and Mass Communication and led site visit teams certifying schools in public relations education for PRSA. She also served on the editorial boards of the "Journal of Public Relations Research" and the "Journal of Promotion Management."

Laurie's areas of expertise, research and publication include strategic communication and issue management, corporate social responsibility and building community partnerships. She consults in those areas and is also an educational consultant to communications programs. In addition to this book, Laurie has co-authored three other communications books. She was a member of the executive board of the local United Way for 20 years, and volunteered for several years at the Humanitarian Center for the Church of Jesus Christ of Latter-day Saints.

Joseph D. Ogden

Joseph is a skilled strategist known for driving innovation and results. He has 20+ years experience in message design, marketing, branding and management. He has been CEO of several enterprises, headed strategy for a Silicon Valley tech company and

been a professor of communications. He founded JDO Communications Strategists, a strategic marketing and communications consultancy, and has worked as an international consultant focused primarily in the hospitality sector.

As one of the country's leading experts in strategic communications, Joseph helped refine the matrix approach to communications and was director of the public relations program at Brigham Young University. He earned a bachelor's degree in communication from Brigham Young University with a minor in music and an MBA in marketing from the Marriott School of Business. He also completed a non-degree program in negotiations at Harvard and MIT.

Before joining the faculty in the school of communications, Joseph was assistant dean of the Marriott School of Business and executive director of the school's national advisory council. In 2010, he received the N. Eldon Tanner award, the school's highest administrative honor. In 2013, he was recognized with the Brigham Young Outstanding Service award.

Before coming to BYU, Joseph worked as corporate communications director for a nearly $1 billion-a-year personal care and nutrition products company. He was the company's spokesperson, directed public relations and marketing in Asia and managed investor communications for the publicly traded firm.

Joseph is a creative thinker who cares deeply about people and the environment. He also likes getting outside to cycle, ski, hike and appreciate amazing architecture.

Christopher E. Wilson

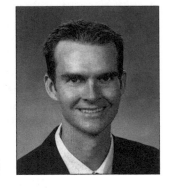

Currently an associate professor of communications and associate chair of undergraduate studies for the school of communications at Brigham Young University, Chris received his Ph.D. in mass communications from the University of Florida where he studied public relations and organization theory. His areas of expertise include public relations management and strategy, measurement and evaluation, and social media. His published research on these topics can be found in the "Journal of Public Relations Education," the "Journal of Communication Management," "Public Relations Review," the "International Journal of Strategic Communication," the "Research Journal of the Institute for Public Relations" and the "Public Relations Journal." He has won top paper awards for his research from the International Institute for Public Relations Research Conference (IPRRC) and the Association of Educators in Journalism and Mass Communication (AEJMC).

Chris worked as a public relations professional for 12 years before pursuing his Ph.D. His undergraduate internship turned into full-time employment in the public information office of West Valley City, Utah's second-largest city, where he helped design and implement communications efforts for city and state emergency operations centers for the 2002 Winter Olympics in Salt Lake City. Among other projects, he also aided the launch of a multimillion-dollar community cultural center. Chris then served as public relations and marketing manager for the BYU Museum of Art, the best-attended university art museum in North America. He directed the adoption of new technologies to enhance the in-gallery experience (cell phone audio tours, MP3 tours and iPad tours) and improve the museum's external communications (RSS feeds, podcasts, websites, ISSUU, Facebook and YouTube).

At BYU, Chris teaches undergraduate courses in public relations research, writing, strategy and campaigns, as well as a graduate seminar in public relations issues and strategy. His graduate students have placed in the communications school division of the annual Arthur W. Page Case Study in Corporate Communication competition. He has also advised BYU's award-winning Rulon L. Bradley Chapter of PRSSA.

When he isn't attending to his administrative duties in the school of communications, teaching in the classroom, mentoring students or working on research and publication, you will likely find him with his family backpacking in the mountains and canyons of Arizona, California, Colorado, Utah or Wyoming.

CHAPTER 1

THE RELATIONSHIP-BUILDING APPROACH TO COMMUNICATION

"Trust is the most basic element of social contact — the great intangible at the heart of truly long-term success."

—AL GOLIN
FOUNDER OF GOLINHARRIS INTERNATIONAL

LEARNING IMPERATIVES

- Understand that an organization's survival is dependent upon building and maintaining trust.

- Understand the characteristics of a relationship-building approach to communication.

- Identify current trends in communications and marketing.

- View the Strategic Communications Matrix as an effective tool for planning and implementing an organization's communications.

T ravis Scott, an American rapper, blew up in 2015 with the launch of his first solo album, "Rodeo," which peaked at No. 2 on Billboard's top albums chart and eventually went platinum.

Scott, known to be exceptionally bright, began bundling concert tickets and merchandise with the launch of his third album, "Astroworld." By fall 2021 Scott had partnerships with Nike, McDonald's, Anheuser-Busch, PlayStation and Dior. Scott's shoes became "quest-worthy must-haves" for sneakerheads. On StockX, a site for reselling luxury clothes, a pair of Travis Scott Nikes regularly sold for 400% above retail. A bright blue pair of Travis Scott X Air Jordan 4 Retros was listed for $10,000 while a purple pair carried a $22,500 price tag.

Travis Scott performing

2021 Astroworld music festival

Organized as an annual event by Travis Scott in 2018, the November 2021 Astroworld music festival sold out in less than an hour. Nearly 100,000 people were expected to attend the general admission festival held at the 350-acre NRG Park in Houston.

On Friday morning, Nov. 5, concertgoers began lining up. By early afternoon people were rushing past security checkpoints and into the venue. Before 4 p.m., at least 54 patients had been treated by medical staff.

The packed crowd began pushing to the stage during the countdown to Scott's performance. At about 9 p.m., minutes after Scott's set began, fans near the stage could be seen struggling to stay on their feet. At 9:25 p.m., Scott stopped the show to draw attention to someone in the crowd who needed help, saying, "Somebody passed out right here." He then continued his performance but stopped two more times in response to the chaos in the crowd, including once when an ambulance drove through.

San Antonio resident Fatima Munoz, 21, described a "domino effect" that took place: "I had fell right on the floor, and that's when everybody started tumbling down, and I tried so hard to get up," she said on ABC News' podcast "Start Here." "There's just too much people like on me, like those legit dog pile on me. I was on the floor. Nobody helped. I tried screaming for my life. I tried screaming for help."

At 9:38 p.m. Houston police officers and firefighters responded to reports of a mass casualty event at the festival, where people were being crushed against the stage and many had already collapsed. Four minutes later Scott stopped the show for a third time to draw attention to someone in the crowd who needed help. At 10:12 p.m., Scott finished the show and left the stage. Police officials later told the "Houston Chronicle" that the promoter, Live Nation, agreed to cut the show short, but Scott continued his set.

Memorial outside NRG Park in Houston

Some 300 people were treated by medical personnel on site and another 25 were transported to the hospital. Ten people ages nine to 27 years old died from their injuries.

Travis Scott's response

Scott reportedly first learned about the severity of the event at a private after party Friday night.

On Saturday, Nov. 6, The remainder of the festival was canceled and Travis released a statement on Instagram saying he was "absolutely devastated by what took place" the night before.

On Sunday, Nov. 7, Scott's girlfriend, Kylie Jenner, posted to her Instagram that Scott was not aware of any fatalities and would not have continued performing had he known. On Monday, Nov. 8, Scott announced he would provide full refunds for all attendees who bought tickets to Astroworld and that he would not perform at the Day N Vegas festival that weekend. He also announced that his Cactus Jack Foundation would team up with BetterHelp, an online therapy platform, to provide Astroworld attendees with one month of free one-on-one virtual therapy sessions.

Scott updated his Instagram and TikTok profiles with a number for the National Alliance on Mental Illness (NAMI) hotline, but it was the wrong number and people thought it was a scam. The BetterHelp website also said that its services are not suitable for minors or those in "an urgent crisis or an emergency situation."

The response to Scott's partnership with BetterHelp was swift, cynical and snarky. Writer Alex Press captured the general mood saying, "'Partnering' with an app typically entails a celebrity being paid to promote a company; is Scott making money off the collaboration? Either way, such a move is more befitting a podcast advertisement than a deadly tragedy — imagine promo code SICKOMODE, or maybe MASSCASUALTYINCIDENT."

On Wednesday, Nov. 9, Scott and his team released a new statement: "Over the last week, Travis Scott and his team have been actively exploring routes of connection with each and every family affected by the tragedy through the appropriate liaisons. He is distraught by the situation and desperately wishes to share his condolences and provide aid to them as soon as possible, but wants to remain respectful of each family's wishes on how they'd best like to be connected."

Scott's response to the deadly tragedy was slow and ill conceived. Instead of putting himself out there for fans, meeting with victims' families and showing sincere empathy, Scott himself remained quiet. It took him more than a month to publicly talk about the Astroworld tragedy in an interview. His partnership with BetterHelp was viewed with suspicion and ineptly executed.

Would fans and sponsors have responded differently if Scott had been more public with his feelings and efforts to help victims? This tragedy shows that trust isn't earned once, but something that must be constantly maintained. It doesn't matter how much you care or how competent you are if people can't see and feel it in your words and actions.

Corporate response

Immediately after the tragedy Nike delayed the release of Scott's Nike Air Max 1 collaboration and did not announce any new collaborations with Travis in 2022. In December, Anheuser-Busch announced that they had discontinued Travis Scott's CACTI Agave Spiked Seltzer. The seltzer debuted in March and was an instant success, completely selling out in the first week of sales.

Travis and Mcdonald's also parted ways. The "Travis Scott meal" was an instant success for the fast-food chain in 2020. It garnered Scott almost $20 million. The chances

Travis Scott X Nike Air Force 1 low Cactus Jack Men's shoe

TRUST

An emotional judgment of one's credibility and performance on issues of importance.

of it returning could now be gone forever. And the luxury fashion house Dior announced, "Out of respect for everyone affected by the tragic events at Astroworld, Dior has decided to postpone indefinitely the launch of products from the Cactus Jack collaboration."

How we respond really matters

People don't actually expect individuals or companies to be perfect. But how they respond to challenges is what sets them apart. The response and communication around problems can shore up or destroy the critical bond of **trust** between an organization and its publics.*

For example, when Hurricane Sandy hit New York City people expected to lose power. But Con Edison, the local provider of electricity, gas and steam actually saw its favorability ratings go up after the storm — despite the fact that Sandy caused more customer outages than any storm in the company's long history.

Con Edison was physically limited in how fast it could restore power, but not in how it could keep people informed. Prior to and immediately following Sandy, the company went into hyper communications mode — delivering real-time updates on the storm and projections of when power would be restored to different parts of the city. If you lived between 14th and 32nd streets, for example, you could expect your power to be restored sometime Tuesday between 5 p.m. and 10 p.m. If you lived between 33rd and 50th streets the power was expected to be restored on Wednesday between 6 a.m. and noon. Knowing what to expect and learning about the utility's extraordinary efforts to mobilize its own workers as well as engineers and maintenance teams from surrounding states gave people the feeling that Con Edison was doing all in its power to get the lights back on.

Con Edison's communications efforts throughout the crisis secured the trust of its publics. But some organizations — companies, governments and nongovernmental organizations (NGOs) — still don't get it.

Trust

As we began a new century, corporate America discovered through sad experience that trust was the primary issue of concern. In fact, it had always been the primary issue. Then, more than a decade into the new century, with aggressive relationship-building strategies, businesses seemed to be recovering somewhat. But it took the events of the early part of this century — 9/11 and its effect on the economy; the demise of Enron, Worldcom, Arthur Andersen and others; the security brokers' scandal; mismanagement by mutual fund managers and many other similar events — for all sectors of our economy to realize that trust among an organization's publics is the single most important factor in organizational survival.

*The term "public" is commonly used in PR to describe a specific group of people who share a common interest. While a "public" and an "audience" might appear to be interchangeable, the term "public" better represents a group of people who are engaged rather than passive observers (see Chapter 6).

Al Golin was a respected senior public relations professional and founder of GolinHarris, an international communications firm with more than 1,700 employees and 50+ offices worldwide. In 2004, he published a significant book, "Trust or Consequences," in which he wrote about his decades-long career as a counselor to CEOs of major corporations intimately involved in building relationships with their publics. He asserted that trust is the key element of strong relationships and the only way to ensure organizational success in the long run. Golin's results with CEOs were mixed. Many, like Ray Kroc of McDonald's, followed his advice, making regular deposits in the "trust bank" and reaping significant benefits over the long term. Others disregarded his counsel in favor of short-term gains, leaving them ill-prepared and at risk when crises hit. And as noted above, the crises did come.

Most trusted groups

In a crisis of trust, organizations looked to professional communicators for counsel on rebuilding relationships with the publics upon whom their survival depended. Leaders in all kinds of organizations began to recognize the need for an integrated approach to communication to build — or rebuild — relationships key to an organization's success. For the last 23 years, Edelman, one of the world's largest public relations firms, has conducted an annual global survey to track public trust in institutions, the Edelman Trust Barometer (see Figure 1.1).

For the first 19 years, NGOs were the most trusted institutions. By 2014, research showed that business held the trust advantage over government and was expected to lead the way in helping government establish and maintain an appropriate regulatory environment. By 2016, trust in all four institutions measured — business, government, NGOs and media — reached its highest level since the Great Recession of 2008. Trust in business had the largest jump in trust, putting it in a prime position to lead in cementing public trust in society's institutions. But by 2018, trust in the four institutions did not just erode, it imploded, particularly in the U.S., which garnered the lowest trust level among the 28 international markets measured. In the year 2020, at the height of the Coronavirus pandemic, governments were seen as the most trusted, but in the last three years, businesses re-emerged as the most trusted institutions.

DISINFORMATION
Information that is intentionally inaccurate or misleading.

ESG PERFORMANCE
How well an organization takes into account social and ecological responsibilities while doing business.

Now, on the heels of the global pandemic, there is a lack of faith in societal institutions triggered by economic anxiety, **disinformation**, mass-class divide and a failure of leadership. Societies across the globe are today deeply and dangerously polarized (Edelman, 2023). But there is hope.

"Business today is the only institution seen as both ethical and competent," says Richard Edelman, CEO of Edelman. "There's been a substantial rise in business ethics over the past three years." He explains the reasons:

- Businesses were seen as a motivating force in doing good during the pandemic.
- Businesses have focused more on **environmental, social and governance (ESG)** issues.
- Over 1,000 businesses left Russia following the invasion of Ukraine.

McDonald's in Minsk, Belarus

© 8th.creator/Shutterstock.com

Figure 1.1
Edelman Trust Barometer timeline

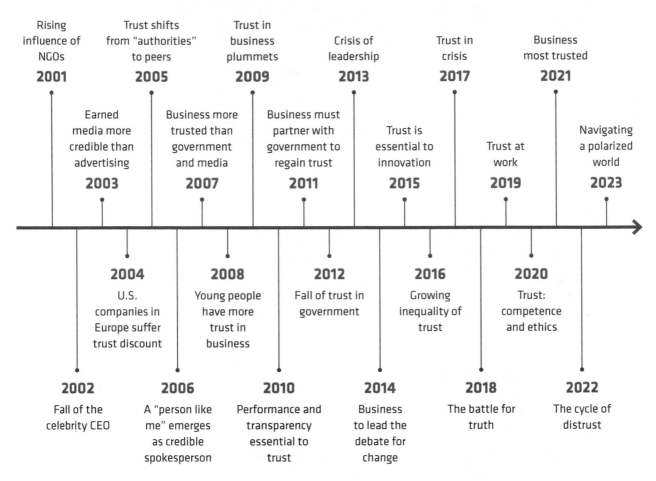

Source: 2001-2023 Edelman Trust Barometers

"The increased perception of business as ethical brings with it higher than ever expectations of CEOs to be a leading voice on societal issues," said Edelman. "By a six-to-one margin, on average, respondents want more societal involvement by business on issues such as climate change, economic inequality and workforce reskilling. But business must tread carefully, more than half (52%) of [people] do not believe business can avoid being politicized when it addresses contentious societal issues."

Nonetheless, societal engagement does put businesses at risk of being politicized. To take action and avoid being seen as politically motivated, Edelman recommends the following.

- Be a trustworthy source regarding an issue but don't take sides.
- Show that actions are based on generally agreed upon facts or well-established scientific evidence.

- Show that engagement on societal issues over time does not consistently align with one political party or another.
- Tie actions to a set of values that the business has consistently supported over time.
- Link actions to the needs of the business and their ability to stay competitive in the marketplace.

It might be time for businesses to figuratively "open the kimono" — show their publics the details behind scientific discoveries, clinical trials and specific efforts to make progress on ESG issues. The more aligned an organization's actions are with its stated values and the more transparent and consistent those actions are over time, the more trust and influence the organization will garner. Many also believe companies should use their influence to support politicians and media that build consensus and cooperation.

The current crisis of trust is not only fueled by deep polarization, but by fears of economic uncertainty and a looming recession. Figure 1.2 shows that people's personal economic worries are now on par with existential fears such as climate change and nuclear war.

 Figure 1.2
Personal anxieties on par with existential fears

Percent who worry about . . .

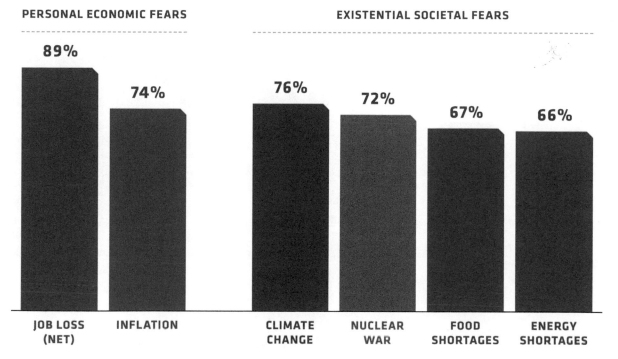

Source: 2023 Edelman Trust Barometer

Further, trust has moved from top down to peer-to-peer to local. One of the casualties coming out of the pandemic is people's lack of belief in information and sagging trust in experts (see Figure 1.3). Media is now among the least trusted institutions in the world, only governments are less trusted. More people put trust in a company newsletter than they do reports from the mainstream media. Similarly, people tend to trust the opinions of a colleague at work almost as much as scientific experts.

Perhaps resulting from the lack of travel and the limited flow of information during the pandemic, people have turned their trust from experts to the people closest to them. They trust people in their own countries more than other countries, people in their own communities more than those in their country and their neighbors more than those in their community. They also trust their coworkers more than their CEO and their CEO more than other CEOs. There is no telling how long this trend will last. But one thing we do know is that trust is something people and organizations must constantly build and maintain.

These data have huge implications for communicating with today's publics. Formal opinion leaders (experts) are still important, but localizing and familiarizing communications is essential. People trust those they are familiar with and closest to. They also expect businesses to lead. CEOs are expected to pay fair wages, ensure home communities are safe and thriving, pay their fair share of corporate taxes,

Figure 1.3
Institutional leaders distrusted

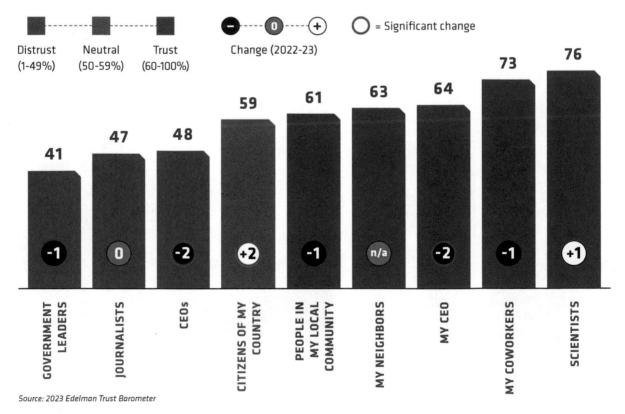

Source: 2023 Edelman Trust Barometer

retrain workers whose jobs are being eliminated, defend facts by exposing questionable science and pull advertising from platforms that spread **misinformation**. Governments should look for ways to collaborate with businesses to solve problems. And NGOs should take a page from businesses to increase their competency in providing solutions rather than just treating societal ills (Edelman 2023).

Consistency and honesty are key elements in reversing the recent declines in trust globally. We know people often need to hear things multiple times before accepting and believing. But the latest research makes it clear that the messages need to be factual and come from sources people trust to be credible.

Trust becomes actionable when it is built on a foundation of honesty and openness. It must permeate the entire organization from the top executives to front-line support and service employees. Increasingly, it is becoming the responsibility of companies and communicators to ensure trust goes beyond the organization to the communities strategic to the organization's survival.

MISINFORMATION
Information that is unintentionally inaccurate or misleading.

An integrated approach

Public relations scholars have been researching and advocating the benefits of **relationship building** for years. The recent findings on trust only underscore the power of this approach. People are clearly more trusting of those they have formed relationships with whether they be personal or professional.

Rather than being fragmented by key publics as organizational functions have been in the past, we recommend an integrated approach to reach all publics and stakeholders in order for the organization to thrive. Long-term success depends on building and maintaining trust across all stakeholders. The importance and role of trust-based relationship building are rooted in **public relations** research and practice.

When public relations emerged from the journalism profession as press representation for corporations in the early 1900s, the public relations counselor was positioned as a key adviser to the CEO. Over time, that status was lost to attorneys and accountants because the PR profession was unable to demonstrate a concrete contribution to the bottom line. Even when business entered an era of keen market competition for products and services where communication now plays a primary role in sales, relationship building was seen as unimportant.

More recently, however, management is recognizing the value of PR in helping articulate and coordinate the exchange of messages across the entire organization as well as with external publics. The need to manage issues and avoid crises has increased with the proliferation of social media channels. Likewise content creation has blossomed and must be managed so that it furthers the goals of the organizations. Finally, whether in person or through artificial intelligence (AI), customers expect ever increasing interaction with companies and organizations. This all requires clear messaging. Public relations practitioners are perfectly positioned to lead these efforts because of their hyper focus on strategic communication. Luckily there are also many tools available today to measure the impact of communication on organizations.

RELATIONSHIP BUILDING
A return to the roots of human communication and persuasion that focuses on personal trust and mutual cooperation.

PUBLIC RELATIONS
Strategically managing communication to build relationships and influence behavior.

© fizkes/Shutterstock.com

Figure 1.4
Integrated marketing communication

PESO model key:
PAID EARNED SHARED OWNED

CONTENT MARKETING

- Websites/SEO
- Emails and SMS
- Blogs and podcasts
- Infographics
- Videos
- Consumer tools

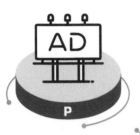

ADVERTISING

- Print
- Broadcast
- Outdoor
- Direct mail

COMMUNITY OUTREACH

- Expertise
- Service
- Sponsorships

INTEGRATED MARKETING COMMUNICATION

- Relationship building
- Strategy
- Message design

PAID DIGITAL

- Search
- Promoted social media
- Display ads
- Influencer marketing

SHARED DIGITAL

- Organic social media
- Shared webinars
- Corporate partnerships

PUBLIC AFFAIRS

- Government regulations
- Sharing expertise
- Lobbying

MEDIA RELATIONS

- Executive interviews
- Product/company news
- Financial results
- Crisis communications

Marketing guru Philip Kotler describes an **integrated marketing communication** approach as, "the concept under which a company carefully integrates and coordinates its many communications channels to deliver a clear, consistent message about the organization and its products."

It is not surprising that those who most carefully and thoughtfully articulate an organization's strategy and messages have great influence over the organization's future and success. Public relations, corporate communications and marketing leaders are well situated to help organizations take an integrated approach. In the end, your title — whether it be marketing or communications — doesn't really matter. What matters is your ability to strategically manage communication across the organization. Figure 1.4 shows the key areas and functions of an integrated marketing communication approach. Consistency and customization of messages to key publics across this array of functional areas is paramount.

Rather than being fragmented and siloed as organizational functions, we recommend a continued push toward a fully integrated approach to marketing communication. This is the only way to strategically build relationships and communicate effectively with publics and stakeholders. The bottom-line impact of this approach can be easily demonstrated.

INTEGRATED MARKETING COMMUNICATION
The process of unifying communication across channels and publics to achieve an organization's goals.

What does it mean to be "strategic?"

In this chapter, we introduce the strategic communications process that drives the tactical decisions made by communications professionals. But first, we must understand what it means to be a **strategic function**.

Very simply, strategy is a well-coordinated approach to reaching an overall goal. In military strategy, the overall goal may be to capture a town. The strategy is the coordinated effort of all units to achieve that goal. Each unit has its specific function to that end. When an organization sets a particular goal in support of its mission, strategy serves to integrate the efforts of all departments to achieve the goal.

Communication is strategic when it aids in formulating the organization's approach to accomplishing overall goals and then supports those efforts in a coordinated and consistent manner, working in concert with all other entities.

Effective strategies require research. They also require a long-range vision and a broad perspective of the organization and its environment. Thinking and acting strategically demand an incisive understanding of an organization's mission and goals. It also requires the ability to clearly articulate the objectives or milestones that must be met in order to achieve those goals. All of our efforts must be **research-based**.

Finally, to be a strategic function means that we must understand how our communications and marketing efforts fit within the greater organization, how they intersect with other functions, and how they contribute to the stated mission. Strategic managers are analytical, pragmatic, visionary and perspicacious.

STRATEGIC FUNCTION
One that contributes significantly to the accomplishment of an organization's mission and goals.

RESEARCH-BASED
When decision-making is rooted in the acquisition, interpretation and application of relevant facts.

The development of communications and PR in business

Business organizations began giving serious attention to communication with publics in the early 1900s. Journalists began serving as press agents and publicists for major corporations such as Ford Motors and AT&T. By midcentury, public relations practitioners were organizational counselors. They responded to traditional American business management practices by manipulating the organization's environment, oftentimes in ways that might now be considered ethically questionable.

By the 1960s, conflicts over issues important to key organizational publics gave birth to **crisis management** as a key function of communicators. Rather than just reacting to crises, good managers began to anticipate problems and mediate them before they could affect the organization's environment and profitability, and issue management was born as a long-term approach to identifying and resolving issues.

The very concept of **issue management** fit well into traditional American business management techniques, based almost entirely on economic principles. Nevertheless, there was obvious conflict between the long-term nature of issue management and the short-term profit orientation of American businesses. Further, there was a more critical conflict between the self-interested rather than public-interested approach of American businesses and the publics who were beginning to demand accountability.

In spite of the conflict, issue management techniques became popular in business communications practice and gave birth to the role of communication in **strategic management**. This meant evaluating all proposed action through a focus on organizational goals, usually defined in short-term contributions to the bottom line. Even though issues must be identified far in advance to be effectively mediated, the purpose is to save the organization future difficulty, not to address the needs of organizational publics because they are intrinsically valued. This focus brought communicators squarely into the camp of purely economically-based, rationalist business management.

It is not surprising that organizational communication ended up here. Throughout its history, public relations and business communications have consistently moved away from a "relations" orientation. Even with all our technological advances, we have been slow to recognize the limitations of mass communication and mass media.

The dynamic emergence of social media, however, has forever altered the landscape as users customize all sources of information and selectively choose their engagement. The latest research on social media usage should convince practitioners of the need to carefully understand and strategically target publics. More than 4.5 billion people are on social media. The average user accesses 6.6 social media platforms on a monthly basis. Facebook says nearly two-thirds of its active monthly users log in to the platform daily.

Social media, along with the explosion of new sources of information such as podcasts, forums and blogs has brought scholars and practitioners back to the roots of human communication and persuasion. These roots emphasize the need to

✂ CRISIS MANAGEMENT
The process of anticipating and preparing to mediate problems that could affect an organization's environment and success.

ISSUE MANAGEMENT
A long-term approach to identifying and resolving issues before they become problems or crises.

STRATEGIC MANAGEMENT
The process of evaluating all proposed actions by focusing on organizational goals, usually defined in short-term contributions to the bottom line.

communicate more directly and personally to build trust and cooperation. The great segmentation and personalization of information offers a more viable approach to reaching key publics and stakeholders than mass communication ever did.

Current trends

Most people are awake for about 15 hours a day. How much of that time do they spend digitally connected? The answer is about half. The time people spend online daily peaked at 6 hours 46 minutes in 2017. We saw a little jump up to 6 hours 56 minutes during the pandemic, but in 2022 that settled back to 6 hours and 43 minutes. At the very least, time spent on mobile, PC, laptops and tablets has plateaued. In some regions of the world time online daily has actually dropped by as much as 30 minutes in the past couple of years.

Knowing this helps us understand two things in our efforts to build relationships with our publics. First, we must compete aggressively for existing time/attention in the digital space. And second, there is increasing interest in non-digital interactions with key publics.

Let's take a look at seven trends affecting the way businesses and organizations communicate with publics and stakeholders: pay for play, consumer activism, community building, AI, livestreaming, secure communication and highly visual short-form content. Understanding this shift in behavior will help you better reach and engage with the individuals your organization cares most about and help you strengthen those relationships.

Pay for play

It has become virtually impossible to build an online presence for an organization or brand without paid media. The concept of "pay for play" in digital marketing began in 2012 when Facebook went public. Since then it has become increasingly important to support organic content with paid media — boosted posts, paid search and online display ads. Many organizations also pay for customer email services, SMS (text message) marketing and search engine optimization (SEO).

As social media and search platforms have matured the costs have gone up. A 2021 study that analyzed over $7 billion in ad spending by advertisers in 150 countries found that the average cost per click (CPC) for paid search ads increased by 34% in 2020. The same study also found the cost per thousand impressions (CPM) went up by 41% over the previous year.

As a result, many organizations are diverting funding to relationship building, community outreach, and owned content. Activities that seemed like expensive luxuries before now look like good bargains. According to a report by "Digiday," consumer brands such as Haus, Parachute and Recess are prioritizing public relations over paid media, having discovered returns of over 100x in earned media, far outstripping the expected return on advertising spend (ROAS) for similar budgets in paid advertising. These tactics are addressed in more detail in Chapter 9 and Chapter 14, including the ethical ramifications for public relations.

Consumer activism

Consumers care about the environment, their communities and how companies treat workers. In fact, 70% of consumers think a business should take a stance on a relevant social issue. A McKinsey poll found that 72% of employees felt their company's purpose should be more than profits.

ESG issues have taken center stage for both consumers and corporations. Many companies have adopted global ESG reporting practices as part of their public relations efforts. ESG is expected to continue to dominate communication efforts as companies, governments and nonprofits are required to reduce their impact on the planet and demonstrate how they are strengthening the social fabric. These kinds of efforts are essential to building strong relationships with publics.

Community building

Online communities are fast becoming one of the best ways for organizations and brands to drive customer engagement and loyalty, building strong relationships with and among key publics. Aside from a friend's personal recommendation, recommendations from an online brand community hold the most sway. More than half of those who follow a brand on social media say they are more loyal to that brand.

Creating a community around a brand increases trust in the brand. If consumers are receiving recommendations from other consumers instead of from the brand itself, they are much more likely to make a purchase. Many of those consumers are also eager for more brand interaction.

A "Harvard Business Review" study found that allowing a brand community to answer customer questions was 72% less expensive than employing customer representatives to do so. Nonprofits and governments could take a page from successful brands' playbooks to invest more heavily in online communities.

Artificial intelligence

AI and machine learning are becoming more and more important in streamlining communications with customers and helping professionals understand sentiment on myriad topics.

First, AI can automatically route calls and chat requests from customers eliminating the need for cumbersome phone trees. Using natural language processing, customers can just write or say what they're interested in. AI can integrate with customer records management systems to schedule appointments, provide updates on order status and accounts, and even process returns without the need to ever speak to a person. Notwithstanding, it is as important as ever to manage this communication. Professionals should take extra care in making this a positive experience where customers still feel like they've been heard. The use of AI in interactions with customers also makes it easier to document and analyze data — making it possible to identify patterns human agents would have never noticed.

Second, AI can be incredibly helpful in processing vast amounts of news and predicting trends. Data show that in the 16 years between 1979 and 1995, 18 million news stories were published by accredited sources. By 2009, 18 million news stories were published in a single year. And in 2021, 18 million news stories were published in a single month.

Using AI as a listening tool to process the ginormous amount of information out there and making sense of it is brilliant. The market for tools capable of social monitoring and sentiment analysis was valued at $1.6 billion in 2020 and is expected to grow to $4.3 billion by 2027. More broadly the market for PR tools like those provided by Cision and Meltwater is estimated to already be more than $10 billion in 2022 and more than $18 billion by 2027.

Organizations that don't take advantage of AI tools to gauge public interest and sentiment will only fall further behind.

MINI CASE

How cyberattacks destroy trust
Target

As Target customers made purchases on the busiest shopping day of the year — Black Friday 2013 — little did they know their credit/debit card information was being stolen. In what was one of the largest data breaches in U.S. history, Target later disclosed that more than 40 million customers' card details — names, card numbers, expiration dates and CVV verification codes — had been stolen by cyberattackers.

The hackers used point-of-sale malware to immediately transfer personal data as customers were checking out in more than 1,700 Target stores between Nov. 27 and Dec. 15. In addition to credit card information, hackers also obtained customers' names and phone numbers as well as home and email addresses.

The security breach was eventually traced to a criminal group in Eastern Europe. Fraudulent charges appeared on about three million credit and debit cards as a result of information stolen from Target. Target faced more than 90 lawsuits as well as an FTC investigation.

It took Target several weeks to acknowledge their system had been hacked despite several threat alerts from the company's own security software. More than two months after the original incident, Target officials revealed that an additional 70 million customers' personal information had also been compromised.

CORE PROBLEM AND OPPORTUNITY
The incident severely damaged Target's reputation and dissolved much of the trust they had built over the years, but a rapid appropriate response could actually enhance their publics' trust and loyalty.

TARGET'S STRATEGY
Target was alerted to the hack in late November, but rather than shut down the system they turned off the security software preferring manual review. As a result, Target continued to allow hackers to steal data for weeks while they investigated. Target finally acknowledged the data breach on Dec. 19, 2013. The company informed affected customers of the actions they were taking to address the issue, assured them that a full investigation was taking place and provided a comprehensive web page offering resources and daily updates related to the breach. Customers were also provided with updates and information through email, Facebook and Twitter. Copies of Target's official email communications were posted online so customers could validate the authenticity of the emails.

To encourage customer spending and foster goodwill, Target announced on Dec. 20 that they would be offering a 10% employee discount to all in-store shoppers on Dec. 21 and 22. They also provided a year's free credit monitoring for all affected customers.

© Tada Images/Shutterstock.com

A few months later, Target hired a new chief information officer, and began a search for a newly-created position, chief information security officer, and a new chief compliance officer. Target also announced they would spend upwards of $100 million to upgrade payment terminals to accept the more secure chip-and-PIN cards.

Nevertheless, Target didn't publicly disclose the breach for 20 days after it was discovered, waiting more than three weeks to issue their first news release about the incident. And it was several weeks more before Target acknowledged security alerts from their own software had been ignored. It took over two months for Target to reveal the full extent of the breach and the customers affected. Customers said Target had a "disheartening" response and many vowed to stop shopping there. The lack of transparency and failure to take responsibility was evident. Clearly, discounts and free credit monitoring for a year was insufficient to rebuild their publics' trust.

RESULTS
- Target's online and in-store shopping traffic hit a three-year low following the breach – only 33% of U.S. households shopped at Target in January 2014 compared to 43% in January 2013.
- Fourth-quarter 2013 profits fell 46% to $520 million from $960 million in 2012, a drop of $440 million. The breach itself cost the company an estimated $291 million.
- In 2017, Target officials said the company would pay $18.5 million in a multistate settlement, the largest data breach settlement at the time.
- Consumer perception scores dropped by more than 54%, and four years later still had not fully recovered.

Livestreaming

Although the first livestreamed video event was a baseball game between the Yankees and Mariners back in 1995, the practice began to gather momentum in 2016 with the introduction of Facebook Live. By 2018, one in every five videos on the platform was a live broadcast. Then we had a global pandemic. Consumption of livestreaming jumped 73% during the first month of shutdowns in the U.S.

The use of livestreaming now includes giant brands like Nike and Microsoft as well as local barber shops and beauty salons. Businesses use livestreaming for interviews, Q&A sessions, product launches and other outreach.

Birchbox, a company which sends subscribers a monthly box of makeup samples, recently did a Facebook Live tutorial video where a rep from Benefit Cosmetics put its new BADgal mascara on the eyelashes of Birchbox's host. The product demonstrated was also featured in that month's Birchbox sample box.

At the beginning of the video, the host and Benefit rep explain that the day before was National Lash Day and that they wanted to celebrate it by highlighting the product. Then the rep explains why the mascara and its unique brush gives eyelashes a more voluminous look. The tutorial begins with one eye getting mascara at a time so viewers can see the difference in volume. Viewers comment asking the host questions. The host also asks trivia questions and allows viewers to answer. She notes that those who engage the most will be entered to win a giveaway.

Birchbox is a great example of a livestream that a brand can do on a budget. The video had no editing, didn't feature any celebrities or influencers and did not appear to require a high production budget.

The current size of the livestreaming industry is around $59 billion, with projections suggesting it will exceed $228 billion by 2028. A significant portion of the growth is expected to come from businesses using livestreams for outreach and relationship building.

Secure communication

In a three-month period from November 2022 through January 2023 PayPal, Chick-fil-A, Twitter, Slack, Dropbox, Mailchimp, T-Mobile, Medibank, AirAsia and password manager LastPass all reported some level of data breach. In the case of T-Mobile, the data breach in late November 2022 cost $350 million in customer payouts alone.

The rise in cybercrime puts more onus than ever on businesses to secure their networks and protect confidential financial and personal information. The consequences of not doing so can be devastating. For example, 60% of small to midsize businesses affected by cyberattacks go out of business within six months.

There is a common misconception that nonprofit organizations are not a target for cybercrime. In truth, nonprofits make great targets for cybercriminals because they offer something of significant value: sensitive information on donors, volunteers and support staff. They are also often much less secure.

Internally, businesses need to secure their collaboration tools and intranet applications. This includes stepping up cybersecurity defenses and the competencies of team members. Externally, businesses need to demonstrate their cybersecurity measures to customers showing that all channels of communication with the business are encrypted and high-level security systems in place to protect customer data. Protecting private identifying and sensitive information is elementary to building trust-based relationships.

Highly visual short-form content

Another avenue of communication that cannot be ignored is high quality short-form content. This is especially true for infographics and short videos.

While traditional methods of customer information such as blogging and email marketing remain important, the trend is toward short and visually captivating content. The rapid growth of TikTok, Instagram Reels and YouTube shorts provide strong evidence of this explosive trend.

Research shows that brief, 60-second or less videos are ideal for capturing and holding audience attention. If you're creating YouTube shorts, be sure that your company name/brand and product appear in the first 15 seconds, the part of the video that automatically plays without users selecting the video. Short-form content is also more likely to be shared on users' profiles and across different platforms.

Branded memes and carefully designed infographics are also capturing significant attention. Neal Schaffer, founder of the digital marketing consultancy PDCA Social says, "Memes are about connection as much as they are about humor. They have the power to build online communities albeit for a short period. Consider the Bernie Sanders mittens meme that went viral. It allowed people to feel good, share a laugh and worked as a social glue in a politically turbulent time."

Most of us are visual learners. Using images and symbols, infographics tell stories visually, and enhance readability. How many times have you been confused about an idea or explanation, then seen an example and said to yourself, "Ah, I get it now." The mind processes images faster than words. As a result, infographics improve message retention and decision-making. They are also highly shareable and can establish your organization or company as industry experts.

Short-form video

Heart Association infographic used by permission

Building relationships with publics

As we have already seen in this chapter, establishing and maintaining trust is critical for any business or organization. With this as a cornerstone, we will briefly look at five characteristics of organizations that have proven successful in building relationships with publics.

The first characteristic is long-range vision. Rather than selecting key publics and issues by their immediate effect on the organization, companies identify all publics or stakeholders and work to establish relationships across a broad spectrum. Organizations use these relationships to identify issues that will be important in the next century, not just the next decade. They have a respect for people and work toward a consensus for action.

The second is a commitment to community, not just to profit. Companies involved in the community are often led by a CEO who is personally committed to charitable work. Commitment at this high level gives the organization's community involvement strength and integrity because it is based on a sincere desire to serve rather than to manipulate for the sake of profit alone. It is understood that what is good for or improves the community almost always benefits the company as well.

The third characteristic is a values orientation that emphasizes the importance of people. Progressive policies and initiatives based on trust of and respect for employees are usually evidence of a people-first orientation. Human dignity is highly valued, and policies and procedures are designed accordingly.

The fourth characteristic is a cooperative approach to problem-solving. Companies that effectively build trust are also those that value collaboration among employees and publics. They provide opportunities to work together to solve problems. Employees are given the latitude to design and implement solutions within their work areas, relying on management to provide an overall vision. Employees are not afraid to stretch themselves and to make mistakes. Management understands that mistakes are indicative of ongoing efforts to progressively solve problems.

Lastly, the fifth characteristic is that such organizations build relationships with all their publics based on mutual respect and mutual gains — not just one-sided manipulation. These relationships engender an environment in which community members seek solutions where all participants win. The community begins to look out for the best interests of the organization because it is in the community's best interest for the organization to thrive.

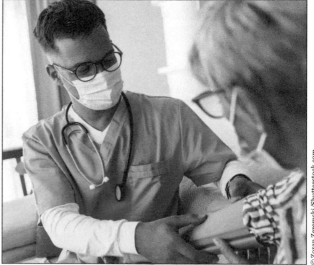

© Zoran Zeremski/Shutterstock.com

Relationships with an organization's publics are based on critical values that have little to do with profit motivation. The values of service, respect and concern for community are at the base of the relationships we establish with people.

This is evidenced in a 2022 Gallup poll, listing nurses as the most honest and ethical professionals

Figure 1.5
The most honest/ethical professions

The results of this poll show the percentage of respondents that considered people in these different fields to be honest and ethical.

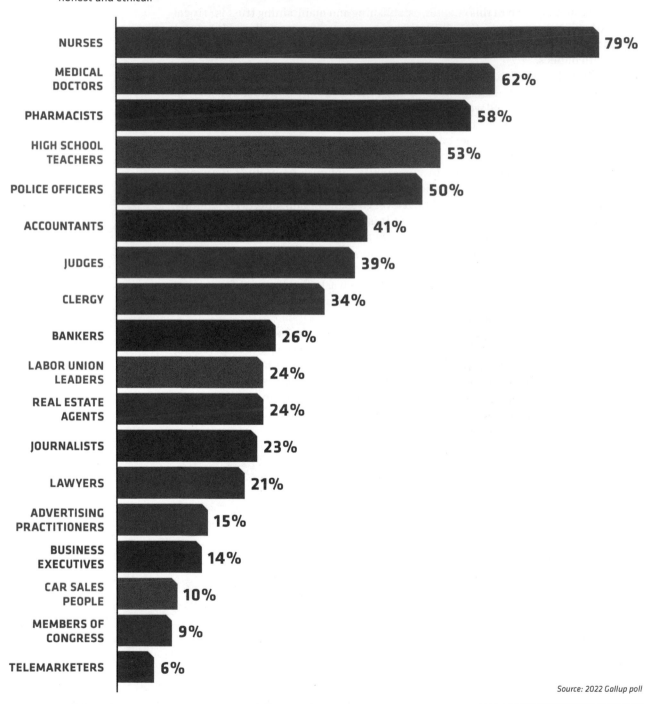

Profession	Percentage
NURSES	79%
MEDICAL DOCTORS	62%
PHARMACISTS	58%
HIGH SCHOOL TEACHERS	53%
POLICE OFFICERS	50%
ACCOUNTANTS	41%
JUDGES	39%
CLERGY	34%
BANKERS	26%
LABOR UNION LEADERS	24%
REAL ESTATE AGENTS	24%
JOURNALISTS	23%
LAWYERS	21%
ADVERTISING PRACTITIONERS	15%
BUSINESS EXECUTIVES	14%
CAR SALES PEOPLE	10%
MEMBERS OF CONGRESS	9%
TELEMARKETERS	6%

Source: 2022 Gallup poll

(see Figure 1.5). Whether we build a relationship with an individual or with an individual representing an organization does not change the fact that the strength of the association is determined by the salience of shared values that place a priority on people.

It is important to note that durable relationships are not created out of rationalist, bottom-line business management techniques. They are created and strengthened through mutual trust, respect, cooperation and benefit.

The Strategic Communications Matrix

Now that we have established a strategic role for communications in developing relationships, we are able to implement the planning and communication that will accomplish specific objectives and is targeted at publics important to the organization. If we have worked to identify and assess our strategic relationships, the selection of key publics for any particular communications or marketing effort will be simplified and much more accurate. We have less chance of omitting a critical public because we know more about all of our publics. Part of our research is already done. We are also better prepared to send messages because our relationships with organizational publics have been maintained and strengthened in our overall approach to marketing and communication.

A strategic, analytical approach to an organization's communication is absolutely requisite. Public relations has used the four-step RACE model — research, action planning, communication and evaluation — but making that process truly analytical is a challenge. To be analytical, each step must be determined by the information acquired and decisions made in previous steps. Incorporating feedback during implementation and making needed alterations to ensure success is even more difficult.

Effective practitioners are doing the kind of research and measurement that helps to make wise decisions. But doing so requires a framework for applying what we have learned through research.

It is not enough to discover the attitudes, values and beliefs of a segmented demographic public; we must interpret those in terms of the issue or problem at hand and predict future behavior. For example, determining that a public's self-interest on a certain issue is "the health and welfare of their children" is of no use unless we formulate messages that emphasize this. Identifying targeted channels to deliver these messages to a key public also does us no good if we then rely on mass media to reach them.

The Strategic Communications Matrix introduced in this chapter, was inspired in the early 1990s by the faculty at Brigham Young University in Provo, Utah. It is designed to direct problem solving analytically, using research to make decisions in each step of communication planning and implementation. This 8-step matrix is the tool we use throughout this book to support the **strategic communications planning** process and campaign implementation. The process begins with the identification of a problem or opportunity that sets the stage for background research and a situation analysis based on the research. It outlines additional research necessary for decision-making that will take place in the planning and implementation processes.

STRATEGIC COMMUNICATIONS PLANNING
An approach to communications planning that focuses actions on the accomplishment of organizational goals.

STRATEGIC COMMUNICATIONS MATRIX

RESEARCH

1. BACKGROUND   A synthesis of primary and secondary research on the industry, external environment, organization, product, service or issue. It includes a stakeholder analysis and segmentation study that identifies current trends in opinions, attitudes and behaviors. Resources such as staffing, facilities and intervening publics are also identified.

2. SITUATION ANALYSIS   Two paragraphs. The first is a statement of the current situation and a description of the challenge or opportunity based on research. The second identifies potential difficulties that could impede success.

3. CORE PROBLEM/ OPPORTUNITY   A one-sentence statement of the main difficulty or prospect, including likely consequences if not resolved or realized.

ACTION PLANNING

4. GOAL AND OBJECTIVES

Goal   A one-sentence statement of the overall result needed to solve the problem or seize the opportunity. It does not have to be quantified.

Objectives   Statements of specific results that lead to achieving the goal. Objectives must be specific, measurable, attainable, relevant, time-bound, written, cost-conscious, and efficient. Evaluation criteria and tools should be included in written objectives. Key publics should become obvious when drafting objectives.

5. KEY PUBLICS AND PRIMARY MESSAGES, BIG IDEA, STRATEGIES AND TACTICS

Key Publics   A description of each group that must be reached to achieve the goal and objectives. Identify:

- Objectives accomplished by each
- Demographics and psychographics
- Relationship with organization or issue
- Opinion leaders
- Self-interests
- Communication channels

Primary Messages   Short summary statements for each public. Similar to sound bites. They identify topical information tied to the action needed from that public and how it meets their self-interest(s). Create a small number of primary messages, typically 1-3 per public.

Big Idea   A creative strategy on which to build your entire campaign. The "big idea" appeals broadly across all key publics. Describe it in one sentence. Include three bullets, one each for strategy, visual representation and slogan/hashtag.

ACTION PLANNING

Strategies	What a public must do to fulfill an objective and the channel(s) to send messages to motivate that action. Strategies are public-specific and multiple strategies may be required for each public.
Tactics	The creative elements and tools used to deliver messages through specific channels. Several tactics are required to support each strategy. Examples are story placements, YouTube videos, Instagram reels, Facebook posts, special events, infographics, websites and podcasts.

6. CALENDAR AND BUDGET

Calendar	Organized by public and strategy showing when each tactic begins and ends. A Gantt chart is recommended. It helps show the work required as well as the flow of the campaign.
Budget	Organized by public and strategy estimating the cost of each tactic. The budget indicates where costs will be offset by donations or sponsorships. Subtotals are provided for each strategy and public.

COMMUNICATION

7. IMPLEMENTATION

Project Management	A list of tasks required to implement each tactic. Use the tactics in the calendar to track all activities required in the campaign. Use the budget to help manage actual costs against estimates.
Tactic Creation	Use strategy briefs to align tactics with strategies. Develop secondary messages to give credibility to the primary messages embedded in each tactic. Facts, testimonials, examples and stories provide the ethos, pathos and logos of persuasion.
Quality Control	Best practices that guide creators and editors in producing quality content. Check to ensure tactics support strategies and objectives.

EVALUATION

8. EVALUATION CRITERIA AND MEASUREMENT TOOLS

Evaluation Criteria	Specific and measurable results taken from each of the objectives. Focus on outputs, outtakes, outcomes and impacts.
Measurement Tools	The methodologies needed to gather the data for the evaluation criteria. These tools must be included in the objectives and in the calendar and budget.

The planning process then starts by setting a goal that directly resolves the identified challenge. This goal may or may not be a tangible, measurable outcome. You next move forward to determine objectives — specific and measurable outcomes — that will ensure the accomplishment of the goal. Specific key publics are next identified. These are important stakeholders we must reach during the campaign. The process naturally flows to the selection of primary messages for each key public. These messages appeal to each key public's self-interest. Next you will want to think creatively about a "big idea." This will be an overarching strategy or theme that will unite the effort among all publics. Once the theme is set, you can choose strategies and tactics for each key public that flow from the big idea. Calendaring, budgeting, implementation and evaluation are also addressed in a strategic way, using research as the foundation for decisions in each step.

The Strategic Communications Matrix enables professionals in marketing communication to address problems and issues of concern to organizations in a strategic way, in concert with their overall goals and objectives. It is enhanced by the understanding of how relationships are built between organizations and their publics.

Summary

Societies across the globe are dangerously and deeply polarized. There is a lack of faith in societal institutions that stems from the proliferation of disinformation, economic fears, a mass-class divide and a failure of leadership. Politicians are less trusted than ever and seen as incapable of bridging the current political divide.

Businesses, however, have seen a resurgence of trust. As a whole, they acted well during the pandemic and people are looking to them to be catalysts for change on societal issues, the environment and the economy. Another shift in trust is to people close to us: our work colleagues, neighbors and friends. The people most trusted today tend to be those we interact with most often.

Communications professionals are well positioned to lead marketing communication efforts by leveraging the relationship-building approach to communications. Adopting an integrated approach to communications, outreach and marketing is more important than ever.

A quick examination of trends tells us that pay for play is here to stay. There are also big opportunities with consumer activism, community building, AI, livestreaming, secure communication and highly visual short-form content.

Finally, we must remember that effective communication is always strategic. We must also understand what our publics and stakeholders want and expect from us so we can best deliver on those expectations. The Strategic Communications Matrix provides an excellent tool to approach all communications challenges and opportunities within the trust-based relationship framework of today's successful organizations.

References and additional readings

ABC News. (2021, November 18). Astroworld Festival timeline: How the tragedy unfolded. Retrieved from https://abcnews.go.com/Entertainment/astroworld-festival-timeline-tragedy-unfolded/story?id=81036039

Anonymous. (2014). The Target breach, by the numbers. *Krebs on Security*. Retrieved from http://krebsonsecurity.com/2014/05/the-target-breach-by-the-numbers/

Bloomberg. (2014). Hacking timeline: What did Target know and when? *Bloomberg Businessweek*. Retrieved from http://www.businessweek.com/videos/2014-03-13/hack-ing-timeline-what-did-target-know-and-when

Brown, Evan Nicole. (2021, December 28). Dior announces indefinite postponement of Travis Scott collaboration line. *Hollywood Reporter*. Retrieved from https://www.hollywoodreporter.com/lifestyle/style/travis-scott-dior-collaboration-postponed-astroworld-tragedy-1235067971/

Buckee, Michael. (2020, March 29). Analyzing company reputation after a data breach. *Inside Out Security Blog*. Retrieved from https://www.varonis.com/blog/company-reputation-after-a-data-breach#:~:text=We%20can%20see%20that%20Target's,increase%20from%202014%20to%202018

Calvario, Liz. (2021, December 16). Astroworld tragedy: All 10 concertgoers' cause of death ruled 'compression asphyxia.' Retrieved from https://www.etonline.com/astroworld-tragedy-all-10-concertgoers-cause-of-death-ruled-compression-asphyxia-176749

Con Edison Media Relations. (2016, October 29). Con Edison close to completing $1 billion in post-Sandy protections. Retrieved from https://www.coned.com/en/about-con-edison/media/news/20161029/post-sandy

Cowen, Trace William. (2022, September 2). Travis Scott after Astroworld: What he's done since festival tragedy. Retrieved from https://www.complex.com/music/travis-scott-astroworld-everything-done-since-festival-tragedy/o2-arena

Dahir, Ikran. (2021, November 10). Travis Scott updated his Instagram bio with the wrong phone number for Astroworld survivors seeking mental health services. *Buzzfeed News*. Retrieved from https://www.buzzfeednews.com/article/ikrd/travis-scott-therapy-instagram-number

Edelman Worldwide. (2023, January 15). 2023 Edelman Trust Barometer reveals business is the only institution viewed as ethical and competent; emerges as ethical force for good in a polarized world. Retrieved from https://www.prnewswire.com/news-releases/2023-edelman-trust-barometer-reveals-business-is-the-only-institution-viewed-as-ethical-and-competent-emerges-as-ethical-force-for-good-in-a-polarized-world-301721906.html

Edelman Worldwide. (2023, January 27). 2023 Edelman Trust Barometer: Global report. Retrieved from https://www.edelman.com/trust/2023/trust-barometer

Edelman Worldwide. (2018). 2018 Edelman Trust Barometer: Global report. Retrieved from https://cms.edelman.com/sites/default/files/2018-01/2018%20Edelman%20Trust%20Barometer%20Global%20Report.pdf

Finkle, J. & Skariachan, D. (2014). Target breach worse than thought, states launch joint probe. *Reuters*. Retrieved from http://www.reuters.com/article/2014/01/10/us-target-breach-idUSBREA090L120140110

Forbes. (2020, November 30). How hip-hop superstar Travis Scott has become corporate America's brand whisperer. Retrieved from https://www.forbes.com/sites/abrambrown/2020/11/30/how-hip-hop-superstar-travis-scott-has-become-corporate-americas-brand-whisperer/?sh=1e93d90074e7

Gallup. (2023, January 10). Nurses retain top ethics rating in U.S., but below 2020 high. Retrieved from https://news.gallup.com/poll/467804/nurses-retain-top-ethics-rating-below-2020-high.aspx

Golin, A. (2004). *Trust or Consequences: Build Trust Today or Lose Your Market Tomorrow.* New York: AMACOM.

Grueter, E. (2014). Deciphering the Target data breach, how POS systems are compromised. *docTrackr.* Retrieved from http://www.doctrackr.com/blog/bid/368859/Deciphering-the-Target-Data-Breach-How-POS-Systems-are-Compromised

Hartzog, Woodrow & Solove, Daniel J. (2022, April 13). We still haven't learned the major lesson of the 2013 Target hack. *Slate.* Retrieved from https://slate.com/technology/2022/04/breached-excerpt-hartzog-solove-target.html

Haworth, Josh. (2023, January 6). 6 Public relations trends in 2023. Retrieved from https://explodingtopics.com/blog/public-relations-trends

Heath, R. L. & Cousino, K. R. (1990). Issues management: End of first decade progress report. *Public Relations Review,* 16(1), 6–18.

Hsu, T. (2014). Target CEO resigns as fallout from data breach continues. *LA Times.* Retrieved from http://www.latimes.com/business/la-fi-target-ceo-20140506-story.html

Jayakumar, A. (2014). Data breach hits Target's profits, but that's only the tip of the iceberg. *The Washington Post.* Retrieved from http://www.washingtonpost.com/business/economy/data-breach-hits-targets-profits-butthats-only-the-tip-of-the-iceberg/2014/02/26/159f6846-9d60-11e3-9ba6-800d1192d08b_story.html

Kaiser, T. (2013). Target data breach compromises 40 million customer credit/debit cards. *DailyTech.* Retrieved from http://www.dailytech.com/Target+Data+Breach+Compromises+40+Million+Customer+CreditDebit+Cards/article33963.htm

Ledingham, J. & Bruning, S. (2000). *Public Relations as Relationship Management: A Relational Approach to the Study and Practice of Public Relations.* Mahwah, NJ: Lawrence Erlbaum Associates.

Lukaszewski, J. E. & Serie, T. L. (1993). Relationships built on understanding core values. *Waste Age,* March, 83–94.

Malcolm, H. (2014). Target sees drop in customer visits after breach. *USA Today.* Retrieved from http://www.usatoday.com/story/money/business/2014/03/11/target-customer-traffic/6262059

McCoy, K. (2017, May, 23). Target to pay $18.5M for 2013 data breach that affected 41 million consumers. *USA Today.* Retrieved from https://www.usatoday.com/story/money/2017/05/23/target-pay-185m-2013-data-breach-affected-consumers/102063932/

Newsom, D., Turk, J. V. & Kruckeberg, D. (2013). *This is PR: The Realities of Public Relations* (11th ed.). Independence, KY: Cengage Learning.

Nolan, Emma. (2021, November 10). Travis Scott's BetterHelp offer after Astroworld tragedy branded 'exploitative.' *Newsweek.* Retrieved from https://www.newsweek.com/travis-scott-betterhelp-astroworld-tragedy-exploitative-backlash-1647872

Schleicher, M. (2014). Data breach case study: Lessons from Target data heist. *TechInsurance.* Retrieved from http://www.techinsurance.com/blog/cyber-liability/data- breach-lessons-from-target/

Press, Alex N. (November 2021). Post-Astroworld, Travis Scott is partnering with an incredibly exploitative therapy app. *Jacobin*. Retrieved from https://jacobin.com/2021/11/astroworld-travis-scott-betterhelp-partnership-exploitation-therapy

Saleem, Hasan. (2022, April 20). 10 business communication trends that are here to stay in 2022. Retrieved from https://readwrite.com/business-communication-trends-for-2022/

Target. (2013). Data breach FAQ. Retrieved from https://corporate.target.com/about/shoppingexperience/payment-card-issue-FAQ

Vitagliano, Joe. (2021, December). More fallout from Astroworld: Travis Scott removed from Coachella, Anheuser-Busch will no longer produce his seltzer brand. *American Songwriter*. Retrieved from https://americansongwriter.com/more-fallout-from-astroworld-travis-scott-removed-from-coachella-anheuser-busch-will-no-longer-produce-his-seltzer-brand/

Wilcox, D. L., Cameron, G. T. & Reber, B. H. (2014). *Public Relations: Strategies and Tactics* (11th ed.). Upper Saddle River, NJ: Pearson Education.

Wilson, L. J. (1994a). Excellent companies and coalition-building among the Fortune 500: A value- and relationship-based theory. *Public Relations Review*, 20(4), 333–343.

Wilson, L. J. (1994b). The return to gemeinschaft: Toward a theory of public relations and corporate community relations as relationship-building. In A. F. Alkhafaji (ed.), *Business Research Yearbook: Global Business Perspectives*, Vol. I (pp. 135–141). Lanham, MD: International Academy of Business Disciplines and University Press of America.

Wilson, L. J. (1996). Strategic cooperative communities: A synthesis of strategic, issue management, and relationship-building approaches in public relations. In H. M. Culbertson and N. Chen (eds.), *International Public Relations: A Comparative Analysis*. Hillsdale, NJ: Lawrence Erlbaum Associates.

Wilson, L. J. (2001). Relationships within communities: Public relations for the next century" In R. Heath (ed.), *Handbook of Public Relations* (pp. 521–526). Newbury Park, CA.: Sage Publications.

Winters, Emma (2021, November 11). Travis Scott loses MAJOR brand deal following Astroworld festival tragedy. *Music Times*. Retrieved from https://www.musictimes.com/articles/83253/20211111/travis-scott-loses-major-brand-deal-following-astroworld-festival-tragedy.htm

CHAPTER 2

APPLYING PUBLIC INFORMATION AND PERSUASIVE COMMUNICATION THEORIES

"Data is only available about the past. . . . The only way you can look into the future [is] to have a good theory."

—CLAYTON CHRISTENSEN
HARVARD BUSINESS SCHOOL PROFESSOR

LEARNING IMPERATIVES

- Understand the role of public opinion and its impact on successful communication with an organization's publics.

- Understand the theory and principles underlying persuasion and how to use them to change behavior.

- Understand how to use persuasive appeals.

- Understand the legitimate role of advocacy in a free-market economy and the ethical standards that apply to persuasive communication.

As communications professionals, we are in the public information and persuasion business. The ethical basis of marketing and public relations is in advocacy. Advocacy means providing "a voice in the marketplace of ideas, facts, and viewpoints to aid informed public debate." Advocacy is an essential societal value deeply rooted in the U.S. Constitution. Notice, for instance, a citizen's right in the U.S. legal system to an attorney or "advocate."

In our function as advocates, we play a critical role in a democratic society with a free marketplace of ideas and a free-market economy. We provide information and advocate products, services or issues honestly, responsibly and in accordance with public and consumer interest. Advocacy is a crucial public service that allows people to make informed decisions for their lives.

Because we are engaged in public information and **persuasion**, what we do is inextricably tied to **public opinion**. What publics think and believe directly affects how they behave. As we established in the previous chapter, an organization that ignores the opinions of its publics simply will not build sufficient trust to survive in today's society.

In this chapter, we will examine a few communication theories that explain the relationship between what people think and how they behave. As Harvard Business School Professor Clayton Christensen (2012) explained, theories are tools that help us learn how to look at a situation in terms of "what causes what, and why."

After sharing his theory of disruption with Andy Grove, the CEO of Intel, Christensen explained: "If I had tried to tell Andy Grove what he should think about the microprocessor business, he would have eviscerated my argument. ... But instead of telling him what to think, I taught him how to think. He then reached a bold decision about what to do on his own." Although this text is not designed to be a comprehensive treatment of the theories of public opinion and persuasion, these theories provide lenses through which we can make sense of communication problems, identify ways to address them and predict likely outcomes if certain actions are taken. Effective advocacy depends upon our ability to understand and apply communication theory.

PERSUASION

Disseminating information to appeal for a change in attitudes, opinions and/or behavior.

PUBLIC OPINION

What most people in a particular public express about an issue that affects them.

Behavior: the ultimate objective

Civilizations have been engaged in public information and persuasion since the beginning of time. While much more is now known about what techniques work and why, not much has fundamentally changed in the processes used to motivate people to act. What has changed is our precision in applying research to shape specific persuasion techniques to more effectively reach and motivate well-defined publics using new and constantly evolving media channels.

In modern times, Walter Lippmann published his seminal work, "Public Opinion," in 1922. His work and the work of subsequent scholars in the field essentially define public opinion as what most people in a particular group think, feel and express about an issue or event of importance to them.

In 1923, public relations practitioner Edward Bernays published "Crystallizing Public Opinion," asserting that knowing what people think isn't enough. To make a difference, we have to get them to act on their opinions and **attitudes**. As important as public opinion is, the savvy communications professional will always remember that behavior is the final evaluation. According to practitioner Larry Newman, in public relations we are ultimately trying to get people to: do something we want them to do, not do something we don't want them to do or let us do something we want to do.

Knowing what our publics think is only useful insofar as it leads us to accurately predict what they will do. Even when we simply disseminate information in the public interest, we typically do so with some behavioral expectation in mind. A public information campaign about the risk of COVID-19 isn't just informing people; its purpose is to motivate people to practice preventive behaviors like getting a vaccine, wearing a mask or washing their hands frequently. We must determine what behavior we are trying to influence, and then lay the groundwork to get there.

 ATTITUDES
Collections of beliefs organized around an issue or event that predispose behavior.

Shaping attitudes to change behavior

According to Milton Rokeach (1968), behavior is based on attitude, which he called a predisposition to behave. Working in the 1960s and 70s, he created a theory of beliefs, values and attitudes (see Figure 2.1), which was further developed by Martin Fishbein and Icek Ajzen as the theory of reasoned action and, subsequently, the theory of planned behavior. Rokeach asserted that the fundamental building blocks of our cognitive system are **beliefs**. Beliefs are inferences we make about ourselves and about the world around us. From observation, we infer that the sky is blue, that dark clouds result in rain and that most leaves are green. Rokeach said that some beliefs are more central to an individual's cognitive system than others. These core beliefs, or **values**, are typically well established and relatively stable. They are difficult to change because they are fundamental to individuals and their belief systems. They function as "life guides," determining both our daily behavior and our life goals.

BELIEFS
Inferences we make about ourselves and the world around us.

VALUES
Core beliefs or beliefs central to an individual's cognitive system.

Figure 2.1
Rokeach's theory of beliefs, values and attitudes

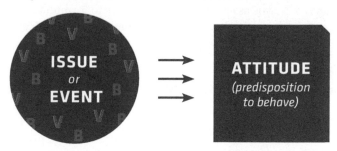

B = Belief   **V** = Value

For example, if someone challenges our belief that leaves are green by pointing out red leaves on certain trees, it doesn't really shake our world. But if someone challenges our value that a supreme being created those trees, it causes dissonance and discomfort because that "value" is central to our cognitions.

According to Rokeach, collections of beliefs and values organize around a focal point, such as an issue, an event or a person, to form an attitude, or predisposition to behave. Attitudes determine an individual's behavior in any given situation. Rokeach uses gardening as an example. The collection of an individual's beliefs — that garden-ing is fun, that it saves money, that it releases tension and that it produces beauti-ful flowers — will result in a favorable attitude toward gardening. Given the absence of intervening attitudes, a person's collection of beliefs and resultant attitudes will motivate gardening behavior.

For communications professionals to motivate behavior then, they must under-stand and tap into core beliefs and values that shape attitudes. Rokeach found that changing the collection of beliefs and values surrounding an issue or event could change the attitude and resultant behavior. Remembering that core beliefs are dif-ficult to change, we may try to tap into a value and base the alteration of peripheral beliefs on that central belief. We may also need to motivate people to change the rel-ative importance of a belief or value to help us build a foundation for attitude change. Or we may introduce beliefs and values into the collection that hadn't before been considered relevant. At any rate, it is important for us to recognize that people do not do something just because we want them to do it or because we think they should consider it in their self-interest. People behave in their self-interest as they define it, according to their own beliefs and attitudes. Changing behavior requires addressing those beliefs and attitudes.

In the 1970s, Fishbein and Ajzen (1980) developed Rokeach's work further to help us understand attitudes and to predict and change behavior. They asserted that behavior was not just a result of the influence of attitudes (collections of beliefs and values) but also of subjective norms (see Figure 2.2.) **Subjective norms** are the way we perceive others expect us to behave. Subjective norms may also be the way we perceive society expects us to behave. Even more critical may be how we think peo-ple important to us, such as peers and parents, would like us to behave. Fishbein and Ajzen's theory of reasoned action advanced Rokeach's model using both attitudes and subjective norms as the foundation of intended behavior, which then becomes behavior. Subsequently, Ajzen (1991) added one additional factor — perceived behav-ioral control — to create the theory of planned behavior.

Rokeach's work primarily addressed the beliefs and values that are the building blocks of attitudes which predispose our behavior. Fishbein and Ajzen studied sub-jective norms as an addition to attitudes to formulate behavioral intention. In 1990, social scientist and public relations practitioner Pat Jackson developed a behavioral

 SUBJECTIVE NORMS
Perceived behavioral expectations.

Figure 2.2
Theory of reasoned action, adapted from Fishbein and Ajzen

model of public relations (Figure 2.3) that focuses on converting attitudes or behavioral intentions into actual behavior. His model addresses a public's progression from awareness to actual behavior change as a result of communication efforts.

In Jackson's model, the awareness stage is the public information process. Word-of-mouth, publicity, online posting, publications and other communications tools create awareness and reinforcement of an issue. They should be designed to tie the message into people's existing perceptions and attitudes, or to adjust those attitudes if necessary. Awareness efforts must be based on quality research to determine the attitudes and perceptions that are the foundation for a certain public's behavior or potential behavior. From this awareness, people begin to formulate a readiness to act — an attitude (Rokeach's predisposition to behave or Fishbein and Ajzen's

Figure 2.3

Pat Jackson's behavioral public relations model

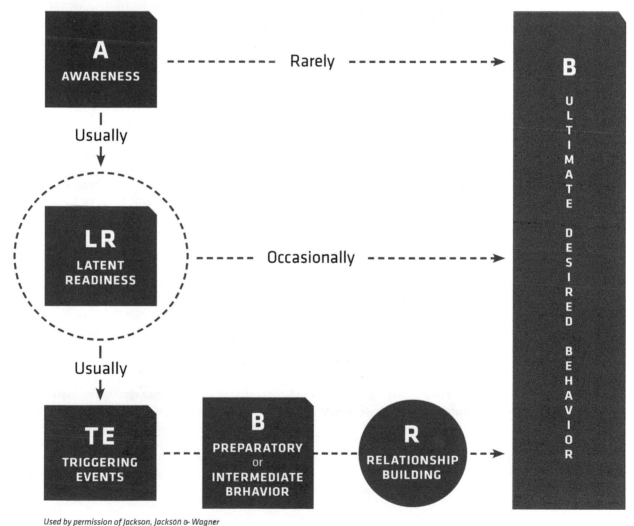

Used by permission of Jackson, Jackson & Wagner

TRIGGERING EVENT

An event that transforms readiness to act into actual behavior.

INTERMEDIATE BEHAVIORS

Actions that build relationships with the organization and prepare publics for the ultimate desired behavior.

behavioral intention). Converting the attitude into action requires some kind of **triggering event** such as an election in a political campaign or a sale at a clothing store. A triggering event transforms readiness into behavior because it helps people overcome barriers to action, including lack of time, money or motivation.

However, triggering events usually start people down the path of engaging in **intermediate behaviors** that eventually lead them to the ultimate desired behavior. According to public relations experts Allen Center, Pat Jackson, Stacey Smith and Frank Stansberry, "Asking right off for the ultimate behavior is usually ineffective." Communication should encourage intermediate behaviors like attending a meeting, interacting with social media content or visiting a website, that help an organization build relationships with publics and increase the likelihood that people will ultimately engage in the desired behavior.

Combining Rokeach's initial formulation, Fishbein and Ajzen's further development of the theory and Jackson's behavioral model, we know that understanding attitudes is essential in understanding and predicting behavior. And we know that influencing and changing the beliefs and values that shape attitudes will allow us to influence and change attitudes, which then changes behavior. For example, research shows that efforts to stop smoking among Hispanic males are far more successful when the appeals focus on family relationships and responsibilities. Smoking behavior among Hispanic males is facilitated by attitudes comprised of beliefs regarding the pleasure and peer acceptance associated with smoking. When beliefs and values are introduced regarding relationships with family and children, and how smoking affects their health and futures, stop-smoking appeals are dramatically more effective. Taking the three models together, we understand that the attitudes underlying behavior must be influenced and changed (by altering the set of beliefs), and then a triggering event, for example, a workplace "smoke out," must be used to begin a process of behavior change. Subsequent public relations efforts are focused on encouraging intermediate behaviors that build relationships and prepare individuals to engage in the ultimate desired behavior.

TIPS FROM THE PROS

Changing behavior one step at a time

Stacey Smith, senior counsel and partner at Jackson Jackson & Wagner, the behavioral management consulting and public relations firm founded by Patrick Jackson, offers additional tips to make changing behavior a bit less challenging.

No one starts out as an Olympic-level athlete, a world-class musician or a Fortune 50 CEO. The behaviors it takes to get people to reach such lofty goals are small and steady, little steps exercised again and again, reinforced, and then celebrated by others. These "steps" are no different than those used to motivate the behaviors we seek from our stakeholders.

1. Before getting to the ultimate desired behavior there is a *series of smaller, intermediate behaviors* which reinforce and create confidence in the behavior itself, and prove that the behavior is socially acceptable (or not). Though these smaller behavior steps are often thought of as being linear, they do not actually happen that way. The most effective intermediate behaviors (those that lead most effectively to other behaviors) must be stimulated again and again until the ultimate desired behavior is reached. Research can help us identify what those intermediate behaviors are likely to be.

2. Different stakeholders will move along the behavioral continuum at different rates and at different times. Therefore this is *not a "one and done" exercise.* Stakeholders who are innovators or early adopters (diffusion of innovation) will need less stimulation as they tend to reach the ultimate desired behaviors more quickly than others. Stakeholders who are slower to act (typically identified as the early and late majority) will need more – and perhaps different – stimulation than others. Finally, laggards (who are by nature the slowest to adopt behavior change) are typically not worth the effort. These individuals change behavior at a snail's pace, if at all. Best to let them be.

3. It is critical to identify *what barriers may prevent stakeholders from adopting a new behavior.* Without this understanding, even the most well-written communications and well-executed tactics will fall short. Barriers can be structural (money, distance, time, etc.) or psychological (fear of a future impact or a past negative experience with a similar behavior). An individual who as a child had many negative school experiences is likely to avoid going to their child's parent-teacher conferences, volunteer at school or help with homework, and may hesitate to hold their own children accountable for violating school policies based on a pre-existing bias. Uncovering these barriers through research will help you set more realistic goals for behavior change and design more effective tactics.

4. *Humans are social animals.* They want – even need – to be part of a group. For this reason, they will often make decisions that are not in their best interest, but are in line with social norms. Motivating behavior requires social rewards from influentials, opinion leaders, family and friends. We need to build those rewards into our plans by considering the four steps of behavior change: coalition, enforcement, engineering and social reinforcement.

5. It is our responsibility as professionals to *make sure these techniques are applied ethically* to the work of our employer or client. We must remember what is in the best interest of society and humanity and not seek behavioral change that can be damaging to an individual, a community or a nation.

Contributed by Stacey Smith. © Kendall Hunt Publishing Company.

The influence of mental shortcuts on behavior

Research in behavioral economics, a field of study that combines principles from psychology and traditional economics, has produced valuable insight into how people make decisions. While these theories don't focus specifically on beliefs, attitudes or social norms, they describe the underlying cognitive processes (including mental shortcuts) that cause people to behave in ways that aren't predictable through classical economic models. In other words, these theories help explain why people do things for reasons other than money. Under certain circumstances these cognitive processes may either make it easier or may pose significant challenges to informing and persuading publics. The Institute for Public Relations (IPR) has established a Behavioral Insights Research Center to "help professionals understand how and why people think and behave the way they do."

Daniel Kahneman (2011) explained that the brain has two different processing modes: system 1 and system 2. System 1 works quickly and automatically, without much cognitive effort and in the background of conscious thought. It allows us to make intuitive decisions by relying on **mental shortcuts** or heuristics. For instance, system 1 enables you to stop your car when you encounter a red, octagonal sign at an intersection without consciously processing its meaning. Conversely, system 2 works slowly, requires focused attention and takes considerable conscious mental effort. This process is more rational, is rule-based and is used to tackle complicated problems involving multiple steps. It allows you to keep several ideas in your mind at once.

Because people generally don't like to exert cognitive effort if they don't have to, they rely on the intuitive and sometimes error-prone system 1 to make decisions. The Arthur W. Page Society (2013) identified a number of cognitive biases emerging from system 1 intuitive decision making that are important for communications professionals to understand. These mental shortcuts may mean the difference between a public being persuaded by your message, ignoring it completely or thinking something other than what you intended. They may also unknowingly influence your thinking as you create plans to communicate with your key publics.

> *Loss aversion.* In situations where people have to weigh the risk of losing one thing against the benefit of gaining another, they become risk averse. This means that the potential pain of loss influences decisions more than the possible pleasure of gain. Accounting for this bias may include considering whether messages should be framed as a loss or a gain for your targeted public (see Rothman et al., 2006).
>
> *Anchoring.* People's decisions are influenced by the most recent idea they have been exposed to. The recent idea becomes the baseline, or anchor, for the decision. Surprisingly, anchoring occurs even if a person consciously understands that the recent idea is irrelevant to the decision. Overcoming this bias may require an approach that engages a target public's system 2. One strategy that showed promise in recent research was to encourage people to consider reasons why the anchor may be wrong (see Nagtegaal et al., 2020).
>
> *Narrative fallacy.* People create meaning out of the limited information available to them by transforming what they know into simple, coherent narratives. However, these stories do not consider the complexities of a situation and do not account for chance. They focus on simplified cause-and-effect explanations. As a result, they may differ significantly from reality and cloud people's judgment of future outcomes. According to the Page Society (2013), this fallacy underscores the need for communications professionals to be "in the business of establishing credible narratives," especially during a time where the internet and social media "have exponentially increased the number of storytellers and made all of them as visible as their stories."
>
> *Outcome bias.* People tend to focus on the outcomes of decisions rather than the complexities and unknowns of the decision-making process. For example, actions or decisions that made sense with information available at the time (foresight) can be seen later as imprudent and irresponsible because of the outcome (hindsight). Research on this bias has shown that it may be the

✂ MENTAL SHORTCUTS
Intuitive decisions that do not rely on conscious cognitive processing.

result of an individual's need for closure, need for control, need to enhance their self-esteem or need to punish or condemn (see Strohmaier et al., 2021).

Confidence bias. People put too much confidence in their own knowledge and expertise, or in the knowledge and expertise of a group of people who think like they do, even when there is convincing evidence that their judgments or decisions are wrong. Research on overconfidence has demonstrated that 75% of Americans overestimate their ability to distinguish between true and false information on Facebook. In addition, "those who overrate their ability more frequently visit websites known to spread false or misleading news. These overconfident respondents are also less able to distinguish between true and false claims about current events and report higher willingness to share false content, especially when it aligns with their political leanings" (see Lyons et al., 2021).

Using behavior to segment publics

While demographic data has always been useful in segmenting publics, much more useful is psychographic data that includes the values, beliefs, lifestyles and decision-making processes of publics. Knowing the behavior of publics — in purchasing, recreation and other activities — helps us segment them and design more effective messages for specifically targeted communications channels.

The notion that publics coalesce around issues and emerge from specific events is also an important one, particularly as we deal with crisis communication and crisis management. Psychographics may be of more help in profiling these kinds of publics than demographics, but even psychographics may be of limited worth when segmenting publics by issues or events of importance to them.

As we will see in the next several chapters, behavior is the ultimate objective. The matrix leads us through the steps to motivate behavior. It helps to determine which publics we need to target and what messages will shape their latent readiness to act (attitudes). It also aids in designing the specific strategies and tactics to deliver those messages and to trigger desired behavior.

Public opinion

Now that we understand how attitudes and cognitive processes influence the behavior of an individual and, by extension, a group of individuals or public, let's examine how we discover the attitudes held by our publics. Essentially, public opinion is the expression of the attitudes of a particular public. Extensive psychological and sociological studies have been done on the phenomenon of public opinion. Its measurement — in an attempt to predict behavior — has become not only a science but also a highly profitable career track. Most of the descriptions of the phenomenon

© saiko3p/Shutterstock.com

Shoppers in Mong Kok, one of Hong Kong's busiest shopping places.

contain similar elements and can be synthesized into a straightforward definition: Public opinion is the collection of beliefs, attitudes and opinions expressed by the majority of individuals within a particular group or public about an issue or topic of interest to them.

Let's examine the elements of this definition.

- Public opinion is collective. It is not what just one individual thinks; it is the collection of what several people think.
- The beliefs and ideas must be expressed to be public opinion. Public discussion usually crystallizes or solidifies opinion into something that can be expressed.
- The opinion must be held by the majority of individuals within the group.
- The opinion is identified with a certain group or public, not the mass or "whoever" is out there. The particular group holding the opinion is identifiable from the mass. Opinion research uses demographics and psychographics to identify the specific groups expressing the opinion.
- The opinion is focused on a particular issue or topic.
- The masses are segmented into groups or publics differently from topic to topic. The issue of embryonic stem cell research will create within the mass audience certain public segmentations that will be different than those created by the issue of Palestinian sovereignty in Israel.
- The topic must hold a particular interest to the individuals within the group. In other words, it must involve their self-interest.
- Interest is typically aroused and sustained by events relating to the topic or issue. The stem cell debate heats up as we begin to lose scientists to other nations that have advanced such research. At some point, other news takes precedence and attention wanes. But the debate is again fueled when someone famous contracts a disease that could potentially be cured through stem cell research.

Opinion formation

Because public opinion is a collection of individual opinions, the logical place for us to begin in determining how public opinion is formed is with the individual. A review of the basic models and principles of human communication will aid us in determining how individuals form opinions.

Opinion is basically a thought process. We attach meaning to the world around us based on the collective influence of our past experience, knowledge, culture and environment. This collective influence is often referred to as our **frame of reference.** Within this frame of reference we establish our own personal beliefs, values and attitudes which were previously discussed as the foundation of our behavior. All of our thoughts, ideas and communicative acts are processed through our frame of

⚛ FRAME OF REFERENCE

The collective influence of experiences, knowledge, culture and environment that forms our perceptual screen.

reference, and no two individual frames of reference are identical. Our frame of reference determines how we perceive or sense our world as well as the communication of others directed toward us.

In the mid-1940s, Hadley Cantril (1944) proposed 15 "laws" of public opinion that demonstrate the influence of an individual's frame of reference. Those laws can be synthesized into a few basic observations that serve as guides in persuasive communication.

- Opinions are more easily influenced by events than words, but opinion changed by events requires subsequent reinforcement.
- Opinion is basically determined by self-interest, and persuasion is only effective if it maintains a consistent appeal to self-interest over time. Opinion rooted in self-interest is extremely difficult to change.
- Information is most effective when opinion is in formative stages.
- If people already trust their leaders, they will allow them the opportunity to handle sensitive situations. People trust their leaders' decision-making more when they feel they (the people) have had a part in shaping the decision.
- Public opinion is focused more on expected results than on methods to achieve those results. People care more about an outcome than the process to reach the outcome.

Elisabeth Noelle-Neumann (1984) has identified another phenomenon of public opinion we characterize as the "sleeper" effect. An individual's fear of social rejection or isolation may cause them not to verbalize an opinion they perceive to be in the minority. In other words, vocal groups may suppress mainstream or majority opinions because the majority believes itself to be in the minority and, therefore, remains silent. This "spiral of silence" as Noelle-Neumann termed it, or the "silent majority" as former President Richard Nixon called it, is a sleeper factor usually unaccounted for in our research unless we dig for it. Noelle-Neumann identified mass media as an accomplice in the spiral of silence because their own voice may often reflect the minority opinion, but it has become one of the loudest and most dominant voices in the free marketplace of ideas. Once the spiral of silence is broken, however, the silenced opinion flows forth like water from a breached dam. People quickly discover that others think as they do and no longer remain silent. Social media now rivals traditional mass media in the public opinion marketplace. It can either exacerbate the spiral of silence or have the opposite effect of stimulating the flow of honest opinion.

The phenomenon of perception

Perception is an unpredictable phenomenon, largely because it is so individually determined. Unless you have a solid understanding of an individual's frame of reference, it is impossible to predict how they will perceive an event, experience or message. In communication we sometimes forget that meaning is in people. Our words and messages do not transfer meaning; they can only evoke images in the minds of our public that we hope will have similar individual meanings.

In addition to being very individual, perception also carries with it the power of truth. What is perceived by an individual is what they believe to be true. We express this in clichés such as "seeing is believing," but the impact of perception is far greater than we usually realize. Whether or not a perception is accurate has no bearing on its power as truth to the perceiver. When police question witnesses of a traffic accident, they get as many different stories as there are observers, each absolutely certain their version is the truth.

Sometimes perception is so intimately tied to an individual's belief and value system that it is difficult, if not impossible, to alter it even when it is flawed. Norris (1984) calls these "cast-iron" perceptions. Further, some perceptions are shared with others in a group and are "preformed." We have already decided how certain things should be and that is the way we perceive them. We call these stereotypes. We often stereotype people (e.g., dumb blondes or computer geeks), but other phenomena can be stereotyped as well (e.g., government is wasteful or red meat is bad for you). Stereotypes are often useful in helping us deal with the world around us, but they become dangerous when they prevent us from perceiving things as they really are. They are also dangerous when they create an environment in which people are denied the opportunity to reach their potential.

As public relations professionals, we should be aware of Klapper's concepts of **selective exposure, selective perception** and **selective retention.** Because of the barrage of stimuli we receive from our environment, including increasing numbers of messages from people trying to persuade us, our perceptual mechanism also works as a screen or a filter to keep us from experiencing overload. As we learn from the uses and gratifications theory of mass media (Katz, Blumler & Gurevitch, 1973-74), we choose the media and channels we pay attention to, and we choose those messages we want to perceive as well as those we want to retain. This is a critical principle in marketing, advertising and public relations. Our professions depend on channels to get messages to key publics, but if those publics are not paying attention to the channels through which we send messages, or are electing not to perceive or retain our messages, our efforts are useless.

For example, think about how you get your news. Few people read every story in their newsfeed from start to finish. As you scroll through an app, you read headlines and look at pictures to decide which stories you want to read. You do the same with email. You check the sender and the subject and often delete without opening. Individuals selectively perceive far fewer messages than are targeted at them in a given day, and they actually retain even less of the content once those messages have been filtered through the perceptual screen to determine whether they are useful. In fact, studies of selective perception in advertising demonstrate that people actually pay more attention to ads and consume more information about a product after they have purchased it than before. Just as agenda-setting theory predicts, they are looking for reinforcement of their purchase decision rather than using the information to actually make a decision.

Selective perception becomes an even more poignant phenomenon when we consider how new technologies have given consumers, or publics, control over how and if they receive information. As people seek information less from mass media and more from increasingly specialized and segmented sources, we must become more sophisticated in appealing to their self-interests. Uses and gratifications theory identifies three motives for media use: environmental surveillance, environmental diversion and environmental interaction. A basic assumption of the theory is that people choose how media will serve them and use media for their own purposes.

A problem with this user-driven access to information — and with social media in general — is the variable reliability of the information. Now, more than ever, misinformation abounds. Anyone with a story to tell, accurate or not, can post it. Blogs, YouTube,

---

⊶ SELECTIVE EXPOSURE

The function of selecting the communications channels one chooses to pay attention to.

⊶ SELECTIVE PERCEPTION

The subconscious function of selecting from the millions of daily stimuli only those messages one chooses to perceive.

⊶ SELECTIVE RETENTION

The function of selecting from the stimuli perceived only those messages one chooses to retain.

Facebook, Twitter, Instagram, Pinterest, Snapchat, TikTok all provide a soapbox for expression. Most people know all online information should be verified for accuracy, but how many actually do that? We typically believe what we read from traditional media news sources. The same goes for what we read online — except online information is much more suspect than information filtered through journalists.

What all this means for communications professionals is that we must make a greater effort to understand the frames of reference of our key publics, use good research to try to predict how messages and events will be perceived by those publics and design messages that those publics will select, retain and act upon. But we must also constantly monitor traditional and social media to find out the information and misinformation reaching our publics and respond accordingly.

Opinion leaders

One of the most important influences in the phenomena of public opinion and persuasion is an **opinion leader**. Opinion leaders are those we turn to for advice and counsel, typically because they have more knowledge or information about the issue in question. We all have a number of opinion leaders in our lives. They may be authority figures of some kind, or they may be your next-door neighbor. When you get ready to buy a car, to whom do you talk about the best value? Before voting on a local referendum, with whom do you discuss it? What blogs or websites do you go to when trying to decide on a purchase or a vote or any kind of action? All of these sources are opinion leaders for those particular issues or decisions. Whether their knowledge and information comes from personal experience, special training, extensive reading or another source, you trust their judgment.

Studies of opinion leaders show that they are usually heavy consumers of media. In the 1940s, Elihu Katz and Paul Lazarsfeld conducted studies of voting behavior that led to their seminal two-step flow theory of opinion leadership. They found that certain individuals within a community search out information from mass media and other channels and pass it on to others. (Subsequent research has altered this hypothesis to a multiple-step flow, finding that the number of relays between media and the final receiver varies.)

Because of their possession of more information, we consider opinion leaders better informed and rely on their advice and counsel. We trust mechanics because they consume the most credible, reliable and current information on automobiles and auto repair. That mechanic also has much more experience identifying problems and making repairs than we do. We trust a doctor to be informed and know where to go to get the best information on medical diagnosis and treatment. We might know a neighbor who has a particular interest in the plants and flowers that grow best in our area. We trust the neighbor's advice because they have acquired knowledge and experience with plants that grow well. And their yard probably looks terrific.

As these examples show, opinion leaders can be formal or informal. They are specialists on particular issues or topics and are better informed on those topics. Research also shows that opinion leaders tend to be

> ✂ **OPINION LEADER**
> A trusted individual to whom one turns for advice because of their greater knowledge or experience regarding a specific topic.

© Goodluz/Shutterstock.com

early adopters of new ideas and products. As noted in the first chapter, some of the most effective opinion leaders are peers, and the internet is the great equalizer for peer-to-peer communication.

Viral campaigns using opinion leaders are a new reality because people trust others who are "just like" them. While the ethics of such viral campaigns are not yet fully sorted out, they are already being used with notable success.

Measuring public opinion

"Saturday Review" world columnist Charles Frankel said, "Majority opinion is a curious and elusive thing." It is certainly not stable. It changes from moment to moment as circumstances are constantly changing. For that reason alone, any measure of public opinion is never absolutely accurate. The moment the survey is completed, the interview is concluded or the focus groups are dismissed, the results are dated material.

James Stimson (1991), a well-known scholar in the field of public opinion measurement, contends that most measures are not accurate predictors of behavior because they measure attitudes and opinions in isolation from other members of the social group. He points out that individuals may formulate opinions on issues when approached, but those opinions are altered, refined and crystallized through discussion and interaction with others. Additionally, people do not behave in isolation; they are part of social systems that strongly influence behavior.

The Coca-Cola Company learned this lesson the hard way when introducing New Coke in 1985 (Schindler, 1992). The new formulation came about in response to the wildly successful Pepsi Challenge advertising campaign that had been eroding Coca-Cola's market share. Pepsi pitted itself against Coke in head-to-head taste tests at malls and grocery stores across the country. A Pepsi representative would set up a table with two unmarked cups: one containing Pepsi, and one with Coca-Cola. Shoppers were encouraged to taste both colas and then select which drink they preferred. The representative would then reveal the identity of the two colas with a consensus choosing the sweeter Pepsi over Coke. As a result, Coca-Cola officials commissioned "Project Kansas," a secret effort to reformulate the company's flagship soda.

Taste tests for the new formula showed a strong preference for it over Coke and Pepsi. In opinion surveys, people expressed the belief that if the majority preferred the new formula, then Coke should change to it. But a curious phenomenon occurred in the focus groups. When the groups began discussion, participants favored a for-

mula change as they did in the opinion surveys. Then, as some members of the groups began to voice their preference for the old formula, the overriding value of personal choice caused individuals within the focus groups to change their attitudes in support of the rights of those who preferred the old formula (because of taste or out of habit).

However, because quantitative opinion surveys were judged, at the time, to provide more credible data than qualitative research, Coca-Cola trusted them instead of the focus groups, changed the formula and scheduled a phasing out of the old. For the first couple of weeks people accepted the new formula; then the outcry of the masses for the rights of die-hard Coke loyalists to continue purchasing the original formula forced the company to create Coca-Cola Classic — leaving the old formula on the market but also scaling back production of New Coke. That is exactly what should have been predicted from observing the focus groups. Opinion surveys that measure opinion and predict behavior in isolation from the group may be inherently flawed. Coke found out that Americans value the right of personal choice more than they value the majority's rule. The New Coke was eventually renamed Coca-Cola 2 and was ultimately discontinued in 2002.

Further, the opinion expressed by individuals in a group may reflect a number of realities other than the opinion on that particular issue. The expression may be indicative of party or organizational loyalty, peer group pressure to conform or a reflection of the opinion of an influential whose judgment the respondents trust more than their own. And the combination of beliefs and attitudes that are the basis for behavior are far more complex and multidimensional than a singular opinion on a particular topic. Singular opinions on an issue do not necessarily directly lead to behavior. Too many other factors, events and attitudes intervene. Unless the measuring device is carefully designed and implemented, it may not measure the most salient opinion and resultant behavior. The results will be misleading, causing costly strategic errors.

In spite of the difficulties, we must still do our best to measure public attitudes and opinions as a foundation for persuasive efforts. Measurement problems are identified to aid us in designing research that corrects for and minimizes difficulties. This is done to help us understand and better interpret results, as well as to design programs that are flexible enough to respond to changing opinions. The methods for measuring public attitudes and opinion are described more fully in the next chapter. The most typical are survey research, which yields statistical results, and personal interviews and focus group research, which provide qualitative results.

Methods of persuasion

More often than not in today's environment, public relations engages in disseminating information rather than in heavy-handed persuasion. Knowledge and information are key cognitive elements that help shape attitudes and opinion. Further, public information provides the awareness foundation necessary for persuasion to effectively motivate publics. Nevertheless, even objective information of benefit to a public must be designed and delivered in such a way as to draw the attention of publics accustomed to filtering out messages to prevent overload. The message itself may not be designed to persuade, but the targeted publics may need to be persuaded to pay attention to the message.

Newsom, Turk and Kruckeberg (2013) contend that people are motivated to action through power, patronage or persuasion. Power may be legitimate

© Pressmaster/Shutterstock.com

authority, peer group pressure or informal status. Patronage is simply paying for the desired behavior, either monetarily, in kind or by favor. Persuasion, the method most used by public relations, typically involves information dissemination and devises appeals to change attitudes and opinions to achieve the desired behavior.

Methods and approaches to persuading typically focus on getting a public to pay attention to a message, accept it and retain it. Yet persuasive attempts fall short if they do not address motivating behavior. Carl Hovland's Yale Approach suffers from just such a shortfall. His four-step approach addresses persuading people to a particular opinion through gaining attention, designing the message for comprehension (understanding), creating acceptance through appeal to self-interest, and finally, ensuring retention through well-organized and presented arguments. Hovland believed attitudes change if you change opinion. But, as we have seen, merely changing opinions is insufficient. Unless attitudes and opinions are changed in such a way that they motivate the behavior we are seeking, we have expended valuable resources (time and money) to no avail. Behavior change is not only the ultimate measure of success, but also provides the reinforcement necessary to retain an attitude change. And as Jackson asserted, changing attitudes is not sufficient; behavior must be triggered in some way.

As noted earlier, opinion leaders are tremendously effective in motivating behavior. A public's reliance on known and trusted opinion leaders is often the key to motivating behavior. Reaching opinion leaders with media messages is one of the most effective persuasive methods.

Using mass media to influence publics

It is important to consider the effect of mass media in persuasion. McCombs and Shaw's agenda-setting theory contends that mass media do not tell people what to think; rather, they tell people what to think about. Media sets the agenda or determines what is important, and, as Lazarsfeld reiterates, they serve to reinforce existing attitudes and opinions. Uses and gratifications theory affirms that people choose the media they pay attention to based on their own needs. Agenda-setting studies have also shown that people select what they pay attention to for the purpose of reinforcing the decisions they have already made. People who had already purchased a car were the heaviest consumers of car ads. The same phenomenon is true across the board. People choose news channels that project their same political and social opinions. The vast majority of Sean Hannity's listeners are people who agree with his political, social and economic attitudes. For all of these reasons, media have not traditionally been considered persuaders.

Nevertheless, additional research has discovered what are called second-level agenda-setting effects (also known as media **framing**) that do have persuasive power. In their delivery of a story, media "frame" it with a set of attributes that affect how the audience perceives the story. In many cases, frames are created by the choice of words used to describe aspects of the story. For example, the term "illegal alien" carries a different meaning than the term "undocumented worker." In an extreme example, media may report that a man drank the water from a well and died. The impression is that the water was contaminated and killed him. But detail omitted from the brief media report may have changed the perception had it been included. Suppose the man was suffering from terminal cancer and had returned to the farm of his youth to drink once more from its pure water before he

FRAMING
Designing a message to influence how an issue or event is perceived.

died. That changes the story entirely. There is no question that media frame stories and thereby inject bias, whether intentionally or not. In public relations, we "frame" messages to persuade publics. But we must always use care to never frame messages in deceptive or manipulative ways.

We live in a world where some media personalities seem to have transcended the role of information provider and agenda setter; certain commentators and newscasters have obtained a celebrity status that has made them as influential as opinion leaders in shaping public opinion. Research has shown that cable news viewers' attitudes about Syrian refugees were influenced by how the networks framed the threat risk of the refugees and whether the refugees were described as Christian or Muslim (Nassar, 2020). Similarly, the frames used to present stories about civil rights protests, whether they were described as legitimate protests or riots, shaped what news consumers thought about the protestors and the police officers who were there (Kilgo & Mourão, 2021). As advancing technology exacerbates the isolation of individuals in our publics, media celebrities like Tucker Carlson, Rachel Maddow, Lester Holt and Anderson Cooper have become increasingly influential.

Out of mass media research have come other theories that prove useful to our persuasive efforts. Media **priming** is one such theory. Research has shown the power of media to "prime" publics at crucial points in a political or social process. The salience or importance of issues is affected by the amount of media coverage those issues receive. While priming effects diminish over time, new stories can be introduced to revive the issue at key points in a debate, election or other decision process. As skilled public relations practitioners place truly newsworthy stories in media, we can activate priming to our persuasive advantage.

PRIMING
Increasing the salience of a public issue through strategically timed media coverage.

A powerful example of this occurred in the Elizabeth Smart case. Elizabeth was abducted at age 14 from her family's Salt Lake City home on June 5, 2002. The story made national news, but the search for Elizabeth turned up nothing in the days that followed. Nonetheless, Chris Thomas, an adept public relations expert hired by the Smart family, kept the story alive locally, releasing new information and details about the investigation every few days or weeks until Elizabeth was found nine months later on March 12, 2003, in Sandy, Utah, 18 miles from the site of her abduction. This is an extraordinary example of media priming — being able to keep the story alive for nine long months. Elizabeth was found because members of the public recognized her captors Brian Mitchell and Wanda Barzee from news pictures they had seen — despite the fact that they were all wearing wigs at the time of their capture.

Another useful mass media theory is Everett Roger's **diffusion of innovations,** which describes how new technologies and ideas are adopted by a society. There are two key elements of this theory that are important for communicators to understand. First, research has shown that adoption follows an S curve; it starts slow, picks up speed in the middle, and then slows down at the end. People can be categorized based on the point in time they are most likely to adopt a new innovation or idea: innovators, early adopters, early majority, late majority and laggards. Early adopters are highly likely to become opinion leaders for those who are likely to adopt the innovation after them. Second, research found that people go through a five-step decision-making process before adopting a new technology or idea.

DIFFUSION OF INNOVATIONS
The process by which a new technology or idea is adopted by a society.

1. ***Awareness.*** The person learns about the innovation or idea, typically through a mass media or social media channel.

MINI CASE

Restoring a tourism industry
Discover Puerto Rico and Ketchum

In 2017, Puerto Rico found itself in the path of two deadly hurricanes: Irma and Maria. Irma, a Category 5 storm, brushed by Puerto Rico's north coast on September 7th. It caused $700 million in damage, left 1 million people without power and killed four people. Just two weeks later, Maria, a Category 4 storm rated as the third-strongest hurricane ever to hit the U.S., engulfed the island, causing catastrophic damage to the island's infrastructure and utilities and killing nearly 3,000 people.

Part of the island's recovery efforts focused on rebooting its tourism industry. A significant challenge for Discover Puerto Rico, a non-profit established by the Puerto Rican government to promote tourism to the island, was the media-influenced perceptions of tourists about the island's recovery. News coverage of the hurricanes showed wide-spread devastation.

CORE OPPORTUNITY
Discover Puerto Rico and its PR agency Ketchum worried that as the one-year anniversary of the hurricanes approached, the news media would again focus on the destruction, reinforcing the narrative that Puerto Rico wasn't a safe place to visit, rather than tell the story of Puerto Rico's recovery.

© NAPA/Shutterstock.com

DISCOVER PUERTO RICO'S STRATEGY

Their communication strategy took advantage of being at the top of the media agenda. It focused on reframing the anniversary coverage by reframing the most iconic visual of Hurricane Maria's destruction — an empty intersection where "S.O.S. Necesitamos Agua/Comida" was written in large letters that were visible from the air — as an image that showed how far Puerto Rico had come in its recovery. The reframed image showed the same intersection full of cheering residents standing next to the words "Bienvenidos #covertheprogress." Ketchum and Discover Puerto Rico used this reframed image to invite the media to share "the true stories and scenes of the resilient people who have brought the island back to life" (Discover Puerto Rico, 2019).

Ketchum and Discover Puerto Rico applied the following theories to address the opportunity.

Agenda setting: Research showed that major media outlets often run anniversary stories about major natural disasters. In other words, Ketchum and Discover Puerto Rico could accurately predict when negative stories about Puerto Rico would be on the media agenda.

Framing: Their research also found that anniversary stories of major natural disasters often "recycle negative images" from the initial coverage. Based on this knowledge, Ketchum and Discover Puerto Rico could predict that anniversary coverage of the hurricanes would be framed in terms of their destruction and devastation, reinforcing the narrative that the island wasn't a good place for tourists to visit.

RESULTS
- 1 billion earned and social media impressions.
- 70% positive coverage.
- 50% growth in positive conversations of tourism in Puerto Rico.
- 23% improvement in positive perceptions of Puerto Rico as a tourist destination.
- 9.4% increase in tourism in 2019.

2. ***Persuasion.*** The person considers the relative advantages and disadvantages of adopting the technology or idea based on their self-interest. They also rely on opinion leaders' experience with the technology or idea to inform their decisions.
3. ***Decision.*** The person decides whether to adopt the innovation or idea.
4. ***Implementation.*** The person uses the innovation or idea and evaluates its usefulness. They may also continue to seek more information about it.
5. ***Confirmation.*** The person seeks information that will validate their decision. New information may cause them to change their decision.

Persuasive appeals

Effective persuasion always requires some kind of appeal to self-interest. As will be fully explored in a later chapter, self-interest should not imply selfishness. Often the most effective persuasive appeals are to our publics' better nature: for the benefit of community or society or disadvantaged populations. Appealing to the self-interest of those you are trying to motivate is an essential element of all persuasive messages.

PERSUASIVE APPEAL

Appeals to self-interest to enhance persuasion and motivate behavior. Most likely involve ethos, pathos and logos.

LOGICAL APPEAL

A claim supported by credible evidence (logos).

EMOTIONAL APPEAL

Creating a positive or negative feeling leading to a behavioral response (pathos).

SOURCE CREDIBILITY

An appeal using an expert or trustworthy source (ethos).

Perhaps the most effective formula for **persuasive appeals** dates back more than two millennia to the philosopher and rhetorician Aristotle. His classic logos (logical argument), pathos (emotional appeal) and ethos (source credibility) are as salient today as they were in ancient Greece. These three appeals constitute the majority of persuasive appeals used in communication. These appeals should be carefully selected to address your public's overriding self-interest.

The message itself is a key element of a persuasive appeal. It should appeal to an individual's self-interest and use appropriate logical or emotional appeals based on research. A message using a **logical appeal** makes a claim, provides credible evidence to support the claim and explains the logical connection between the claim and the evidence. Logical appeals require people to actively evaluate the evidence and reasoning of the appeal, which they are more likely to do when they are highly involved with an issue and enjoy thinking deeply about different ideas.

A message with an **emotional appeal** seeks to influence a person's interpretation of their current situation, which leads to either a positive or negative feeling about it. For example, if you encounter a large, wild animal during a daytime trip to the local zoo, your interpretation of that situation will produce a different emotional response than if you encounter the same large, wild animal wandering freely into your mountain campsite. Emotional appeals are powerful because they can produce physical reactions within us, such as an adrenaline rush or increased heart rate, which lead predictably to a behavioral response. In the case of the zoo visit, we are thrilled to get close and watch the animal wander around its habitat. In the case of the campsite, we fear for our lives and may try to scare the animal away. Common emotional appeals in strategic communications include fear, guilt and shame on the negative side and love, humor, pride and joy on the positive side. Carefully consider the use of emotional appeals that invoke negative feelings. Trying to persuade using guilt or shame can often cause a defensive reaction to our attempt to persuade.

Equally as important, the source of the message must be carefully selected. Research on **source credibility** has found that our perceptions of a message source matter more than the actual credibility of the source. Typically, people evaluate the credibility of a source using two criteria: trustworthiness and expertise. A trustworthy source is one that a target public believes will tell them the truth. Similarly, an expert source is one that the target public believes is well informed on a particular topic. Research by psychology expert Robert Cialdini (2006) found that we are more likely to be influenced by a message when it comes from someone we perceive as an authority or from someone we like.

Authority. People follow the advice of someone they trust who has knowledge on the subject.
Liking. People are more likely to be influenced by people they like. People like others who are similar to them, who pay them compliments and who cooperate with them.

Research-based persuasion efforts

As you can see from the preceding discussion, while much research has been done to understand and perfect the persuasion process, there are too many variables in the human psyche and behavior for persuasion to be an exact science. Every public, every situation, every purpose is different and requires extensive examination and analysis. No perfect formula exists. Every effort to persuade is different; no two are alike, although some similarities may exist. Each effort will require fresh thought and new ideas, based on solid research. We need to do research to understand our publics intimately. We need to know their demographics and psychographics and refrain from relying on old research for that information. Fresh data and ongoing research is necessary to understand the continually changing publics we address.

Further, new research into persuasion techniques and appeals is constantly emerging. For example, we know from research that widespread use of product-warning labels may be responsible for consumer desensitization to their safety information. They are no longer an effective communications tactic to convey safety procedures. Research also tells us that when we want to get a public to adopt a preventive behavior such as getting a flu shot, that a gain-framed message is more effective (e.g., avoid getting sick this winter.) But when trying to motivate screening behavior such as getting a mammogram, loss-framed messages work best (e.g., failure to detect tumors early limits your treatment options.)

Similarly, much research has been conducted on different public segments. We have extensive data on the attitudes, lifestyles, values, behaviors, preferences and media use of every conceivable public segment. We have available to us extensive and continually updated profiles of publics based on age, ethnicity, religion, recreation, political leanings, special interests, hobbies, professions and every other possible segmentation. We know their media habits, their information preferences, their opinion leaders. In today's data-rich environment there is no need for guesswork.

We have information literally at our fingertips to construct persuasive efforts that have high probabilities of success. If we fail, we probably didn't do the research. The point is that we need to access the most current data and studies to select our channels and tactics and to construct our messages and appeals so they are the most effective. The techniques shown in Figure 2.4 are only a sample of the kinds of tips we can glean with a little careful research.

The ethics of persuasion

At the heart of much of the conflict between journalists and marketing, advertising and public relations professionals is the question of ethical practice. Whereas ethical codes for journalists are based on objectivity, the ethical basis for our communication efforts is in advocacy. That foundation does not make the practice of persuasive communication less ethical. In fact, advocacy is key to the effective functioning of a democratic society and a free-market economy.

Because of the influence of marketing, advertising and public relations in our society, it is of primary importance that persuasive appeals be used in an honest and ethical manner. The Institute for Propaganda Analysis has formulated a list of persuasive appeals designed to mislead (Figure 2.5). Sometimes called "propaganda devices," these appeals raise the question, is there a difference between persuasion and propaganda? Some consider persuasion ethical and propaganda unethical because of its attempt to distort or mislead. Others contend they are the same, the judgment of propriety being a matter of perspective.

Whereas some of the "propaganda devices" in Figure 2.5 are clearly unethical, others are used quite ethically in persuasive campaigns. For example, "name-calling" is widely used as labeling an issue or event for ease in reference. A short label

Figure 2.4
Guidelines for changing attitudes and opinions

SOURCE CREDIBILITY (ETHOS)

- A highly credible communicator is more likely to persuade opinion change than someone with low credibility; nevertheless, the communicator's credibility is less of a factor over time since people tend to remember ideas longer than they remember sources.

- Communicators' motives affect their ability to persuade and motivate.

- Communicators are more effective if they express some views shared by the audience.

- The audience's opinion of the persuader is often directly influenced by its attitude toward the message.

RATIONAL APPEALS (LOGOS)

- The people who are most likely to be influenced by a rational appeal are those who already have a high level of involvement and are motivated to think deeply about your argument.

- Successful persuasion considers the beliefs and values underlying attitudes as well as attitudes and opinions themselves.

- The quality of your evidence will make or break the persuasiveness of your message.

- The most effective messages contain supporting and opposing viewpoints and provide a refutation of the opposing view.

- Desired opinion change is more likely if you explicitly state your conclusions rather than letting the audience draw its own.

EMOTIONAL APPEAL (PATHOS)

- A strong threat may be less effective than a mild threat in inducing the desired attitude change.

- The effectiveness of a fear appeal depends on the audience's attitudes and behavioral intentions.

SELECTIVE PERCEPTION

- The people you most want to reach in your target audience are the least likely to be present or to choose to perceive your communication.

MESSAGE REPETITION AND STRENGTH

- Over time, the effects of a persuasive communication tend to wear off, but repeating a message tends to prolong its influence.

- The more extreme the opinion change requested, the more actual change is likely to result.

GROUP INFLUENCE AND SOCIAL NORMS

- Opinions and attitudes are strongly influenced by groups to which a person belongs or wants to belong.

- A person is typically rewarded for conforming to the standards of the group and punished for deviating from them.

- People with the strongest ties to a group are probably the least influenced by messages that conflict with group standards.

- Opinions expressed or shared with others are typically harder to change than opinions held privately.

- Audience participation helps overcome resistance.

reference is selected based on the perception or image it conveys. The same revolutionaries in a developing nation are alternately considered both terrorists and freedom fighters, depending on your point of view. The label is consistent with the labeler's perception, not necessarily intended to mislead. To detractors, such a label is considered "propaganda;" to supporters it is an accurate depiction of reality.

In fact, persuasion actually began as propaganda and was not considered "evil" until World War II when Nazi Germany engaged in the practice. In the 17th century, Pope Gregory XV established the College of Propaganda to train priests to proselyte to propagate the faith. The United States engaged in propaganda efforts in both world wars, not only directed at the populations of Europe but also at Americans (e.g., Rosie the Riveter). Perhaps the most reasonable approach to evaluating persuasive methods and appeals is to avoid the persuasion versus propaganda debate and to simply follow ethical standards that prevent us from manipulating information and publics.

Appendix C contains the codes of ethics from a number of research and advocacy-based professional associations such as the American Marketing Association, the American Advertising Federation, the Association of Institutional Research and

 Figure 2.5
Persuasive appeals or propaganda devices

Name-calling: Giving an idea a label, either good or bad, to encourage the public to accept and praise or reject and condemn the idea without examining evidence.

Glittering generality: Associating something with a "virtue word" that is designed to encourage the public to accept and approve the idea without examining the evidence.

Transfer: Transferring the aura of authority and prestige of a celebrity or opinion leader to a product, person or idea to persuade the public to accept or reject it.

Testimonial: Endorsement of a product by a celebrity or opinion leader who actually uses it.

Plain folks: Attempting to convince the public that a speaker's (often a politician's) ideas are good because they are "of the people" or because the speaker is "one of us."

Card-stacking: Selective use of facts to tell only one side of the story, often obscuring the other side.

Bandwagon: Appealing to conformity with the majority to persuade by encouraging the public to join their friends and neighbors because "everybody's doing it."

Emotional stereotypes: Evoking an emotional image like the "ugly American" or a "PR flack."

Illicit silence: Withholding information that would clarify a situation or correct an incorrect impression or assumption.

Subversive rhetoric: Attacking the spokesperson rather than the idea, a device frequently used in political campaigns.

Source: The Institute for Propaganda Analysis

the Public Relations Society of America. Following those codes will help us ethically engage in persuasive communication.

According to retired television commentator Bill Moyers, the challenge for communications professionals engaged in persuasion is to do so ethically. Although many practitioners are held to ethical codes of conduct either through their employers or professions, anyone using persuasive devices should meticulously examine the integrity of their methods. Researchers Sherry Baker and David Martinson (2001) developed a tool called the TARES test to help communicators evaluate the ethics of their persuasive intentions and communication. TARES is an acronym that encompasses the following ethical guidelines.

> ***Truthfulness (of the message).*** Ethical communicators must tell the truth. However, sometimes the truth can be used to deceive. At its heart, the principle of truthfulness depends on the intention of the persuader. True information should be communicated without an intent to deceive.
>
> ***Authenticity (of the persuader).*** Ethical communicators must have integrity and personal virtue. Not only must they do the right things, but they must also have the right motivations for doing those things. Ethical communicators are also sincere and genuine. This means they should support and believe in the company, product or person they are advocating. Finally, ethical communicators must be loyal to their employer and, at the same time, maintain independence to follow their own moral compass.
>
> ***Respect (for the persuadee).*** Baker and Martinson wrote that respect for those who we attempt to persuade is the heart of the TARES model. We must think of those we are persuading as human beings with individual worth, and respect their right to make choices that are different than what we intend.
>
> ***Equity (of the persuasive appeal).*** Ethical communicators cannot take advantage of another's circumstances or lack of knowledge to notch a victory. Persuasion attempts must be fair. This means that communicators must work to level the playing field so persuadees aren't manipulated. This principle can be characterized as the Golden Rule of persuasion: "Persuade others as you would want to be persuaded."
>
> ***Social responsibility (for the common good).*** Ethical communicators must think about the impact of their persuasive efforts on society and not just on their employer's bottom line. Will advocating for a client, product or idea do harm to individuals or society at large? This principle is the embodiment of the relationship approach to public relations discussed in Chapter 1.

Ethical decision-making is critical to our reputation as professionals. Although ethical codes and behavior are addressed more fully in a later chapter, it should be noted here that all decisions we make as communications professionals affect the profession itself, as well as our own status and reputation. No decisions are free from ethical considerations; every decision we make as practitioners has ethical consequences. Being aware of those consequences and carefully examining our proposed plans and behaviors according to sound ethical principles will help us avoid the ethical land mines that some of our colleagues unwittingly encounter.

Persuasion in and of itself is not unethical. Advocacy has a strong history and important role in our free society. Nevertheless, it must be conducted according to principles that support not only the public interest but also the public's right to know and choose.

Summary

Marketing and public relations is the business of disseminating information, persuading opinion change and motivating behavior. Since behavior is based on values, beliefs and attitudes, it is imperative we understand how to influence those cognitive elements or we will not meet with success. It is equally important to understand the cognitive processes publics apply in making their behavioral decisions. Sometimes providing public information is enough; often it is not. Persuasive methods, used ethically and responsibly, are inextricable elements of advocacy communication.

Application case

Consequences of climate change: Spreading Lyme disease

from New Hampshire's public health system and Jackson Jackson & Wagner

In 1975, researchers wondered why a large number of children were being diagnosed with juvenile rheumatoid arthritis in Lyme, CT, and two neighboring towns. They found that tiny deer ticks infected with a spiral-shaped bacterium were responsible for the outbreak. Thus, Lyme disease got its name.

As summers have lengthened and gotten warmer, these ticks have spread across the country (reported in nearly all states in the U.S.), but 95% are concentrated in the coastal Northeast, mid-Atlantic states, Wisconsin, Minnesota and northern California.

New Hampshire's public health system was determined to find a way to lower the transmission and impact of this disease and asked for assistance in raising awareness and changing behaviors among adults and children when they are outside. Yet, as always in the public health arena, there was limited funding. It was determined to target those: (1) who are most at risk of Lyme disease, (2) who could serve as role models for others, and (3) who could be more easily — and inexpensively — reached.

Assume you have been hired by New Hampshire's public health system to provide an analysis of the potential publics and how best to reach and persuade them. Use the information provided in this case and principles from this chapter to complete the following tasks.

1. Use Klapper's concepts of selective exposure, selective perception and selective retention to determine which potential publics could be most easily and inexpensively reached regarding the issue of Lyme disease. Show your thinking. Explain how specific insights from these theories influenced your analysis.

2. Apply what you learned about opinion leaders and public opinion to determine which potential publics could serve as role models for others on the issue of Lyme disease. Show your thinking. Explain how specific insights from these theories led to your recommendations.

3. Use either Rokeach's theory of beliefs, values and attitudes or Fishbein and Ajzen's theory of reasoned action to determine which potential publics could be most at risk (i.e., achieve the greatest value in changing their behaviors) of contracting Lyme disease. Show your thinking. Explain how specific insights from these theories affected your thinking.

4. Identify a public that meets all three of the criteria specified in the campaign strategy. Use Pat Jackson's behavioral model to outline a communication strategy that could move that public from awareness of Lyme disease to engaging in outdoor behaviors that reduce the transmission of the disease.

References and additional readings

Arthur W. Page Society. (2013). *Building Belief: A New Model for Activating Corporate Character and Authentic Advocacy*. http://www.awpagesociety.com/thought-leadership/building-belief

Ajzen, I. (1991). The theory of planned behavior. *Organizational Behavior and Human Decision Processes*, 50, 179–211.

Baker, S. & Martinson, D. L. (2001). The TARES test: Five principles for ethical persuasion. *Journal of Mass Media Ethics*, 16(2-3), 148-175.

Baran, S. J. & Davis, D. K. (1995). *Mass Communication Theory: Foundations, Ferment, and Future*. Belmont, CA: Wadsworth.

Behavioral Insights Research Center. (n.d.). *Institute for Public Relations*. https://instituteforpr.org/behavioral-insights-research-center/about-birc/

Broom, G. M. & Sha, B. (2013). *Cutlip and Center's Effective Public Relations* (11th ed.). Upper Saddle River, NJ: Pearson Education.

Cantril, H. (1944). *Gauging Public Opinion*. Princeton, NJ: Princeton University Press.

Center, A. H., Jackson, P., Smith, S. & Stansberry, F. R. (2014). *Public Relations Practices: Managerial Case Studies and Problems* (8th ed.). Upper Saddle River, NJ: Pearson Education.

Christensen, C. M., Allworth, J. & Dillon, K. (2012). *How Will You Measure Your Life?* New York: Harper Collins.

Cialdini, R. B. (2006). *Influence: The Psychology of Persuasion*. New York: Harper Business.

Coto, D. (2020). Report: FEMA fumbled in Puerto Rico after storms Irma, Maria. *Associated Press*. Retrieved from https://apnews.com/article/puerto-rico-hurricane-irma-storms-latin-america-hurricanes-8bfd2865519e79a2109bab7edb625436

Dillard, J. P. & Pfau, M. (2002). *The Persuasion Handbook: Developments in Theory and Practice*. Thousand Oaks, CA: Sage Publications.

Dillard, J. P. & Shen, L. (2013). *The SAGE Handbook of Persuasion: Developments in Theory and Practice*. Thousand Oaks, CA: Sage Publications.

Discover Puerto Rico. (2019). #CoverTheProgress. PRSA. Retrieved from https://apps.
    prsa.org/Awards/SilverAnvil

Disruptive Innovation Explained. (2012, March 30). *Harvard Business Review.* Retrieved
    from https://www.youtube.com/watch?v=qDrMAzCHFUU

Fishbein, M. & Ajzen, I. (1980). Predicting and understanding consumer behavior: Attitude-
    behavior correspondence. In Ajzen, I. & Fishbein, M. (eds.). *Understanding Attitudes
    and Predicting Social Behavior* (pp. 148–172). Englewood Cliffs, NJ: Prentice Hall.

Jackson Jackson & Wagner. (n.d.).Four steps to public relations behavior change
    thru public relations campaigns. Retrieved from https://patrickjacksonpr.com/
    Theories%20&%20Models/4%20Steps%20to%20Public%20Behavior%20
    Change%20thru%20PR%20Campaigns.pdf

Jackson, P. (1990). Behavioral public relations model. *PR Reporter,* 33(30), 1–2.

Kahneman, D. (2011). *Thinking, Fast and Slow.* New York: Farrar, Straus and Giroux.

Katz, E., Blumler, J. G. & Gurevitch, M. (1973–1974). Uses and gratifications research. *The
    Public Opinion Quarterly,* 37(4), 509–523.

Ketchum. (n.d.). Discover Puerto Rico: #CoverTheProgress. Retrieved from https://www.
    ketchum.com/work/covertheprogess/

Kilgo, D. K. & Mourão, R. R. (2021). Protest coverage matters: How media framing
    and visual communication affects support for Black civil rights protests. *Mass
    Communication and Society,* 24(4), 576-596.

Larson, C. (1983). *Persuasion: Reception and Responsibility.* Belmont, CA: Wadsworth
    Publishing Company.

Littlejohn, S. W. & Foss, K. A. (2010). *Theories of Human Communication* (10th ed.). Long
    Grove, Ill.: Waveland Press, Inc.

Lyons, B. A., Montgomery, J. M., Guess, A. M., Nyhan, B. & Reifler, J. (2021).
    Overconfidence in news judgments is associated with false news susceptibility.
    Proceedings of the National Academy of Sciences, 118(23),1-10.

Martin, D. & Wright, D. K. (2016). *Public Relations Ethics: How to Practice PR Without
    Losing Your Soul.* New York: Business Expert Press.

Nagtegaal, R., Tummers, L., Noordegraaf, M. & Bekkers, V. (2020). Designing to debias:
    Measuring and reducing public managers' anchoring bias. *Public Administration
    Review,* 80(4), 565-576.

Nassar, R. (2020). Framing refugees: The impact of religious frames on U.S. partisans and
    consumers of cable news media. *Political Communication,* 37(5), 593-611.

Navarro, M. (2017). Puerto Rico on her mind: How to help a stricken island called home.
    New York Times. Retrieved from https://www.nytimes.com/2017/11/03/travel/
    puerto-rico-virgin-islands-hurricane-maria-irma-volunteer-tourism.html

Newsom, D., Turk, J. V. & Kruckeberg, D. (2013). *This is PR: The Realities of Public
    Relations* (11th ed.). Independence, KY: Cengage Learning.

Noelle-Neumann, E. (1984). *The Spiral of Silence.* Chicago: University of Chicago Press.

Norris, J. S. (1984). *Public Relations.* Englewood Cliffs, NJ: Prentice-Hall, Inc.

O'Keefe, D. J. (2013). The elaboration likelihood model. In Dillard, J. P. & Shen, L. (eds.).
    The SAGE Handbook of Persuasion: Developments in Theory and Practice. Thousand
    Oaks, CA: Sage.

Rice, D. (2018). 2017's three monster hurricanes — Harvey, Irma and Maria — among
    five costliest ever. *USA Today.* Retrieved from https://www.usatoday.com/story/
    weather/2018/01/30/2017-s-three-monster-hurricanes-harvey-irma-and-maria-
    among-five-costliest-ever/1078930001/

Rogers, E. (2003). *Diffusion of Innovations* (5th ed.). New York: Free Press.

Rokeach, M. (1968). *Beliefs, Attitudes and Values: A Theory of Organization and Change.* San Francisco, CA: Jossey-Bass.

Rothman, A. J., Bartels, R. D., Wlaschin, J. & Salovey, P. (2006). The strategic use of gain- and loss-framed messages to promote healthy behavior: How theory can inform practice. *Journal of Communication,* 56, S202-S220.

Sarkis, S. (2019). Anchoring bias can weigh you down and make you settle for less. *Forbes.* Retrieved from https://www.forbes.com/sites/stephaniesarkis/2019/05/31/anchoring-bias-can-weigh-you-down-and-make-you-settle-for-less/?sh=73a63f92396b

Schindler, R.M. (1992, December). The real lesson of new Coke: The value of focus groups for predicting the effects of social influence. *Marketing Research,* 22–27.

Stiff, J. B. & Mongeau, P. A. (2016). *Persuasive Communication* (3rd. ed.). London: Guilford Press.

Stimson, J. A. (1991). *Public Opinion in America: Moods, Cycles, and Swings.* Boulder, CO: Westview Press.

Strohmaier, N., Pluut, H., van den Bos, K., Adriaanse, J. & Vriesendorp, R. (2021). Hindsight bias and outcome bias in judging directors' liability and the role of free will beliefs. *Journal of Applied Social Psychology,* 51(3), 141-158.

Wilcox, D. L., Cameron, G. T. & Reber, B. H. (2014). *Public Relations: Strategies and Tactics* (11th ed.). New York: Allyn & Bacon.

CHAPTER 3

COMMUNICATIONS RESEARCH METHODS

"Communications research provides a foundation for the entire public relations process from landscape assessment to objective-setting to strategy development to tactical creativity and performance evaluation."

—MARK WEINER
CHIEF INSIGHTS ADVISER, PUBLICRELAY

LEARNING IMPERATIVES

- Understand the necessity of research as a foundation for decision-making.

- Recognize the variety and sources of information available.

- Understand the basic research methodologies for effective communications research.

RESEARCH
Gathering and using information to clarify an issue and solve a problem.

In the last two decades, **research** in the communications field has exploded. Before this time, it was often considered an unaffordable luxury. Now we seem to abound in data, so much so that we sometimes drown in it. The key, now, is to sort through and synthesize data into usable information to help us make wise decisions.

Not only do most successful organizations now do research, but there are a plethora of specialized consultants and research firms which have taken market, social media, environmental, communications and organizational research to levels of sophistication never before dreamed. Whereas in the past, communications practitioners found themselves begging for a pittance to find out what their publics thought, they now have executives whose first question is, "What does the research say?"

As a result, our challenge is no longer to convince practitioners to do research. At this point in your education or career, you have probably learned the value of research and measurement and how to do it or how to buy it. Further, there are now dozens of texts and handbooks as well as online resources for conducting research. The challenge is to provide the basic framework for thinking about and organizing research and analysis, and then, in the next chapter, to apply it in the strategic planning process.

The role of research in communication

FORMATIVE RESEARCH
Research used as a foundation for campaign planning.

EVALUATIVE RESEARCH
Research used to determine the effectiveness of campaign implementation.

Research is only as good as its application to the problem-solving process. Research can contribute to this process in two ways. First, communications professionals use **formative research** to guide their planning efforts. This might involve conducting research to better understand an organization, to identify problems or opportunities or to analyze and segment publics. Second, **evaluative research** helps communicators gauge the effectiveness of tactics, techniques or strategy. Copy testing, monitoring progress during a campaign and determining the overall success of a campaign are all examples of evaluative research. In other words, communications professionals are involved in research at every step of the strategic communications process.

To be research-oriented means gathering and basing decisions on information as part of your daily routine. To be effective in communicating with an organization's publics, we must be constantly listening to them and scanning the organization's operating environment for information. We should establish good communications channels so information is constantly flowing to us — resulting in adjustments and refinements of our efforts as plans proceed.

Research helps us to:

- Save time and money.
- Understand our publics.
- Make sound decisions.
- Avoid mistakes.
- Discover new ideas.
- Identify potential publics.
- Identify communications channels.

- Justify plans.
- Connect with communities.

As professional communicators we should be wary of "gut reactions," knowing what we know about how people perceive and misperceive, as well as how our brain's mental shortcuts can produce biased decisions. Always test the information that leads to conclusions, and especially to key decisions. The next chapter provides a research guide of the information you need to meet the various challenges of an organization and to plan strategically to seize opportunities. In this chapter, we identify some of the best sources of information and the methodologies used to obtain it.

Research methods and the diversity of tools

Research methods are often categorized as formal and informal, quantitative and qualitative, and primary and secondary. Nevertheless, these categorizations are not parallel. For example, formal research is not necessarily quantitative research, nor is it always primary research. A few definitions regarding research will help to avoid confusion.

Formal and informal research. **Formal research** implies a structured study. It is governed by the rules of the scientific method that include previously identifying what you hope to learn, how and from whom. Because it follows universal rules of research, the findings are more accurate and reliable. **Informal research** is less structured and more exploratory. It does not follow specific rules. Nevertheless, it often provides valuable insight to lead us in directions of more formal discovery.

Quantitative and qualitative research. **Quantitative research** transforms information about individuals into numerical data that can be interpreted by statistical analysis. While descriptive statistics provide basic summaries of this type of data, such as frequencies, percentages and averages, inferential statistics use the laws of probability to draw conclusions about a larger population based on data collected from a representative sample of that population. This type of research is valuable for determining how many people hold certain beliefs, values and attitudes and statistically examining the relationships among those concepts. **Qualitative research** is focused on understanding how individuals and groups make sense of the world. This type of research can uncover rich insights about why a particular group of people has certain beliefs, values or attitudes, or how that group of people developed a particular view on an issue. While qualitative research may be supported by some descriptive numerical data, the data themselves are usually comprised of transcripts of spoken words that can be analyzed for patterns and themes. Even though this type of research is not statistically representative of a given population, it can still be governed by the rules of the scientific method. Focus groups, for example, are a qualitative tool. They may be informal discussions but are more often formal research yielding important insights into a public's

FORMAL RESEARCH
Data gathering structured according to accepted rules of research.

INFORMAL RESEARCH
Less-structured exploratory information gathering.

QUANTITATIVE RESEARCH
Using research methods that yield reliable statistical data.

QUALITATIVE RESEARCH
Using research methods that provide deeper insight into attitudes and motivations but don't provide statistical significance.

perceptions, attitudes and motivations. Now that focus group methodology has actually become a dominant method of market research, the rules of research governing this methodology are meticulously followed to ensure the most accurate insights. Although the method is classified as formal research because it follows rules and structure, it is still typically a qualitative approach that yields in-depth understanding but no statistical data.

Primary and secondary research. **Primary research** implies gathering the information firsthand for a specifically identified purpose. It doesn't necessarily refer to survey research. Personal interviews and focus groups, as well as mail and telephone call analysis, yield primary information. Primary research is any type of qualitative or quantitative research that you implement yourself or contract out for a particular purpose. **Secondary research** is primary research data originally collected for a different purpose that is now being drawn upon for a new use. Typically, it is cheaper and faster to use secondary research. In this era of omnipresent data, you should exhaust secondary sources before embarking on any costly primary research efforts.

Given these definitions, the research tools become more difficult to categorize. Focus groups may be formal or informal. They are typically qualitative, but if enough groups are conducted, some quantitative data analysis may be done on the results. Results are primary research when you organize and conduct them for the immediate purpose, but reviewing transcripts and analyses of focus groups conducted for other purposes is secondary research that may shed light on the problem you are trying to solve.

Similarly, personal interviews may be informal and qualitative research. They may be one of your "listening" techniques. Or, given more structure and an appropriate research design, they may be formal and quantitative, allowing statistical analysis with a high degree of confidence that the results reflect the opinions of the larger population. They would be a primary research tool if conducted for the project at hand, yet may be useful as secondary data in subsequent programs.

Whether the research you do is formal or informal, quantitative or qualitative, primary or secondary, depends largely on what you need and how you structure it. You should determine your purpose (what you are hoping to accomplish with the research) and what you are trying to find out from whom, before you decide on the best tools to use and how to structure the effort.

Secondary research

Organizational research

The first place to begin in gathering information is within the organization itself. Many kinds of research tools are available to help gather and assess the information available to you. A communications audit examines all of the organization's communications to see if it supports the organization's mission and message. Environmental scanning within an organization monitors the mood and feelings that exist among the employees, customers, investors, suppliers and many other publics of the organization. Online, mail and telephone analysis helps you track what issues cause concern among your publics. Social media analytics help to monitor your reach and

---

PRIMARY RESEARCH
Firsthand information gathered specifically for your current purpose.

SECONDARY RESEARCH
Information previously assimilated for other purposes that can be adapted for your needs.

relationships. Certainly customer service and complaint sites help you track opinion trends and potential problems.

Important background information about your company or your client is found in the publications, websites and social media sites of the organization. Employee publications, blogs, digital communications, annual reports, brochures and marketing materials, policy and procedures manuals, organizational charts, sales and accounting records, histories and any other material available from the organization, either in hard copy or electronically, can be valuable information. Keep in mind that such material usually possesses an inherent bias, and you need to look outside the organization as well as inside to make sure you have the complete picture. Organizations do not often open their closets to display the skeletons through their own printed and electronic material. You will get rich information about the organization through its material, but you will not usually get the bad news. And, not knowing the bad news may sabotage your communication efforts. While the organization itself is the place to start your research, it should never be your only source.

The organization may also have data from past surveys or research. You may need some primary research to determine the mood and opinion of employees. Most organizations would benefit by taking a searching look inside before focusing research efforts externally.

Internet and library research

Information technology and the computer revolution have given us access to incredible resources for research. Information that would take weeks or months to find from original sources is now readily available at our fingertips. The communications professional of today and of the future must understand how to get good data from the internet to compete in this new environment.

Online research gives the researcher access to the collections held by thousands of libraries and organizations and to databases full of information and references. Nevertheless, much is still available in library documents that may be difficult to find or expensive to secure elsewhere. Most of us underestimate the value of the data available in our local college and public libraries. And unless you actually take the time to investigate, to talk to a resource librarian or to just explore the collection, you will not appreciate the vast amount of information at your fingertips.

Remember the latest census? It's available on the internet. In that census, some people received a more in-depth questionnaire than the rest of us, and the psychographic data are accessible as well. Further, the census is continually updated with interim studies. Also accessible is a host of government documents and studies published every year, along with many private research studies. You can find national and local newspapers and magazines that date back years, sometimes to the beginning of publication. Often the results of opinion polls can be found, as well as rich economic data on local, state, national and international markets.

Some universities have separate libraries for their business schools. In that case, the business library probably contains detailed market analysis and other such valuable information. While most of this information may be available electronically, there are volumes of information that can only be accessed by visiting a library in person. The more current the information, the more likely you will be able to get it via the internet. Nevertheless, there may be significant risks in ignoring the deeper background that older documents contain.

Organizational information is also readily available on the internet. And increasingly, you will find many independent websites, blogs and other internet sites that contain valuable information. Be careful of the source of the information and seek secondary confirmation when possible. The information may be credible, such as that from an industry analyst with a professional responsibility to provide such information, or it may be a site constructed by a disgruntled customer or employee containing extremely biased or inaccurate information, rumor and innuendo.

External organizations

Our tax dollars support local, state and national government offices that have a charge to operate in the public interest. Providing public information is often an integral part of that responsibility. Much of the information is now available over the internet, but some of the valuable information you seek may only be available upon request, or by digging through studies and papers. Sometimes the bureaucracy can be difficult and getting information can take weeks or even months. Nevertheless, the information available is often critical.

Most cities and states have economic development offices of some kind that collect invaluable information on industries and markets. State, and sometimes local, governments have information on population, wages, education, unemployment, health and just about everything else you can imagine. Data regarding the political, social, economic and even physical environment are readily available from area chambers of commerce and travel councils. Be persistent; the information you want may be part of something else. You will have to do most of the searching, so start specific but be ready to broaden your search until you find documents and reports that will provide the information you need. You have to ask broad and searching questions to get to the right documents and studies.

For example, asking a clerk for any studies on how much college students spend on e-books might not get you the information you want. But studies of online use or income and expenditures of 18- to 24-year-olds or the costs of a college education would all contain information on e-book expenditures.

Inherent in the missions of associations, advocacy groups or professional societies is gathering and disseminating information. One of the most valuable benefits of membership may be access to the research they gather. You may be able to access the information you want from them through their publications or resource libraries. You may have to pay a search or use fee to access the material. In some cases, you may need to get the material through an association member. But the data available are generally very rich, current and valuable.

A word of caution: When you receive data from these kinds of organizations, especially from activist groups, check the sources and methodologies used. Be aware that any information published by an interest group of any kind will be inherently biased to some degree. Make sure you understand and allow for that bias and seek confirming and/or disputing information from other sources, or carefully examine the research methodology used and adjust for distortion.

Media research

Media research straddles the line between secondary and primary research. Depending on the purpose, it could be either. Nevertheless, it is crucial in today's media environment. A number of publishing houses produce internet-accessible media guides and services that provide current and valuable information about media throughout the nation by category: newspapers, magazines, radio stations, television stations, cable stations, websites, social media channels and so on. Media services such as Agility PR Solutions, Cision, Meltwater, Muckrack, Notify and Prowly track editors and reporters by assignment, how to submit pieces and what is typically accepted. The guides also indicate readership, viewership or listenership and will sometimes provide additional **demographic** information that may be of help in profiling key publics. They at least provide a way to contact the media organization to request more detailed information. Most media organizations can provide detailed viewer, listener or reader profiles because they sell advertising. And advertisers want to know who they're buying access to.

Media and internet analysis are a critical part of communications research and evaluation. Whether in-house or a contracted service, tracking such coverage is essential. Nevertheless, because of the time it takes to be thorough, you will usually get more comprehensive and cost-effective analysis if you contract a clipping service. Clipping services may do as little as simply clip, or provide you with a digital copy of, anything (print, broadcast and other digital media) that mentions the company or an issue of interest to the company. At the other end of the spectrum, they may engage in extensive analysis and evaluate the positive or negative impact of the pieces that discuss the organization and its competitors or any of the issues faced by the industry. You can specify the level of service you want and pay accordingly.

Monitoring the internet is particularly important to organizations today. And the methodology has become more sophisticated as tracking tools have been developed and refined. Social media monitoring services such as Brandwatch, Meltwater, Netbase Quid, Sprout Social and Talkwalker allow organizations to "listen" to what people are saying about them online. The data are usually pulled from legacy internet publishers as well as blogs, forums, reviews and social media sites. Using a combination of keywords and Boolean logic, communicators can search for specific conversations and gauge the volume, sentiment (positive or negative) and other attributes of the content. They can also pinpoint specific days and times when conversations are happening, and parse out topic themes and audience characteristics. Media monitoring and analysis companies like Fullintel and Buzzsumo now use artificial intelligence and natural language processing to uncover trending online and social content. Most organizations have given up trying to monitor all the online conversations, but a selective approach to online listening related to issues of concern to your organization is imperative.

At the same time, in the wake of myriad violations of personal data privacy, organizations need to exercise care in the way they "listen" to online conversations. Sadly, the theft of millions of files of personal information is an almost weekly occurrence. For example, in 2021, LinkedIn was hacked and data for 700 million users was posted on the dark web. And in 2019, Facebook apps allowed data from 530 million

DEMOGRAPHIC DATA
Information used to segment publics according to tangible characteristics such as age, gender and socioeconomic status.

users to be accessible on the internet. Also, data mining operations have caused concern since Cambridge Analytica, a UK-based political consulting firm, harvested Facebook data with the intent of using the data to target people with political advertising. As a result, Cisco's most recent consumer privacy survey found that 89% of respondents said they cared about data privacy and 82% said they were willing to act to protect their online data.

We need to be careful that our online listening does not negatively affect the trust we work so hard to build with key publics. Large-scale violations of public trust typically result in government regulation, like that recently enacted in the European Union (EU). The General Data Protection Regulation (GDPR) that became effective in May 2018 requires that all organizations doing business in the EU issue notification of data breaches and be transparent about what data are being collected and why. Going forward, consent to collect and use data from online users will have to go beyond the simple click boxes agreeing to "terms and conditions."

Since the GDPR became law, numerous states in the United States have passed data privacy laws, including California, Colorado, Connecticut, New York, Virginia and Utah.

Primary research

Focus groups

Focus group research has become an important and reliable source of data to understand our publics. A focus group is a moderator-led discussion with four to 14 participants. The moderator asks open-ended questions to garner qualitative responses on attitudes and behavior.

Moderators must be careful not to bias the discussion by injecting personal opinion or information into the group. They should encourage participation from all members of the group and probe for in-depth understanding. The moderator must also create an atmosphere of openness, honesty, safety and confidentiality to engender free and open discussion. With the permission and knowledge of the participants, the session is usually recorded (audio or video), and the discussion transcribed for further evaluation and data tabulation.

Focus group research is generally easier to conduct than survey research and provides rapid results along with depth of opinion and attitudes within the group. The discussion-based nature of focus groups shapes, refines and crystallizes opinions and attitudes (see Figure 3.1). Further, while not always less expensive than other kinds of research, it is often more cost-effective. Focus groups used to be conducted in communications and marketing research primarily as discussion forums for advisory committees or idea panels to supplement quantitative research. The information was often used as a precursor to survey research to assist in developing a questionnaire that adequately probed attitudes and opinions. In today's research-oriented marketplace, many practitioners recognize that, while survey research is becoming less credible as an accurate representation of publics, focus groups provide the kind of information needed to immediately address and resolve problems.

As discussed in the previous chapter, people do not behave in isolation. The discussion and refinement of opinions and attitudes which occur in focus groups often provide problem-solving behavioral information that surveys cannot. The example

⬡ FOCUS GROUP RESEARCH

Moderator-led discussions with fewer than 15 participants providing in-depth information on attitudes and behaviors.

Figure 3.1
Uses and abuses of focus group research

USES

IMMEDIATE RESULTS. Focus group research is relatively easy to organize, implement and analyze. That often makes it much less costly as well.

COMFORT IN NUMBERS. A small group is usually less intimidating than a personal interview. People feel more comfortable expressing opinions.

FLEXIBLE AND RESPONSE-ORIENTED. Because the structure is less rigid, the group takes the discussion where it wants to go, and a broader investigation of the topic is possible. The focus is on responses (attitudes and opinions), not on the questions, so information emerges on salient topics through the natural flow of discussion.

GAUGE OF GROUP BEHAVIOR. Rather than researching individual behavior or potential behavior, focus groups explore attitudes and behavior influenced by the group or society, a far more reliable measure and predictor.

ISSUES EXPLORED AND OPINIONS CRYSTALLIZED. Because the group is discovering and examining attitudes and behaviors they may not have thought about before, it allows time for discussion and rumination to discover motivations.

SENSITIVE ISSUES ADDRESSED. When members of the group can empathize with one another because of similar experiences, they are more open in the discussion of sensitive, value-laden issues like stem cell research or domestic abuse.

ATTITUDES OF ACTIVISTS INCLUDED. A focus group provides a cooperative atmosphere which may encourage the participation of activists and organizational detractors not willing to participate in other kinds of research.

ISSUES AND JARGON IDENTIFIED. The responses from a focus group identify the issues of most concern to the group as well as the language they use and can understand in discussing those topics. Such a foundation provides solid ground for subsequent research and message development.

ABUSES

WEAK OR DOMINANT MODERATOR. A weak moderator may allow some members of the group to dominate, and others may be intimidated or refrain from offering opinions. The group result will be biased and probably useless. A moderator who dominates the group will impose opinions and attitudes rather than probing the attitudes of the group.

NOT HOMOGENEOUS. A focus group should be homogeneous, or the members will be intimidated and uncomfortable with sharing their attitudes. Broad representation is achieved by conducting multiple focus groups among several homogeneous publics, rather than mixing representation within a single group.

TOO FEW GROUPS. For the research to be valid, a number of groups must be conducted among various homogeneous publics. Then the information can be consolidated to provide a more comprehensive look.

GENERALIZING TO A POPULATION. Focus group research is qualitative, not statistical. You cannot generalize your conclusions to any "general public." Your conclusions are very much issue- and group-specific. They may be indications that will lead you in problem-solving or in designing quantitative research, but they do not represent public opinion.

cited in the previous chapter of the introduction of New Coke is a case in point. Both research techniques were used, yielding opposite results. Yet because of the reputation for validity of survey research over focus-group responses, the company chose to rely on predictions of behavior based on attitudes expressed in isolation. They should have more carefully considered the group behavior that emerged from the focus groups.

Further, focus group research can demonstrate the process of opinion formation. While not representative, the group is a social microcosm of a larger public. The analysis of how attitudes and opinions change based on the flow of the discussion can help us know what information people need to make sound decisions and what appeals will be most effective in the larger arena. Innovations in focus group research now allow quantification of results if certain conditions are met. Conducting large numbers of groups and employing some content analysis techniques can make the data statistically reliable.

The internet provides an interesting resource for traditional focus group research. Scheduled online chats can produce similar results without the geographic restrictions. Nevertheless, care must be taken that participants are invited and known. Otherwise, the data may not be useful for the researcher's purpose. Face-to-face group discussion is still preferable but can be simulated using tools such as Zoom or Microsoft Teams.

Copy and product testing

One classic use of focus groups is for copy and/or product testing. But this is not the only method by which to test. Copy testing simply selects individuals within your

TIPS FROM THE PROS

How to use research methods in the day-to-day practice of PR

Angela Dwyer, head of insights at Fullintel, a media monitoring and analysis company, and member of the Institute of Public Relations (IPR) Measurement Commission tips you off on different research methods that can help answer the burning questions that keep clients up at night.

When I hear the phrase "strategic public relations," I quickly rephrase it to "research-based public relations." That's because if I want to help clients be strategic—and make smarter communications decisions—I need to use research.

It's just not enough to have a good idea or to tell clients the solution without explanation. You need to show your clients through data insights. The gathering, analysis and communication of that data is called research.

How do you apply the research methods you learned in school to answer real-world questions?

- *Start* by determining a research question that aligns with a specific objective. Because there's an overwhelming amount of data out there, focusing on a specific question can help narrow the approach and save you from drowning in semi-relevant data.
- *Next,* review the research you already have—secondary data or any data that clients have access to that can help identify gaps.
- *Finally,* choose an initial research method, knowing that you may use more than one tool in your research toolkit.

To make this process more tangible, let's walk through some common questions I often hear from clients across different industries. As we go through each, you'll notice the tools are similar, but the magic is in the details of the application.

Here are five frequent questions I get and the research methods I use to answer them.

1. *How do I measure the quality of my media coverage?* Through a review of secondary research, identify multiple factors in media that might influence reader recall or perceptions such as branded visuals, headline mentions, brand prominence, spokespeople and sentiment. Then conduct a survey to test these factors and weight their impact in a media impact score. With that score, next do content analysis to measure these factors and score the quality of coverage. The score can be tracked over time and benchmarked against competitors.

2. *How can I show that my PR work drives sales?* One of the greatest challenges for PR professionals is showing that the work they do impacts actual business outcomes, such as sales. In this case, use a combination of media analysis and survey data to show the impact of PR. Media analysis measures the quality of content and can even predict the likelihood of coverage impact. Secondary research shows—and the use of primary research survey data could confirm—that exposure to news content has an impact on purchase intent, which is a proxy for sales.

3. *Which influencers should I use for my campaign?* To identify the right influencers, start with a focus group consisting of members of your key audience. Ask questions aimed at understanding who they relate to, trust and find the most credible. Following this, conduct a social media analysis to see which influencers drive the most engagement with your target audience.

4. *How can I increase trust in my brand?* Trust is the currency of business and the key to reputation. To increase trust, start by defining a trust baseline. Secondary research reveals three well-tested factors of trust: ability, benevolence and integrity. Through a survey, rank which factors are most important to building trust that also impact reputation and purchase intent. From there, help your clients prioritize factors to maximize trust-building goals.

5. *How do I quantify the impact of PR relative to other marketing efforts for my CEO?* Quantifying the impact of PR can be difficult, especially relative to other communication methods with more clear attribution, such as advertising. Start with a survey measuring exposure to news content and brand advertising, as well as purchase intent. Showing the C-suite that authentic, organic news content leads to more purchase intent than advertising is a great way to start the conversation about the financial impact of PR—and might even lead to a redistribution of the total communications budget.

Contributed by Angela Dwyer. © Kendall Hunt Publishing Company.

target publics and requests their review of copy, whether survey copy or communications copy (brochures, advertising and the like). In product testing, individuals are asked to examine and use a product and provide feedback on everything from packaging and sales methods to product quality. Product tests may be done individually by personal interview, by mail, in focus groups or online.

Honest responses in copy and product testing help avoid costly mistakes. Survey research instruments should always be tested before being implemented. Testing copy helps ensure that the messages are coming across in such a way as to produce the desired result. Marketers test promotional campaigns or products in areas representative of the overall market. Sometimes, two or three different versions of a product or a campaign will be tested in similar geographic areas to determine which will be the most effective to roll out nationwide. Copy and product testing is one of the most valuable kinds of research available to the practitioner. Its greatest value lies in its ability to prevent mistakes — saving money, effort and time.

Psychographic studies

PSYCHOGRAPHIC DATA
Information used to segment publics according to values, attitudes, lifestyles and decision-making processes.

Values and Lifestyles Segmenting, developed by SRI International in 1978, is a research methodology that classifies publics not just by demographic data, but also by **psychographic data** or attitudes, beliefs, lifestyles and decision-making processes. Found to be far more effective in segmenting publics than demographics alone, psychographic studies help us to know what motivates individuals within a particular public. The VALS categories — achievers, survivors, sustainers, belongers and so on — have been used extensively in advertising and marketing to segment and tailor messages to specific target publics. They provide the same valuable segmentation for communication with all the organization's publics. Communicators should know the VALS categories, both the original and the more recently revised segmentations, and understand the motivations tied to the differences in attitudes and lifestyles.

Other market research firms have subsequently developed similar categorizations. In the 1990s, Claritas developed PRIZM, segmenting American consumers into 14 groups with 66 demographically and behaviorally distinct types like "Cosmopolitans" and "Kids & Cul-de-Sacs." PRIZM was subsequently purchased by Nielsen, the company known for rating what people watch on television. Oftentimes, local media and other similar organizations will have segmented and profiled their own target audiences using a combination of demographic and psychographic data. Whereas some will be unwilling to disclose the information, which is quite costly to compile, others may be persuaded to share the data, especially if the request comes from a nonprofit organization or is for a charitable purpose.

Another valuable tool for understanding key publics is Values in Strategy Assessment (VISTA), a process developed by Wirthlin Worldwide which was subsequently purchased by Harris Interactive and is now part of the Harris Brand Platform market segmentation tool. This tool's premise is that values are the fundamental determinant of an individual's behavior and decisions. Understanding the fundamental values of a public provides the strategy to motivate action.

Social media analytics

A new reality of today's communication environment is pervasive social media. With the range of networks available today, organizations must carefully choose those with which they will engage — those most appropriate for building relationships with key publics. Facebook was perhaps the first to become an essential presence for the organization. Now Twitter, Pinterest, Instagram, Tik Tok and a host of other social media networks have become channels through which we interact with our publics. Since the effort to build and manage a social media presence is so costly and time-consuming, it is critical that organizations employ research methods to ensure the effectiveness of their social media efforts in delivering the messages of the organization, building relationships with key publics and providing the interactions key publics desire.

Quite simply, social media analytics are the tools used to measure, analyze and interpret the interactions and relationships with our key publics. Using analytics is essentially "online listening" to help us better meet the needs of publics. The Eastman Kodak Company used online listening several years ago to determine what features consumers wanted in a digital camera. They discovered through their research that no existing camera offered the combination of features consumers were buzzing about on Facebook. Kodak engineers quickly went to work and within a few months were able to bring a new product to market that contained all of the features people wanted most at an affordable price. The new camera sold extremely well, but unfortunately wasn't enough to save the struggling company from bankruptcy in 2012.

This kind of measurement is so important that many of the social media networks have embedded their own monitoring and analytical tools to track social media efforts. In addition, a host of external tools — some free, some for a fee — integrate measurement of all social media efforts. It is essential, nevertheless, that you are careful about what you are measuring. Measuring the number of "likes" or "friends" or "followers" doesn't measure whether publics are actually retaining and acting on your message. Don't confuse interactions with individual pieces of content with overall campaign success. Remember that behavior — or action — is the final evaluation. It doesn't matter how many "followers" you have if they don't actually perform the action that will satisfy your objectives.

Survey research and opinion sampling

A popular quantitative research method is survey research, although its credibility has declined somewhat in recent years because of the difficulty in securing a truly random and representative sample. Several events have affected the ability of researchers to secure statistically generalizable samples. Mail surveys have always been extremely unreliable, not only because of low response rates but also because of sampling bias introduced by those who choose to respond. Only certain kinds of people will take the time to respond to a mail survey, making it anything but representative.

Telephone surveys have also declined in credibility for the same reason. And the "do not call" registry has made telephone surveying more difficult than ever. Although telephone surveys are not prohibited by the registry, the very existence of a "do not call" list seems to have given people the courage to refuse calls they would have previously endured.

Nevertheless, survey research has been a popular research technique in communications and will probably continue to be in some form or another. For example, researchers may find the personal drop-off method to still be effective because of the personal contact involved in dropping off and/or picking up a survey. It is not as easy to turn down someone face to face as it is to say "no" over the telephone.

Online survey companies like Qualtrics make surveying easier but still face the challenge of securing representative samples. Professional research firms have developed other techniques that can also improve response rates.

Survey research is a difficult and exacting approach. It requires meticulous attention to detail at every step of the process: questionnaire design, sample selection, survey implementation, data processing and data analysis. A mistake or misjudgment at any point will skew the results, often without the researcher knowing the data are skewed.

To be valid and reliable, survey research must follow strict rules of research. The idea behind survey research is to take a sample from a population. If we follow good random sampling procedures, we should be able to make that sample relatively representative of the larger population, although we can never be absolutely

MINI CASE

Making peanut allergies history
National Peanut Board and Golin

A government study released in 2016 upended common knowledge about children and peanut allergies. The study showed that introducing peanut-containing foods to infants as early as four to six months old could reduce the likelihood of developing a peanut allergy. In 2017, the National Institute of Allergy and Infectious Diseases (NIAID) issued new allergy prevention guidelines for parents based on the new study. Because the new guidelines contradicted previous advice given to parents, naturally there was some skepticism and confusion among parents about which advice to follow.

CORE OPPORTUNITY
Because the National Peanut Board recognized that it was part of the peanut allergy problem, it saw an opportunity to educate parents about the new guidelines and potentially reduce the number of children who develop peanut allergies.

THE NATIONAL PEANUT BOARD'S STRATEGY
The National Peanut Board's strategy was informed by the following research.
- *Formal, primary, quantitative research:* A survey following the 2017 release of the NIAID peanut-introduction guidelines found that most parents were not aware of the guidelines. It also discovered that parents needed to hear the information from sources they trusted to alleviate their concerns about introducing peanut-containing foods to their infants on their own at home.
- *Formal, secondary, quantitative research:* A survey conducted in 2017 by Children's Hospital Colorado confirmed the results of the National Peanut Board's survey – parents were afraid to give peanut-containing foods to their infants at home.
- *Formal, primary, quantitative research:* The National Peanut Board and Golin conducted a large scale, national survey of 1,000 pregnant women and 1,000 millennial parents in 2018. The results showed that the survey

respondents were unaware of the guidelines, afraid to introduce peanuts to their infants, and disagreed with the recommendations of the NIAID. The survey results also showed that parents needed to hear from trusted sources and see successful examples of parents introducing peanut-containing foods to their children.

To generate additional credibility for their campaign, the National Peanut Board partnered with the American College of Allergy, Asthma and Immunology and the Food Allergy and Anaphylaxis Connection Team. They also secured a celebrity influencer who their target public of parents with infant children could relate to. Actor Justin Baldoni, a star of the show "Jane the Virgin," was also a new dad and a frequent writer on the role of fathers. The campaign featured a series of videos that showed Baldoni introducing peanut-containing foods to his infant son. Baldoni's videos and campaign-related information were hosted on a campaign website: PreventPeanutAllergies.org. The campaign also featured earned media outreach to traditional media and "mommy bloggers," as well as a coordinated owned and social media blitz from the National Peanut Board and its partners during Food Allergy Awareness Week.

RESULTS
- 6.1 million views of Baldoni's videos.
- 34% increase in the number of people who agreed that peanut-containing foods are safe to feed children less than 12 months old.
- 29% increase in the number of people who said they intended to introduce peanut foods to their children at home before 12 months.

© Mr.Alex M/Shutterstock.com

sure of our accuracy unless we survey every individual in the population (a census). The total number of individuals surveyed in the population and the way they are selected will determine how accurately the results reflect the actual population.

Statistical research on very critical issues, or in close political campaigns, needs to have a high level of confidence and a low sampling error, also known as **margin of error**. The **confidence level** reflects the researcher's percentage of certainty that the results would be the same (within the margin of error) upon replication of the survey. The margin of error reflects the percentage points that the sample results, on any given question, may vary from the population as a whole. Increasing the sample size increases the confidence level and decreases the margin of error. The only way to be 100 percent confident and eliminate the margin of error would be to survey the entire population or take a census. Research regarding an organization's publics generally requires at least a 95% confidence level, and a margin of error of +/-5% or less. Further, the more important or controversial the issue, the greater the need for a lower margin of error.

There are two basic kinds of survey sampling: probability and nonprobability. Probability sampling is scientifically random; every individual in the population has a known and equal probability of being selected by chance. Nonprobability samples survey whoever is available, for example, intercepting students during the lunch hour as they enter the student center or interviewing people at a grocery store on Saturday afternoon.

There are also two kinds of errors: sampling error and nonsampling error. **Sampling error** is inherent in survey research because we are collecting data from a portion of the population and not the entire population. As a result, sampling error is the known and expected variance between a random sample's answers and the answers that would be obtained from surveying the entire population. We decrease sampling error by increasing sample size; the closer we get to surveying the whole population, the smaller the sampling error. Sampling error is unavoidable in survey research (unless we take a census) and is measured as a percentage called margin of error.

MARGIN OF ERROR
Also known as sampling error, the inherent possible percentage variation of sample data from the whole population.

CONFIDENCE LEVEL
The percentage of certainty that the results of a survey would be the same if replicated with a different sample.

SAMPLING ERROR
Measured as margin of error, it indicates the possible percentage variation of the sample data from the whole population.

TIPS FROM THE PROS

Beyond sampling error

Dee Allsop, Ph.D., CEO and managing partner of Heart+Mind Strategies and former president of Harris Interactive Solutions Groups—producers of the Harris Poll—tips you off on understanding key factors in survey accuracy.

With the current emphasis on "big data" for critical decision-making, survey and sampling science are all about accurately measuring a small number of people to understand the attitudes and predict the behavior of an entire group. Accuracy in survey research is the direct result of identifying, eliminating or correcting for all types of error or bias that can enter into research. While sampling error is the most visible indicator of survey accuracy reported in the media, your success depends on understanding both sampling and nonsampling errors.

SAMPLING ERROR

Sampling error is the statistical estimate of variation that will occur when using a small number of people (a sample) to approximate a result from a much larger population. One way to think of sampling error is the range of results that would occur if you were to repeat your survey hundreds of times. For example, many surveys report a sampling error of plus or minus 3% at the 95% confidence interval. This simply means that if you were to repeat this study 100 times, 95% of the time your results would fall within a range of 6 percentage points.

NONSAMPLING ERROR

Sampling error is inherent in all surveys. We understand it well and can predict it. Other sources of error are more elusive, yet far more important to accuracy and utility of survey results.

Sample frame. Make sure the sample was taken from the group of people that matter. For example, if the survey is about who will be elected president, the sample should come from people who can actually vote for president: registered voters.

Nonresponse error. Several factors influence a respondent's likelihood to respond (e.g., mode effects, interviewer effects and sensitivity effects). Rather than sampling error, I would much prefer to know the response rate for a survey. A low response rate indicates the survey is less likely to reflect the population in question.

Construct validity. Questions can be worded or constructed to generate just about any result desired. Always read the questions that were asked before interpreting the results. Biased wording will produce biased results.

Institutional reputation. Always check to see who conducted the survey and who paid for it. Reputable companies invest significant time and resources to produce objective findings and eliminate nonsampling errors.

Take a lesson from marketing and survey research companies. Instead of worrying about sampling error, focus on understanding how to reduce nonsampling error through good survey design, questionnaire construction, interviewing execution and data processing and correction.

Nonsampling error is all other types of errors introduced into the process. Mistakes made in questionnaire construction, survey implementation, data entry and tabulation are all nonsampling errors. Great care must be taken in designing and implementing the questionnaire. Question and answer categories must be worded to avoid the introduction of bias so that answers accurately reflect the information the researcher needs.

Bias can also be introduced in the implementation of the survey. Ensuring strict confidentiality of responses can lessen courtesy bias, or the tendency of respondents not to answer questions honestly so as not to offend the researchers. Training interviewers to ask questions without injecting value inflection or personal comments, explanation or other bias is also critical. Further, great care must be taken in coding the surveys and entering the data. Data processing converts the observations and responses into statistics for interpretation. Data analysis manipulates the data to make logical inferences. For the inferences to be reliable, the data must be accurately entered and processed.

Finally, the inferences made must be fully supportable by the data set. A few years ago, a ballot measure in Utah proposed a light rail transportation system to

NONSAMPLING ERROR
Mistakes made in designing and implementing a questionnaire that may include definitional differences, misunderstandings and misrepresentations as well as coding errors and/or problems that negatively influence response rates.

be funded by a small tax increase. When the measure was soundly defeated, many analysts concluded it was a vote against light rail. In reality, it was more likely a vote against the funding method, not the light rail system itself. When we deal with statistics and make inferences from data, we must be very careful that the data support the conclusions. Otherwise, we have established a faulty foundation for decision-making.

In addition to the types of survey research discussed above, other variations have specific purposes and benefits. The following short descriptions will provide a basis upon which to investigate the techniques for any given research situation.

>   ***Purposive sampling.*** Based on Katz and Lazarsfeld's two-step flow theory, purposive sampling identifies and surveys opinion leaders to determine attitudes and behaviors. The researcher must devise a procedure that selects the target publics' influentials (or causes them to self-select), and then survey opinion and behavior. It is also helpful to know a little bit about opinion leaders, such as where they get their information about certain issues. Understanding opinion leaders helps us understand how they will influence others. The Edelman Trust Barometer is an example of purposive sampling.
>
>   ***Stratified sampling.*** Truly random sampling should yield a cross section of the population representative of the characteristics within the population (i.e., proportionate numbers of women and men and so on). Whenever we skew the randomness of the sample by using techniques that make it easier for us to complete the research, like surveying every "nth" number from a local telephone list, we risk jeopardizing the representativeness of our sample. If obtaining a truly proportionate representation is critical, the research sample should be stratified so that it includes appropriate proportions of the key segments of the overall population.
>
>   ***Internet surveys.*** A growing area of survey research is conducting surveys over the internet and through social media. While there is inherent bias because of the nature of accessible respondents, this data can be extremely valuable if the purpose is consistent with the population sample. Increasingly, organizations use this method to survey their members, employees or customers. Commercial firms with access to email lists may further facilitate this method. The low-cost nature, ease of conducting and rapid feedback of internet surveys have fueled their popularity.
>
>   ***Personal interviews.*** Very sensitive issues and research that requires deep probing for attitudes and behaviors are best addressed through personal interviews. The personal interview ensures greater control over the sample and the data. But not only is this method costly, it requires a lot of time and well trained interviewers. Nevertheless, in certain circumstances, it is the only viable method to secure reliable and useful information.
>
>   ***Benchmark surveys.*** This type of survey is simply a periodic reexamination of attitudes and opinions within the population. An initial survey is done to set a benchmark against which subsequent survey results are compared. Benchmark surveys are good tools for measuring change as well as for evaluating the success of a program.
>
>   ***Panel studies.*** Sometimes you will want to study attitudes and opinions on a variety of issues over a period of time. Panel studies select respondents who will be available for follow-up surveys at least once and often several times. For example, a newspaper will select individuals from its readership to follow

a specific issue or election and respond to queries at specific points in the campaign. Behavioral studies are also sometimes conducted by a panel to assess whether a change in behavior is temporary and what motivates permanent change.

Omnibus surveys. One of the easiest and least expensive methods of obtaining survey data is to add a few questions to an omnibus survey being prepared by a professional research company. These surveys, sometimes called tag-on surveys, usually have multiple research clients that share the costs and the common demographic data collected. Specific data gathered from the questions each client adds remains proprietary. The advantages are the cost saving shared by multiple clients and the currency of the data because the surveys are ongoing and conducted regularly. In addition, the reliability of the data is high as the sample size is usually large.

Summary

The communications environment has changed. CEOs require "big data" to make decisions, and they expect our recommendations to be logically based on reliable information. To secure a constant flow of the kind of information you need to make reliable decisions, to effectively meet challenges and to plan strategic action, you must find the right combination of continuous research techniques. The purpose of the research and the kind of information desired drive the selection of methodology. Otherwise your research will be useless because it is inaccurate or because it doesn't provide the information you need to design persuasive campaigns.

Application case

Thrive Indianapolis electric vehicle campaign
from the City of Indianapolis Office of Sustainability and Pivot Marketing

The City of Indianapolis developed a plan to make the city more resilient and sustainable called "Thrive Indianapolis." The plan reflects the city's goal to become carbon neutral by 2050. It was developed in response to the city winning a bid for support from the American Cities Climate Challenge, which provided Indianapolis with support from Bloomberg Philanthropies, "including additional staff capacity, technical assistance from world class partners, access to intensive peer-to-peer networking and support in launching communications, outreach and education campaigns."

The City of Indianapolis' Office of Sustainability administers the Thrive Indianapolis plan. A key part of the plan is to increase electric vehicle adoption in Central Indiana.

Assume you have been hired by the City of Indianapolis' Office of Sustainability to conduct initial research for a strategic communications campaign focused on increasing electric vehicle adoption. Use the information provided in this case and principles from this chapter to complete the following tasks regarding campaign research.

1. Think through the types of secondary research (listed below) that you might use to develop this campaign. Identify specific sources you would use. Provide links (URLs) and a brief description of the kind of information you would expect to find from each source.
   a. Which organizations would help you secure the research you need and why?
   b. What internet or library sources could you consult to help you learn more about electric vehicle adoption?
   c. What external organizations could help you learn more about electric vehicle adoption?
   d. What kinds of media research could you conduct to help you learn about what the media and/or Indianapolis residents are saying about electric vehicles or the Thrive Indianapolis plan?

2. Determine which primary research methods would give you the data necessary to build this campaign. Provide a description about why each of the following primary research methods would either be useful or not useful. If you think a research method would be useful, provide an additional description of the population(s) the data should come from, as well as what you would expect to learn from the data.
   a. Focus groups
   b. Copy and product testing
   c. Psychographic studies
   d. Social media analytics
   e. Survey research and opinion sampling

References and additional readings

Babbie, E. (2020). *The Practice of Social Research* (15th ed.). Boston, MA: Cengage Learning.

Bloomberg Philanthropies. (n.d.). American cities climate challenge. Retrieved from https://www.bloomberg.org/environment/supporting-sustainable-cities/american-cities-climate-challenge/

Brown, T. J., Suter, T. A., & Churchill, Jr., G. A. (2018). *Basic Marketing Research: Customer Insights and Managerial Action* (9th ed.). Boston, MA: Cengage Learning.

Cisco. (2022). *Data Transparency's Essential Role in Building Customer Trust*. Retrieved from https://www.cisco.com/c/dam/en_us/about/doing_business/trust-center/docs/cisco-consumer-privacy-survey-2022.pdf?CCID=cc000160&DTID=esootr000875&OID=wprsc030156

DiStaso, M. W. & McAvoy, J. (2018, May 25). What PR pros need to know for GDPR compliance day. *Institute for Public Relations*. Retrieved from https://instituteforpr.org/what-pr-pros-need-to-know-for-gdpr-compliance-day/

Fink, A. (2002). *The Survey Kit* (2nd ed.). Newbury Park, CA: Sage Publications.

Golin. (n.d.). National Peanut Board: Peanut-powered parents. Retrieved from https://golin.com/work/national-peanut-board-peanut-powered-parents/

Griggs, I. (2018, March 22). "A watershed moment:" Have people woken up to how their Facebook data is used following the Cambridge Analytica scandal? *PR Week*. Retrieved from https://www.prweek.com/article/1460137/a-watershed-moment-people-woken-facebook-data-used-following-cambridge-analytica-scandal

Greenbaum, T. L. (1997) *The Handbook for Focus Group Research*. Newbury Park, CA: Sage Publications.

Grunig, J. E. & Grunig, L. A. (2001). Guidelines for formative and evaluative research in public affairs: A report for the Department of Energy Office of Science. *Institute for Public Relations*. Retrieved from http://www.instituteforpr.org/wp-content/uploads/Guidelines-for-Formative-and-Evaluative-Research-in-Public-Affairs.pdf

Hill, M. & Swinhoe, D. (2022, Nov. 8). The 15 biggest data breaches of the 21st century. *CSO*. Retrieved from https://www.csoonline.com/article/2130877/the-biggest-data-breaches-of-the-21st-century.html

Hood, I. (2018, March 22). Facebook and Cambridge Analytica — it's time to make choices. *PR Week*. Retrieved from https://www.prweek.com

Indianapolis Office of Sustainability & Pivot Marketing. (2022). Highly EVolved campaign steers drivers away from fossil fuels. *PRSA*. Retrieved from https://www.prsa.org/conferences-and-awards/awards/search-silver-anvil-case-studies

LEAP. (n.d.). Peanut allergy guidelines. Retrieved from https://www.leapstudy.co.uk/peanut-allergy-guidelines#.Y69SWezMITU

Lindenmann, W. K. (2006). Public relations research for planning and evaluation. *Institute for Public Relations*. Retrieved from http://www.instituteforpr.org/wp-content/uploads/2006_Planning_Eval.pdf

National Peanut Board & Golin. (2019). Making peanut allergies history — Driving parents to be the change. *PRSA*. Retrieved from https://www.prsa.org/conferences-and-awards/awards/search-silver-anvil-case-studies

Office of Sustainability. (n.d.). Retrieved from https://www.indy.gov/agency/office-of-sustainability

Paine, K. D. (2011). *Measure What Matters: Online Tools For Understanding Customers, Social Media, Engagement, and Key Relationships*. Durham, NH: Paine Publishing.

Paine, K. D. (2007). *Measuring Public Relationships: The Data-Driven Communicator's Guide to Success*. Durham, NH: Paine Publishing.

Stacks, D. W. (2016). *Primer of Public Relations Research* (3rd ed.). New York: Guilford Publications, Inc.

Stacks, D. W. & Michaelson, D. (2014). *A Practitioner's Guide to Public Relations Research, Measurement and Evaluation* (2nd ed.). New York: Business Expert Press.

Thrive Indianapolis. (n.d.). Retrieved from https://www.thriveindianapolis.com/home

Weverbergh, R. & Vermosesen, K. (n.d.). GDPR for PR and corporate communication: A checklist. *Finn*. Retrieved from https://www.finnpr.com/blogs/gdpr-pr-and-corporate-communication-checklist

CHAPTER 4

STRATEGICALLY APPLYING RESEARCH AND SOCIAL INSIGHTS

"Today one of the big faults that we run into time after time is we get exquisite answers to the wrong problems."

—HAROLD BURSON
FOUNDER OF BURSON-MARSTELLER

LEARNING IMPERATIVES

- Understand how to organize research and draw inferences that support strategic planning.

- Learn how to use stakeholder research to facilitate communication and relationship building with key publics.

- Learn how to determine publics' self-interests, opinion leaders and preferred communications channels.

- Understand how to use information to determine strengths, weaknesses, opportunities and threats.

- Learn how to synthesize broad information into a concise situation analysis and core challenge/opportunity statement.

INTERNAL ENVIRONMENT
Events or conditions inside an organization that influence how it operates. Factors that influence internal environment can be categorized as strengths or weaknesses.

EXTERNAL ENVIRONMENT
Economic, political and social developments that occur outside an organization but have an influence on it. The source of opportunities, challenges and risks.

STAKEHOLDER
A broad group of individuals that has a vested interest, or "stake," in an organization.

R esearch should be an established and ongoing process in any organization. Successful organizations are always scanning both the **internal environment** and the **external environment**, gathering data and feedback from key **stakeholders** and **publics**, as well as measuring the effectiveness of their communication in moving toward established goals. At some point, the key information is pulled together to support planning, but that does not signal an end to research.

The savvy professional is always looking for new information that may adjust plans at any point or reconfirm the validity of current efforts. Research that we call "evaluation" in the Strategic Communications Matrix focuses on measuring our success rather than gathering information to chart a course. Nevertheless, what we find out from evaluation integrates with the constant flow of other information to become the foundation of new efforts, programs and campaigns.

Research helps us identify the right problems to solve and provides the information that helps us find solutions that work. It also demonstrates our credibility to our clients or to management. If the research process can be said to have a beginning, it starts when someone first states a problem or discovers an opportunity. Someone — a client, a customer, a colleague, a supervisor or you — identifies an **issue** or an opportunity. Then we start to organize what we know around that issue or opportunity. We also reach out to gather what we don't know but need to know.

That's when the real work begins. Facts and information are gathered from all sources and organized to be sorted and evaluated. Figure 4.1 is a graphic depiction of an organization's operating environment. This diagram illustrates a variety of possible stakeholder groups, both external and internal, with which an organization may need to communicate about a particular issue or opportunity. It also highlights characteristics of an organization that stakeholders evaluate in forming their perceptions of reputation and relationship. This visual representation highlights the breadth of perspective necessary to gain an accurate understanding of how the issue or opportunity impacts an organization and related stakeholders.

STRATEGIC COMMUNICATIONS MATRIX

RESEARCH

1. BACKGROUND	A synthesis of primary and secondary research on the industry, external environment, organization, product, service or issue. It includes a stakeholder analysis and segmentation study that identifies current trends in opinions, attitudes and behaviors. Resources such as staffing, facilities and intervening publics are also identified.
2. SITUATION ANALYSIS	Two paragraphs. The first is a statement of the current situation and a description of the challenge or opportunity based on research. The second identifies potential difficulties that could impede success.
3. CORE PROBLEM/ OPPORTUNITY	A one-sentence statement of the main difficulty or prospect, including likely consequences if not resolved or realized.

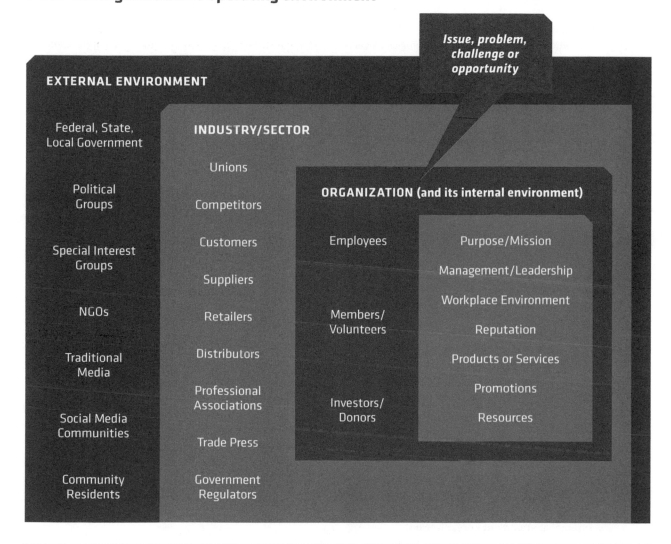

Figure 4.1
The organization's operating environment

The Communications and Marketing Research Guide in Figure 4.2 shows in more detail the depth of research you will need for each area of the diagram in Figure 4.1. It gives suggestions about the types of information that should be considered in analyzing the external environment, the industry in which the organization operates and internal organization factors. Translate the concepts in both figures to whatever economic sector you are representing. Your analysis may have a commercial product orientation, a corporate issue management focus, a nonprofit fundraising challenge or any number of other purposes. Figures 4.1 and 4.2 suggest areas for research that can be universally applied.

If you are designing the first-ever communications effort or strategic communications plan for your client or company, the research section of your plan may take a significant amount of time to complete. It may require an exhaustive search

PUBLIC
A specific group of people who share a common interest.

ISSUES
Problems or disputes that arise between organizations and publics. Issues can evolve over time changing from emergent to current to crisis to dormant.

Figure 4.2
Communications and marketing research guide

1. External environment
- Political, economic, social, technological, legal and/or environmental (i.e., climate, weather, geography) conditions within which the organization operates and the problem, challenge or issue has occurred.
- Current state of the problem, issue, challenge or opportunity.
- History, evolution and future direction of the problem, issue, challenge or opportunity.

2. Industry
- Organizations, companies, sales, distribution patterns, control and regulation, promotional activity, geographic characteristics, profit patterns, strengths, challenges.
- Industry growth patterns, primary demand curve, per capita consumption, potential.
- History, technological advances, trends.
- Impact of the problem, issue, challenge or opportunity on the industry.

3. Market share and competition
- Share of the market in terms of dollars, units, clients, donors, services, etc.
- Market potential.
- Competitors and their potential.
- Competing attitudes, ideas and lifestyles.

4. Stakeholder research
- Stakeholders affected by the problem, issue, challenge or opportunity.
- Current attitudes, opinions and values of stakeholders pertaining to the problem, issue, challenge or opportunity.
- Active or aware publics that may have formed in response to the problem, issue, challenge or opportunity.
- Demographic and psychographic data (beliefs, values, attitudes, lifestyles and decision-making processes).
- Relationship quality between stakeholders, publics and the organization.
- Social media conversations about the issue, challenge or opportunity, including hashtags, search terms, key words, volume, sentiment, trends, engagement, macro and micro influencers, content authors and publishers.
- Motivating self-interests.
- Intervening publics and opinion leaders.
- Information sources and preferred media channels.

5. Internal environment - organization
- Purpose: Mission, values, character, history.
- Management and leadership: Scope of business, corporate governance, senior leaders, size, growth, financial performance, social responsibility, environmental responsibility, ethical standards.
- Workplace environment: Personnel, structure, culture, employee engagement, diversity and inclusion.
- Reputation: Visibility, distinctiveness, authenticity, transparency, consistency, responsiveness.
- Impact of the problem, issue, challenge or opportunity on the organization.

6. Product or service
- Development, quality, design, packaging, pricing policies and structure, sales and profit history, market share, demand, trends, distribution.
- Sales features: Exclusive, nonexclusive, differentiating qualities, competitive position in publics' minds.
- Sales force or service providers: Size, scope, ability, cost/sale.
- Product or service research and planned improvements.

7. Promotions
- Successes and failures of past policy, sales force, advertising, publicity.
- Expenditures, budget emphasis, relation to trends.
- Ad/PR/marketing strategies, themes, campaigns.
- Promotions of competitors and like organizations.

8. Resources
- Intervening publics and opinion leaders.
- Attitudes and opinions toward product, issue or organization.
- Physical facilities, budgets, personnel, client support.
- Current and/or potential partnerships.

---

and synthesis of new data. If, however, ongoing communications functions have systematically gathered and organized research data into easily accessible and usable information, your research task will be more of an update. Always take the time to record and file pieces of information you come across in your daily routine. Continually gathering information will make the research task for any given effort or issue much easier.

The next several chapters in this book take you through each step of the Strategic Communications Matrix. The Matrix Applied sections, introduced in this chapter, provide practical application of that process. As we progress through the steps of the matrix in this and subsequent chapters, the Matrix Applied examples illustrate each step as it is discussed in the text. (Appendix D is a complete sample strategic plan.)

This chapter is designed to help you pull together information and analysis into a succinct document focused on a specific purpose. That purpose might be a complete strategic plan, a budget request for a new communications effort, a solution to a problem or challenge, a response to a perceived threat or a proposal to take advantage of an emergent opportunity. For our purposes here, we call this part of a plan or proposal the research section to facilitate parallelism with the Research, Action Planning, Communication and Evaluation (RACE) model. As depicted in the Strategic Communications Matrix and Matrix Applied example, the research section consists of the background, situation analysis and core problem/opportunity.

Background

The background is a summary of pertinent facts and information drawn from primary and secondary research. It must be comprehensive, but written concisely. It does not contain everything you discovered in research, only the information necessary to establish credibility with your client or manager and build the foundation for your plan. A good background will often depict data and more detailed information in the form of figures and graphs. Data is more easily understood in graphic form. Figures 4.1 and 4.2 should guide the development of content that may be appropriate for the background. At the very least, they represent how comprehensive your understanding of organizations, issues, stakeholders and publics should be.

The background sets the stage for understanding the situation at hand. It contains information about the industry and the client or organization, specifically past efforts and events affecting organizational success and where the client currently

TIPS FROM THE PROS

Channeling data into reservoirs of insight

Sean Williams, assistant teaching professor at Bowling Green State University and founder of Communication AMMO with previous experience working in communications roles with KeyCorp, National City Corporation, The Goodyear Tire and Rubber Company and True Digital Communications tips you off on how to channel an overwhelming sea of data into reservoirs of insight.

Think of data like water. Too little of it and you're parched and thirsty, too much and you're drowning. Just enough and you're healthy and happy.

We are awash in data! PR data is everywhere, from Google Analytics, to SEM Rush, to Facebook Insights, to survey data, poll data, formal research data... And not a drop to drink?

How do we cull it, categorize it, make sense of it and apply it to issues and problems? It all comes down to three steps, at least for me in my nearly 30 years of working in the practice of public relations, marketing and communication.

Step 1: Scan for patterns. When I read an article or essay, I pass through the document and identify the main themes, thoughts, ideas or situations. I'm looking to recognize the perspectives and angles of the subject matter, the author and their intentions. What do they want me to think, feel or do? Scan data in the same way.

Step 2: Group like things. Where are the similarities in the data, where are the differences? What do I think or feel when I examine both? Am I looking at a snapshot that shows me a theme, or a series of correlations that push me to extrapolate?

Step 3: Draw conclusions. What are my takeaways? How do these data apply to the issues I'm exploring, the problems I'm attempting to solve, the objectives I'm striving to attain? What are the proof points that support these conclusions?

Following this three-step process is essential for me to apply the tools of sense-making, to direct the sea of data to reservoirs of insight. And yet, it's just the start of how I use these insights.

My favorite planning tool is one of my own making: AMMO – Audiences, messages, methods, objectives. It is even the name of my company, Communication AMMO. The insights fuel understanding of each of the elements of the tool.

Audiences: Seeking insights about stakeholders, publics and constituents is intrinsic to strategic planning. So we start with the "who?" Who do we want to communicate with, interact with or draw into discussion? Closely defining these stakeholders narrows our focus critically.

Objectives: What do we want these people to think, feel and/or do? It's the same question I ask myself about the data I'm examining. Each audience might share some elements of the same objectives, but most often require different objectives. These are the results that can be qualitative or quantitative, but must follow the SMART acronym. Some people use "goal" in the place of "objective," but for my purposes the former is general and the latter specific.

Messages: Only after articulating the audience and objective do we move to messaging. What do we have to get across to the audience to reach the objective? Messaging isn't copy, by the way. It's the thinking that inspires creative copy and design. Messaging is, "We want to be an employer of choice among public relations professionals." We might never see those words explicitly in a news story or other communication. What we *should* see is stories demonstrating and illustrating how we are an employer of choice or should be.

Methods: What channels and outlets will we use to engage our audiences with our messaging and fulfill our objectives? Note that the selection of the "how" happens *last*. How many times have you had someone say, "We need a video! We need an ad!"? The method has to fit the message and the objective for each audience. A TikTok video isn't going to reach retirees very effectively. A legal document won't be particularly inspiring and touch people's hearts.

The essence is that all of our AMMO work needs insights to be an effective planning method, and data is just so much noise without organizing principles to help us derive insights.

Contributed by Sean D. Williams. © Kendall Hunt Publishing Company.

stands in the marketplace or in relationship to the issue. Remember that it selects and highlights only those bits of information that build the foundation for the solution or plan you will propose. Although you have not yet fully defined the problem or begun the planning process, some obvious alternatives will emerge as your team gathers and evaluates the research. The background should organize the information and present it in a way that will demonstrate to your client or manager the wisdom of the solutions you propose.

Stakeholder research

Stakeholder research provides the foundation from which you can make informed decisions about segmenting and targeting publics. It also helps you step into the shoes of those affected by an organization's decisions and see the issue from their perspective. As shown in the diagram in Figure 4.1, you can conduct research on any of the stakeholder groups you think may be affected by the problem or opportunity.

Remember that you cannot select key publics at this point because you have not set objectives. You have to decide what you need to do to meet the challenge/opportunity (objectives) before you decide who (key publics) you need to reach and motivate to act. Nevertheless, this research will be invaluable to you as you proceed to plan. With good stakeholder research, you will be armed with the knowledge and understanding you need to select the best combination of key publics when the time comes.

A good place to start when researching stakeholders is to understand the reason for their connection to your organization. Categorizing stakeholders in this way can help you prioritize your research efforts, spending more time to research the groups that are most likely to be affected by the current situation. Research in the fields of public relations and business have identified four types of stakeholders based on four different types of connections (Rawlins, 2006).

> ***Enabling stakeholders*** have some degree of authority or control over your organization. They restrict organizations from or enable them to acquire resources and pursue their goals. Examples include shareholders, lawmakers and government regulators.

Functional stakeholders are essential to make your organization function properly. They provide the labor (e.g, employees or subcontractors) and resources (e.g., suppliers) your organization needs to produce and deliver products and services. They are also consumers of your organization's products and services.

Normative stakeholders share a common interest, have similar values, seek related goals and experience similar problems as your organization (e.g., competitors and industry associations).

Diffused stakeholders have infrequent interactions with your organization. Usually, these interactions are caused by your organization's actions or decisions. They often get involved during a crisis (e.g., media and activist groups).

Communication theorists also suggest that stakeholder research can define the attributes of each group selected for study. Business scholars have identified three attributes that can help you determine which stakeholders should receive the most attention (Mitchell, Agle & Wood, 1997). These attributes include power, legitimacy and urgency.

Powerful stakeholders can convince the leaders of your organization to make decisions they otherwise wouldn't make. Legitimate stakeholders have invested something of value in your organization and have legal or moral standing to influence its decisions. Urgent stakeholders want your organization to do something that is important to them right now. The more of these attributes a stakeholder group has, the more important it is to your organization.

From the ranks of these broad stakeholder groups, you can begin segmenting publics. Research on publics should contain both demographic and psychographic information (gained through primary and secondary research) as well as any information that will help you reach publics (like media preferences and habits). It includes attitudes, values, opinions, behaviors, lifestyles, purchasing preferences, recreation habits, media usage and much more. Some of the information is hard data such as census reports, opinion research or social media analytics. Other information may be from focus groups, secondary research, personal observation and informed stereotypes.

As explained in Chapter 2, behavior can be used to segment publics. Studies done by James Grunig in the early 1980s concluded that publics are situational. That is, they form around specific issues or events and can be segmented by their communication behavior. Non-publics are not affected by the issue. Latent publics are affected but do not realize it yet. Aware publics recognize that an issue affects them but are not doing anything about it. And active publics are trying to address it through communication.

Researchers expanded on these initial ideas in this decade to more accurately explain how people use information to help them solve problems (Kim & Grunig, 2011). Generally, problems arise when people experience differences between what they expect and what they experience. Naturally, people want to solve problems, but they need information to do so. Their motivation to communicate about a problem depends on their awareness of it, their level of involvement with it and the extent to which they feel they can do something about it. When gathered, this psychographic information can be used to predict how latent, aware or active public segments might engage in three different communication behaviors: information acquisition, information selection and information transmission.

Figure 4.3 has more details about the specific passive and active behaviors in each category. Observational research on the current communication behaviors of each

Figure 4.3
Passive and active communication behaviors

COMMUNICATION BEHAVIOR	PASSIVE	ACTIVE
Information acquisition	*Information attending* People pay attention to messages about a specific problem.	*Information seeking* People actively seek out messages about a specific problem.
Information selection	*Information permitting* People accept any information related to the problem.	*Information forefending* People avoid certain types of information, are systematic about their search and want specific and relevant information about the problem.
Information transmission	*Information sharing* People only share their opinions about a problem when asked to by others.	*Information forwarding* People proactively share information about a problem without it being solicited by anyone.

Source: Kim and Grunig (2011)

public segment can help inform the development of psychographic profiles. Keep in mind that research has shown that passive publics only exhibit passive communication behaviors. However, active publics use both passive and active communication behaviors to solve problems.

Identifying self-interests

Your research helps you determine motivating **self-interests** in connection with the problem or issue at hand as well as with opinion leaders. This will be important in designing messages that will motivate key publics. Remember that people don't do what you want them to do just because you want them to do it. They act in their own self-interest, and unless you can plainly identify those self-interests and appeal to them, publics will not do what you want them to do. But don't confuse self-interest with selfishness. People are often motivated to act from intrinsic values like care and concern, community improvement, quality of life, welfare of family and friends and because it is the "right thing to do."

Clearly, it is in our self-interest to feel good about ourselves, to take care of our families and friends and to improve the quality of our community and living situation. That doesn't mean money and power are not motivators, but relying upon them as the primary or overriding self-interests for our publics will probably limit

SELF-INTEREST
The fundamental motivation for an individual's behavior.

our success. Refer back to the discussion in Chapter 1 about the critical values underlying trust and relationships. Your stakeholder research should help you understand publics at this deeper level, and you will be more successful as a result.

As you will see in the following chapters, appealing to the self-interest of a public is necessary at two levels. You already know you must use a self-interest appeal to move a public to action. But with the clutter of messages and information bombarding everyone today, we must also appeal to self-interest just to get a public to pay attention to our message. People choose to perceive a message only when they believe it is in their self-interest to do so, otherwise they just tune out. Regardless of the channels used, you have to get over the perception hurdle before you can complete your primary task of informing or motivating.

Identifying opinion leaders

The stakeholder research should also tell you who influences different publics. Who are the opinion leaders regarding the particular issue or challenge to be addressed? As discussed in Chapter 2, a public's opinion leaders are individuals (either by personal acquaintance, social media connection or reputation) who have the credibility to effectively give advice, affect opinion or call for action. They are typically heavy consumers of media and usually possess significant information and expertise. Most importantly, they are trusted.

How do you identify who a public's opinion leaders are? Formal opinion leaders are relatively easy to determine. We see them every day (e.g., political officials) or know who they are by the issue or influence involved (e.g., religious leaders). Nevertheless, just because someone may hold a position of authority does not mean they can actually sway the opinion of our public.

Identifying informal opinion leaders can be tricky. So how do we find out who actually influences a public? The answer is deceptively simple: Ask them. Part of research is asking people whose advice they trust when making decisions. Focus groups and surveys are particularly useful in this process. We can also observe behaviors — watching how people react when they receive messages from different sources or analyzing who they follow on social media channels.

Opinion leaders are best used to persuade and motivate. Nevertheless, their credibility is based upon our publics' assessment of their character and judgment. Opinion leaders lose influence if they are perceived to be manipulated or manipulative. Using them in that manner is unethical and will ultimately lead to a decline in their influence.

Assessing relationships

It is also important to use stakeholder research to assess the current state of the relationship your client or organization has with its publics. This assessment may use a formal methodology like establishing a scale of strength indicators of the relationship — or the assessment may be more informal. Research has shown the key factors or dimensions to be considered in a relationship include levels of: loyalty, trust, openness, involvement, community investment, commitment, satisfaction and influence (Bruning & Ledingham, 1999, 2000; Ki & Hon, 2007).

Significant research has been conducted within the relationship building and the relationship management schools of thought in public relations. While those

MINI CASE

Data-driven glamping
Kampgrounds of America (KOA)

Kampgrounds of America (KOA) started in 1962 with one basic campsite along the Yellowstone River in Montana that featured a picnic table, a fire ring and level ground to pitch a tent. KOA now owns or franchises nearly 500 locations in the U.S. and Canada that feature standard camping conveniences such as RV hookups, showers, laundry facilities, swimming pools, restrooms and playgrounds. In recent years, however, KOA has upgraded many of its sites with resort-style pools, RV sites with patios, deluxe cabins with full baths, premium tent sites and pet parks. Most also offer access to modern amenities like Wi-Fi internet access.

CORE OPPORTUNITY
KOA needed to generate media and consumer interest in its upgraded campgrounds.

KOA'S STRATEGY
KOA's strategy was informed by the following research.
- In January 2016, KOA worked with a marketing research firm with expertise in the hospitality and services industries to develop a survey instrument and draw a random sample of people from the U.S. and Canada that represented the overall populations in terms of age, gender and ethnicity. The online survey was distributed to a U.S. sample that included 2,418 households, with a margin of error of +/- 1.9%. The Canadian sample included 500 households, with a margin of error of +/- 4.3%.
- Results from the survey led to the conclusion that "diversity in the outdoors is slowly increasing." The data showed that 40% of new campers were Latino, Asian-American or African-American.
- Another finding of the survey was that younger generations are getting into camping. Data revealed that 44% of new campers were millennials.
- Not surprisingly, the data showed that people are not disconnecting from technology when they camp. The survey found that 76% of people access the internet while camping. However, research discovered that this might not be a bad thing as 4% of campers who check their email while outdoors spend an average of three additional days camping per year compared to those who don't check email.
- Finally, the data indicated a 25% increase in the number of people who said they intended to camp more often in 2016.

KOA worked with a public relations firm to develop an integrated marketing campaign to attract new campers to its properties. In addition to its ongoing media relations efforts, as well as its established digital, email and social media marketing communication, KOA and its agency partner packaged and positioned its research as a camping industry trend report: The 2016 North American Camping Report. Public relations efforts to pitch the findings of the report to key industry opinion leaders and media influencers landed KOA national media coverage in "USA Today" and the "New York Times," as well as coverage in regional media outlets such as Indiana's "South Bend Tribune."

In addition, KOA and its agency used the research findings to target its messages about KOA's upgraded amenities to audiences that the research indicated were interested in camping. For example, they reached out to millennial travel bloggers and invited them to experience, and write about, "glamping" in a deluxe KOA cabin. They secured coverage about KOA amenities on regional family and travel-related websites like "ArkontheGo.com" and

"ParentMap.com." And they created a partnership with "Hispanicize 2016" in Miami, Florida, to reach out to potential Hispanic campers.

RESULTS
- Campaign evaluation data showed that 77% of current campers and 52% of new campers named KOA their top-of-mind campground. According to KOA, this was the highest the awareness statistics had ever been.
- Business from new campers in 2016 generated $30 million in revenue, a 2% increase.
- Overall occupancy rates at KOA campgrounds in 2016 increased by 5% and registration revenue increased by 11%.
- KOA reported that 2016 was the most successful year in the company's history.
- The 2016 North American Camping Report was so successful that KOA has issued a new report every year since (see http://www.koapressroom.com/).
- In 2022, KOA issued its first North American Glamping report (see http://www.koapressroom.com/).

© SCK_Photo/Shutterstock.com

disciplines have been advocating a relationship building approach to dealing with all organizational publics since the mid-1980s, it is only recently that research has led to the methodology to measure the strength of those relationships. The eight factors identified above are those most often used and measured. Loyalty, trust, satisfaction and influence are arguably two-way factors, the strength of which is measured both from the perspectives of the organization and the publics. The other four primarily measure the publics' perception of the organization's performance. The openness, involvement, community investment and commitment of the organization to publics and issues are typically seen as responsibilities of the organization.

The purpose of your communication, particularly long term, is to strengthen relationships with publics and move them to mutually beneficial action. Communication that highlights the organization's performance on these eight factors will help you do that.

Without stakeholder research, you won't be able to make sound decisions about key publics when the time comes. It is equally important to have research about

intervening publics. You gain their cooperation in the same way you motivate action in key publics: by making it in their self-interest. For this reason, you need to know about them, understand their self-interests as they relate to your problem, know who influences them and understand the status of your relationship with them.

SWOT analysis

As you have organized and synthesized your data and information about the factors in the Communications and Marketing Research Guide in Figure 4.2, you have probably begun to make some inferences and draw some conclusions relative to the issue or opportunity you are addressing.

At this point, take some time to do a **SWOT analysis** — strengths, weaknesses, opportunities, threats. According to Stacy Collett, a SWOT analysis is: A way to analyze a company's or a department's position in the market in relation to its competitors. The goal is to identify all the major factors affecting competitiveness before crafting a business strategy.

Although typically designed to support development of marketing strategy, a SWOT analysis is useful in supporting plans to address an organization's relationships with all of its stakeholders and publics, not just customers. It is equally valuable to analyze the internal and external factors affecting issues and the operating environment within which the organization exists. When conducting a SWOT analysis, remember that your organization's relationships with key publics as well as the key publics' opinions and values can also be considered strengths or weaknesses.

This analysis is a great way to sum up your research and focus your knowledge on the opportunity you face and the barriers to be overcome. The process takes pages of information and focuses them into a few key words that will help shape a successful campaign.

Situation analysis

Although the problem or challenge was identified for us initially as we began the research process, it is important to redefine the situation after we have synthesized all available and pertinent information. The client or manager's initial perception of the problem or opportunity may be quite unlike the actual situation. You may have initially believed people didn't donate to a cause because they didn't see the need.

Research may have discovered the real reason was that they didn't know how. A local drive-time radio show in a Western city made an impassioned appeal for donations for a young local boy who would be dropped from the organ donor list by the next day for lack of funding. But they failed to tell listeners how and where to donate, frustrating the tens of thousands of listeners who wanted to help.

Based on the background, assess and describe in one paragraph the situation as it appears after the data has been organized and analyzed. This paragraph should include those most pertinent pieces of data that will become benchmarks upon which to later base your objectives. That means your analysis of the data should yield numerical markers that must be improved to resolve your problem or meet the challenge.

In describing a problem, you might know that 75% of public opinion is that your organization doesn't care about the community. Obviously that is a statistic that

INTERVENING PUBLIC
An influential individual or small group of people used to carry a message to a key public.

SWOT ANALYSIS
A structured analytical tool set up in a 2-by-2 matrix that examines strengths, weaknesses, opportunities and threats.

MATRIX APPLIED

Research background, situation analysis and core problem/opportunity

The State Department of Corrections is planning to construct a new prison in Green Valley, a small farming town 50 miles from an interstate highway. The 7,500 people in the town and 2,500 more in the surrounding area are concerned for the safety of their families and property. The state will face expensive opposition unless attitudes can be changed so that the town is reassured of its safety and welcomes the economic development that will come with the new facility.

BACKGROUND

The external environment: Like the rest of the country, Green Valley is struggling to emerge from the economic downturn that hit this farming community particularly hard. Unemployment and underemployment have been problems, and the construction project, and the staffing and maintenance of a prison in town would be a definite economic boon. Politically, the residents are conservative and supportive of the penal system, but highly publicized incidents of violent crime have them wary of the kinds of people and criminal culture that would be introduced into their community and to their children.

The industry: While the penal system would introduce the seamier side of society to Green Valley, the prison and all the services needed to support the prison would mean several million dollars injected into the area economy annually, and it would mean 750 new jobs with the prison alone, not to mention the jobs that would be added as the town's business community expanded to meet the needs of such a facility. While many of those jobs would be blue collar, hourly positions, a fair percentage would be professional positions in education, health care, management, finance and other professions. Technology, strict regulation and control in this industry renders safety less of an issue than the public may think. That means growth for Green Valley as people move into town to support the new prison, and employment for people in Green Valley who have been without work because of the recent recession.

Competition: The only competition is the publics' perceptions, attitudes and values. Fear for safety and fear for a loss of innocence present opposition. Those can be overcome with accurate information and recognition of the benefits. There is also a potential for legal opposition to a project like this.

Stakeholder research: Green Valley residents are diffused stakeholders. They do not typically interact with the State Department of Corrections, but because the proposal to construct a prison in their town will have a significant impact on their lives, they are more likely to become involved with the department throughout the approval process. The prison proposal will also have an impact on their attitudes about and opinions of the department. Green Valley residents have some power over the elected officials making decisions about the prison through the ballot box and public pressure. They have a legitimate claim on the issue because the prison will be built in their community, which will be left to deal with both the positive and negative impacts. Also, they will feel a sense of urgency for government leaders to address their concerns as deadlines approach for community input and government approvals that move the prison from idea to reality. This broad group of Green Valley residents can be segmented into publics that will respond to the issue in different ways. This requires a full demographic breakdown of each segment in terms of ages, income, employment and other characteristics. It also requires psychographic data on attitudes, values and beliefs on political, social and economic issues, as well as about the prison specifically. The psychographic breakdown would include lifestyles, recreation and other similar data. It would also include identification of opinion leaders, self-interests, information sources and preferred media channels.

The organization: The state prison system keeps a low profile, and has been able to do so because of virtually no incidents threatening public safety in the last couple of decades. The system is efficiently managed, and employees are competent. Its reputation is unsullied.

The service: The service provided by the taxpayer-funded state penal system is necessary. In this conservative area, the justice system is supported, and the concept of prisons is understood and accepted. There is little, if any, opposition to the idea of a prison; there was simply concern that it would be located here. The issue of safety is the primary concern in the minds of citizens, and the exposure of children to the idea of violent crime in society is a close secondary concern. In a small town like this, children and families would see the prison facility daily, a constant reminder of their vulnerability and the criminal element in society.

Promotions: Research shows that other states that have faced this challenge have been most successful when they have invited the community's voice in the process. Providing full information on location, plans, timelines, construction and operation along with inviting public discussion and comment have typically allowed communities to weigh the pros and cons and come to a decision of support. Economic benefits, safety procedures and safety records of other state facilities have all been powerful messages. When communities have a voice in the process, are assured of the safety of their families, recognize the economic benefits and see the meticulous planning for the least disruption of their lives, they tend to be supportive of a prison in their community. A pervasive public information effort, the support of local opinion leaders and community forums have been the most effective tools to engage publics and gain support.

Resources: Opinion leaders will be critical resources in this public information and persuasion campaign, particularly local officials, school administrators and local media. The community's need for economic growth and stability, as well as jobs, can be considered a resource. City hall, the high school and the local recreation center are established community meeting places that can be used for community forums. A weekly newspaper and a local radio station will also be resources for information dissemination, as well as social media, particularly those also used by local government and police to keep citizens informed.

SWOT analysis:

STRENGTHS
1. Economic benefits
2. Penal system safety record
3. Support of local leaders

WEAKNESSES
1. Construction inconvenience
2. Daily visibility of negative element

OPPORTUNITIES
1. Jobs
2. Local media and social media

THREATS
1. Safety
2. Family values
3. Legal opposition

SITUATION ANALYSIS

The announcement that the state is planning to construct a new prison facility in Green Valley has been met with initial resistance. While residents are generally supportive of the state's penal system, which has an excellent record of safety and competence, they fear the introduction of the criminal element into their peaceful community. Safety has been the overriding concern of residents, overshadowing the economic benefits that would come from the construction and maintenance of this facility. This project would bring in several million dollars annually and 750 jobs to this economically struggling community. It would boost the business and professional communities, improve medical facilities, strengthen funding for education and provide an economic injection that would significantly improve the quality of life for the vast majority of area residents. A solid 80% of residents have expressed concerns over safety, but only 35% could name a potential economic benefit. Fewer than 20% thought the new facility would improve other local services like education and health care. Nearly three-quarters of residents have a favorable opinion of the State Corrections Department, but only one-quarter indicate that they would be fully supportive of a prison in Green Valley. While only 30% are outright opposed to locating the prison here, 45% have significant concerns. Should those concerns not be alleviated, the opposition could potentially mobilize a legal challenge to the project.

The primary challenge seems to be public awareness and education. Other efforts have shown that giving the community a voice in the process and being completely transparent and open about plans and operation have improved community support, especially given the economic benefits. Safety will always be an issue, but the reputation and safety record of the Department of Corrections as well as procedures in place to ensure safety can assure the community that there is low risk associated with housing a prison in the community. Local opinion leaders and local media are well-informed on relevant issues and are supportive. But if opposition can't be converted to support, Green Valley will likely lose the opportunity to improve the standard of living for residents by locating the prison there.

CORE PROBLEM/OPPORTUNITY

Raise public awareness of safety and the benefits of the new prison to gain public support and neutralize opposition so that the Green Valley prison project can go forward without costly delay or legal opposition.

must be improved to meet your challenge. Those are the critical pieces of data that must be included in the situation analysis. If you can explain a problem or challenge using measures from research data, then writing measurable objectives to meet the challenge is easy. Further, using actual data — numbers — to summarize the attitudes, opinions and behaviors that must be changed will inspire confidence in your superiors that you have a realistic grasp of the problem and understand how to overcome it.

So don't just say your publics don't trust the organization; identify what the specific trust levels are among which publics. Don't just conclude people lack information; find the statistics to describe which publics lack which specific understandings or pieces of information. Find the critical data that not only describe publics, attitudes, opinions and behaviors but also provide the benchmarks to measure success.

In a second paragraph, identify any related issues, problems or difficulties. Honestly assess potential barriers to success that must be overcome, but use your research as a confidence builder so your client or manager will be certain that the difficulties can be overcome. Identifying difficulties and then suggesting reasonable ways to neutralize them may be the best approach.

Core problem or opportunity

Based on the synthesis of research in the background, you have narrowed the issue or challenge to a short assessment of the situation and any related difficulties. Now cut to the heart of the problem or opportunity in one sentence.

For example, "Because key publics are not getting adequate and timely information about mobile blood drives, blood donations have declined, threatening the local hospital's immediate access to needed lifesaving units." The statement gets right to the central core of the problem and translates it to a tangible consequence if the problem is not solved.

Be careful not to mistake symptoms of a problem for the problem itself. Like an onion, problems are made up of many layers. The layers surrounding the problem often take the form of symptoms and effects. In order to identify the core problem you need to peel back the symptoms and effects to find out what is really causing the difficulty.

Summary

Organizing background research according to the Communications and Marketing Research Guide helps lay the foundation for decision-making. The background, SWOT analysis and stakeholder research help to focus everything we know into a solution or plan. It funnels research into the problem-solving and planning process because it has driven us to think analytically, to evaluate what is known and to identify how that will assist in the selection of publics and resources to solve the problem.

Application case

Park City, Utah

Tourism campaign

Park City, Utah, is a mountain town located 25 miles east of Salt Lake City. It has established a reputation as a ski town. Park City has two ski resorts — Park City Mountain and Deer Valley — that draw skiing enthusiasts from around the world to experience Utah's "greatest snow on earth." The city was also a venue during the 2002 Winter Olympics. Utah Olympic Park in Park City still has four working sliding (bobsled, luge, skeleton) tracks and six Nordic ski jumps that are used in the winter and summer. Park City is also known for being a high-end destination. It has the largest concentration of luxury ski accommodations in North America and annually hosts celebrities and filmmakers during the Sundance Film Festival with a variety of restaurants and spas.

Recently, Park City and its county government partner, Summit County, developed a sustainable tourism plan. The report produced for this plan outlines the city and county's vision for tourism in the area: "Our vision embraces our Olympic spirit, our love of the outdoors, and the health of our environment as the beating heart of the Summit County experience. We see a future in which locals, governments, business groups, nonprofits and land managers share a mission to integrate tourism with stewardship and preservation, engaging visitors as partners who care about—and for—our community. We will adapt our community systems, seeking to become the most sustainable ski destination in the world."

Assume you have been hired by Park City and Summit County to conduct initial research for a strategic communications campaign focused on establishing Park City as a sustainable destination among leisure travelers. Use the information provided in this case and principles from this chapter to complete the following tasks regarding the first three steps of the matrix.

1. Using secondary research, complete a background research report for Park City and Summit County. Apply the skills you learned in Chapter 3 to find appropriate secondary research sources. Follow the guidelines provided in the Communications and Marketing Research Guide in Figure 4.2 to determine which topics to conduct research on. Synthesize the data you find into a concise background research report like the example shown in this chapter's Matrix Applied. Here are some ideas to get you started.
   a. IbisWorld: Ski & Snowboard Resorts Industry in the US–Market Research Report (may be available through your university library).
   b. Expedia: Travel trends reports (https://welcome.expediagroup.com/en/research-and-insights/the-traveler-value-index).
   c. Utah Office of Tourism: Utah tourism statistics and trends (https://travel.utah.gov/research-planning/utah-tourism-industry-metrics).
   d. Park City Visitors Bureau: Economic data and resources (https://www.visitparkcity.com/members/resources/); Sustainable Tourism Plan (https://www.visitparkcity.com/sustainabletourismplan/).
   e. Park City: City information (https://www.parkcity.org/).
   f. Summit County: County information (https://www.summitcounty.org/).

2. Conduct a SWOT analysis based on what you learned from creating your background research report.

3. Write a two-paragraph situation analysis using the information you gathered in your background research report and what you learned from conducting the SWOT analysis. The first paragraph should be a statement of the current situation and a description of the challenge or opportunity. The second paragraph should identify potential difficulties that could impede success. Remember to use actual data — numbers — to summarize the attitudes, opinions and behaviors that must be addressed in the campaign.

4. Write a one-sentence core problem or opportunity based on what you wrote in the situation analysis. Try to get right to the central core of the problem and translate it to a tangible consequence if the problem is not solved.

References and additional readings

Booker, T. (2016, May 18). Millennials a test for RV industry. *South Bend Tribune*, A7.

Bruning, S. & Ledingham, J. (1999). Relationships between organizations and publics: Development of a multi-dimensional organization-public relationship scale. *Public Relations Review*, 25(2), 157–170.

Bruning, S. & Ledingham, J. (2000). Organization and key public relationships: Testing the influence of the relationship dimensions in a business-to-business context. In Ledingham and Bruning (Eds.) *Public Relations as Relationship Management: A Relational Approach to the Study and Practice of Public Relations*. Mahwah, NJ: Lawrence Erlbaum Associates.

Cairn Consulting Group. (n.d.). Portfolio. Retrieved from http://www.cairnconsultinggroup.com/portfolio/

Cairn Consulting Group. (2016). The 2016 *North American Camping Report*. Retrieved from http://koa.uberflip.com/i/654141-2016-north-american-camper-report/0?m4

Collett, S. (1999, July 19). SWOT analysis: Quickstudy. *Computerworld*.

DenOuden, J. (2016, September 15). Camping with KOA. *GirlontheMoveBlog.com*. Retrieved from http://www.girlonthemoveblog.com/2016/09/15/camping-with-koa/

DiBlasio, N. (2016, June 1). Roughing it, with some social media. *USA Today*, 2A

Gibson, A. (n.d.). The captivating story of KOA campgrounds. *KOA Blog*. Retrieved from https://koa.com/blog/the-captivating-story-of-koa-campgrounds/

Gruber, T. (2016, January 6). Campground living at the KOA in Mystic, CT. *We3Travel.com*. Retrieved from https://we3travel.com/mystic-koa-camping-cabins/

Grunig, J. E. (1983). Communication behaviors and attitudes of environmental publics: Two studies. *Journalism Monographs*, 81 (March), 40–41.

Ki, E. J. & Hon, L. C. (2007). Testing the linkages among the organization–public relationship and attitude and behavioral intentions. *Journal of Public Relations Research*, 19(1), 1-23.

Kim, J. N. & Grunig, J. E. (2011). Problem solving and communicative action: A situational theory of problem solving. *Journal of Communication*, 61(1), 120-149.

Kirkland, E. (2016, June 13). Camping in America: The KOA mission and vision carries on. *ArkontheGo.com*. Retrieved from http://akonthego.com/blog/camping-in-americathe-koa-mission-and-vision-carries-on

KOA. (n.d.). KOA history [backgrounder]. Retrieved from http://www.koapressroom.com/press-kit/koa-history/

KOA. (2016, May 1). New, multicultural generation of campers benefitting from time spent outdoors [news release]. Retrieved from http://www.koapressroom.com/press/new-multicultural-generation-of-campers-benefitting-from-time-spent-outdoors-2/

KOA. (2016). Franchise benefits guide. Retrieved from http://koa.uberflip.com/i/677214-2016-koa-franchise-benefits-guide/9?m4

McClary, R. (2016, May 12). The 101 on KOA, your new favorite camping experience. *ParentMap.com*. Retrieved from https://www.parentmap.com/article/the-101-onkoa-campgrounds-for-puget-sound-families

Mitchell, R. K., Agle, B. R. & Wood, D. J. (1997). Toward a theory of stakeholder identification and salience: Defining the principle of who and what really counts. *Academy of Management Review*, 22(4), 853-886.

Moon, F. (2016, Sept. 30). Six ways to save money (and sanity) on a road trip. *New York Times*. Retrieved from https://www.nytimes.com/2016/10/02/travel/budget-familyroad-trip-six-ways-to-save-money.html

Paine, K. D. (2011). *Measure What Matters: Online Tools for Understanding Customers, Social Media, Engagement, and Key Relationships*. Durham, NH: Paine Publishing.

Paine, K. D. (2007). *Measuring Public Relationships: The Data-driven Communicator's Guide to Success*. Durham, NH: Paine Publishing.

PRWeek Staff. (2018, March 16). PRWeek U.S. Awards 2018: The winners. *PRWeek*. Retrieved from https://www.prweek.com/article/1458806/prweek-us-awards-2018-winners#DataInsight

Rawlins, B. L. (2006). Prioritizing stakeholders for public relations. *Institute for Public Relations*. Retrieved from https://www.instituteforpr.org/wp-content/uploads/2006_Stakeholders_1.pdf

Stacks, D. W. (2016). *Primer of Public Relations Research* (3rd ed.). New York: Guilford Publications, Inc.

CHAPTER 5
SETTING GOALS AND OBJECTIVES

*"If you fail to plan,
you are planning to fail!"*

— **BENJAMIN FRANKLIN**
AUTHOR, INVENTOR, SCIENTIST AND STATESMAN

LEARNING IMPERATIVES

- Be able to turn a problem/opportunity statement into a goal.

- Understand the characteristics of good objectives.

- Learn how to write objectives to support the accomplishment of a goal.

- Learn to create evaluation criteria and tools as you write objectives to ensure evaluation is accomplished.

The second step of the RACE model is action planning. **Planning** and the programming it generates is how we get from here to there. "Here" is where we are now. It is our current situation as we have described it after synthesizing our research and redefining the challenge or opportunity we face. "There" is where we want to be; it's our **goal**. Planning helps us to look ahead, to chart our course to ensure we get there. Like sailing a boat, planning must be flexible and open to course correction as we receive feedback or obtain new information. Nevertheless, unless we know where we are going and have some idea of an appropriate course to get there, our arrival at the destination will be left to chance. The more complete our planning — based on good research — the better our chances of arriving at our destination.

The matrix approach to planning

The heart of the Strategic Communications Matrix is the action planning section. The research process — including the collection, organization and analysis of information and honing it into a situation analysis and core problem/opportunity — lays the foundation for the action planning process. Broom and Sha (2012) call this a "searching look backward," a "wide look around," a "deep look inside" and a "long look ahead."

Similarly, the action planning step in the matrix lays the foundation for the communication or implementation step. As such, planning must be dynamic or flexible enough to allow for feedback and adjustment during implementation. It must also be based firmly on stakeholder research to ensure the right publics are selected, the messages motivate them to do what needs to be done and the right channels are used to get the messages to the publics in a way that they will perceive them and act on them. Planning must also integrate an outline for evaluation so the plan is truly results-oriented.

Planning occurs at two distinct levels within any organization: long-term planning for the entire organization and short-term planning for communications efforts. Long-term planning occurs at the top level of an organization and looks at the entirety of the organization and its mission. It identifies goals, **objectives**, publics and messages that address the long-term accomplishment of the organization's mission. Planning at this level involves all entities within the organization and requires the use of stakeholder research to truly understand the organization's publics. Doing so helps us avoid costly mistakes like that made by Mylan, the maker of EpiPen, which treats life-threatening allergic reactions. From 2009 to 2016, the company hiked the price of the product more than 500 percent from $103.50 to $608.61. The price hike put it out of reach of many for whom using EpiPen is the difference between life and death. It meant that schools could no longer afford to keep them on hand to treat children who have allergic reactions to something like peanuts or a bee sting.

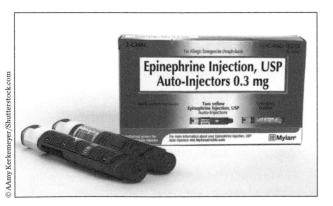

Although the American Medical Association and politicians urged Mylan to reduce the price, CEO Heather Bresch called the price hikes "fair," revealing that the drugs in the pen cost about $2 while the majority of the price tag is in the design of the auto-injector. She blamed the Affordable Care Act (aka Obamacare) and distributors for the high cost. Eventually Mylan said it would release a cheaper generic version of EpiPen but it was too little, too late. The anger of consumers, legislators and regulators — all key publics of the organization — resulted in Mylan stock value plummeting 70%, an antitrust investigation, lawsuits and employee layoffs.

Short-term planning is designed to target more immediate needs such as managing a crisis, launching a new product line and repairing a damaged reputation. Effective higher-level, long-term planning should, nonetheless, inform planning for more specific short-term campaigns. Although they are focused on a more specific challenge, short-term communications efforts should always reinforce the key messages, goals and objectives of the long-term plan. Nevertheless, by their nature, they may also address publics that may not be long-term key publics to the organization but that are crucial to the accomplishment of the short-term effort.

Research helps us define the challenge and the current environment within which the opportunity has occurred or will occur. As shown in the complete matrix in Chapter 1, planning identifies what specifically needs to be accomplished (goal and objectives) to overcome the challenge, who (key publics) we need to reach and/or motivate to accomplish the goals and objectives, what we need to convey (messages) to those publics to stimulate action and help us achieve our objectives, and how (strategies and tactics) to get those messages to those publics so they both receive and act upon them. The matrix also includes the big idea strategy to better tie together the who, what and how of a campaign under a unifying creative theme.

As shown in the simplified example in Figure 5.1, the planning process is analytical, with the decisions made and actions planned in each step driving the decisions made and actions planned in each subsequent step. Further, each step must be taken in turn. For example, the key publics for a particular problem-solving effort cannot be selected until we have determined the goal and the objectives necessary to achieve that goal. Only then can we select the publics that are needed to accomplish those objectives. Similarly, we can only design effective messages after we have selected key publics, know what we need them to do and have determined their motivating self-interests. The decisions we make about the information a public needs, what will motivate the public to act and who should deliver the message to the public are prerequisite to designing messages that result in action that accomplishes objectives.

Effective informational and motivational messages cannot be designed for a given public without a thorough analysis of its research profile, examination of the status of the current relationship with that public and knowledge of its self-interests as they pertain to the problem at hand and related issues. Strategies and tactics appropriate to send the designed messages to the selected publics cannot be determined until we know what those messages are. Quite simply, the matrix approach requires us to decide what we want to do, who we need to reach to do it, what messages we need to send to obtain cooperation and how we can most effectively send those messages to those publics. The steps must be taken in order or our planning is left to chance and could easily get off-track.

A Google search using the keywords "worst PR marketing campaigns" will reveal a list of industry websites documenting communication efforts that failed miserably. Irma Jakić, a writer for Mediatoolkit.com, explained that campaigns fail because

Figure 5.1
Simplified example of the matrix analytical process*

Delaware Department of Natural Resources and Environmental Control

CORE OPPORTUNITY   Because the Delaware General Assembly passed a new law banning plastic carryout bags, the Department of Natural Resources had to inform and persuade retailers and residents about the benefits of complying with the law.

GOAL   Inform Delaware residents about the ban on plastic carryout bags.

OBJECTIVE   Increase awareness about the ban on plastic carryout bags by 25% by the end of the campaign, as measured by a post-campaign online survey.

KEY PUBLIC   Delaware residents who frequently shop in retail stores affected by the ban on plastic carryout bags.

PRIMARY MESSAGES
1. Starting Friday, Jan. 1, 2021, plastic carryout bags will be banned in Delaware.
2. Choose to reuse, or bring your own bag (BYOB). The law helps us reduce our waste in landfills and reduce the number of plastic bags that litter our roads and waterways.

STRATEGY   Inform Delaware residents about the ban on plastic carryout bags by partnering with the Retail Trade Association to develop in-store display signage about the ban.

TACTIC   In-store signs and flyers posted at the point of sale.

* To demonstrate the analytical process, this example focuses on only one of the objectives, one of the key publics, one of the strategies and one tactic. To accomplish the goal, more objectives, publics, strategies and tactics would be necessary.

---

they were "not thought through enough, to put it nicely." To put it in terms of the matrix approach, somehow these campaigns misconnected in the planning process.

One poignant example mentioned on many of the "worst PR and marketing campaign" web pages is the release of PepsiCo's 2017 short film, "Live for Now," starring Kendall Jenner, an American model and social media celebrity. The video shows Jenner posing for a photo shoot while a large group of happy protestors walk down the street holding generic signs. A line of police officers is waiting for the protestors. Someone invites Jenner to join the protest. She is shown walking through the protestors with a can of Pepsi in her hand. Finally, she reaches the front of the protest, walks up to the police line and hands her can of Pepsi to one of the officers. The police officer drinks the Pepsi and all of the protestors cheer.

Reaction to Pepsi's video was immediate and fierce, especially on social media. Many accused Pepsi of insensitively co-opting the Black Lives Matter movement to sell soda. Elle Hearns, former Black Lives Matter organizer, was quoted in the "New York Times" saying that the video "plays down the sacrifices people have historically taken in utilizing protests." And Bernice King, the daughter of Martin Luther King Jr. and Coretta Scott King, tweeted a picture of her father and other civil rights protestors being pushed by a line of police officers with the caption, "If only Daddy would have known about the power of #Pepsi."

Pepsi quickly issued an apology and pulled down the video from their social media accounts. Interestingly, Pepsi's apology revealed the goal of their campaign: "Pepsi was trying to project a global message of unity, peace and understanding. Clearly, we missed the mark and apologize. We did not intend to make light of any serious issue."

So how did a communications campaign that was intended to "project a global message of unity, peace and understanding" veer so far off the mark? According to Thomas Hobbes of "Marketing Week," one reason Pepsi's in-house marketing team might have produced such a tone deaf message is because they didn't seek an outside perspective that could have exposed the flaws in their thinking. Another reason is likely that the Pepsi team didn't do research to understand protestors and protest movements. While both of these reasons seem likely, the bottom line is that the Pepsi marketing team obviously didn't understand their publics well enough to communicate in an authentic, respectful, equitable or socially responsible way.

Pepsi's marketing team had a clear goal. But they clearly did not conduct enough research to help them understand the situation or their publics. Yet, based on their faulty and incomplete understanding, they proceeded to design a message that angered and alienated the people they were targeting, as well as many people who they didn't intend to target. The Pepsi team also sent the message through multiple social media channels, which ensured that the viral criticism and backlash to the video would be seen by a large number of social media users and the traditional news media.

Each step of the matrix planning process must build on the previous step. The logic must flow consistently and coherently. As the Pepsi example shows, disregarding the information accumulated, the decisions made and the actions planned in one step will almost always ensure that the decisions made and actions planned in the subsequent step are off target and headed for failure.

With this important lesson in mind, the next few chapters address the action planning steps of the Strategic Communications Matrix. This chapter begins that discussion with identifying what needs to be done to meet the challenge or to seize the opportunity at hand.

Establishing goals

Once the core problem or opportunity is accurately established, setting the goal is a simple task. The goal is actually a positive restatement of the core problem. If your challenge is declining confidence among investors leading to a low stock price, your goal is to reestablish confidence and boost your stock price. If your problem is a lack of accurate information regarding the process of organ donation, thereby causing a shortage of available organs for transplant, your goal is to increase the number of

STRATEGIC COMMUNICATIONS MATRIX

ACTION PLANNING

4. GOAL AND OBJECTIVES

Goal   A one-sentence statement of the overall result needed to solve the problem or seize the opportunity. It does not have to be quantified.

Objectives   Statements of specific results that lead to achieving the goal. Objectives must be specific, measurable, attainable, relevant, time-bound, written, cost-conscious, and efficient. Evaluation criteria and tools should be included in written objectives. Key publics should become obvious when drafting objectives.

organs donated by overcoming misperceptions about the process. The goal should be broader and more general than the objectives that follow. A goal also does not have to be specifically measurable. The measured achievement of strategic objectives should ensure that the overall goal is reached.

Nevertheless, determining the goal may not be as simple as it appears. Too often, organizational communications and marketing personnel act unilaterally to set goals. But those are not isolated functions within an organization; they should be integral parts of the overall management approach. Setting campaign goals in isolation, or without consideration of the organization's overall mission and goals, is dangerous and can lead to a lack of internal support.

Three precautions can aid you in avoiding this problem. First, be sure you closely align campaign goals with the organization's mission. Doing so will also align your campaign's communication goals and objectives with the organization's long-term plan. A campaign goal is not as broad as a mission statement, but should be seen as a significant step toward achieving the organization's mission.

Second, verify that the campaign goal does not conflict with existing goals and objectives. Does your campaign goal mesh with what marketing, advertising, sales and public relations are already trying to accomplish? Will the campaign be cooperating with or competing against existing initiatives?

Third, gain an understanding of the role other departments in the organization play in accomplishing the overall mission and goals. The communications department will contribute something different to accomplishing the organization's goals than the human resources or finance departments. But, there may be some overlap between communications, marketing and sales. Understanding the role that communications plays within the organization will help you know how to work together effectively with colleagues in other departments. It will also help you clearly define communication goals that demonstrate your unique contribution to the overall effort.

Truly sound and defensible communication goals and objectives will enhance and support the overall organization's mission and goals. Figure 5.2 identifies three examples of how communication goals can and should flow out of an organization's mission and goals. As you read through the examples, identify what makes each communication goal unique to the communications function. It may help you to review

Figure 5.2
Examples of organization and communication goals

For-profit business: Formica Corporation

CORE PROBLEM — "Despite being an iconic brand and the inventor of laminate, awareness and consideration of Formica Corporation and its offerings is declining with its core audience of architects and designers and is even lower with the next generation of these pros."

BUSINESS MISSION — "Our mission is to make top quality surfacing products accessible to all. That's why we offer products that provide a broad range of creative options that allow you to achieve the look you want, whatever your design challenge or budget."

BUSINESS GOAL — Ensure that future generations of designers and architects will consider Formica products.

COMMUNICATION GOAL — "Get as many students as possible familiar with the company's products and build affinity so they might consider using them in future projects."

Nonprofit organization: The Cleveland Museum of Art

CORE PROBLEM — Because of the COVID-19 pandemic, the Cleveland Museum of Art had to shut its doors to the public after a period of record-high in-person attendance, which meant the museum had to find a way to keep its visitors engaged during the shutdown.

ORGANIZATION'S MISSION — "The Cleveland Museum of Art creates transformative experiences through art, 'for the benefit of all the people forever.'"

ORGANIZATION'S GOAL — Maintain high levels of visitor engagement.

COMMUNICATION GOAL — "Through amplified virtual engagement with Northeast Ohio audiences and beyond, position the CMA for a strong reopening once the stay-at-home orders are lifted."

Government organization: Washington State Department of Natural Resources

CORE PROBLEM — "Washington saw more wildfires in 2021 than the first six months of any year on record since the state's comprehensive tracking began in 2005."

ORGANIZATION'S MISSION — "Manage, sustain and protect the health and productivity of Washington's lands and waters to meet the needs of present and future generations."

ORGANIZATION'S GOAL — Protect Washington State residents from the devastating effects of wildfires.

COMMUNICATION GOAL — "Motivate residents in three of Washington State's highest risk counties to take action to protect their home, property and neighbors from wildfires."

Chapter 1 about relationship building and Chapter 2 about public information and persuasion. Remember that effective communication with key publics is necessary to create the environment in which the organization can reach its goals. Any single campaign — whether designed to solve a problem or to proactively position the organization — must be planned within the framework of the organization's goals.

Identifying objectives

According to Mark Weiner (2021), chief insights officer at PublicRelay, "Striving for success without objectives is like trying to reach a destination without a map or a GPS." Once the goal is set, the challenge is to break down what you want to accomplish into more specific communication-oriented outcomes. If your company's goal is to expand a research program, your communications campaign may need to set

Figure 5.3

Examples of communication goals and objectives

For-profit business: Formica Corporation

COMMUNICATION GOAL	"Get as many students as possible familiar with the company's products and build affinity so they might consider using them in future projects."
OBJECTIVES	1. Increase brand awareness of Formica's products by 50% among students by the end of the campaign. 2. Increase participation in Formica's annual FORM Student Innovation Competition by 20%.

Nonprofit organization: The Cleveland Museum of Art

COMMUNICATION GOAL	"Through amplified virtual engagement with Northeast Ohio audiences and beyond, position the CMA for a strong reopening once the stay-at-home orders are lifted."
OBJECTIVES	1. "Increase Collection Online visits and Open Access Collection Online visits by 30% from the same quarter the previous year." 2. "Earn at least a combined 75 local, national and art trade media hits." 3. "Amplify engagement across CMA's three social media platforms (Facebook, Instagram and Twitter) by 10% from the onset of the campaign."

Government organization: Washington State Department of Natural Resources

COMMUNICATION GOAL	"Motivate residents in three of Washington State's highest risk counties to take action to protect their home, property and neighbors from wildfires."
OBJECTIVES	1. Get "1,800 Wildfire Ready Neighbors sign-ups." 2. "Get 600 residents to sign up for home visits."

objectives that involve securing public approval, generating funding, attracting personnel and building community support for the renovation of facilities. Figure 5.3 illustrates how the organizations featured in Figure 5.2 crafted objectives that broke down their communication goals into measurable outcomes.

Objectives are specific, measurable statements of what needs to be accomplished for the goal to be reached. Whereas a goal may be somewhat ambiguous (e.g., not defining how much is enough funding or profit), objectives must be absolutely precise. Figure 5.4 lists the Institute for Public Relations' six reasons for setting specific and measurable objectives.

 Figure 5.4
Why specific, measurable objectives are important

- They allow team members' actions to be prioritized.
- They focus the team on ensuring that strategies and tactics support and achieve them.
- They keep everyone on the same page, reducing the potential for disputes.
- They increase efficiency by concentrating resources where they will make a difference.
- They focus attention and action on the criteria by which the program will be evaluated.
- Ultimately, they allow an organization's decision makers to determine if the public relations campaign was successful.

Source: The Institute for Public Relations, The Communicators Guide to Research, Analysis, and Evaluation

We strongly recommend that objectives meet the following eight criteria that have been carefully refined by communications and business professionals. The first five criteria are based on the well-known SMART acronym. Keep in mind that precision is important in not only being able to carry out but also in effectively measuring your objectives.

Specific. Objectives should be free from ambiguity. What you are hoping to accomplish should be specific and clearly articulated. Each objective should address only one outcome. You shouldn't write an objective to increase awareness and improve sales. Similarly, achieving general awareness may not be enough. Be specific about what kind of awareness you are seeking. Do you want to increase awareness of an organization's existence or of a specific product line? Are you targeting awareness of a new coronavirus variant or, more specifically, its effect on the unvaccinated? And what levels of awareness are you seeking based on current levels of public knowledge? Having specific objectives helps you more clearly understand what publics you need to reach and what you need each public to do. Your approach to achieving these outcomes and the associated tasks will become the strategies and tactics used to reach key publics later in the planning process.

Measurable. Objectives must be improvement-oriented and quantifiable. To be improvement-oriented, objectives must work together to achieve your overall goal. Rarely will one objective suffice. Plan a number of objectives that all measure progress toward the goal. For example, if your goal is to open a new food bank, objectives could focus on fundraising, citizen support, government support and determining the best location.

○—○
○—○ **BENCHMARK**

A standard or point of reference against which communications outcomes may be compared or assessed.

To be quantifiable, each objective must have a number tied to it that can be used as a **benchmark** or starting point. Benchmarks should come from your research. These benchmark numbers can be represented in percentages or simple figures. Examples of percentage-based objectives are: a 20% increase in sales, a 50% jump in donations and a 60% decline in the number of high school students who have experimented with drugs before graduation. Examples of simple figure objectives are: raising $200,000 for the women's shelter, getting 3,000 participants in a 5K and engaging 6,000 people on an issue through social media.

When working with percentages, remember to carefully state the percent increase or decrease and use clarifying phrases. Otherwise, you might set yourself up to disappoint management's expectations created by your own objectives. If you want to increase the percentage of elementary school kids brushing their teeth at least twice a day, you should follow up that number by specifically stating the benchmark. You might write an objective like this: to increase the number of elementary school children in Arizona who brush their teeth at least twice a day from 25% to 75% by May 1, 2024.

Make sure you know the difference between a 50% increase and a 50 percentage point increase. The first is dependent on the starting point to calculate the actual increase. Fifty percent of 25 is 12.5, which would make your target 37.5% of school children brushing their teeth. A 50 percentage point increase takes you from 25% to 75% of school children brushing — two very different results. Similarly, a 20% increase in participation among a total population of 100 is not 20 people. The percent increase depends on the current level of participation, not the total population. If 50 of 100 people are currently participating, a 20% increase would be 10 people (20% of 50), from 50 to 60 participants, or a 10 percentage point improvement. Be very precise when planning and writing your objectives.

Sometimes benchmark statistics on opinion, awareness and action are not readily available. If you are certain the current level of knowledge or participation is minimal, you can reasonably state the level it needs to rise to in order to accomplish the goal. If you don't have statistical measures for something, find another way to count the improvement.

Attainable. Objectives need to be realistic if they are to be attainable. Keeping objectives specific and clear will help you set realistic targets. But you still need to set your sights on significant improvement. Management will scorn objectives that don't cause the organization to stretch and are too easily achieved. Executives have little respect for employees and managers who are unwilling to reach a bit, to take some risks and to challenge themselves. Nevertheless, if you shoot for the moon and just hit the stars, you may be branded as having fallen short, even if the stars were all you really needed to reach. According to the Institute for Public Relations, the key to setting attainable objectives is to openly negotiate them "with the executives who evaluate and fund public relations programs and confirm what the public relations function can realistically be expected to deliver."

Relevant. As previously discussed, objectives must be in line with and support the organizational mission and goals. Objectives are required to address issues, problems, opportunities or improvements that management perceives as valuable.

Keep in mind why the company is in business or why the organization exists. What are the key factors that have and are contributing to its success? Then ask yourself if your objectives will contribute to or detract from the organization's main purpose. Always doing this makes you strategic — of value to your organization because you help it accomplish its mission.

Time-bound. Objectives need to have a deadline. They should clearly outline when you expect to achieve a specific outcome. Setting time-bound objectives also determines when you will measure your success or failure. The duration of a campaign will be determined by the problem or opportunity being addressed. Some campaigns may require short, quick efforts (a few days, weeks or months) while others may necessitate long-range efforts. Some campaigns have built-in deadlines (e.g., attendance at a special event for a product launch). Others are designed to change perceptions and attitudes, which happens slowly.

Every objective, however, must include a target date. In some cases, interim measures may be helpful in measuring progress along the way and keeping you on track to reach the objective. For example, you might have a fundraising objective to raise $30 million for the construction of a new community theater. Benchmarking the objective to raise $10 million in the first six months may be necessary to give the project the momentum it needs to succeed.

Written. Objectives must be written down and published (at least shared with the communications and marketing teams). This may seem obvious, but too often organizations assume everyone knows about and understands the campaign's purpose and objectives. Unless they are written and shared, they have probably not been well thought out, and there may be differing perceptions of what the objectives are. One member of the team may be working toward something entirely different than the other members because their perception of the desired outcome is different than others on the team. Putting your objectives in writing helps to solidify and refine the plan while avoiding confusion over what you are trying to accomplish.

Further, written objectives serve as reference points throughout the planning process. When you come to a point of disagreement on any element of the planning process or when you run out of ideas somewhere in the process, it often helps to go back and review exactly what it is you are trying to accomplish. Finally, written objectives serve as tangible guides for evaluation. They allow you to demonstrate how far you've come — not only in a campaign but also as a professional.

As you write each measurable objective, also plan its evaluation. Specifically state the evaluation criteria and the tool to be used to access that number. While evaluation (further discussed in Chapter 12) is the last step in the RACE process, and criteria and tools are in the last step of the matrix, this is merely their chronological position. You do evaluation at the end of a communications effort to see if you achieved your desired results. But unless the evaluation is planned as you set objectives, it likely will not be carried out. You may run out of energy and just not get to it. Or you run out of money and can't complete the evaluation research. Or you didn't include a plan to gather data as the campaign progressed and lost your opportunity to evaluate. Or you didn't really have a viable tool to measure your results. Those are all typical excuses for not doing evaluation. You avoid those pitfalls if you actually write into your objectives what data will be gathered, when and how. Gathering this data — the results of your efforts — is critical to proving your success, and your worth to your organization. Figure 5.5 illustrates the formula for writing an effective objective.

Efficient. Objectives should also look for the easiest way to reach the goal. There are indeed many roads that lead to Rome. Whenever possible, pick the most direct route. As discussed above, when you write your objectives, you need to think about how you will measure them. Determining exactly how you will evaluate whether you reached your desired outcome will help you keep objectives simple and efficient.

Trying to measure the percentage of students on a university campus distracted by electronics after 10 p.m. will not be easy, and will be even more difficult to validate. By contrast, measuring the reported number of hours students sleep per night is much more straightforward. Similarly, measuring interest in a new product is more difficult than tracking sales of the product.

Cost-conscious. Objectives must take into consideration the available budget. It goes without saying that you should choose the most cost-effective ways to achieve the desired outcomes in any campaign. There will always be organizational pressure to accomplish more with less. Smart strategists look for low-cost options first.

Although you won't always know what budget will be available for a specific program when you are at this preliminary stage of planning, be sensitive to the organization's internal climate. A recession, slow sales, a global pandemic or downsizing may necessitate objectives that create more modest expectations. They may also force greater creativity in your planning. So keep perspective when crafting your objectives. It is not feasible, for example, to spend 50% of a campaign budget on opinion research. You will need money to develop and deliver your messages and motivate action.

While you must set objectives to solve the problem and reach the goal, the objectives you set also shape the organization's expectations of you and your team.

Figure 5.5
Formula for writing an effective objective

FORMULA: Criterion (communication metric) + benchmark (current state) + amount of improvement desired (desired state) + timeframe for achieving the desired improvement + research method used to measure the criterion.

EXAMPLE: Raise awareness of the company's efforts to respond responsibly to the oil spill from 60% to 80% within three weeks, measured by a contracted survey of the community.

MATRIX APPLIED

Writing goals and objectives

The local oil refinery has a good record of community involvement and an approval rating among local publics of 75% (measured by ongoing research conducted by the company every six months). Nevertheless, it continually faces scrutiny and even opposition from environmental activists. Recently, one of the pipelines sprung a leak. Before the leak was found and fixed, the equivalent of 100 barrels of oil seeped out into a small creek that runs through a residential neighborhood. The company immediately mobilized teams of experts, employees and local volunteers to clean up the small spill and restore the area (as much as possible) to its original pristine condition.

GOAL
To restore the company's approval rating and neutralize regulatory threats.

OBJECTIVES
1. Raise awareness of the company's efforts to respond responsibly to the spill from 60% to 80% within three weeks, measured by a contracted survey of the community.
2. Raise awareness of the company's local contribution to the community and economy from 65% to 80% within six months, measured by the organization's routine community survey.
3. Restore public approval to its previous 75% level within six months, measured by the organization's routine community survey.
4. Ensure no new state or local regulations (resulting from the spill) are enacted within the next three years, measured by monitoring legislation and regulation and tracking any changes.

Strategic approaches to setting objectives

Output, outtake and outcome objectives

In addition to the characteristics of good objectives, it is important to recognize there are four categories of communication objectives: output, outtake, outcome and impact. Each serves a different purpose, but all four are integral to the overall accomplishment of any campaign. At this stage of the planning process, we recommend that you focus on identifying outcome objectives.

Outcome objectives will help you define the overall success of your campaign. Think of it like this: outcome objectives usually are measured at the end of your campaign to determine its success. If you keep these desired outcomes in mind as you think through the rest of the campaign planning process, you will be much more likely to stay on the right track to success.

Output objectives and **outtake objectives** are valuable for tracking the performance of the individual tactics that make up your campaign. However, since you shouldn't be thinking about tactics at this stage of the planning process, we will

OUTCOME OBJECTIVES
Objectives that focus on the overall effect of a communication campaign on key publics.

OUTPUT OBJECTIVES
Objectives that focus on the dissemination of information and messages to key publics.

OUTTAKE OBJECTIVES
Objectives that focus on key publics' response or reaction to your messages.

further explain how to use outputs and outtakes in Chapter 12. In that chapter, we will also discuss the ways you can link your campaign outcomes to desired organizational **impact objectives**.

⅋⅋ IMPACT OBJECTIVES
Objectives that focus on the communication campaign's contribution to the organization or society at large.

Outcome objectives are meant to capture the overall effect of your communication on your key publics. In addition, outcome objectives can help you focus on the elements of information dissemination and persuasion you learned about in Chapter 2. Did your communication efforts make your key publics aware of something they weren't already aware of? Did your campaign messages reinforce a value that is important to your key public? Did your communication about your organization change the beliefs of any of your target publics? Did your key public better understand your organization's position on a controversial issue? Did your key public feel more positively about your organization? Did your campaign influence your key public to do something? Because we are dealing with the effect of communication on human beings, the outcomes you are trying to accomplish will usually have to do with how people think, feel and behave. The Institute for Public Relations describes outcome objectives as "the ultimate goal and related KPIs [key performance indicators] to which leading senior communicators aspire." Other examples of potential outcomes include:

- Advocacy
- Purchase intent
- Consideration
- Reputation
- Loyalty
- Satisfaction
- Preference
- Trust

There are two basic kinds of outcome objectives: informational and motivational. Each serves a different purpose, but both are integral to the overall accomplishment of any campaign.

Informational outcome objectives lay a foundation of understanding and awareness necessary for any kind of persuasive effort. They address the dissemination of information and an increase in awareness among key publics. This is a necessary step for publics to develop attitudes that will drive the behavior we are seeking. Informational objectives are usually easy to accomplish because you are just spreading information, not attempting to change anything. In fact, much of today's corporate communications practice is heavily engaged in information dissemination and awareness- or consciousness-raising. Nevertheless, Wilcox, Cameron and Reber (2014) contend that it is difficult to measure the accomplishment of such an

TIPS FROM THE PROS

The advantages of smaller objectives

Jesper Andersen, independent adviser and owner of Quantum PR Measurement in Copenhagen, Denmark, and a member of the International Association for the Measurement and Evaluation of Communication (AMEC), tips you off on the advantages of breaking "big objectives" into several, smaller objectives.

My clients often come to me with one specific problem related to objective-setting in communication measurement and evaluation: It is "too big."

The problem with communicating in a competitive market (where several parties are trying to influence the same target audience but with individual, conflicting objectives) is that it will require very specific (and most likely costly) data to correctly assess the influence of each party on the audience, i.e., how much was your communication a success, but how much do you then need to "subtract" from that success due to outside conflicting influence?

For example, the Danish Heart Foundation works to prevent heart disease. They work with research in cardiovascular diseases, prevention of heart diseases and support of patients. Like other health-related NGOs, who may focus on cancer, AIDS, or Alzheimer's disease, the Heart Foundation operates with an overall vision – in their case, a world in which heart disease is not a threat to the general public's health.

But if you measure the success of the organization's communication by that overall goal alone, you are not only in violation of the principles of SMART objective setting – you are also confronted by the problem that the Heart Foundation alone does not have the final say in whether they will eventually succeed or not. Other NGOs will lobby politicians for a limited amount of funds and political reforms, socio-economic developments like a recession may force families to eat less healthy food, thus increasing the risk of heart disease, and researchers and scientists may direct their efforts toward other health issues. Thus, there are numerous other factors at work that obstruct or counter what the Heart Foundation is working to achieve.

The solution – in terms of communication measurement – is to go smaller.

BREAKING A BIG OBJECTIVE INTO SMALLER OBJECTIVES

By breaking one large goal or objective into several smaller objectives, you gain several benefits:

- Each sub-objective will be easier to make SMART, because once you go down to a more tactical, operational level instead of a lofty strategic level, you naturally start getting more specific; going for something attainable becomes easier.
- You will have an easier time orchestrating a communications initiative that is less vulnerable to "noise" from opposing parties, thus making it easier for you to measure the outcome and impact of your own efforts.
- Having three, five or even ten smaller objectives that all "feed back" into the original overall objective means that you essentially have a greater chance of succeeding with some of your communications initiatives, rather than just frustratingly failing at the one. By evaluating your results, you can learn more easily from your mistakes and try again, and you will have something to show for all your work because it becomes obvious what your communication accomplished.

To illustrate, in the case of the Heart Foundation we might imagine they could come up with several relevant smaller communications objectives such as:

- Making sure relevant politicians have the best possible information on which to base informed critical healthcare-related decisions.
- Targeting wealthy potential donors with influence campaigns with the aim to secure a steady pipeline of funding for scientific research over a multiyear period.
- Motivating as many people as possible in the general population to attend courses in resuscitation and cardiac massage.
- Creating a broad awareness and understanding of the benefits of a healthy lifestyle.

Each of these examples are easier to work with than the overall vision because the goal no longer is: "Have we eradicated heart disease as a threat?" Now it is something much more tangible and with less noise from other interest groups and outside activities. But once you get to evaluating the impact of the Heart Foundation's communications, you can point to these specific activities and their outcomes and how they played an important role in reaching the overall goal.

objective because you are trying to measure a cognitive function (increase in information or understanding) on a sliding scale (how much information or understanding). In other words, have you simply achieved name recognition, or does your public have an understanding of what you do?

Although informational outcome objectives are necessary to lay a foundation to persuade people to act, they are never enough by themselves. It is recommended that most of your objectives focus on motivating action.

Motivational objectives are directly tied to behavior. As a result, they are usually easier to measure and harder to achieve. It is a relatively simple matter to measure a desired behavior. People voted for your candidate or they didn't; consumers bought the product or they didn't; children were inoculated or they weren't. Nevertheless, changing attitudes and opinions and creating the triggering event to move the public from awareness to action is much more difficult than just disseminating information and raising awareness of an issue or problem.

Use informational objectives to lay the foundation for persuasive efforts and motivational objectives to get publics to act. People can't vote the way you want them to on an issue if they are not aware of the issue and its effect on their lives. Consumers cannot buy a new product that will make life easier or more pleasant if they are not aware of its existence and benefits. Create awareness and information objectives, with all the characteristics of good objectives, to lay the foundation to accomplish your motivational objectives.

Remember that disseminating information is easy, but motivating behavior is more difficult. You will be able to reach a far higher level of awareness than you will behavior. You may be able to inform upwards of 90% of your target population on a particular issue. Nevertheless, 90% awareness does not translate to motivating 90% of a public to act. The achievable percentage of behavior will always lag behind the level of awareness. On some issues it may be only slightly lower; on other issues there may be a dramatic difference.

Summary

The Strategic Communications Matrix guides the planning process in communication and problem solving. It is the analytical tool that ensures research data and information are applied to solving the problem or seizing the opportunity. The matrix requires that good information, sound reasoning and clear logic drive decisions regarding the objectives needed in a campaign, what publics you need to reach, what messages you need to send to motivate those publics to act and what communications tools (tactics) will ensure key publics perceive and act on your messages.

The matrix transforms each step of the RACE model into strategic functions. It ensures that the communication process is not just a succession of steps to be completed, but that it is an interactive, integrated methodology for finding the best and most timely solution for the lowest cost. The process must be guided by specific, measurable, attainable, relevant, time-bound, written, cost-conscious and efficient objectives that lead to the accomplishment of a clearly articulated goal.

Remember that a campaign goal is a positive restatement of the core problem identified in the research section of the matrix. Objectives lay the foundation for the selection of the campaign's key publics you must reach. They also help determine the big idea, the messages, strategies and tactics necessary to inform and motivate publics to act. Objectives should also establish the evaluation criteria and tools necessary to effectively measure the success of your efforts.

Application case

Choose Topeka

from the Greater Topeka Partnership and Violet PR

In 2019, the Greater Topeka Partnership launched an initiative to get people from around the U.S. to move to Topeka, Kansas. Called "Choose Topeka," the initiative centered on a relocation incentive of up to $15,000 cash for college-educated workers who were willing to move to Topeka.

CORE OPPORTUNITY

Due to the COVID-19 pandemic and subsequent Great Resignation, more companies and workers were willing to consider telework and telecommuting.

BACKGROUND RESEARCH

A visit to Topeka revealed that the city was more diverse and more attractive as a destination than many people might expect. Topeka has a thriving arts scene (the NOTO Arts and Entertainment District), an outdoor concert venue (Energy Plaza), as well as other performing arts venues and organizations. The city also prides itself on its diversity, supporting racial justice and LGBTQ+ inclusion. Topeka hosts a variety of cultural festivals every year ranging from Fiesta Mexicana to Indiafest to Chinese New Year. Secondary research found that the cost of living in Topeka was 10% lower than the national average and one to two times lower than the cost of living in major metropolitan cities. Research about Topeka on social media and in the traditional news media found that awareness of Topeka was low and that most of the current conversation was about the city's chain restaurants and the anti-LGBTQ+ views of a church located in the city.

The Greater Topeka Partnership is made up of the Greater Topeka Chamber of Commerce, GO Topeka, Visit Topeka, and Downtown Topeka, Inc.

MISSION OF THE GREATER TOPEKA PARTNERSHIP

To be the catalyst for economic prosperity within our community.

BUSINESS GOAL OF THE GREATER TOPEKA PARTNERSHIP

Encourage college-educated workers to move to Topeka.

Assume you have been hired by the Greater Topeka Partnership to create a strategic communications campaign for the "Choose Topeka" initiative. Use the information provided in this case and principles from this chapter to complete the following tasks regarding campaign goals and objectives.

1. Write a communication goal for the "Choose Topeka" campaign that flows out of the Greater Topeka Partnership's mission and business goal. Provide a brief

rationale that explains why the goal you wrote is appropriate for communications to address and how it contributes to accomplishing the Greater Topeka Partnership's mission and business goal.

2. Write one informational outcome objective for the campaign using the formula in Figure 5.5 and following the eight criteria for objectives focusing on the overall behavior the campaign is seeking. What changes need to occur in terms of awareness, knowledge or understanding before the key publics will be ready to take action (i.e., move to Topeka)? Make sure to include a description of the tool you will use to measure the successful accomplishment of this objective. Provide a brief rationale that explains how the objective you wrote will help you demonstrate that you have accomplished your communication goal.

3. Write one motivational outcome objective for the campaign using the formula in Figure 5.5 and following the eight criteria for objectives focusing on the overall behavior the campaign is seeking. What changes need to occur in terms of the key publics' beliefs, values, attitudes or opinions that will motivate them to take action (i.e., move to Topeka)? Make sure to include a description of the tool you will use to measure the successful accomplishment of this objective. Provide a brief rationale that explains how the objective you wrote will help you demonstrate that you have accomplished your communication goal.

References and additional readings

Anderson, F. W., Hadley, L., Rockland, D. & Weiner, M. (2009). Guidelines for setting measurable public relations objectives: An update. Institute for Public Relations. Retrieved from https://instituteforpr.org/wp-content/uploads/Setting_PR_Objectives.pdf

CBS News. (2017, January 27). Mylan CEO on EpiPen drug price controversy: "I get the outrage." Retrieved from https://www.cbsnews.com/news/epipen-price-hike-controversy-mylan-ceo-heather-bresch-speaks-out/

Choose Topeka. (n.d.). Retrieved from https://choosetopeka.com/

"Choose Topeka" PR campaign. (n.d.) Persuading young professionals to make Topeka their new home. Retrieved from https://www.violetpr.com/choose-topeka

Cleveland Museum of Art. (n.d.).Mission, vision, promise. Retrieved from https://www.clevelandart.org/about/history-and-mission/mission-statement

Cleveland Museum of Art. (2021). Home is where the art is: The Cleveland Museum of Art's response to the COVID-19 quarantine. PRSA. Retrieved from https://www.prsa.org/conferences-and-awards/awards/search-silver-anvil-case-studies

Cutlip, S., Center, A., Broom, G. & Sha, B. (2012). *Effective Public Relations* (11th ed.). Englewood Cliffs, NJ: Prentice-Hall, Inc.

Delaware Department of Natural Resources and Environmental Control. (n.d.). BYO bag: Plastic bag ban. PRSA. Retrieved from https://www.prsa.org/conferences-and-awards/awards/search-silver-anvil-case-studies

Formica Corporation. (n.d.). Who we are, what we do. Retrieved from https://www.formica.com/en-us/who-we-are-what-we-do

Formica Corporation. (2022). Formica Corporation nurturing the next generation of designers. PRSA. Retrieved from https://www.prsa.org/conferences-and-awards/awards/search-silver-anvil-case-studies

Greater Topeka Partnership. (2021). "Choose Topeka" - $15,000 relocation campaign. Retrieved from https://www.prsa.org/conferences-and-awards/awards/search-silver-anvil-case-studies

Hobbes, T. (2017, April 7). Pepsi's ad failure shows the importance of diversity and market research. Retrieved from https://www.marketingweek.com/pepsi-scandal-prove-lack-diversity-house-work-flawed/

International Association for the Measurement and Evaluation of Communication. (n.d.). Integrated evaluation framework. Retrieved from https://amecorg.com/amecframework/

International Association for the Measurement and Evaluation of Communication. (n.d.). Barcelona Principles 3.0. Retrieved from https://amecorg.com/resources/barcelona-principles-3-0/

Jakić, I. (2022, June 20). Bad PR examples. Retrieved from https://www.mediatoolkit.com/blog/bad-pr-examples/

Newsom, D., Turk J. V. & Kruckeberg, D. (2013). *This Is PR: The Realities of Public Relations* (11th ed.). Independence, KY: Cengage Learning.

The Greater Topeka Partnership. (n.d.). Retrieved from https://topekapartnership.com/

The Institute for Public Relations (2021). *The Communicators Guide to Research, Analysis, and Evaluation*. Institute for Public Relations. Retrieved from https://instituteforpr.org/wp-content/uploads/IPR-Guide-to-Measurement-v13-1.pdf

Victor, D. (2017, April 5). Pepsi pulls ad accused of trivializing Black Lives Matter. Retrieved from https://www.nytimes.com/2017/04/05/business/kendall-jenner-pepsi-ad.html

Washington State Department of Natural Resources. (n.d.). About the Washington Department of Natural Resources. Retrieved from https://www.dnr.wa.gov/about-washington-department-natural-resources

Washington State Department of Natural Resources, & C+C. (2022). Wildfire ready neighbors. PRSA. Retrieved from https://www.prsa.org/conferences-and-awards/awards/search-silver-anvil-case-studies

Weiner, M. (2021). *PR Technology, Data and Insights: Igniting a Positive Return on Your Communications Investment*. Kogan Page: NY, New York.

Wilcox, D. L., Cameron, G. T. & Reber, B. H. (2014). *Public Relations: Strategies and Tactics* (11th ed.). New York: Allyn & Bacon.

CHAPTER 6

KEY PUBLICS AND PRIMARY MESSAGES

"To genuinely connect with your audience, you need to know what makes them tick. What strikes them as funny? What makes them sad? What unites them? What will cause them to rise up and act?"

—NANCY DUARTE
CEO OF DUARTE, INC.,
A GLOBAL LEADER IN VISUAL MESSAGING

LEARNING IMPERATIVES

- Learn how to effectively select key publics based on research insights.

- Learn how to use research to profile and analyze publics to discover motivating self-interests and opinion leaders.

- Craft primary messages that inform and motivate publics.

- Use research to discover the best channels to reach each public so messages are received and result in desired behaviors.

KEY PUBLIC
Segmented group of people whose support and cooperation is essential to the long-term survival of an organization or the short-term accomplishment of specific objectives.

I n Chapter 5, we discussed setting the objectives to be accomplished to meet the challenge or resolve the core problem. Now, we can identify the **key publics** whose cooperation will be essential to achieving our objectives and design the messages that will motivate those publics to act, or to allow the organization to act. In the following chapters, we will discuss how to deliver those messages effectively to your publics.

Public versus audience

We use the term "public" to describe a multidimensional active and interactive group of individuals with a few common characteristics that allow us to group them

for the purpose of building relationships through communication and cooperation. In essence, we stereotype based on key factors that help us understand, effectively communicate with and motivate a public.

In public relations, we tend to avoid referring to target groups as audiences. Audiences are often defined as spectators or listeners at an event and are therefore more passive than a public. Publics are groups we want to engage with through dynamic **two-way symmetrical communication**. Thinking about publics as groups to have a conversation with — a certain give and take — will help you identify those you need to work with to accomplish your objectives and goal.

Objective-focused

TWO-WAY SYMMETRICAL COMMUNICATION
A dialogue between organizations and publics that maintains mutually beneficial relationships.

For some communicators, it has become habit to select key publics before setting objectives. As a result, objectives are determined by who you want to reach rather than what you need to accomplish. Every organization should have identified publics who are key to its long-term success. And the organization should systematically work to build relationships with those publics. But when a problem or challenge emerges, assuming this same set of publics is all that's required to solve it is a prescription for failure. You may be successful at reaching the organization's existing key publics, but you risk missing other publics who are key to seizing the opportunity at hand.

Think about it: if there is a problem, then either your communication is failing or you've missed some key publics. Either way, the problem won't be corrected until you've analyzed it and set objectives to overcome it. Only when you know what you need to do can you identify who you need to motivate to help you do it.

Don't waste time and money informing and motivating publics that won't necessarily help you accomplish your goal. First identify the outcomes (objectives) you need to accomplish and then select those publics that you need to reach and motivate to achieve those outcomes. Your strategies for a public then identify the specific tasks (tactics) you must accomplish with that public to achieve your objectives.

STRATEGIC COMMUNICATIONS MATRIX

ACTION PLANNING

5. KEY PUBLICS AND PRIMARY MESSAGES, BIG IDEA, STRATEGIES AND TACTICS

Key Publics A description of each group that must be reached to achieve the goal and objectives. Identify:

- Objectives accomplished by each
- Demographics and psychographics
- Relationship with organization or issue
- Opinion leaders
- Self-interests
- Communication channels

Primary Messages Short summary statements for each public. Similar to sound bites. They identify topical information tied to the action needed from that public and how it meets their self-interest(s). Create a small number of primary messages, typically 1-3 per public.

Determining key publics

By this time in your study and practice of marketing communications and public relations, you should be well aware that there is no "general public." Targeting a general public is useless because people won't pay attention to a message that isn't tailored to their self-interests and received through a channel they use. Yet as communicators, our use of so-called mass media seems to perpetuate our tendency to generalize publics. In fact, communicators will often **segment** publics and then devise a single message to reach all of their segmented publics through the mass media. The segmentation was a waste of time and resources, and the message sent even more of a waste. Remember that just because a medium is designated mass does not mean that the publics consuming the information provided therein are mass.

Think for a moment about how you get your news. Do you read every story in your newsfeed? How about every word in the stories you choose to read? Probably not. When you read a news story you choose what you read based on headlines and pictures. Then you continue to read a story only as long as it is of personal interest. The same perceptual behavior applies to new digital and social media tactics like websites, blogs, Instagram, Tik Tok and email. You look at a photo, video, headline or subject line. If that draws you in by appealing to your self-interests, you continue to read. But the minute the story loses its appeal to you personally, you move on. No matter the channel or tactic, people choose to perceive our messages only when we design them specifically to appeal to their interests. It is clear that for a message to be selected, perceived and retained by our publics from any kind of medium, it must be carefully and specifically targeted to a segmented public

SEGMENTATION
Defining and separating publics by demographics and psychographics to ensure more effective communication.

included within the viewership, readership, followership or listenership of that medium. If its appeal is general, no public will consider it for perception and retention. It may get sent, but if it doesn't obviously address the self-interests of specific target publics, it will be ignored.

TIPS FROM THE PROS

Segmenting drives effective communication strategy

Maury Giles, chief growth officer of Heart+Mind Strategies, an insights-based communications consulting firm, tips you off on a practical way to use segmentation to drive strategy.

To drive behavior, effective communication must persuade by reason and motivate through emotion. Both are required. But they only resonate when you convey a natural outcome of how people will feel because of the functional benefit you offer. Emotion does not work on its own. Rational arguments alone do not move people.

We call this sweet spot the strategic hinge for communication. This is where the magic happens. It is the center of effective messaging that will drive the outcome you seek.

The growing challenge in today's market reality is that you must identify the primary strategic hinge and then be able to deliver nuanced versions to myriad unique groups of people. Communicators today have the ability through digital channels to create and serve up custom messaging and personalized experiences. This is how we consume information in our everyday lives. It is how we expect to receive it. So, marketers must deliver it this way.

You can build this type of messaging playbook when you break down and understand the people you need to reach in smaller subgroups with shared characteristics: segments. What makes them tick? What do they need? In what ways do they matter to your success?

The simplest form of segmentation is born out of the political arena. It is mapping your "core," your "swing" and your "anti" groups. It is looking at your public through the eyes of those who are with you, those who could be convinced to support you and those who are against you.

CORE
In politics this is simple. Who are your "definite" voters? The concept extends across sectors beyond voting. Who is already doing the things you want them to do? These are the people you need to do more, say more or be more in some context. They are critical to your success. They are likely the 20% who account for 80% of your success.

SWING
These are the people who can be moved. They are open to your message, but they need a reason to act, change or think differently. They are the most important public for you to drive the outcome you need because they will make the difference.

ANTI
These are your opposition. You may need to avoid them. You may need to inoculate against their attacks. Or you may need to engage to move them. It is important to understand this group in context of the communication strategies you are building.

Identify these three groups based upon the decisions that are most important for you to influence. In politics this is voting. In times of crisis, it might be defined through reputation or trust. In market growth, it is likely centered on purchase or preference or loyalty or awareness. These are the filters through which you decide who are your core, swing and anti publics. Get creative in your definition. Make certain to relate to the human-centered reality of the people you seek to reach and influence. That matters!

STEPS IN USING A SIMPLE SEGMENTATION

Profile your core, swing and anti publics by demographics. Who are they? But don't stop there. Consider the characteristics that make them fall into one of your three segments.

Think about how you'll find them. These are the identifiers of behaviors, interests, channels or preferences you'll be able to use later. Include all of these in your segmentation and how you define each public.

Decide exactly what you need each audience to think, feel or do. This is key! It's essential to uncovering your strategic hinge for messaging and experience planning.

Anchor on the most important answer to step three for each public. Map the functional benefit you offer that matters most to each group and link it to the feeling that makes that important. That is your strategic hinge.

Now adapt it to your three groups as you reach out and connect.

Good luck!

Contributed by Maury Giles. © Kendall Hunt Publishing Company.

Segmenting publics

There are lots of ways to segment publics. The way you choose to segment publics for a particular campaign depends on the issue and your purpose. If you are addressing the quality of education in the community, public segmentation would include parents, teachers, administrators and future employers. If the issue is zoning regulations within that very same community, your segmentation would re-categorize the community members as nonproperty owners, residential property owners, commercial property owners or business people, and civic and government leaders. In both campaigns, they are the very same people, but how you group people together and describe them for the purpose of reaching and motivating them is based upon the issue at hand and their self-interests tied to that issue.

© Monkey Business Images/Shutterstock.com

In the background step of the research section, you access stakeholder research to understand public segmentation using both demographic and psychographic data. The primary and secondary data gathered on publics includes their opinions, attitudes, values, beliefs and lifestyles. The stakeholder research tells you their media habits and the best channels to use in communicating with them. Your research describes their current relationships with the issue and organization as well as identifies self-interests and opinion leaders. Because you have gathered and studied that research, you have a deeper understanding of the potential publics needed to meet your current challenge. Now, review your objectives and determine which public segments are essential in helping you achieve those objectives. Remember that more than one public may need to be reached to accomplish each objective and that a key public may help you achieve more than one objective.

Bear in mind that there may be several different combinations of key publics that can help you accomplish the objectives. As described in Figure 6.1, your task is to discover the combination that: first, does the best job of combining to solve the problem; second, is most logical in terms of ongoing organizational efforts to build relationships; and third, provides the most benefit for the lowest cost in terms of resources (time, money and effort).

 Figure 6.1
Priorities in selecting the best combination of key publics

1. Which publics working together will produce the best overall solution?

2. Which publics make the most sense for long-term organizational relationships?

3. Which combination of publics will get the desired result for the least amount of additional time, money and other resources?

Consider, for example, a presidential election campaign. Political campaigns are probably one of the best examples of using thorough research to guide decision-making. The research consultant to a presidential candidate has access to thousands of pieces of information from a variety of research techniques including, at a minimum, focus groups, panel studies and opinion polls. The consultant has divided the voting population into dozens of different segments and has an in-depth, research-based profile of each. The research profiles the attitudes, behaviors and voting preferences of every demographically segmented public by age, income, education, gender, religion, geography, occupation and any other descriptor you can imagine. Further, the consultant has included in the profiles their lifestyles, consumer preferences, habits and other psychographic and value-based characteristics.

With all those segments, there are literally hundreds of combinations of publics that could accomplish the task of electing the candidate for president. A strategist might, for example, choose a combination that includes, among others, 24- to 32-year-olds, Catholics, blue-collar workers and Northeastern voters. The job of the strategist in a political campaign is to select, from the dozens of profiled segments, the combination of voter publics that will best assure victory in the election (priority one in Figure 6.1). In selecting publics to bring victory, the strategist should also consider those publics whose cooperation will be most crucial to the long-term success of the newly elected president (priority two in Figure 6.1). Finally, the strategist should consider the combination of publics that will bring the most benefit for the least cost (priority three in Figure 6.1).

Too often in the past, business has operated with that third priority as the first consideration. Leading our decisions with only cost considerations has landed us in the current crisis of trust among those publics who are most essential to the survival of organizations in our society. The key publics selected to meet any challenge we face should be those best combined to facilitate proper resolution and long-term success. If cost considerations become a concern, they should be addressed in more creative use of resources rather than by jeopardizing the long-term health of the organization.

Message design

Primary messages

Now that you know what you need to do to resolve your problem and who you need to reach to accomplish that, you are ready to design the messages to motivate your key publics to do what you want them to do. Messages are public-specific. As a result, how you segment publics to achieve your objectives and the self-interests you identify dictate the messages for each public. Your messages should contain two essential elements:

- Your purpose — what you need a key public to think, feel, believe or do in order for you to accomplish your objectives.
- Your appeal to a key public's self-interest — what will motivate them to act favorably to accomplish your objectives.

As mentioned before, you cannot successfully incorporate a public's self-interest into a message generalized to all publics. Each public will need a different appeal based on its particular self-interests.

It is essential that messages be based on the insights you have gained from research. Applying your research on key publics, including specifics about their demographics, psychographics, self-interests and the way they receive messages, will make it more likely that your messages will be received and acted upon.

Seasoned communicator, Ann Wylie of Wylie Communications suggests six keys to making messages more meaningful.

Start with your goals. "Stop thinking like a news bureau; your job is to change behavior, not report news."

Simplify messages. "It doesn't matter how great your message points are if nobody can understand [or remember] them." Keep them short and simple.

Make messages credible. If the public doesn't believe your messages, they won't act on them. Substantiate messages with factual evidence.

Focus on the audience. People care about themselves, not about your organization. Segment your audience, think like your audience and focus message points on your audience.

Let the messages drive your content. If a tactic — a news story, photo or even a caption — doesn't help communicate one of your key messages, don't use it.

MATRIX APPLIED

Selecting key publics and crafting primary messages

Arizona's State Department of Health has verified that bubonic plague has been discovered in rats in rural areas of the state, with one confirmed human case. Research shows that while 60% of Arizonans know plague is carried by fleas, only 40% are aware that rodents in Arizona may be infected. Only 40% could identify symptoms of plague, although 45% could identify preventive behaviors. Only 35% identified antibiotics as the cure. Without treatment, bubonic plague kills about two out of three infected humans within four days. Because symptoms mimic the flu, treatment is often delayed.

Bubonic plague is generally believed to be the cause of the Black Death that swept through Europe in the 14th century and killed an estimated 25 million people. Today, the plague occurs mostly in rural areas, so rural residents are at risk. Outdoor recreationalists are at risk, as are farmers, ranchers, pets and pet owners. Those most commonly affected are men ages 20 to 45.

KEY PUBLICS

1. ***Outdoor recreationalists.*** This public includes all those who participate in outdoor recreation in Arizona's rural areas. Their activities include hunting, fishing, hiking, camping, biking, boating, rock climbing, ATV riding or any other type of outdoor recreation. While they range in age from children to seniors, those most commonly at risk are middle- to upper-class men ages 20 to 45. Most in this group tend to feel invulnerable to risk. They are typically informed about Bubonic plague and plague prevention but may be unaware of the current outbreak.

   Self-interests: enjoying nature, outdoor fun, health and safety.
   Opinion leaders: peers, family, outdoor activity bloggers, personal medical professionals, park rangers.
   Channels: recreational venues; recreation retailers; blogs and social media, particularly sites featuring opinion leaders with news, information and tips on outdoor recreation and venues; targeted cable television programming.
   Primary Messages:
   1. There is a recent outbreak of the plague in this area that is likely to increase your risk of contracting the disease.
   2. Remember to practice smart plague prevention. Your life depends on it.

2. ***Rural residents.*** This public includes residents of small towns as well as farmers and ranchers. They are typically middle-class individuals and families whose roots go back for generations in close-knit communities throughout rural Arizona. They live in the midst of the recreation venues that draw enthusiasts from all the Western states. They participate in recreation activities as well as provide services to visitors who come for that purpose. They would know about the plague outbreak, preventive behaviors, symptoms and treatment. They are opinion leaders and information sources for outdoor recreationalists.

   Self-interests: health and safety and sustaining lifestyle and community while enjoying the outdoors.
   Opinion leaders: peers, family, respected local public servants such as sheriffs.
   Channels: local community media, word-of-mouth and opinion leaders.

Primary Messages:
1. You can keep your community safe by reminding tourists about smart plague prevention.
2. If you encounter a visitor who has symptoms of plague infection, help them seek immediate medical attention. Their life depends upon it.

3. Pet owners. Because plague is carried by fleas and fleas are attracted to animals, pet owners are important in preventing the spread of disease. A significant portion of the population own at least one pet, many two or more, typically cats or dogs. Demographics of this public are diverse, encompassing all ages and income ranges. Many owners are vigilant in the care of their animals involving grooming and veterinary professionals, but just as many do not invest in such services. Nevertheless, all pet owners purchase pet food and supplies. They would have little awareness of plague in Arizona or the recent outbreak and possibly limited knowledge of symptoms, treatment or prevention.

Self-interests: their health and the health of their animals.
Opinion leaders: neighbors, family, friends, co-workers and pet care providers.
Channels: mass media, social media, opinion leaders, pet-related retailers and service providers.
Primary Messages:
1. You can keep your pet healthy and safe by practicing smart plague prevention.
2. Know the symptoms of plague infection in your pet and seek immediate medical attention if your pet has any symptoms. Both your lives depend upon it.

4. Medical professionals. This public includes all medical professionals whether in private practices, clinics, insta-cares or hospitals. These are upper middle-class to upper-class, well-educated individuals. They are opinion leaders to other publics. They would be familiar with plague routinely occurring in rural areas but unaware of the recent outbreak.

Self-interests: welfare of patients and their professional reputations.
Opinion leaders: employers, patients, state and county health officials.
Channels: state and county health departments, employers and local mass media news.
Primary Messages:
1. There is a recent outbreak of the plague in this area that is likely to increase the number of patients you see with plague symptoms.
2. Alert your patients who spend time recreating outdoors about the symptoms of plague infection. Their lives depend upon it.

Repeat messages. Research shows a message repeated or reinforced seven times over 30 days yields 90 percent retention. Relevance is equally important. If information is personally relevant to the audience, fewer exposures are needed to make an impression.

In the Strategic Communications Matrix, messages are written in two parts: primary and secondary. **Primary messages** are the leading drivers of the campaign and are crafted in this step of the matrix. Secondary messages are more specific details that fill out the primary messages and make them believable. Secondary messages are identified and developed when you build out your tactics in a later step. We will discuss secondary messages in more depth in Chapter 11.

 PRIMARY MESSAGES
Sound-bite statements that encompass what you need the public to do and an appeal to the public's self-interest to act.

Primary messages are topical. They focus on the specific information each public needs to spur them to action. The topics of your primary messages will depend on the objectives you are trying to accomplish and the key publics you are trying to reach. Topics that need to be communicated are indicated by the specific evaluation criteria included in your objectives. The Matrix Applied in this chapter about Bubonic plague prevention provides a good example. Objectives for the Bubonic plague campaign would need to achieve the evaluation criteria of understanding the symptoms and treatment of the disease, knowledge of plague prevention measures and awareness of the current outbreak. The key public of outdoor recreationalists wants to spend as much time outdoors as possible while staying safe and healthy. While members of this public are typically informed about Bubonic plague and plague prevention, they may be unaware of the current outbreak. As a result, informative messages about the topics of Bubonic plague symptoms and plague prevention measures may not be needed for this public. But, outdoor recreationalists will need an informative message to make them aware of the current outbreak and probably a motivational reminder to practice smart plague prevention while they recreate outdoors.

Primary messages often resemble sound bites that might be given during a media interview. They should be relatively short and easy to understand and remember. Keep in mind that primary messages are not empty sound bites or clickbait. They have to be thoughtfully crafted in order for them to help you accomplish your objectives. Each primary message should have embedded within it information about what you want the public to understand, believe or do. They also should include a short self-interest appeal. Your public needs to clearly see why this information is relevant and useful to them so they will be motivated to act on it. A helpful way to think about primary messages may be as a claim you are making to your public about how they will benefit if they believe and act on your message. Later, we will develop secondary messages that will provide the support or evidence needed to back up your claim.

A campaign to reduce obesity among children, for example, will have a number of primary messages directed at specific key publics. For parents of children 12 and under, a primary message might be designed to encourage parents to take a more proactive role in looking after the nutrition of their children. One way to craft that message could be, "Healthy adults come from healthy kids — ensure your child's future with a healthy diet today." In this case, the information we want our public to understand or believe is that if children eat a healthy diet when they are young, it will help them be healthy when they grow up. This is our claim. The appeal to the public's self-interest embedded in this message relies on the desire that parents have for their children to grow into healthy, happy and successful adults. If the message is successful, parents shouldn't just believe our claim, they should act on it.

The number of primary messages for a key public will depend upon the number of topics you need to communicate about, as well as the breadth and duration of the campaign. This is best determined by the objectives you have set. For example, if you only need the help of one key public and you are only trying to accomplish one objective, you may need only one primary message that provides the information specified by the evaluation criteria of that objective. If you need the support of multiple publics to accomplish several different objectives, you will likely need primary messages that address the topics indicated in evaluation criteria of each objective and are tailored to the self-interests of each key public. Naturally, this will result in more primary messages. Typically, a key public will have two to three primary messages.

At the heart of the planning process are the decisions we make about the messages we want to send to our key publics and the best way to get those messages to those publics. It is in this central part of the process that we need most to be guided by our research. Yet, we are most tempted to rely on instinct alone. Not that instinct is necessarily bad. It is often a subconscious process of integrating bits and pieces of knowledge and information and charting an appropriate course given the data. But, it can also be an unwillingness to believe information and data because it conflicts with limited personal observation. In the latter case, instinct usually leads us to follow courses that fail to solve — and often exacerbate — the problem. To avoid that error, we would be wise to always test our instinct against the information and data gathered through research.

If you learn through your research that a particular target public is motivated on a given issue by its self-interest in quality of life for their children, your message must convey the importance of that result. For example, parents concerned about their children's safety from gang violence are motivated by messages that promise a safer environment, not reductions of taxpayer cost. ("We have to find a way to keep our children safe at school and at play.") On the other hand, if your target public is more concerned about higher taxes and the government's growing demands on their income to solve social problems, they will be more motivated by messages that focus on perceived low-cost solutions. ("Lock them up; we can't keep spending money on expensive programs for law breakers!")

Intervening publics

An intervening public is one that carries our message to the publics we ultimately need to reach and influence. Media and opinion leaders are intervening publics that are often used in communication and persuasion. Teachers or PTA volunteers in school are sometimes good channels to get a message to a parental public. Health care workers are good intervening publics on health issues. Intervening publics are not typically designated as key publics unless you need to persuade them to help you. If you need to develop or strengthen a relationship with an intervening public to ensure its cooperation, you might designate it as a key public. For example, if you've had a problem with media being hostile, unresponsive or inaccurate, you may need to identify them as a key public and develop message strategies and tactics that will improve your relationship with them. Otherwise, media are typically an intervening public or channel we often use to reach our key publics.

TV anchor Anderson Cooper shakes hands with Debbie Gibson at the 39th Annual Daytime Emmy Awards in Beverly Hills.

Yes! to Census 2020
City of Houston and Harris County with Lopez Negrete Communications, Inc, UP Art Studio and January Advisors

Every 10 years, the United States conducts a census of its population. The data collected by the census has a significant impact on the lives of all Americans. Census results are used to determine the number of seats for each state in the U.S. House of Representatives and to draw boundaries of state legislative districts. They also guide the distribution of federal funds to local communities.

CORE PROBLEM
The City of Houston was at risk of its population being undercounted in the 2020 Census. Houston had the lowest predicted census self-response rate. In addition, it had a large number of hard-to-count groups. Because the census is used to allocate federal funding, every Houston resident who was not counted in the 2020 Census meant fewer federal resources for the city.

HOUSTON 2020 CENSUS STRATEGY
Prior to creating the campaign, Lopez Negrete Communications conducted a series of focus groups with Hispanic, Vietnamese, Chinese, African American, Urdu, Hindi, Vietnamese, Chinese, LGBTQ+ and non-Hispanic White individuals living in Houston. Some of the focus groups were made up of opinion leaders of these hard-to-reach individuals. Other focus groups included members of hard-to-reach populations. Their qualitative research produced insights about what each population segment knew about the census, their main barriers to participation, their main motivators of participation (self-interests), trusted opinion leaders and primary messages. Here are two examples.

1. ***Hispanic Population.*** The majority of the Hispanic population had little knowledge about the census or its benefits. They were afraid that the government would use the information they provided on the census against them. Those who lived in the U.S. for less than 10 years were apathetic about the census because of the belief that they might return to their home country soon. The main motivators for Hispanics were that census information is protected by law, that the census has an impact on the future of their children and community, and that the census can be taken in Spanish.

   Self-interests: family, benefits, education, children, wellness, future, trust.
   Opinion leaders: well-known Hispanics from TV, radio, sports and music.
   Channels: TV, radio, social media, shopping, outdoor events.
   Primary messages:
   1. The immigration question is OUT.
   2. Your census information is private.

2. ***African-American Population.*** While the African-American population had little knowledge about the purpose of the census, they had more knowledge than any other hard-to-reach segment. This group had a historical distrust of and disappointment in government that affected their census participation. They were also afraid

© lev radin/Shutterstock.com

that their participation would result in the loss of government-funded social benefits. The main motivator for African-Americans was seeing tangible evidence of the benefits of census participation. They felt more comfortable filling out the census in a secure location.

Self-interests: community, civic duty, safe participation, representation.
Opinion leaders: religious leaders.
Channels: TV, radio, social media, mail, outdoor signage (posters, signs, etc.).
Primary messages:
1. Your participation is an opportunity to make a difference and have fair representation.
2. It is your right to have a say in what happens in your neighborhood in the next 10 years.

Using similar insights for all of the hard-to-reach segments, the campaign communicated motivational messages about completing the census through earned media and a variety of opinion leaders including local government officials, church leaders and social media influencers.

RESULTS
- Harris County's self-response rate (62.9%) was slightly higher than the self-response rate for the entire state of Texas (62.8%).
- Twenty-nine neighborhoods had self-response rates as high as 71%.

Summary

Once objectives are set, we can select the most effective combination of publics to accomplish them. To be holistic in accomplishing the goal, we need to remember that more than one key public may be needed to reach an objective and that a key public may help satisfy multiple objectives. Stakeholder research, including demographic and psychographic data, can be used to segment and profile each key public.

Once we thoroughly understand each key public, we can design primary messages that will result in the behavior that accomplishes our objectives. Key messages are public-specific, communicate your purpose and focus on a key public's overriding self-interests, which are crucial in designing messages that publics will pay attention to and act on. At this point, we may also identify intervening publics to help us get our messages to the key publics.

Application case

Planet Fitness openings in Wasilla and Eagle River, Alaska

from Planet Fitness of Wasilla and Eagle River with Helvey Communications LLC and Embley Communications

CORE PROBLEM

A new Planet Fitness franchise owner was getting ready to open two new gyms in Wasilla and Eagle River, Alaska. However, residents of Wasilla and Eagle River were skeptical of a national franchise opening in their cities because they have a lot of community pride in their traditional, small-town feel.

BACKGROUND RESEARCH

Research about the Planet Fitness franchise found that the company's purpose involves: (1) breaking down "barriers of intimidation and affordability to make fitness truly accessible to all;" (2) creating an "inclusive, engaged and judgment free culture" for employees and members; and (3) adopting business practices that "acknowledge the inextricable link between human health and planet health."

In addition, research found that Planet Fitness has a reputation for inclusivity, positivity and kindness. One challenge about Planet Fitness operating on a franchise model was that all brand social media accounts are controlled by the corporate office. Local franchisees are not allowed to have their own, branded social media accounts. Research about the attitudes of local residents found that most people in Wasilla had a negative attitude about national brands coming into their community. And research about competition in the area discovered that Wasilla already had a number of fitness options available.

BUSINESS GOAL

To get Wasilla and Eagle River residents to purchase Plant Fitness memberships.

COMMUNICATION GOAL

To excite Wasilla and Eagle River residents about Planet Fitness coming to their communities.

Objective 1: To secure [confidential number] members by 30 days prior to opening day.

Objective 2: To secure at least one high-profile local community partnership in each community by close of the campaign.

Objective 3: To secure positive stories from the four main media outlets at least twice by the end of the campaign.

Assume you have been hired by the owner of the Wasilla and Eagle River Planet Fitness locations to create a strategic communications campaign for the Planet Fitness openings. Use the information provided in this case and principles from this chapter to complete the following tasks regarding key publics and primary messages.

1. Identify and segment the key and intervening publics that you need to reach and motivate to achieve the campaign goals and objectives.

2. Determine which combination of publics will best enable you to accomplish your goals and objectives.
   - Which publics working together will produce the best overall solution?
   - Which publics make the most sense for long-term organizational relationships?
   - Which combination of publics will get the desired result for the least amount of additional time, money and other resources?

3. Following the examples in the Mini Case and Matrix Applied, write a short paragraph that describes each segmented public. In each paragraph, include information about the segment's demographics, psychographics and relationship with the organization and the issue. In bullet points beneath each paragraph, identify each public segment's:
   - Self-interests,
   - Opinion leaders,
   - Viable communications channels, and
   - Primary messages.

References and additional readings

Broom, G. M. & Sha, B. (2013). *Cutlip and Center's Effective Public Relations* (11th ed.). Upper Saddle River, NJ: Pearson Education.

City of Houston. (2021). Yes! to Census 2020. Retrieved from https://www.prsa.org/conferences-and-awards/awards/search-silver-anvil-case-studies

Houston in Action. (n.d.). 2020 Census research report. Retrieved from https://drive.google.com/file/d/1aDO_5ZGXmyxyFCMqoKrVuCviy-8fT4qx/view

Newsom, D., Turk, J. V. & Kruckeberg, D. (2012). *This is PR: The Realities of Public Relations* (11th ed.). Independence, KY: Cengage Learning.

Planet Fitness of Wasilla and Eagle River, Helvey Communications LLC, & Embley Communications. (2021). New gyms show community how to "exercise kindness." Retrieved from https://www.prsa.org/conferences-and-awards/awards/search-silver-anvil-case-studies

Planet Fitness. (n.d.). PF purpose. Retrieved from https://www.planetfitness.com/pf-purpose

Stern and Company. (2007). Targeting key publics and message definition. Retrieved from asternglance.com/sternco-essays-2/targeting-key-public-and-message-definition

Wilcox, D. L., Cameron, G. T. & Reber, B. H. (2014). *Public Relations: Strategies and Tactics* (11th ed.). Upper Saddle River, NJ: Pearson Education.

Weiner, M. (2021). *PR Technology, Data and Insights: Igniting a Positive Return on Your Communications Investment*. Kogan Page: NY, New York.

Wylie, A.. (n.d.). On message. Retrieved from https://www.wyliecomm.com/

Yes! to Census 2020. (n.d.). Retrieved from https://www.lopeznegrete.com/yes-census-2020/

CHAPTER 7

CREATIVITY AND BIG IDEAS

"It's kind of fun to do the impossible."

—WALT DISNEY
ANIMATOR, FILMMAKER AND CREATIVE GENIUS

LEARNING IMPERATIVES

- Appreciate the importance of creativity in developing winning campaigns.

- Develop the skills and techniques needed for creative thinking.

- Be able to design big ideas that capture attention and appeal to an organization's key publics.

Buzz Lightyear from Pixar's "Toy Story."

CREATIVITY

The process of looking outside ourselves and our routine to discover new ideas and innovative solutions.

Creativity

It took roughly 100 men and women five years — including a lot of holidays, weekends and late nights — to create the first feature-length film fully animated on a computer. But when "Toy Story" debuted Thanksgiving weekend in 1995, it forever changed the landscape for animated films. Disney executives had advised the upstarts at Pixar to fill the movie with songs, but the company resisted. "Despite being novice filmmakers at a fledgling studio in dire financial straits, we had put our faith in a simple idea: If we made something that we wanted to see, others would want to see it, too," says Ed Catmull, president of Pixar. "For so long, it felt like we had been pushing that rock up hill, trying to do the impossible.... Now, we were suddenly being held up as an example of what could happen when artists trusted their guts."

"Toy Story" became the biggest grossing movie of the year, earning $358 million worldwide. The name Pixar has become synonymous with **creativity** and innovation. In 2006, Disney paid $7.4 billion to acquire Pixar. As of 2023, Pixar-Disney has won an incredible 18 Academy Awards, nine Golden Globes and 11 Grammys for its animated films including the "Toy Story" series, "Monster's Inc." and "Monster's University," "Finding Nemo" and "Finding Dory," "The Incredibles," "Ratatouille," "WALL-E," "Up," "Brave," "Inside Out," and "Coco."

Many people say, "I'm just not creative." As a result, they miss out — leaving the creative aspects of campaigns to others. This is no different than claiming, "I'm not strategic" or "I'm not a good writer." These conditions may be true, but they are not terminal. Creativity, like any other skill, can be learned.

Just like a glassblower has to learn what temperature, pressure and movement are needed to create beautiful objects, learning to be creative means mastering the process and practicing. Sometimes desperate times cause us to break with our routine.

Not long after the Airbnb founders blew up three air mattresses in their San Francisco apartment and rented them to complete strangers, the startup (now worth more than $75 billion) found itself with a binder full of maxed out credit cards. The debt collectors started calling around the 2008 presidential election between Obama and McCain. But Airbnb CEO Brian Chesky and his buddies had an idea. "Boys, what if we designed and sold limited edition cereal boxes and called them Obama O's & Captain McCain?"

They had 1,000 custom boxes printed, bought loads of cereal (Cheerios and Captain Crunch), put the boxes together with a hot glue gun in their apartment and slapped on a $40 price tag. The stunt was featured on national television and Airbnb sold 1,000 cereal boxes in a day, making $30,000 after expenses — easily covering the $20,000 they owed.

A more recent example comes from Citizen Brick, a Chicago-area toy company known for making far-out versions of LEGO mini figurines. In March 2022, owner Joe Trupia watched the Russian invasion of Ukraine and wanted to do something. President Zelenskyy's leadership had also caught his attention. Using toy parts the store had on hand Citizen Brick created a LEGO-based figurine of the Ukrainian president and tiny Molotov cocktails featuring the Ukrainian flag.

The Zelenskyy figurines sold for $100 each. The Molotov cocktails were $20. Both sold out within hours, raising more than $145,000 in proceeds benefiting the nonprofit aid group, Direct Relief. "We just wanted to do a small fundraising effort," Trupia said. "But this one seemed to hit the bull's eye with some people."

Trupia admits that a month earlier he, like many others, could not have told you who Zelenskyy was. But there was a moment in time that he captured the world's attention. "It really impressed me that he was kind of staying there for his people and really kind of leading the way that they needed him to at the minute."

"On its face, making a toy Molotov cocktail is an absurd idea," Trupia said. "And I kind of enjoyed the twist of turning that into medical supplies for refugees. That seemed like a good deed. But...I'm not really sure why that was the thing that caught people's eye."

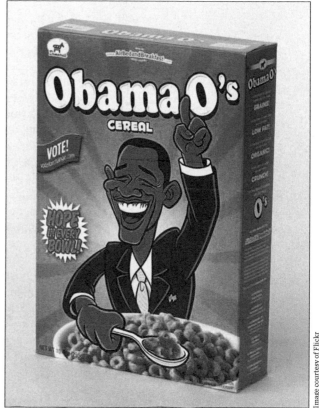

Image courtesy of Flickr

Just because you have a crazy idea, doesn't mean you are crazy, it could actually mean you're brilliant.

Knowing what will stick

Why do some ideas stick and some fade? The answer is how creative the idea is or in other words how unusual, timely, salient, relevant and/or humorous the idea is. Throw in a sprinkling of luck and voilà.

Learning how to evaluate the "creativeness" of ideas is as important as learning how to generate those ideas. But in order to evaluate something, we need a tool, a way to measure it. This can be challenging since creativity, like humor, is not universally appreciated.

As a result we need a tool and some shared language to be able to express and evaluate creative thinking. You may have noticed that people tend to avoid discussing things they don't know how to talk about. To overcome this obstacle we turned to the marketing team at Dutch brewing company Heineken. They found a way to both evaluate and talk about creativity that really works.

Claire Bridges, in her book, "In Your Creative Element" (2016), describes how marketers at the beer company developed the Heineken Creative Ladder. The 10-point scale (see Figure 7.1) with descriptors on each rung of the ladder are a stroke of genius. Rather than just say, "we need something more creative," the tool provides a description of what an idea might be missing. For example, saying your 5K blood drive fundraiser is cliché is probably a fair statement, but it does little good to just say it needs to be more creative. When you say it needs to be more "ownable" or "fresh" we move up the creative scale in a way that is easier to understand.

Most ideas we generate, for example, are forgettable. Using the Heineken descriptors, we'd call them "cliché." We've seen or heard them before. Cliché ideas aren't going to grab attention and certainly aren't going to drive your campaign. But don't worry, they could be worse! Your ideas could be "confusing," get "hijacked" or be outright "destructive" to your organization or brand.

On the other hand, the better your ideas are, the further up the scale you go to describe them. Is an idea "groundbreaking?" "Contagious?" Could it be a "cultural phenomenon?" Maybe over time it becomes "legendary."

Take a look at a big idea from outdoor retailer REI highlighted in the Application Case at the end of this chapter. The company's idea to close its stores on Black Friday became a cultural phenomenon. The REI #OptOutside campaign generated 2.7 billion media impressions within the first 24 hours and more than 1.4 million people decided to go outside the Friday after Thanksgiving.

The move not only reinforced REI's market positioning as an authentic outdoor co-op but also boosted the company's bottom line contributing to a significant increase in revenue. The campaign was so successful, REI continues to build on it. In 2016, REI began partnering with nonprofits including the National Parks Service. By 2017 more than 700 other organizations had joined the company in encouraging people to get out and experience nature. Rideshare operator Lyft even jumped on the bandwagon offering free rides to local parks. By 2018, the "good purpose" focus of the campaign took center stage.

© Suzi Pratt/Stringer/Getty Images

In 2019, as the global threat of climate change dominated news, REI sought to leverage the popularity of #OptOutside into environmental awareness. The 2019 campaign was subbranded "Opt to Act: 52 weeks of action to leave the world better than we found it." REI sought to extend both the purpose and the timeframe of the movement. REI committed to reduce its own environmental impact — pledging to be a zero-waste company by expanding its gear trade-in and rental programs and eliminating poly packaging for shipped orders.

The campaign has now reached legendary status with more than 14.2 million uses of #OptOutside on Instagram alone. REI's big idea inspired its members and employees to create motivating YouTube content around "Will You Go Out With Me?" Hundreds of partners joined in eschewing consumerism and taking steps to save the planet. REI increased its short-term profits, but more importantly reaffirmed its purpose "...to awaken a lifelong love of the outdoors, for all."

Creativity is, in many ways, another word for experimenting — taking existing ideas and adding something to them or putting them together in new ways. The 80-minute experiment we know as "Toy Story" was really the answer to a question: "Can an animated film be made using only computers?" The answer launched a company and a new industry of computer graphic animation or CGI that is now used across many disciplines including communications, medicine, education and engineering. Creativity in communications and marketing is a critical part of any winning campaign. Without it, ideas will be cliché, fail to captivate or, worse, damage the organization.

Figure 7.1
Heineken's Creative Ladder

10	LEGENDARY
9	CULTURAL PHENOMENON
8	CONTAGIOUS
7	GROUNDBREAKING
6	FRESH
5	OWNABLE
4	CLICHÉ
3	CONFUSING
2	HIJACKED
1	DESTRUCTIVE

Source: Fast Company 2015

Creativity is essential

All good campaigns require a high level of creativity. The number one challenge for all communications is capturing attention. You simply can't do that with a boring or cliché campaign.

Step five in the Strategic Communications Matrix begins with key publics and primary messages followed by the **big idea**. Once you know who you need to reach and what types of messages will motivate them, it should be easier to generate a big idea to capture their attention and motivate them to act.

To break through the din of messages bombarding our key publics, we need something new, something fresh. This is where the big idea fits in the Strategic Communications Matrix. Once you have your big idea, you'll create strategies and tactics for your campaign that tie back to your big idea. It's essential that you take the time to come up with something that is at least ownable and potentially legendary. Give yourself permission to be creative. Go to work **brainstorming** your next big idea as well as the strategies and tactics to support it.

BIG IDEA
A creative idea or theme on which a campaign is built.

BRAINSTORMING
A structured group creative exercise to generate as many ideas as possible in a specified amount of time.

The matrix provides a framework to focus your creativity, ensuring it is on target to reach the right publics with the right messages and the right motivation. You will need your target publics to do more than agree with you. You will need to motivate them to act on those beliefs. For example, getting people to agree with a candidate's views does little unless you motivate those people to get out and vote.

You'll first use creative tools to help you develop a big idea. A handful of these are outlined in this chapter. Use these tools to put together the components of your big idea: big idea strategy, visual representation and slogan/hashtag. The elements that make up a big idea are discussed later in the chapter. Once you have your big idea you'll be ready to create campaign strategies and tactics to support it.

STRATEGIC COMMUNICATIONS MATRIX

ACTION PLANNING

5. KEY PUBLICS AND PRIMARY MESSAGES, BIG IDEA, STRATEGIES AND TACTICS

Big Idea   A creative strategy on which to build your entire campaign. The "big idea" appeals broadly across all key publics. Describe it in one sentence. Include three bullets, one each for strategy, visual representation and slogan/hashtag.

Marrying creativity and strategy

Only by channeling your creativity within the analytical process will you avoid a common mistake: allowing a creative idea to drive your campaign. Just because you have a great opportunity to use a celebrity in a campaign doesn't mean that approach will serve your public, purpose and message. Creative ideas not founded in a logical analysis of publics and messages will result in lots of money wasted on campaigns that accomplish nothing. Nationwide's "Dead Child" Super Bowl campaign is a prime example. The company spent millions on airtime alone, but the vast majority of the public, including the people they were targeting, were appalled by such dark messaging. The insurance giant experienced a huge backlash and was forced to issue a statement explaining the ad's purpose was to begin a conversation. However, the public felt the campaign was a manipulative way to sell insurance.

If you get a creative idea that doesn't work for a specific purpose, public and message, put it on the shelf to be adapted and possibly used for something else. No good idea is wasted in the long run. You'll be surprised how ideas resurface and how they can be redeployed for use in another campaign. A good idea is only wasted if you try to use it where it doesn't fit. Save it for the future.

Breaking habits

French naturalist Jean-Henri Fabre wrote of the processionary caterpillar. Processionary caterpillars feed on pine needles as they move through the forest in a long procession, with each one's head fitted snugly against the behind of the caterpillar before. In his experiments, Fabre enticed a group of these caterpillars onto the rim of a flower pot where he got the first one connected with the last so they were moving in an unending procession around the top of the pot.

Caterpillars following one another in a procession.

Fabre expected the caterpillars would catch on to their useless march and move off in a new direction, especially since he had placed food nearby. Not so. The force of habit caused them to continue moving in their unending circle, round and round the rim of the flower pot. Even though food was visible nearby, the caterpillars continued their march for seven days and nights, and probably would have continued longer had they not collapsed from sheer exhaustion and ultimate starvation. The food was outside the range of the circle, off the beaten path. They followed instinct, habit, custom, tradition, precedent and past experience. They confused activity with accomplishment. They were in constant motion, but they made no progress.

Take a look at the square and circle diagram. Most people see this pattern as rows of squares and circles. Some might see a large square composed of smaller squares and circles. Few, however, see it as columns of alternating squares and circles. Once this is pointed out, it's very easy to see columns of alternating shapes. One creativity expert, Michael Michalko, explains it this way, "We have become habituated to passively organize similar items together in our minds. Geniuses, on the other hand, subvert habituation by actively looking for alternative ways to look at and think about things."

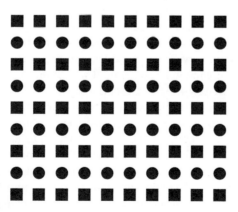

Creativity is the process of looking outside ourselves, our habit, our custom and our tradition to find new solutions and innovative ideas. The strategic communications planning process is designed to analytically drive our planning and decisions. But it should not limit our creativity in searching for solutions. In fact, unless we develop creative big ideas, strategies and tactics, our publics are not likely to stop long enough to pay attention to any of the messages we're trying to deliver.

Brainstorming and ideation

Many people believe that creativity is inborn — you either have it or you don't. This simply isn't true. The greatest scientific discoveries and inventions came out of years of experimentation, trial and error. It actually took Thomas Edison 2,774 attempts to arrive at the carbonized bamboo filament that made the light bulb a commercial success.

The Royal Bank of Canada tells its employees that innovation is like playing hockey: The best players miss more shots than they make. But they also try more often. The more you shoot, the more you score. That's why one of the rules of brainstorming is not to evaluate or criticize while in the brainstorming session (see Figure 7.2). The object is to get as many ideas on the table as possible, no matter how ridiculous they might initially appear. Those ridiculous ideas, reevaluated, rearranged and recombined, frequently become the innovative solutions that are praised, awarded and used as examples of exceptional creativity.

Many people also think brainstorming doesn't work. They are simply wrong. Most of the big ideas mentioned in this chapter — including the REI #OptOutside campaign — came out of brainstorming sessions. Some techniques for brainstorming or **ideation** work better than others, depending on the group you are working with and the challenge you are facing.

⊶ **IDEATION**

The formation of ideas or concepts.

One of the challenges with most brainstorming sessions is that participants are put on the spot to come up with fresh, creative ideas. Rarely do the best ideas emerge on command in the few minutes allocated for a brainstorming session. Experience has proven it's best to prime people in advance. For example, giving people two or three questions or topics to think about several days in advance puts the creative process in motion long before they see a white board.

Give the group a topic and the vision of where you'd like to end up so that ideas can be percolating before the session begins. Have your team thinking about the problem or opportunity while biking to work, mowing the lawn, taking a shower or dozing off at night. It's brain time and subconscious bandwidth you don't have to pay for, but that will reward you with better ideas and happier people. Creativity is spawned through observation and association. Giving people some time will not only produce fresher ideas, but also will give those ideas time to percolate and morph into other ideas before you officially meet. In addition, it will build confidence in participants' abilities to contribute in new and more creative ways.

Once you meet as a team to brainstorm, try experimenting with different techniques other than the blue-sky, free-for-all sessions typically used. For example, try using the "pass the paper" method. This begins with a brief orientation and introduction to the topic. The goal is stated and the team is separated into groups of two or three people to write a series of questions that lead back to the goal. When you've drafted the questions (e.g., "How do you want people to feel during your event?"), transfer each question to the top of its own poster-sized sheet of paper (try using giant Post-It pads). These questions are then posted around the perimeter of the room.

Participants are each given a stack of 20 to 25 sticky notes and asked to write down a short phrase or idea for each question. The process of sticking ideas under each question is repeated as individuals rotate around the room four or five times. This ideation method puts everyone participating on the same footing and values ideas equally. It also encourages subordinates and shy participants to share their ideas. With each idea on a sticky note, grouping related ideas together and analyzing the results becomes much easier.

Hilton hotels, which completed the largest initial public offering for a hospitality company ever on Dec. 12, 2013, brainstormed how to generate media interest and investor momentum for its stock offering. The communications team came up with the idea of turning the New York Stock Exchange into a hotel for the day. The company, which has 18 brands and more than 7,000 hotels in 122 countries or territories, used its own people — putting a doorman at every door of the exchange, serving food and having team members on the platform. Company executives also donned hotel bathrobes for the occasion. The money shot seen around the world and shared through social media was of the Hilton CEO wearing a bathrobe on the floor of the NYSE. Creative approaches like this often come from the most unexpected places. Make sure you invite new people — those from outside your work group or department — to help with each brainstorming session.

Figure 7.2
Rules for brainstorming

1. ***Assemble a diverse group of people (at least three).***

2. ***Set a time limit for the brainstorming session.*** Plan no fewer than five minutes but no more than 20-30 minutes to ensure urgency and, hence, a rapid flow of ideas.

3. ***Record the session for later transcription.***

4. ***Do not evaluate ideas while in the session.*** Even laughter can be an act of evaluation that may stifle the flow of ideas (although in a truly free-flowing session, it Is difficult not to laugh).

5. ***Engage in freewheeling.*** Verbalize any idea that comes into your mind. Otherwise you are silently evaluating your own ideas and perhaps censuring those that are most creative.

6. ***Reserve the details for the post-session evaluation.*** Use your time to generate as many ideas as possible, not to explain your ideas in any detail.

7. ***Piggyback on ideas.*** For example, if someone mentions a tactic like bumper stickers, try to spiral off with similar transportation-related ideas like bus boards or sun visor wraparounds.

8. ***Take some time as a group after the session to evaluate each idea for its merits.*** Try to find ways that each might work. Try modifying, combining and rearranging before discarding an idea.

Observing and seizing opportunities

Several years ago, a newly hired marketing and communications director at Blendtec, a manufacturer of commercial blenders for the food service industry, walked by the research and development suite and noticed wood shavings on the floor. Inquiries led to the discovery that one of the R&D guys liked to play around blending odd things to test the sturdiness of Blendtec's heavy-duty blenders. The marketing director got a video camera and began shooting as they blended rakes, iPods, golf balls and everything imaginable. He posted

iPad: will it blend?

MINI CASE

Miracle at Calgary International Airport
WestJet

The mission of Canadian air carrier, WestJet, is to provide its customers with safe, affordable and friendly air travel. Its core values include being fun, caring, positive and passionate in everything it does. Combining all these values into one big idea, WestJet created one of the greatest Christmas stunts ever attempted: the "Christmas Miracle" campaign. The campaign was not only fun and memorable, but became a viral hit on YouTube because of its creativity, unexpectedness and flawless execution.

CORE OPPORTUNITY
WestJet wanted to use the holiday season to show appreciation to its customers and engender their loyalty by demonstrating its core values.

WESTJET'S STRATEGY
In late November 2013, while passengers waited to board flights to Calgary from Toronto Pearson and John C. Munro Hamilton airports, they were greeted by a virtual Santa booth. After scanning their boarding passes, Santa asked passengers what they wanted for Christmas over live video chat.

© Heather Dunbar/Shutterstock.com

While both flights were en route, WestJet employees in Calgary had roughly four hours to dash around the city and purchase gifts customers had asked for from Santa. As passengers awaited their baggage, fake snow began to fall and Christmas music played over the speakers as customers' hoped-for presents suddenly started to fill up the carousel. WestJet surprised 250 unsuspecting passengers with 357 personally wrapped gifts that included a 50-inch TV, cameras, smartphones, tablets, toys for the kids and even some socks and underwear.

WestJet captured the event on 19 hidden cameras placed in the airport terminals, onboard one of the planes and at the baggage claim area. Filming took place on Nov. 21, 2013. WestJet then posted the video on YouTube Dec. 8, 2013. Mosaic was responsible for the PR efforts, Globacore handled the design and fabrication of the virtual Santa booths, and Studio M created the campaign's YouTube video. Promotion of the campaign's video cost WestJet less than it would have cost to rent billboard space In Toronto for three months.

In order to keep within budget, WestJet decided to approach several companies to participate in the campaign in return for positive exposure in the video. The airline also wanted to involve its own employees in the execution of the "Christmas Miracle" campaign – reinforcing the fun and passionate ideals of the company. Finally, WestJet understood its key publics are active in social media. It intended to appeal to these groups by reaching out to several influential bloggers who would then share the video, generating greater exposure for the company.

RESULTS
- In the two weeks following the release of the video, traffic to WestJet's website increased 100%, bookings increased 77% and revenue rose 86%.
- The YouTube video, "WestJet Christmas Miracle: Real-time Giving," went viral, receiving 27 million views in one week. It became the number one trending topic globally as well as the most shared viral ad in Canada during 2013.
- The video generated more than 1 billion Impressions on Twitter in one month.
- The story has been covered more than 1,600 times by media outlets globally.
- The Christmas Miracle campaign has been so successful that WestJet has continued the campaign each year with different creative ways to give and serve, documenting them for YouTube and other social media channels.

the videos on YouTube to launch a new line of home blenders. The "Will It Blend?" series went viral.

Sales of Blendtec's blenders doubled in a month; large retailers such as Costco started carrying the company's products. Blendtec's YouTube channel soon had about a hundred videos and 1 million subscribers. Some of the videos had nearly 20 million views. Blendtec also engaged with thousands of customers responding to suggestions on what it should blend next. The Blendtec viral campaign cost less than $100 to initiate. A savvy marketing and communications director saw an opportunity and took a chance. With a supportive CEO, it paid off handsomely.

The Blendtec campaign is the result of looking at a blender differently. It wasn't designed to pulverize a 2"-by-4" piece of lumber, a Bic lighter or a "human" skeleton for Halloween, but it certainly can. This leads us to the big idea. Blendtec blenders are so tough they can take on just about anything — leaving no question they can crush the ice in your next fruit smoothie. Big ideas like this are born of curiosity, observation, adaptation and experimentation.

Edison said that creativity is "10% inspiration and 90% perspiration." It may well begin when you realize that there is no particular benefit in doing things as they have always been done. It also does not require complete originality. Creativity often means borrowing and adapting ideas. Modify and rearrange, make things bigger or smaller. Brainstorm ways to change and adapt an idea. We suggest practicing your

Figure 7.3
Roger von Oech's mental locks to creativity

BE PRACTICAL. Don't disregard impossible suggestions, rather use them as stepping stones to workable solutions.

THE RIGHT ANSWER. Looking for the one right answer keeps us from realizing that there may be many possibilities.

THAT'S NOT MY AREA. Specializing causes us to miss out on a lot. Interdisciplinary answers are better solutions.

FOLLOW THE RULES. Creativity is often enhanced by breaking the rules, going outside the normal parameters.

DON'T BE FOOLISH. Poking fun at proposals provides feedback that prevents group think.

THAT'S NOT LOGICAL. Don't disregard thinking outside the boundaries because it doesn't fit the analytical approach.

I'M NOT CREATIVE. A self-fulfilling prophecy. Allow yourself to be creative.

PLAY IS FRIVOLOUS. Fun environments are productive, creative environments.

TO ERR IS WRONG. Get over the stigma that being wrong is all bad. Use mistakes to learn.

AVOID AMBIGUITY. Introducing ambiguity into a creative session can help generate answers. Also use humor and paradoxes.

---

brainstorming on a random topic just to see how many different ideas you can come up with. Try free association. Piggyback on ideas. Practice saying whatever idea comes into your head.

Give yourself permission

These are all good exercises, but to be creative, you must first give yourself permission to break the barriers to creative thinking identified in Figure 7.3. Explore your imagination. Create fantasies and play with ideas. And then cultivate the habit. The more you challenge yourself to think creatively, the better you will become. In her book, "Teaching Creative Behavior," Doris Shallcross (1981) provides several exercises that require you to challenge the parameters of your thinking. For example, how many squares do you see in the illustration below? The expected answer would be 16, but count all the squares.

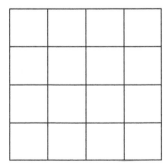

Assuming this diagram is on a flat plane, there are 30 of them, all different sizes. One is the outside square. You will also see 2-by-2 squares and 3-by-3 squares. A door is opened to our creative brain when we obtain permission — indeed are given direction — to look outside the traditional boundaries and expected perception!

The next test from Shallcross is one you may have seen before, but it powerfully illustrates the need to go outside the boundaries we set for ourselves. Connect all nine dots with four straight lines. Go through each dot only once and do not lift your pen from the page. Take a few minutes to take this test before reading on. (The solution is located at the end of the chapter.)

$$\bullet \quad\quad \bullet \quad\quad \bullet$$

$$\bullet \quad\quad \bullet \quad\quad \bullet$$

$$\bullet \quad\quad \bullet \quad\quad \bullet$$

This test is specifically designed to show us that we set our own artificial boundaries. There was no instruction indicating the connecting lines had to be kept within the invisible boundary set by the dots in the diagram. Yet we are accustomed to setting those boundaries ourselves.

One of the greatest marketing ploys of all time was to print a margin line an inch in from the edge of notebook paper and on legal pads. Most of us automatically observe that margin and leave the space on the left side of the line blank. Most notepaper and pads are used for taking notes no one else will ever see. What does it matter if we observe the margin? But much more notepaper is sold to students and companies each year because the artificial boundary restricts what fits on the page.

It is interesting to note how powerfully ingrained these artificial boundaries are. In using the Shallcross dots test each semester over three decades, we have found that most students have seen it before and have been shown that the solution is to go outside the artificial boundary. But the vast majority of those can't remember the principle and revert to trying to connect the dots inside the perceived boundary. They are accustomed to staying within perceived limitations, even when no limitations actually exist.

Where did we learn to set these kinds of invisible boundaries? Remember when you began coloring? What are some of the first lessons — or rules — you were taught? One was to always color inside the lines. That rule was so ingrained that some of us even traced the lines with the crayon before coloring to make sure we didn't accidentally breach the boundary.

We were also taught to choose the appropriate colors. Frogs are green, not purple or blue. So we always

© Channar/Shutterstock.com

had to choose the right color for the item pictured, so much so that fights erupted in grade school over crayons. Now, grade school kids buy their own set of crayons so they don't have to fight with anyone to get the green crayon for their frog. But in graphic design, wouldn't a purple frog get more second glances than a green one? Or better yet, one wearing cowboy boots and a bikini?

Creative ideas and solutions are, by nature, out of our typical range of experience. Problems with obvious, traditional solutions seldom require much time. To find truly innovative solutions to challenges we face, we must reach outside our comfort zone and the artificial boundaries we have created for ourselves.

Overcoming fear

Fear is probably the single greatest barrier to creative behavior. Author John Holt has said that the real test of intelligence is "not how much we know how to do, but how we behave when we don't know what to do." What do we fear? We fear failure and rejection. No one likes their ideas to be rejected, laughed at or ridiculed. We often fail to contribute our ideas for fear we will look silly or stupid. We think that

TIPS FROM THE PROS

Stoking creativity for award-winning ideas

Grace Leong, APR, CEO and partner of Hunter Public Relations, who leads a team that services the nation's top consumer products companies, tips you off on coming up with "big ideas."

Be an everyday student of creativity. Build a database of great ideas. The best brainstormers are those who read, see and retain good ideas daily. Keep a file of "great ideas" that catch your eye: a new product launch that used an innovative strategy or a clever idea for a media kit or website. Your personal library of ideas will serve you well when you are asked to be creative "on the spot."

Never respond to the question: "What's the big idea?" To get to the big idea in a brainstorm you need to put people's minds at ease. Play creative games, ask seemingly unrelated questions, make the environment fun. When minds are stimulated in a creative atmosphere, ideas flow and a big idea will emerge naturally.

Strive for singles and doubles, and you will hit more home runs. Hank Aaron was the home run king of baseball, but he also ranks high on the all-time strike-out list. Allow yourself hundreds of strikes, singles and doubles for every home run. People who are not afraid of striking out are more likely to hit the ball out of the park.

Create an environment that inspires your creativity. At Hunter PR, we assembled a team of people with diverse backgrounds and outlooks on life, and we inspire each other to look at opportunities from multiple perspectives. We are a culture that regularly permits people to slay the sacred cow. No idea is a bad idea even if it goes against convention. If you do not live in a culture like this, fix that first, and then watch the creativity flow.

people who fail don't get promoted. They don't get raises. But if you never take risks, you won't grow into that new position or be valued for your ideas either.

Think about the hockey player and work to create a risk-friendly environment. Applaud those that take shots and surface new ideas. Don't get stuck on the mistakes made in the process. Praise the courage and effort taken to experiment and to see things differently. Companies that foster this kind of environment are known for their creative products and solutions, and are those that survive disruption. Target, for example, has invested heavily in online shopping — creating experiences that leverage both the in-store opportunity to see, touch and feel with the convenience and selection of the online experience. Target facilitates price-matching with online sales, scanning to look up options not stocked on shelves and choosing store pick-up or home delivery. And while it's hard to compete with a giant like Amazon, Target's online sales at the end of 2022 were growing much faster than Amazon's.

To reinforce the need to fail and fail often, some companies even give annual awards for the most spectacular failure because management recognizes that if employees are afraid to be creative, the company will lose its competitive edge in the marketplace.

Creative environments and people

While you may not be working for an organization that openly rewards failure, you can still create an environment that stimulates ideation and innovation. Not all business environments work for all people, but there is strong consensus among creativity and innovation experts that surroundings affect performance. One of the most important considerations in planning a workspace is an organization's culture. Does the work environment support the culture? The company HubSpot, for example, values an open culture and the free exchange of information and ideas. To facilitate this, no one in the company has an office. They all rotate desks on a regular basis and assign seats by pulling names out of a hat.

Many companies — especially tech companies — have moved to an open work environment. Max Chopovsky, founder of Chicago Creative Space, says that even traditional companies need to think about how the work environment reflects the corporate culture. "Baby boomers are retiring and [Gen Zs] have a different perspective of what a work environment should be," he says. "It all comes down to two trends: technology and demographics. Literally, my phone can be my office," Chopovsky says. "If I have a laptop and all other tech available, I literally never have to come into the office. I come in because of ideas, collaboration. That's where creativity happens."

Marriott International, the world's largest hospitality company, has given new focus to innovation in recent years to reinvigorate its brands and appeal to a growing number of **Gen X**, **Gen Y** and **Gen Z** travelers. The company recently opened a new headquarters in Bethesda, Maryland that includes nearly 20,000 square feet of open, flexible, modular, and virtually collaborative workspace for individuals or group meetings. The new building will also serve as a global hub for Marriott's research and development operation, featuring its Innovation and Design Lab, a premium test kitchen and beverage bar, as well as "model" hotel rooms in the adjacent Marriott

GEN X
Generation born between 1960 and 1980.

GEN Y
Generation born between 1980 and 1999, also called millennials.

GEN Z
Generation born in 2000 and after.

Interior design concept at Marriott's new Design Lab.

hotel, where new concepts, design elements, service approaches and amenities will be tested for potential use across the company's portfolio of 30 brands.

Many companies, like Disney, encourage employees to decorate their workspace. Others build creative spaces to support their culture, like the Groupon office's enchanted forest which fosters employees' creativity. The important thing is to make sure there are places for people to gather, talk, exchange information and ideate — you can never have too many white boards.

In the end it's about people. Creativity researcher Claire Bridges shared the top six things creative people value:

- Curiosity
- Courage
- Creativity
- Fun
- Freedom
- Grit

You can read more about these values in her book, "In Your Creative Element" (2016). Consciously putting in place processes that acknowledge and support these values will lead to a culture of creativity bereft of micromanagement. This culture will be the most important factor in attracting employees with fresh ideas and perspectives.

Big ideas

The concept of the "big idea" comes from advertising. In the 1960s advertising genius David Ogilvy coined the term, which had an immediate impact in the field of advertising. It later spread to marketing and public relations.

According to Ogilvy, "You will never win fame and fortune unless you also invent big ideas. It takes a big idea to attract the attention of consumers and get them to buy your product. Unless your advertising contains a big idea, it will pass like a ship in the night."

Ogilvy believed that such ideas sprang from the unconscious mind. "Your unconscious has to be well informed, or your idea will be irrelevant," he said. "Stuff your conscious mind with information; then unhook your rational thought process."

Researchers and communications experts believe there are ways to stimulate the unconscious mind to draw out creativity. A few of the tools and concepts used to do this were discussed earlier. We refer you to the references and additional readings for more tools and examples.

What is a big idea?

A big idea is more than a unique selling point used by advertisers and marketers to sell a product. It's more than the articulation of a competitive advantage. A big idea is the hook on which your entire campaign hangs. It might be helpful to think about it the same way you would think about telling a story. What is the climactic

© Todd Gipstein/Corbis Historical/Getty Images

David Ogilvy, widely hailed as "The Father of Advertising."

Figure 7.4
Booker's seven basic archetypes

OVERCOMING THE MONSTER	THE QUEST	COMEDY	RAGS TO RICHES	TRAGEDY	REBIRTH	VOYAGE AND RETURN

surprise or element that captures the attention of your reader and appeals to their self-interest? In his book, "The Seven Basic Plots," Christopher Booker identifies seven story archetypes (Figure 7.4). Chances are, whatever big ideas you generate will fit one or two of these.

Big ideas shouldn't be complicated and shouldn't require much explanation. They should pretty much stand on their own. If you can't tell a friend in a text or IM what your big idea is, then you haven't yet nailed it. That said, the hardest part about building a campaign around a big idea may very well be learning how to recognize one. Ogilvy suggested asking these five questions:

1. Did it make me gasp when I first saw it?
2. Do I wish I had thought of it myself?
3. Is it unique?
4. Does it fit the strategy of the product?
5. Could it be used for 30 years?

Long-lasting, he believed, was one of the most important concepts behind big ideas. A good example of a big idea with staying power is Dove soap. For more than 60 years, Dove advertisements have made the claim in one way or another that "Dove doesn't dry your skin the way soap can." More recently the brand message is, "Dove is one-quarter moisturizing cream." While these questions and the Dove soap example may belong more to advertising than public relations and marketing, they help describe the origins and thinking behind big ideas: to serve as a unifying theme.

Crafting big ideas

The big idea is strategically placed in the middle of the Action Planning section of the matrix. This is done because it is at the heart of the campaign. You will already have determined your key publics and primary messages, but you won't have crafted your strategies and tactics just yet.

The big idea is a campaign's master strategy and overriding message. If it doesn't work with some of your key publics, you either chose the wrong key publics or, more likely, came up with a bad big idea. They must all fit tightly together.

The best way to write down your big idea is to start with a sentence or two that succinctly describes it. You can then identify the three components that are part of every big idea.

Big idea strategy. The **big idea strategy** is a story hook or archetype. It is based on research, pop culture or brand relevance. It must be memorable and have broad appeal to accomplish your goals and objectives. The best big ideas often

BIG IDEA STRATEGY
A story hook or archetype.

Coca-Cola Australia 'Share a Coke' campaign

Red Bull #PutACanOnIt campaign

have an almost universal appeal. The "Share a Coke" campaign is a prime example. The Coca-Cola Company discovered through research that young people in Australia were losing their connection to the brand; they no longer felt it was relevant. The response was a campaign where the most popular first names were printed on the cans of the beverage. This personalized the experience with the brand and reconnected Coke with a rising generation of consumers. The campaign was so successful, it was eventually rolled out globally.

Visual representation. The **visual representation** of the big idea is the element that excites and connects target publics to the strategy. The more tangible and interactive the visual, the stronger the idea. Frito-Lay didn't have money for an expensive Super Bowl campaign but was determined to get noticed. It created the Tostitos Breathalyzer bag. Each bag had a black steering wheel on it that turned red when you breathed on it after consuming alcohol. The limited-edition packaging garnered massive media attention and went viral on social media.

Slogan or hashtag. A clever **slogan**, motto, **hashtag** or handle captures the essence of the big idea and conveys the primary message. The strongest slogans and hashtags are those that are easy to spell and remember. Red Bull noticed a few customers posting pics on social media that looked like oversized cans of Red Bull were being carried by people, pets, cars — you name it! To **amplify** the idea, Red Bull came up with the hashtag #PutACanOnIt and the campaign went viral.

In 2013, American Express (Amex) celebrated the 50th anniversary of the "Member Since" date being added to the card. Amex created the notion that having their card was an exclusive and desirable thing — a badge of honor. Its strategy was to make people who had Amex cards feel special. The visual representation was a stamp of the initiation year on the front of each person's card. The slogan "membership has its privileges" became famous.

The message that you are joining an elite club and you are special has allowed American Express to charge higher fees on each card transaction than Visa, MasterCard and Discover. Big ideas don't have to be expensive. The cost of this big idea was zero, yet it's a concept that continues to yield dividends.

To celebrate the 50-year milestone of the "Member Since" idea, Amex launched a special members since app. The company asked users to select the year they became Amex cardmembers. Then, it presented a tidbit from American Express history for that year along with the opportunity to post on users' Facebook timelines and on Twitter. One 81-year-old man who's been a cardmember since 1958 tweeted that

VISUAL REPRESENTATION
A physical or digital example of a big idea.

SLOGAN
A short, memorable phrase linked to primary messages.

HASHTAG
A word or short phrase preceded by a hash (#) used to search for and group together related posts on social media.

AMPLIFY
To increase the volume or intensity of something to greatly broaden its reach.

he was one of the original charter members alongside Elvis Presley. Another woman jokingly shared that she got her card when she was planning her wedding 10 years ago. She still has the card, but not the husband.

Slogans, tag lines and hashtags

Slogans, taglines and hashtags are good ways of reducing your strategy and overriding message to a few words. We recommend experimenting with slogans to see how much information you can convey in a phrase. Slogans should be short, compelling and attention-getting. They should be general enough to relate to all of the publics you will target, and focused enough to appeal to some of their shared self-interests. Some examples of pervasive slogans with high retention value include Apple's "Think Different," Nike's "Just Do It" and Dollar Shave Club's "Shave Time. Shave Money."

Image courtesy of Flickr

MATRIX APPLIED

Big idea

When the Marriott School of Business at Brigham Young University was getting ready to celebrate the 25th anniversary of the school being named for Marriott Hotel founders J. Willard and Alice S. Marriott, the school's external relations team came up with a big idea to drive its year-long celebration. The research insight was that business students were perceived as caring only about themselves and money.

BIG IDEA

The big idea was to tie the school's anniversary to the Marriott company's "Spirit to Serve" initiative and log 25,000 hours of service during the year. Here are the components of their big idea.

> *Big idea strategy:* Motivate students and alumni to serve 25,000 hours in the anniversary year by showcasing service opportunities and visually tracking progress in a creative way.
>
> *Visual representation:* Build a giant glass "M" in the school's atrium and add a blue tennis ball for every hour of service by students and alumni.
>
> *Slogan:* "Marriott 25 Spirit to Serve" and marriott25.byu.edu.

© Bradley Slade/Courtesy of BYU Marriott School of Business.

Another successful slogan was developed in 1992 for the American Plastics Council, "Plastics Make it Possible." The campaign built around this theme redefined the debate about plastics. The big idea of the campaign, summarized in the tagline, focused key publics on the positive associations they have with plastics such as keeping food fresh, keeping people safe and making possible many of today's life-saving medical technologies. Instead of directly taking on the environmental concerns people have about plastics, the campaign worked to generate appreciation for the material's unique properties. "Plastics Make it Possible" was so successful that the American Plastics Council used the tagline for 25 years.

Notwithstanding their utility in summarizing key messages, slogans and advertising taglines cannot stand alone as messages to your publics. They are useful in creating synergy among all publics in a campaign and can dramatically affect recall of public-specific messages sent in other channels. A slogan like "Working Toward a Healthier Community" will bring to mind public-specific messages regarding economic well-being to a business public, messages of physical and mental health to the health care public, and messages of combating drug and alcohol abuse to a parental public. The slogan in and of itself is not an effective message. It is only as good as the public-specific messages and visual representations that support it.

Generating big ideas

Generating a big idea is a process of insighting, ideating and developing. Insighting means to analyze the current situation, problem/challenge and culture using research to glean a few key findings or insights. What is on the minds of your key publics? Look for market trends, cultural trends, changes in perceptions, what you are known for, what has worked before and what is current and in the news. Examine the social media chatter. From this insight, you will find a story hook, something which will help you generate ideas.

The next step is to apply the creative process described earlier to ideate. Brainstorm around the insights you gained from your research. Use the best practices to make ideating productive and valuable. This is where big ideas first surface. Remember to find creative surroundings for the process, and try new brainstorming techniques. Break the routines and patterns that often block ideation. Invite different people — people outside your circle — to your brainstorming session. Great ideas often come from unexpected places and people. Go for quantity over quality — generate lots of ideas — and plan sufficient time at the culmination to thoroughly examine all the generated ideas. Rearrange, recombine and modify to fully evaluate each idea's potential.

The last step is developing. Take your best ideas and build them into a campaign. Concisely write down the three components of a big idea: big idea strategy, visual representation and slogan/hashtag. Test the "bigness" of the idea. Build out your messages, strategies and tactics to reach and engage with your key publics. Ask yourself: "Does my idea appeal to our key publics' self-interests?" "Will it achieve our objectives and ultimately accomplish our goal?" Most importantly, "Did we settle?" If the answer to the last question is yes, then go through the process again until you have something amazing.

We recommend using the Heineken Creative Ladder in Figure 7.1 to evaluate your big idea. Most big ideas, even those resulting from brainstorming sessions, are cliché. Strive for ideas that rank above cliché. Legendary ideas are few and far

MINI CASE

Breathing new life into the fight against tobacco
Tobacco Free New York State

Tobacco advertising to minors is an old story. State legislators have debated for decades how to regulate advertising, trying to strike a balance between free enterprise and expression and public health. But many of the key facts have been obscured.

Over $200 million is spent on tobacco ads annually in New York state alone, not to mention in-store discounts and promotions. The average age of a new smoker in New York is 13 years. Evidence shows that seeing cigarettes makes kids far more likely to try them. Tobacco advertising is big business. Tobacco Free New York State (TFNYS) is a non-profit that was determined to do something to curb tobacco addiction among minors and adults.

CORE CHALLENGE
The challenge was to raise public awareness and build support for stricter tobacco advertising laws in the state of New York.

TFNYS' STRATEGY
TFNYS wanted reporters all over the state to write about tobacco advertising on "World No Tobacco Day." The big idea was to use an illustrated children's book to capture reporters' attention and encourage them to write about the issue. Jack and Jill (and Tobacco) is an 11-page illustrated book that was printed and mailed to 200 reporters in the state. The book is peppered with key facts about tobacco and children, dramatically showing how youngsters are bombarded with cigarette advertising. TFNYS also produced a video version of the animated children's story that was shared online. The visual representations were the children's book, video and landing page. The slogan was #SeenEnoughTobacco.

RESULTS
- More than 70 media outlets covered the TFNYS campaign.
- Engagement on social media was about 20%.
- More than 540,000 people watched the video.
- TFNYS gathered more than 20,000 signatures and emails of support that were shared with legislators.
- A 2018 poll showed New Yorkers were overwhelmingly in favor of raising the purchasing age for tobacco to 21 years.

between, but at least shoot for fresh or groundbreaking. The higher your idea is on the ladder, the better it is.

Executing big ideas

The difference between big ideas that take flight and those that fail is often the level of engagement you have with your key publics. Ideas need to be amplified through multiple channels. Use a good mix of social and digital channels to send your message. But don't ignore the traditional channels. Look for ways to involve people, ask them to do something. Make sure that your messages are strategically timed — many traditional channels require more lead time. Plan for that so your messages in traditional channels correspond with those in social and digital channels.

Remember the importance of timely messages. Social media provides great opportunities to engage with your audiences. Most of your content should be pre-programmed to go out at just the right time. Others should be created daily to mirror what's going on in society, popular culture and online conversations. Engaging with people is what brings the personality of your organization or product/service to life. That's where you can develop one-on-one connections with your publics. That's when they feel you care.

A big idea at HP

Hewlett-Packard used a big idea to help turn around the company's reputation by rethinking employee communications. In 2011, HP hired Meg Whitman, the sixth CEO of the company in as many years. HP's reputation was at an all-time low. It had been blasted by the media as one of the worst-run companies in the world. Analysts had called for it to be broken up and sold off.

Headlines such as "Is HP's Autonomy the Worst Place to Work on the Planet?" and "Why a Bad CEO is a Company Killer— Sell Hewlett-Packard" and "How

Hewlett-Packard Lost Its Way" were not uncommon. HP employees were, understandably, depressed, frustrated and, in some cases, downright angry. The company was in crisis. But the new CEO was committed to keeping the company together. Whitman believed the company had great products and a powerful global workforce of 330,000 employees. But it had to change. And the change had to start from within.

Whitman believed the company could draw upon the power of HP employees as an engine to drive internal change. The company selected Stacey MacNeil, an experienced communications and news practitioner, as a new VP of employee communications to help restore faith in the future of the company and trust in its leadership. The internal communications team came up with a big idea: to give employees permission and encouragement to generate, produce and share company news.

Employee communications needed a huge shot of credibility. So MacNeil and her team turned their focus to organic storytelling within the company. "We needed to connect with employees and absolutely build trust," MacNeil says. "We had to activate the employee voice in our communications."

The slogan, "We make it matter," was adapted from HP's "Make it Matter" mantra. The overriding message being shared was that HP employees matter in big ways — that they believe in the company, and that they are a force for innovation and good that generates thousands of products used throughout the world.

The tangible representation of the big idea at HP was the introduction of HP News Now, an online source for employees posted securely outside the company's firewall. This was done so employees could access it anywhere, including on their mobile devices. HP News Now focused on transparency: sharing the good and the bad. "We want to talk about where things have gone wrong. We call these 'Teachable Moments.' These are sometimes tough stories that are not easily consumed by all employees," MacNeil explains. "We are on a mission to change the behavior of the company. Meg asked for us to do this. It's a vibrant conversation."

Another visual tactic for HPs big idea was to erect giant walls at company locations around the world where employees could write comments expressing their support for and commitment to the future of the company. Surprisingly, despite the problems HP had faced, the vast majority of comments were positive. The comment walls were put up in advance of Whitman's visits to different HP locations. The walls were so successful in engaging employees in conversation that some were left up and preserved as photo backdrops.

HP employee signs wall at "Make it Matter" event in India.

Summary

The ancient Romans didn't believe that an exceptionally gifted person was a genius. They believed that gifted people had a genius within them. This brilliance was something they harnessed and used.

When you understand the creative process and how to apply it you, too, can unlock the power of genius. Creativity is a skill that can be learned and honed over time.

Creativity plays a critical role in effective campaigns. Give yourself permission to be creative. Once you have license to ideate, you can overcome your fears and begin to train yourself to be curious, to observe, to adapt and to experiment by joining concepts together in new ways.

Big ideas are useful in tying a campaign together. Use brainstorming and other creativity exercises such as priming to help generate fresh ideas. Big ideas have three distinct components: big idea strategy, visual representation and a slogan/hashtag/URL, etc. Successful big ideas appeal to your key publics' self-interests and will motivate them to act.

Being able to evaluate the quality and power of new ideas may be just as critical as the ability to generate them. Use the Heineken Creative Ladder to measure your ideas. And don't give up until you have something that truly captures attention and meets your campaign objectives.

Harnessing the creativity of your organization is the only way to achieve the impossible.

Application case

Creatively embracing your mission

Recreational Equipment, Inc. (REI)

REI started in 1938 as a "group of 23 mountain climbing buddies" attempting to pool their resources for access to better, more affordable outdoor gear. The outdoor retailer has since grown to become the nation's largest consumer cooperative with 179 stores and 24.5 million members. In spite of the growth, REI has tried to stay true to its mission: "We inspire, educate and outfit for a lifetime of outdoor adventure and stewardship."

The key question brand executives were trying to answer during a brainstorming session for the 2015 holiday shopping season was, "How do we want to be represented during the holidays?"

REI's Chief Creative Officer Ben Steele said REI's answer to that question began as a seemingly wild suggestion from one of the company's leading merchants: "I know we could never do this, but what would happen if we closed on Black Friday?" According to Steele, the others in the meeting didn't dismiss the idea, even though it meant potentially missing out on sales revenue from one of the biggest shopping days of the year. In fact, Steele said, they started to wonder, "Well, why couldn't we do that?"

REI executives were soon convinced that closing all of their stores on Black Friday would help the brand demonstrate its authenticity — that it was committed to living its values, not just talking about them. "How do we be authentic as an outdoor company the day after Thanksgiving? asked REI CEO Jerry Stritzke. "We came to the conclusion that for us, encouraging people to go outside was one of the most authentic things we could do. We're passionate about it."

REI explained its big idea this way, "We believe that a life outdoors is a life well lived. Within that simple statement is the genesis of #OptOutside, the idea to close our stores on Black Friday, pay our 12,000 employees to spend time outside and invite America to join us."

Big idea strategy: Go against the grain on Black Friday by highlighting REI's commitment to getting people outdoors. Stritzke says the strategy was to create a stark "contrast between what is happening on Black Friday and the joy that is associated with being outside." The purpose of the strategy was to build brand loyalty among co-op members and employees.

The strategy also had value as a news story that people wanted to talk about and share. The story resonated with many people because it was a narrative of rebirth. REI was bucking conventional wisdom and guaranteed profits to return to its roots of focusing on the outdoor experiences of its members. As Charles Trevail explained in an article for "AdAge," "REI's decision reflects its fundamental empathy for its customers, who have zero desire to stand in line for the best deal on a gorgeous fall Friday, when they could be hiking Mt. Moosilauke."

Visual representation: Large, black banners on REI stores announcing that they would be closed on Black Friday. Employee-created YouTube channel videos asking, "Will you go out with me?"

Slogan/hashtag: #OptOutside.

Assume you are a part of the REI creative team and have been tasked to come up with a big idea for the summer season demonstrating brand authenticity as they did with the holiday strategy described above. Narrow your brainstorming ideas down and select one for which you create the big idea strategy, visual representation and slogan/hashtag.

Solution to Shallcross test

How easy the answer appears when we give ourselves permission to breach the perceived boundaries.

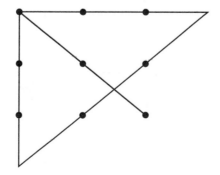

References and additional readings

Androich, A. (2013, December 9). WestJet gives shocked travelers gifts in real-time. *Marketing Magazine*. Retrieved from http://www.marketingmag.ca/news/marketer-news/westjet-gives-shocked-travelers-gifts-in-real-time-96106

Anonymous. (2014, February 13). WestJet's social Christmas campaign: "Nothing short of astounding." *EyeforTravel*. Retrieved from http://www.eyefortravel.com/social-media-and-marketing/westjet's-social-christmas-campaign-'nothing-short-astounding'

Anonymous. (2014, February 22). WestJet's Christmas Miracle — Statistics from social media. *WordPress*. Retrieved from http://westjetcase.wordpress.com/author/rmithanoisscc/

Beer, J. (2016, June 27). How values and purpose made REI's #OptOutside a big winner at Cannes. *Fast Company*. Retrieved from https://www.fastcompany.com/3061312/how-values-and-purpose-made-reis-optoutside-a-big-winner-at-cannes

Blendtec. (2014). "Will It Blend?" Retrieved from http://www.youtube.com/user/Blendtec

Booker, C. (2010). *The Seven Basic Plots: Why We Tell Stories*. London: Continuum.

Bridges, C. (2016). *In Your Creative Element: The Formula for Creative Success in Business*. London: Kogan Page.

Catmull, E. & Wallace, A. (2014). *Creativity, Inc.: Overcoming the Unseen Forces that Stand in the Way of True Inspiration*. New York: Random House.

CBS "This Morning." (2015, Oct. 27). Bucking Black Friday: REI CEO on closing stores on big shopping day. Retrieved from https://www.youtube.com/watch?v=QlVZdnuNiJY

Coffee, P. (2016, June 28). How one brave idea drove REI's award-winning #OptOutside campaign. *AdWeek*. Retrieved from https://www.adweek.com/brand-marketing/how-one-brave-idea-drove-reis-award-winning-optoutside-campaign-172273/

Financial Services Team. (2013, Nov. 12) Amex's "Member Since" legacy goes social. Retrieved from http://www.business2community.com/social-business/amexs-membersince-legacy-goes-social-0679822#!9Bweg

Irwin, T. (2013, Nov. 26). American Express celebrates "Member Since." *Marketing Daily*. Retrieved from http://www.mediapost.com/publications/article/214065/american-express-celebrates-member-since.html

Jack, L. (2015, June 23). How Cannes' Marketer Of The Year codifies creativity. *Fast Company*. Retrieved from: https://www.fastcompany.com/3047609/how-cannes-marketer-of-the-year-codifies-creativity

Kannenberg, Lizz. (2020, Jan. 22). Social spotlight: REI's #OptOutside and how a campaign becomes a movement. Retrieved from https://sproutsocial.com/insights/social-spotlight-rei/

Kuchinskas, S. (2013, December 13). Inside WestJet's Christmas marketing miracle. *Clickz*. Retrieved from http://www.clickz.com/clickz/news/2319134/story-behind-west-jets-Christmas-marketing-miracle

Lampstand Comm. (2015, Oct. 27). Why #OptOutside is the best marketing of 2015. *Medium*. Retrieved from https://medium.com/opt-outside/why-optoutside-is-the-best-marketing-of-2015-fa84e98ab124

Marriott International. (2022, Sept. 19). Marriott International debuts its new global headquarters, unveiling technology and design for an intuitive workplace. Retrieved from https://news.marriott.com/news/2022/09/19/marriott-international-debuts-its-new-global-headquarters-unveiling-technology-and-design-for-an-intuitive-workplace

Master's in Marketing Degree Guide. (2023). 5 Super Bowl advertisement fails. Retrieved from https://www.masters-in-marketing.org/lists/5-super-bowl-advertisement-fails/

Michalko, M. (2001). *Cracking Creativity: The Secrets of Creative Genius*. Berkeley, CA: Ten Speed Press.

Mudd, J. (n.d.) What made WestJet's "Christmas Miracle" PR stunt so great. *Axia Public Relations*. Retrieved from http://www.axiapr.com/blog/thepublicrelationsblog/made-westjets-christmas-miracle-pr-stunt-great

NPR.org. (2022, March 31). A toymaker raised $145,000 for Ukraine by creating a Lego-based Zelenskyy figurine. Retrieved from https://www.npr.org/2022/03/31/1089308679/ukraine-ukrainian-refugees-lego-zelenskyy-collectible

Ogilvy, D. (1983). *Ogilvy On Advertising*. New York: Vintage Books.

Posternatsky, O. (2014). 10 steps to establishing a marketing "big idea" that sells. *Japkin. com*. Retrieved from http://www.japkin.com/websites/blog/10-steps-to-establishing-a-marketing-big-idea-that-sells/

Prendergast, C. (2014, May 8). More from EMS 2014: WestJet's Christmas Miracle. *AgencyEA*. Retrieved from http://www.agencyea.com/news/blog/more-from-ems-2014- westjets-christmas-miracle/

REI Staff. (n.d.). REI history: It started with an ice axe. *REI Co-op Journal*. Retrieved from https://www.rei.com/blog/camp/rei-history-it-started-with-an-ice-axe

REI Staff. (2017, Oct. 29). The history of #OptOutside. *REI Co-op Journal*. Retrieved from https://www.rei.com/blog/social/the-history-of-opt-outside

REI website. (n.d.). About REI. Retrieved from https://www.rei.com/about-rei

Shallcross, D.J. (1981). *Teaching Creative Behavior*. Englewood Cliffs, N.J.: Prentice-Hall, Inc.

Shorty Awards. (2014, February 12). WestJet Christmas Miracle: Real-time giving. *Shorty Awards*. Retrieved from http://industry.shortyawards.com/category/6th_annual/travel/iK/westjet-christmas-miracle-real-time-giving

Tomer, C. (2014). Chicago Creative Space sheds new light on office culture. Retrieved from http://techli.com/2014/02/chicago-creative-space-sheds-new-light-on-office-culture/

TFNYS. (2018, Nov. 26). Seen enough Tobacco. Retrieved from https://seenenoughtobacco.org/

Trevail, C. (2015, Nov. 3). Why REI's #OptOutside is a model for the future of marketing. *AdAge*. Retrieved from https://adage.com/article/digitalnext/rei-s-optoutside-a-model-future-marketing/301177/

von Oech, R. (1990). *A Whack on the Side of the Head: How to Be Creative*. New York: Warner Books.

von Oech, R. (1983). *A Whack on the Side of the Head: How to Unlock Your Mind for Innovation*. New York: Warner Books.

WestJet. (2013, December 9). WestJet Christmas Miracle: Real-time giving. *WestJet*. Retrieved from http://blog.westjet.com/westjet-christmas-miracle-video-real-time-giving/

WestJet website. (n.d.). About WestJet. Retrieved from https://www.westjet.com/guest/en/about/

CHAPTER 8
STRATEGIES AND TACTICS

"Strategy without tactics is the slowest route to victory. Tactics without strategy is the noise before defeat."

—SUN TZU
CHINESE MILITARY GENERAL,
STRATEGIST AND PHILOSOPHER

LEARNING IMPERATIVES

- Be able to design strategies that reach a public with a message through effective communications channels and tactics to motivate a desired behavior.

- Understand how to select the best channels to deliver messages to key publics.

- Understand how to select the best tactics to deliver messages through specific channels.

STRATEGIES

Public-specific approaches specifying the channel to send the messages to achieve objectives.

TACTICS

Strategy-specific communications products that carry the message to key publics.

O nce key publics have been identified, primary messages have been careful-ly crafted and a big idea developed, you can now design strategies and tactics to carry your messages to their intended publics. **Strategies** and **tactics** are pub-lic-specific — they are designed with one public in mind. They are the best way to give a key public its own message to motivate desired behavior.

We can draw a simple analogy to military strategy. In an overall challenge to win a battle, one objective might be to secure a certain piece of ground or a particular town. A strategy would be devised on how to approach this objective. The strategy may be to weaken the town's defenses and attack through a particularly vulnerable spot in the wall. The tactics supporting the strategy may be an artillery barrage, aerial bombing, a special operations force to plant explosives to create a breach and a ground assault through the wall into the town. The strategy provides the overall approach to a par-ticular objective answering what and, very generally, how it will be accomplished. Tactics are the specific step-by-step activities necessary to achieve the strategy.

Strategies

In communicating with an organization's publics, the strategies are the approaches to reaching a designated public through a specific communications channel for a particular purpose with the message that will inform or motivate that public. As we said earlier, your strategy for message delivery is public-specific. In other words, you don't determine how you are going to send a message until you know who you are trying to reach and what you are trying to tell them. The strategy inherently identifies the public, and then addresses what you are trying to do in support of your objectives and the **channel** you propose to use to send the appeal.There are many different ways to craft a strategy. Figure 8.1 provides a proven formula for writing an effective strategy.

A strategy is an approach, not a list of tasks. Strategies are public-specific and identify a channel or group of related channels you will use to reach a key public to accomplish an objective by appealing to the public's self-interests through a message.

The tactics that support each strategy identify in greater detail the specific tasks required to send your messages (e.g., blog posts, local news stories, tweets, employee meetings, podcasts, newsletter articles, payroll envelope inserts, special events and emails from the company president). Tactics are strategy-specific because they sup-port a single strategy targeted at a particular public.

CHANNEL

The conduit or medium through which messages are sent to a specific public to accomplish a specific purpose.

Figure 8.1
Formula for writing an effective strategy

FORMULA: *Action verb* the *key public* through *communications channel(s)* that *the objective* will satisfy the *key public's self-interests*.

EXAMPLE: *Convince* the *Orange County Commissioners* through *in-person meetings with company officials and engineers* that *approving the new plant* will have *a positive economic impact on the community and minimal impact on the environment.*

STRATEGIC COMMUNICATIONS MATRIX

5. KEY PUBLICS AND PRIMARY MESSAGES, BIG IDEA, STRATEGIES AND TACTICS

Strategies   What a public must do to fulfill an objective and the channel(s) to send messages to motivate that action. Strategies are public-specific and multiple strategies may be required for each public.

Tactics   The creative elements and tools used to deliver messages through specific channels. Several tactics are required to support each strategy. Examples are story placements, YouTube videos, Instagram reels, Facebook posts, special events, infographics, websites and podcasts.

Plan each public separately

Keep in mind that a key public will usually be helpful in accomplishing more than one of your objectives. As a result, strategies for those publics should be planned with a complete view of all you need to accomplish with them. Otherwise strategies for separate objectives will be isolated from each other and may not tie to your big idea. They may also result in tactics that don't integrate well into the overall campaign plan, and in some cases even conflict with each other. Separating publics and strategies by specific outcomes or objectives tends to fragment your efforts and lose the advantage of overlapping reinforcement.

When drafting your plan, focus on one public at a time. Write all of the strategies and tactics for that public before moving on to the next public. This approach will help you maximize the whole of their contribution and create synergy among your strategies and tactics. Use your stakeholder research to help you make decisions about strategies and tactics that will yield results. That research will tell you where you stand in terms of your current relationship with each public and give you a baseline to know what you need to do to deliver your messages effectively to each key public.

Informational versus motivational strategies

Strategies directly support the objectives by identifying what action or behavior is desired. The action part of a strategy may be informational or motivational. Informational strategies (also known as awareness or educational strategies) lay a significant foundation of information for the motivational strategies that ask the key public to act in some way.

As with objectives, it may not be necessary to have a separate informational strategy. If a public is already sufficiently educated and is ready to act, necessary information can be carried by the motivational strategy to avoid the risk of fragmenting your strategies and messages. All motivational strategies will contain some informational messages either in separate tactics or within each tactic. A tactic that appeals for a citizen's vote will almost always include some information to justify the action. Your job is to determine whether a separate informational strategy is necessary for that public. If there is a significant lack of knowledge and understanding, you probably need an informational strategy to lay a foundation before you can implement strategies to motivate behavior. If the information is already pervasive and people just need to be reminded, the informational tactics within a motivational strategy will be sufficient.

For example, many people still do not understand that many mental illnesses — like depression — have a physiological cause that must be addressed with medication. Any effort to motivate people with mental illness to see a doctor would require creating a better informed public environment. But to motivate people to give blood, you may only need to tell them where and when to show up. Virtually everyone understands the need and the process.

As you know, objectives always require a metric of some kind. Each objective must specify improvement that can be measured. The action identified in a public-specific strategy may also be stated in measurable terms. While not all strategies will detail the action this specifically, it may be necessary for some to do so. If a campaign supporting a local municipal bond requires 55% of the vote to pass, public-specific strategies may break that overall percentage down into manageable pieces for each public. A 55% overall vote may translate to 85% of business leaders, 65% of white-collar workers, 45% of blue-collar workers and 58% of stay-at-home parents. The strategies for each public may include these specific measurements to support the overall objective.

Take a look around, some marketing and communications strategies have become so pervasive in our society that we don't give them a second thought. What

has become the almost exclusive strategy to market beer to an age-segmented male audience? To deliver beer-drinking messages to that target public, the big idea is typically to use humor and celebrity athletes, while the channel is usually sporting events. This channel has literally hundreds of potential tactics to carry the message. What is the predominant fundraising strategy of your local United Way? It is an annual campaign that leverages workplace peer pressure. The main channel is workplace communications from which you can select specific tactics such as personal invitations from management, department competitions, posters and personalized emails. United Way annual campaign messages are focused at a specific public with the ability to give using tactics that overlap and reinforce one another to accomplish the purpose.

NASCAR driver Kasey Kahne watches cars practice at the Food City 500 race in Bristol, Tenn.

© Action Sports Photography/Shutterstock.com

Another example is an objective to double participation in educational programs for children with disabilities. Parents of children with disabilities would be a key public. They would require an informational strategy to inform them of the resources available and a motivational strategy to persuade them to tap into those resources. An informational strategy for this public would be to increase awareness of the resources available to parents of children with disabilities through a health fair sponsored by the state that showcases the services available to them. Tactics would probably include things like personal interaction with service providers, printed materials, videos, websites, Facebook groups and others.

A motivational strategy would be to persuade parents of children with disabilities to sign up for one or more of the state's free health services through one-on-one consultations with health care professionals. Tactics for this strategy might include email invitations to meet, referrals from health care professionals and a sign-up at the health fair for an in-home consultation.

As we've already seen, opinion leader influence is best exerted by people the parents perceive to be operating credibly in a relevant issue environment. In the above example, nurses and other health care providers would have high credibility. Peers — in this case, other parents who have children with disabilities — would also have very high credibility. Teachers and volunteer PTA leaders may also wield significant influence with this key public. Design strategies and tactics so that you can use opinion leaders to both inform and motivate your key publics.

The channel stipulated in a strategy should be the best way to get the message to the public for the outlined purpose (e.g., health fair, workplace communications or opinion leaders). To be sufficiently planned, each strategy requires the development of specific tactics within the channel (communications tools like signage and T-shirts at staged events, brochures and personalized emails in the workplace and meetings with printed collateral material or tablet presentations for opinion leaders).

How communications channels help focus your tactics

The tactics specify the communications tools within the channel more precisely. In the previous example, one of your health fair-related tactics might be to create a mobile app that parents of children with disabilities can download at the fair that explains the services available to them. Other health fair-related tactics could be social media posts, an infographic, a YouTube video or a printed brochure. Perhaps a follow-up tactic would also be helpful, such as an email survey following the health fair to see how beneficial it was and what parents learned.

By focusing tactics within a specific channel, you ensure that members of the key public will receive the message at least once, but hopefully more than once. Such focused overlap makes it more certain the message will be selected to be perceived, retained and acted upon.

Research suggests that a person must be exposed to a message seven times for its content to be remembered. The point is that you must carefully consider your public in determining the best ways to reach them. How a particular public best receives a certain type of message for a specific purpose is the relevant question. You must also carefully consider the message being sent to ensure the channels and tactics selected are appropriate for the message.

© Alexey Mark/Shutterstock.com

Choosing strategic communications channels

Determining the right channel or group of channels to send the message to a key public is critical to the effectiveness of your communications campaign. It is important to recognize that the effective and extensive use of mass media to communicate with key publics mostly belongs to past decades. While mass media can still be highly

TIPS FROM THE PROS

How to avoid the focus group of one (FGOO)

Marc Stryker, vice president of channel and content management at Penna Powers, a full service communications agency that offers creative advertising, public relations, digital and social media services, tips you off on how to resist the urge for a FGOO and ensure that your channel selection is strategic.

I've never met anyone who disagrees with taking a strategic approach to media channel selection. Strategy is not a word that conjures derision or skepticism. It is pretty much a universally respected word. Who would argue against it? Yet you're reading this book because taking a strategic approach must be learned. We take a strategic approach because our natural tendency is to do the opposite.

Nowhere does this natural aversion to strategy occur more often than in what I call the "focus group of one" or FGOO. When you "FGOO," you are making observations and decisions based on your own personal experience, or even the experiences of your own peer group. And you project your own experiences to the general public or even to your specific audience target. You'll hear this when people say, "No one watches television anymore," or "Everyone's on Twitter and TikTok." The act of FGOO-ing is natural, and something that most of us are guilty of committing.

Here are three ways you can avoid the FGOO and make the best media channel choices.

Question your own assumptions. I had a client who was a power user on Twitter and was convinced that over 60% of the market was on it. They lived and breathed the tool and it seemed to them that most people were on it, too. When I told them that only 29% of the market even visited the app in the last 30 days, they were shocked. Twitter is an influential and loud platform, but for the majority, it is an unused space only mentioned on news reports.

Do your research. Before you decide how you're going to reach your target audience, find out where they spend their time. There are several resources you can use to find this from proprietary customer information to local and national data providers like Nielsen, MRI-Simmons or Resonate. Don't let someone's gut tell you where your audience is, let dispassionate third-party research providers reveal media consumption patterns to you.

Consider all the factors. Even when your target audience is using a platform, that doesn't always mean it's the best fit for your message. In a world of skipping and scrolling, can you place a 60-second product demonstration video on Snapchat? Yes, but will your audience stay to watch it? Your FGOO might want to use it but if you haven't considered clutter, audience attentiveness and your message's uniqueness and complexity, you may need to find a better match.

Contributed by E. Marc Stryker. © Kendall Hunt Publishing Company.

effective in generating name recognition, their information-disseminating utility is not as great as before because of the proliferation of options and declining trust in them. While mass media channels have their place, in an environment where media are not trusted, it is unwise to rely on them too heavily. In fact, with neighbors and coworkers being among the most credible sources of information today, social media has largely overtaken traditional media as a preferred channel for messages.

We are accustomed to segmenting publics for the purpose of persuasion. We have long recognized that identifying a group of people who share common interests and lifestyles (and who may interact with one another) is the best way to devise an appeal that will motivate them. Now, segmentation is required not just to persuade, but to reach our desired publics.

Readership of traditional newspapers has declined sharply and is almost non-existent among millennials and Gen Zs. But even those who still read a newspaper have increased their selectivity in what they read and how they read. Most broad audience magazines have disappeared. Some of these broad audience publications are still available online, but many have been replaced by highly segmented special interest and professional or trade publications.

The explosion of video streaming channels (e.g., Disney+, Hulu, Netflix, Peacock) is creating highly segmented viewership, which will continue to increase. A similar explosion of social media channels (e.g., Mastodon, TikTok, Parler, Clubhouse, BeReal), some of which are oriented to political ideologies, allows social media users to self-select into networks of like-minded people. Sebastiaan Crul of the future-focused think tank Freedom Lab predicted that social and cultural forces would cause "social media to become more fragmented, with different platforms playing different roles and users switching freely between them." For example, he observed that users craving authenticity and community are now gravitating to TikTok and BeReal. While Instagram currently dominates the landscape for people who follow celebrities and influencers and consume brand promotional content, he envisions a future where "instead of [a] single dominant one-stop-shop social media platform, a more fragmented and unbundled social media landscape will arise in the years ahead."

The lesson to be learned is that mass media (which arguably never did reach a mass public) are declining in their ability to reach our publics with the messages we need sent. The good news is that as a medium becomes more specific and segmented, it becomes more effective in terms of reaching the public segments we need to target. So while our jobs may be a bit more difficult in that we need to exercise a greater range of creativity and expertise in using differentiated communications channels, we are promised higher rates of success because of the emergence of social media and the narrowing of mass media audiences.

As described in Figure 8.2, this step of the strategic planning process requires you to select the combination of communications channels that will help you accomplish your objectives, reach each of your key publics and effectively inform or motivate them through effective message delivery.

 Figure 8.2 _____
Choosing strategic communications channels

Questions to answer in selecting the best combination of channels to reach each key public:
- Which channels have the appropriate level of interactivity to accomplish your objectives?
- Which channels provide you with the reach necessary to accomplish your objectives?
- Which channels does your key public or its influencers find relevant and trustworthy?
- Which channels are best suited to delivering the message intended for the key public or its influencers?
- Which combination of channels will result in enough repeat exposure of the message that your target public will perceive and remember it?

Personalization and interactivity of communications channels

To select the best combination of communications channels, it is sensible to compare them in a chart (see Figure 8.3). Across the top of the chart, communications channels are grouped into three categories: personal communication, segmented media, and mass-produced mass media messages. In the second row of the chart, you can see examples of the communications channels and tactics that fit into each of the three categories.

The remaining rows of the chart will help you answer the questions posed in Figure 8.2. A thorough analysis of the possible channels you identified in your target public profiles will ensure that you select the most effective channels to reach your publics, inform or persuade them with your messages and accomplish your objectives. In the third row of the chart, you can compare the **interactivity** of the communications channels in each of the three categories. As you move from the left side of the chart to the right, the level of interaction with the key public changes from highly interactive (two-way communication) to moderately interactive to noninteractive (one-way communication). In the fourth row of the chart, you can compare the reach of the communications channels in each of the three categories. On the left side of the chart, highly personal communication has a low reach because messages are designed to appeal to specific individuals. On the right end of the chart, mass-produced mass media have a wide reach, so messages should be designed for a mass appeal. Finally, the fifth row of the chart identifies key uses for each of the three categories of communications channels.

PUMA hosts annual shareholder meeting in Nuremberg, Germany.

INTERACTIVITY
The degree to which the channel or tactic provides interaction between the sender of the message and the receiver.

Looking at interactivity (row 3), reach (row 4) and key uses (row 5) together suggests that when we need to increase the likelihood of message attention, selection and retention, we should choose a communications channel that is highly personal and highly interactive. The tradeoff is that it will be difficult to reach very many people using this approach. Similarly, when we need to build awareness among a large group of people, using mass-produced mass media will help us achieve it. The tradeoff is that the message will have little or no interactivity. In the middle of the chart are highly segmented media like special interest magazines and topical social media communities. These channels are moderately interactive, reach targeted groups, and can be used to provide detailed information and reinforce existing beliefs and attitudes.

Highly personal and interactive

The basis of the relationship building approach to public relations is the overwhelming power of personal and interactive communication. The personal influence of opinion leaders, subject matter experts and peers is particularly important in a persuasion campaign.

A personal delivery system engenders interactivity. Interactivity is important in several ways. First, interaction has a basis of strong relationships and cooperation. Second, as discussed in the chapter on persuasion, it is a key to the crystallization of

Figure 8.3
The personalization and interactivity grid

1. Type of Communications Channel	Highly Personal Communication	Segmented Media	Mass-Produced Mass Media
2. Examples of Channels and Tactics	• In-person conversations • Email • External or internal mail • Telephone • Digital messaging	• Websites • Blogs • Podcasts • Social media • Magazines • Cable / streaming TV • Mobile apps • Meetings • Special events	• Television • Radio • Print • Websites • Movies • Trade shows • Conventions
3. Level of Interactivity	• Highly interactive (two-way communication)	• Moderately interactive	• Non-interactive (one-way communication)
4. Reach	• Low, individual appeal	• Medium, targeted appeal	• High, mass appeal
5. Key Uses	• Influence opinion • Build relationships • Encourage action	• Provide detailed information • Respond to questions • Reinforce existing beliefs and attitudes • Foster community	• Build awareness

Adapted from L.J. Wilson (1995) and K. Hallahan (2001)

opinion. Third, interactivity provides a personal commitment and stimulus for action. For these reasons, this kind of communication is highly effective. Nevertheless, it is also time-consuming and often expensive. The advantages must be weighed carefully against the costs (time and money) to determine the best circumstances in which to use personal communications channels. Although not quite as personal, social media channels offer a low-cost way for many opinion leaders to connect with key publics. The ease of sharing through social media makes these tools less labor-intensive and less expensive. The tradeoff for those benefits is that you must largely relinquish control of the message to other social media users and its distribution to algorithms.

In some situations, it's possible to create the one-on-one communication hierarchically. A good example is United Way's workplace campaign. Companies that support the United Way in their community by running workplace campaigns identify a company representative (communications channel) who is trained by local volunteers to hold an employee information meeting (communications tactic) and to personally ask each individual in the company to support local community social service efforts through monthly payroll deductions (message). Often the company provides an endorsement of the campaign by making a corporate donation. In larger organizations, the company representative trains employees in each department to do the personal asking. This hierarchical system uses opinion leadership, personal influentials and one-on-one communications channels supported by tactical collateral materials to reach hundreds of thousands of people within a community. Nevertheless, it is highly labor intensive, even though the laborers are volunteers.

Segmented and moderately interactive

Communications channels in the middle of the grid — segmented and moderately interactive — combine elements of mass and personal as well as interactivity (see Figure 8.3). Although not nearly as personal, this category still provides a highly targeted message to a larger target audience than personal communication can. These channels are specifically designed for an already segmented public and are effective at providing detailed information, responding to questions, reinforcing existing beliefs and attitudes, and fostering a sense of community. Good examples include digital channels like blogs, podcasts and mobile apps, and special interest media that are clearly designed and targeted to meet the needs of a very specific group. Another example might be shareholder meetings for all stockholders which, in some companies, can be thousands of people. The segmentation of cable and streaming television channels allows for the effective use of this kind of approach.

These types of channels are more interactive than mass media. Because the target public is an interest group, it tends to be more responsive to surveys, and more active in initiating feedback, phone calls and emails. This environment is perfect for communicators to build in response mechanisms that provide the interactivity necessary for two-way symmetry in communication with the organization's key publics. Further, because the segmented channel has already identified the needs of its audience, it is a fairly simple matter for the public relations practitioner to tap into and help satisfy those needs. Such channels are often shorter on funding than traditional media channels and are therefore hungry for material that honestly meets the needs of their audiences. It is to the practitioner's advantage to identify channels that target the organization's key publics and to include them within the plan to build strong, mutually beneficial relationships.

The savvy practitioner will always remember that today's publics differ from publics of the past in that they have much more control over their access to information. Past practitioners had the control over channels, messages and their delivery. With the rise of internet communication and particularly the explosion of social media, our publics now control how, when and where they receive messages, and they are also in a new role as senders of messages. They vacillate between being hungry for information and tuning it out because of overload. And they control the switch. In this environment, public relations has become the content provider, giving rise to the mantra "content is king." Such an environment reinforces the necessity of public-specific messages (or content) delivered by channels publics themselves choose to access.

Mass-produced mass media

Although we pronounced mass media nearly dead, mass-produced and mass media channels still have their place in some campaigns. The use of electronic media to broadly disseminate messages will undoubtedly keep this category alive for years to come. The technology facilitates broad coverage of certain publics that probably would not be reached any other way. As public relations scholar Kirk Hallahan explained, the primary value of mass-produced mass media "lies in its ability to create broad public awareness of organizations, causes, products and services." Nevertheless, it is important to remember the advantages and disadvantages of specific mass media channels and to use them appropriately. In general, Hallahan says that one of the biggest disadvantages of using mass media channels is the difficulty in capturing audience attention because of intense message competition and clutter. Further, just because we use mass media does not mean we are targeting a mass audience. It is just as important to segment publics and design public-specific messages for mass media as it is for segmented media.

Matthew McConaughey at the 86th Academy Awards in Los Angeles.

The special case of events

Events lend themselves to all three categories of channels. A special event, for example, may be designed to be personal and interactive (like a private dinner for a major donor), segmented and moderately interactive (like a media tour of facilities or an awards ceremony) or mass-produced mass media (like the Democratic or Republican national conventions).

Turning a special event into a media event requires that care be taken to stage the event with messaging for the immediate attendees, but it must be packaged in such a way that the messages will also appeal to those who view or listen over other media channels. Just remember that even though a special event is organized as a celebration or some other routine commemoration, you've wasted the organization's opportunities and resources if you don't also use it to convey primary messages to key organizational publics.

The 2016 Democratic National Convention in Philadelphia, Pa.

Controlled versus uncontrolled channels

Another consideration in selecting the best combination of channels is the degree to which communicators control the media. Broadly, there are two types of media channels: controlled and uncontrolled. Communication scholars and industry practitioners have developed four categories to distinguish between different types of controlled and uncontrolled media channels. Collectively, these categories are referred to as the **PESO model**, an acronym that stands for paid, earned, shared and owned media.

PESO MODEL
A categorization of media channels into paid, earned, shared and owned.

MINI CASE

Have you got ALLERGY FACE™?
Zyrtec and Hunter Public Relations

Zyrtec was struggling to compete with category leaders Allegra and Claritin, who saturated the marketplace and dominated allergy advertising with messages about functional benefits. Zyrtec was outspent nearly 3 to 1 and needed an innovative strategy to build loyalty and core customers. Research showed that 66% of women with allergies felt ugly or unattractive due to their symptoms – watery eyes, puffy faces and red noses. Additionally, half of all female allergy sufferers said they missed out on something important because of allergy-related beauty challenges. Surprisingly, only 5% of stories in the beauty media talked about the way allergies made people look.

However, nearly 70% of women said they used beauty products to maintain their appearance. And 30% said they used beauty products to manage their mental and emotional health. Latinas showed the most loyalty to name brand health and beauty products and 80% considered aesthetic beauty to be a core value.

CORE PROBLEM
In the crowded over-the-counter allergy relief market, Zyrtec needed to differentiate its product from the host of other similar medications by helping women feel better about themselves when they have allergies.

HUNTER'S ZYRTEC STRATEGY
Focusing on the target consumer – female allergy sufferers 25-49 – Hunter created a campaign called "Allergy Face," to provide women tips and techniques to look and feel their best during allergy season – positioning Zyrtec as an

© Dragana Gordic/Shutterstock.com

ally in conquering beauty issues. The goal was to break into the English- and Spanish-speaking lifestyle, health and beauty media. Here are examples of the communications channels and tactics they used to implement their strategy.

Highly personal and interactive channel: Beauty counters in shopping mall cosmetic departments.
   Tactic: Hunter engineered a partnership between Zyrtec and Macy's to create the first-ever allergy-related beauty counter in the cosmetic department at a leading Macy's location. The beauty counter provided personalized ALLERGY FACE™ makeovers in conjunction with the annual Macy's Flower Show.

Segmented and moderately interactive channels: Zyrtec website (owned media) and YouTube channel (shared media).
   Tactic: The campaign teamed with actress Debra Messing and two well-known health and beauty experts to create web videos for the Zyrtec website and YouTube channel. These spokeswomen provided exercise, health and beauty tips for women suffering from allergies. For Latinas, Zyrtec teamed with beauty expert Carmen Ordoñez to customize ALLERGY FACE™ beauty solutions.
   Tactic: The Zyrtec website also featured an allergy survival kit with a tutorial on outdoor exercising in allergy season and other topics the research showed would capture the attention and loyalty of female allergy sufferers.

Segmented and moderately interactive channels: Social media (shared media).
   Tactics: Social media use was pervasive. The campaign was well covered by bloggers and drove viral interest through Facebook, Twitter, Instagram, Pinterest and other social media channels.

Mass-produced mass media channels: Leading women's health and beauty media (earned media).
   Tactics: In only five months, the campaign generated 440 million media impressions and top-tier coverage in the leading women's health and beauty media. Much of the coverage focused solely on Zyrtec, without mentioning the brand's competitors. And the campaign's key message (look good, feel good) was present in 75% of the coverage.

RESULTS
Zyrtec considered the Clio and *PRWeek* award-winning campaign so successful that it trademarked ALLERGY FACE™ and made it a central feature of its 2014 brand plans, expanding it beyond public relations. According to Grace Leong, managing partner at Hunter Public Relations, "Listening to consumer insights . . . was key to making this program a success. ALLERGY FACE™ allowed Zyrtec to start a new conversation about allergies and extend coverage to a new space – beauty."

Controlled channels allow the practitioner to dictate the content, placement or distribution of messages. In the PESO model, paid media channels give practitioners the most control.

Paid media channels are owned and operated by someone other than your organization and have their own established audiences. But, the owners of these channels are willing to sell your organization time or space on their channel. This allows you to put your organization's messages in front of the channel's audience members, though usually in a way that interrupts the regular news or entertainment content on that channel. Organizations can purchase access to the preexisting audiences of a wide variety of media channels, from television and radio to outdoor displays to the internet to mobile phone apps and social media. Paid media allows communicators to have complete control over every aspect of message design, no matter the format. In addition, internet and social media channels have tools that allow advertisers to target their advertising at specific groups of people and track their interactions with the ads.

CONTROLLED CHANNELS
You dictate the content, timing and placement or distribution of messages but messages lose credibility.

PAID MEDIA
Communications channels owned by a third party who is willing to sell time or space.

Keep in mind that the advantages of paid media are tempered by higher costs and lower credibility. Not only do you have to pay for the time or space to run an ad, you also have to pay for the production of the ad itself. And, as you can see in Figure 8.4, the 2022 Edelman Trust Barometer found that only 49% of people said they would either automatically believe an advertised message (8%) or would believe an advertised message if they saw the ad more than once (41%). Additionally, 21% of people said they would never believe a message if they only saw it in an ad. Publics are well aware that paid media convey exactly what the organization paying for the space wants. There is no doubt in the consumer's mind when they are reading or watching paid advertising, that the advertiser is telling only one side of the story to motivate consumer purchase.

Uncontrolled channels require the sacrifice of control over a message in exchange for inclusion in a media channel's regular news or entertainment content. In the PESO model, practitioners have the least amount of control over **earned media** channels.

A more common term for earned media is publicity, or the coverage an organization receives from a third-party media source. This might include a story about your organization in the "New York Times," a piece about your organization on a popular topical website, or a post about your organization by a social media influencer. Practitioners don't pay for this type of media coverage. They earn it by providing relevant and newsworthy stories about their organizations to news reporters, content editors and social media influencers. These media **gatekeepers** assess the value of the organization's information to their audiences. If the information has value for the audience of a particular media outlet, a news reporter or social media influencer will then create and publish their own version of the organization's story. As a result, the practitioner loses control over the exact wording of the message, its placement and its timing. However, the message gains credibility because of the intervention and scrutiny of a trusted third party. The message is also disseminated to the media outlet's audience. The risk that the message may be buried or distorted is the price paid for credibility gained through perceived third-party objectivity and no-cost exposure of the message to the outlet's audience.

Media relations is the function of building relationships with media gatekeepers and earning coverage in media outlets that will reach your key publics. Practitioners need to be strategic about which media outlets and influencers they work with so their messages ultimately reach their intended publics. It's not enough to earn media coverage for your organization. If you are serious about accomplishing your objectives, you must earn coverage in the media outlets that your key publics trust and pay attention to. This is especially important in an era of declining trust in the news media.

The latest Edelman Trust Barometer data, illustrated in Figures 8.4 and 8.5, show that traditional news media are still among the most trusted sources for news and information. However, there seems to be a limit to the amount of trust people are willing to extend to the news media. Just over half (57%) of the study's participants said they would either automatically believe a news media report with a named source (10%) or would believe a news report with a named source if they saw it more than once (47%). While these results are better than those for paid media, when news reports use unnamed sources, people's trust in the news media drops below the trust levels of paid media. Only 48% said they would either automatically believe a news report with an unnamed source (8%) or would believe a news report with an

---

⚇ UNCONTROLLED CHANNELS

Someone else dictates the content, placement or timing of messages but messages gain credibility.

⚇ EARNED MEDIA

Communications channels owned by a third party who can be persuaded to tell your organization's story using their own resources.

⚇ GATEKEEPER

A reporter, editor or social media influencer who controls the flow of information that appears on their media channel.

⚇ MEDIA RELATIONS

The function of building relationships with reporters, editors and social media influencers so that your information becomes more trusted and relevant.

unnamed source if they saw it more than once (40%). Similar to paid media, 21% of people said they would never believe a message if they only saw it in a news report with unnamed sources. Clearly, practitioners attempting to earn media coverage for their organization need to be transparent with information and sources to get the credibility boost they are seeking.

Shared and owned media channels are neither completely controlled nor uncontrolled. They fall somewhere in between. While both owned and shared media give practitioners control over the content of the original message, the technologies used to publish the message can impact its distribution and timing. They also allow publics to interact and engage with the message in ways the practitioner cannot control. To help you understand the similarities and differences between shared and owned media, we will break from following the order suggested by the PESO model acronym and discuss owned media first followed by shared media.

Owned media are communications channels created and maintained by an organization. While organizations may use some printed materials (e.g., magazines and brochures) to communicate with publics, the ability to publish and distribute engaging and interactive forms of communication on the internet, such as emails, ebooks, websites, webinars, blogs, videos and podcasts, has transformed organizations into media publishing outlets. According to David Meerman Scott, author of "The New Rules of Marketing & PR," owned digital media channels allow organizations to "communicate directly" with their publics "in a form they appreciate." Today, organizations don't have to pay to use someone else's channels to talk to their publics. They also aren't dependent on a media gatekeeper to vet their message before it sees the light of day. Owned media enables organizations to cut out the middleman and talk directly to the publics they care about. Now, some corporations and nonprofits even rival traditional media publishing companies in their ability to produce content and generate an audience.

© Audrey Popov/Shutterstock.com

OWNED MEDIA
Communications channels that are created and maintained by an organization.

This owned media approach is often referred to as content marketing or brand journalism, where the goal is to attract an audience that keeps coming back to your organization's channels to consume, engage with, and hopefully share your organization's content. As Ann Handley and C.C. Chapman explain in their book "Content Rules," "Produce great stuff, and your customers will come to you. Produce really great stuff, and your customers will share and disseminate your message for you." Because owned media is used to pull publics to the organization's message, it is usually thought of as the hub of the PESO model. Paid and earned media extend the reach of an organization's message by pushing it out through third-party media channels. After this initial exposure to an organization's message, publics can find more information on an organization's owned media channels. Once publics become part of the organization's owned media audience, the organization can develop a relationship with them over time by publishing content that cultivates the relationship.

According to the 2022 Edelman Trust Barometer data in Figure 8.5, owned media is trusted less overall for news and information than traditional news media. However, the trust people ultimately have in owned media channels seems to depend on the source of the information. As you can see in Figure 8.4, employees tend to believe

messages from their employer the most. Specifically, 65% of people said they would either automatically believe information from their employer (13%) or would believe information from their employer if they saw it more than once (52%). This means that organizations shouldn't miss the opportunity to communicate with their employees through their own media channels. Citizens of national governments also tend to believe government messages (58%). While the percentage of citizens who believe government messages is not as high as the percentage of employees who believe employer messages, government messages were still believed by more people than both earned and paid media. Major corporations, however, had lower levels of believability (54%) than media reports with a named source, but higher levels of believability than paid media.

⊶ SHARED MEDIA

Interactive, open access communications channels owned and operated by a media technology company.

Shared media are communications channels that are owned and operated by a third-party media technology company — think Meta, Google or Twitter — that allows organizations and individuals to use their platform to share messages and interact with other users. While there is typically no cost to use shared media platforms, these companies make money by selling advertising that shows up in their users' feeds. Social media channels, such as Facebook, Instagram, LinkedIn, Pinterest, Snapchat, TikTok, Twitter and YouTube, are all examples of shared media. Like owned media, shared media allow practitioners to disseminate messages and engage directly with members of their organization's key publics. Because of the vast number of people who regularly use shared media, these channels have become the go-to media for generating awareness, humanizing faceless organizations, demonstrating thought leadership, driving traffic to owned media channels, managing reputation, dealing with crisis situations and fielding customer service questions.

Some may question why shared media needs its own category. While it's tempting for your organization to think that it "owns" the social media account it created for itself on any of the popular platforms, the truth is, it doesn't. Karen Freberg, author of "Social Media for Strategic Communication," compared using social media platforms to renting an apartment. The media companies that own and operate the platforms set the terms of use, and you and your organization are expected to abide by the service agreements even when the media company decides to change them.

Shared media differ from owned media in at least two other important ways. First, the distribution of messages on social media is governed by mathematical algorithms. This means you can post a message on a social media channel, but you don't get to determine who sees it. The algorithm does. Social media platforms used to display content in users' feeds chronologically. Now, sophisticated algorithms use data generated by social media users' online behavior to serve up content to their feeds that is relevant to their interests. One way to deal with algorithms is to understand how they work on each social media platform so you can effectively target content to the users who are part of your key publics. The other way is to pay for advertising, which bypasses the algorithm altogether. You will learn more about these approaches in the next chapter.

Second, no one controls the conversation on shared media. Your organization is one voice in a sea of thousands, or sometimes even millions, of voices. Once you share your message on a social media channel, the conversation around that message is now largely out of your hands. Your organization can still participate in these conversations as they develop, but there are so many other voices involved in these conversations that there is no way for your organization to control any of them. In addition, because anyone with a social media account can share anything on that platform (within the terms of service), misinformation and disinformation are rampant. So, not only are people having conversations based on the information you post about your organization, but they also are having conversations about information that someone else posts about your organization, which may or may not be accurate, may or may not be positive, and may or may not be malicious.

The effect of untrustworthy and deceptive information on shared media channels can be seen in the 2022 Edelman Trust Barometer data shown in Figures 8.4 and 8.5. Social media channels had the lowest levels of trust as a source for news and information. In addition, only 38% of people said they would either automatically believe information that showed up in their social media feed (6%) or would believe information in their feed if it showed up more than once (32%). Strikingly, 27% of people said they would never believe information from their social media feed if it was the only place they saw it. This was the highest level of disbelief for any of the sources considered in the 2022 Trust Barometer research.

Figure 8.4
Media source believability

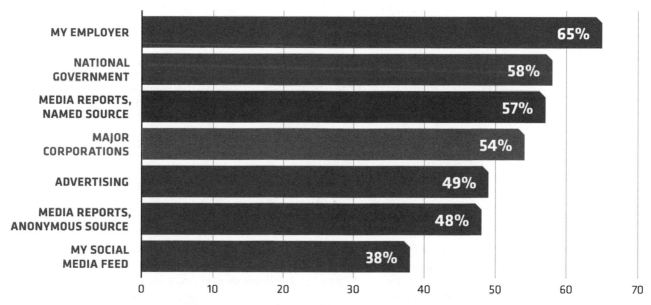

Source: 2022 Edelman Trust Barometer

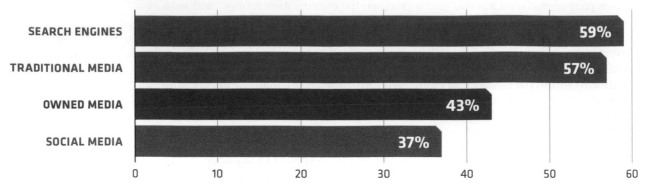

Figure 8.5
Trust in sources of news and information

Source: 2022 Edelman Trust Barometer

Tactics

The first thing that students and many practitioners do when presented with a challenge is jump to tactics. It is what communicators and marketers do the best — and the worst. We're pretty good at developing catchy slogans, social media contests, fun special events and attention-grabbing visuals. The problem is not a lack of ideas for interesting tactics; it is rather not enough careful calculation to ensure the tactics will accomplish your strategies and objectives. Tactics, or communications tools, always need to be approached in the context of your research and the problem/opportunity you're tackling. Following the matrix approach and developing tactics only after your objectives, publics, messages, strategies and communications channels have been determined will ensure they are aligned to help you accomplish your goal. The creativity required of good tactics must be carefully channeled to ensure strategic alignment with your campaign.

Tactics as strategic tools

Tactics are the tools — the hammer, nails, lumber and paint — you need to build a successful campaign. You can also think of them as the tasks you must perform in your campaign. The activities you undertake to implement your campaign are all tactics. Everything that costs money, aside from research and measurement, is a tactic. This is why the items that show up on your calendar and in your budget are all tactics. So regardless of how well you have planned your strategy, the success of your campaign will ultimately rest on the implementation of your tactics. The majority of business strategies fail not because they were ill-conceived, but because there was a breakdown in implementation. Their tactics either did not support the strategies or they were poorly executed. To avoid this scenario, we strongly recommend you use strategy briefs for all tactics. Strategy briefs are concise design tools that help you plan each tactic around your strategy. We'll explain more about them and about how to create effective tactics in Chapter 11.

MATRIX APPLIED

Strategies and tactics

Once the Arizona State Department of Health has identified which key publics need to be motivated to meet the challenge faced by the recent outbreak of bubonic plague in rural areas, the state must develop effective message delivery strategies for each public. This example will cover message strategies, channels and tactics for outdoor recreationalists.

OUTDOOR RECREATIONALISTS' MESSAGE DELIVERY

Strategy one: Raise awareness among outdoor recreationalists of the bubonic plague threat and prevention through retailers of recreation products and rental equipment outlets.

   Communications channel: Retailers of recreation products and rental equipment outlets.

   Tactics:

- Letter from state health director and governor explaining threat and asking for cooperation and participation in an awareness and prevention campaign.
- Follow-up calls to retailers and rental outlets to encourage participation in the AZ Fights Plague campaign.
- Information kits containing:
   - Posters to be displayed in stores.
   - Flyers to be distributed as bag stuffers with each purchase.
   - Fact sheet for employees with suggested preventive measures and products.
- Links to participating retailers on the www.AZfightsplague.org website, Facebook page and Twitter.

Strategy two: Raise awareness among outdoor recreationalists of the risk of plague in certain areas through targeted recreational venues.

   Communications channel: Targeted recreational venues.

   Tactics:

- Signs prominently placed at trailheads, camp sites and other recreational venues with QR code link to AZ Fights Plague website, Facebook page and Twitter.
- Posters at fee stations and information booths.
- Flyers distributed by park rangers and venue employees at fee stations, information booths and park shops and restaurants.
- Information and AZ Fights Plague links on official BLM, Forest Service and state and National Park Service reservation and permit websites as part of the purchase process.
- Tag relevant Facebook and Twitter posts with #AZfightsplague.

Strategy three: Use the official AZ Fights Plague website to educate outdoor recreationalists about the need to employ plague prevention behaviors and seek immediate medical treatment when necessary.

   Communications channel: Website.

   Tactics:

- Launch official AZ Fights Plague website at www.AZfightsplague.org, which includes:
   - Attention-grabbing landing page.
   - Facts about bubonic plague.
   - Interactive map of areas of confirmed plague and number of cases in each area.

- Preventive measures checklist.
- Bubonic plague infection warning signs.
- Medical treatment options.
- Embedded YouTube AZ Fights Plague video.
- Infographic about plague risks, prevention and how to identify symptoms.
- FAQs.
- Participating retailer links with downloadable posters and flyers.
- Links to recreationalists' blog posts.
- Establish backlinks to official plague website on state and county venue sites as well as on websites of groups, clubs and associations organized around outdoor recreational activities such as four-wheeling, rock climbing, hiking and mountain biking.
- Optimize website for search.
- Pay for search engine advertising on Google and Bing.

Strategy four: Use social media to motivate outdoor recreationalists to employ plague prevention behaviors and seek immediate medical treatment when necessary.
  Communications channel: Social media.
  Tactics:
- Set up Instagram, Twitter and YouTube accounts featuring news and information (similar to website) on plague and plague prevention linking to participating retailers and rental outlets.
- Links to campaign social media accounts on state and county venue sites as well as on websites of groups, clubs and associations organized around outdoor recreational activities such as four-wheeling, rock climbing, hiking and mountain biking.
- YouTube videos and Instagram reels about plague prevention and warning signs that can be shared through social media channels.
- Boost video posts on Facebook and Instagram to ensure exposure to key publics and encourage follower growth.
- Target paid video ads on Twitter and YouTube to key publics to encourage follower growth.
- Infographic about plague risks, prevention and how to identify symptoms.
- Tag all Instagram and Twitter posts with #AZfightsplague.

The difference between strategies and tactics

One of the hardest things to work through when learning the matrix is the difference between strategies and tactics. It's simple, really, when you think about it this way: A strategy is an approach and a tactic is a task. You need many tasks to accomplish a strategy. A helpful question to ask is, "Can the tool be broken down any further?" If the answer is no, it's a tactic. An earned media approach to communicating on a mass media channel, for example, can be broken down into many different tactics — an email or telephone pitch, a news release, a radio actuality, a public service announcement or an op-ed piece. A brochure, on the other hand, can't be broken down any further so it's a tactic. You can see a few more examples of the differences between strategies and tactics in Figure 8.6.

A special event is trickier. It can be either a strategy or a tactic. If it's a large event with many elements to it such as a conference or the FIFA World Cup, it's probably a strategy. If your special event is small and simple, like an employee awards ceremony, it's probably best treated as a tactic.

A diversity of tactics

In addition to not always tying tactics to strategy, another problem has been the tendency to rely on the same tactics or communications tools over and over. Although there is nothing wrong with reusing tactics that work well with particular publics, communicators should be careful not to fall into the routine of the processionary caterpillars described earlier in Chapter 7. Using a tactic repeatedly sometimes causes us to select that tactic without thinking about its appropriateness to get a particular message to a particular public for a particular purpose. We fall into a pattern of selecting tactics because we've always used them, or because the tactic worked before.

Remember to review the analytical process to select communications tools each time you design messages and strategies for publics. Change is one of the only constants in business and marketing. Publics change, circumstances change, purposes change, messages change and communications channels change. If communicators stay with the same plan for the same publics without recognizing the constantly changing environment, communication efforts will miss their targets. A practitioner will be left (possibly without a job) wondering why it didn't work this time since it had always worked before.

The other inherent danger in using the same tools continually is stifling creativity. Communicators may ignore new creative and innovative ways to get messages to publics. But in a society flooded with messages in the typical media channels, creative and innovative delivery of messages is necessary to cut through the message clutter to reach our targets. Remember the challenge is twofold: You must motivate the members of your key public to choose to perceive the message (and retain it), and to choose to act upon it. Both require an appeal to the public's self-interests, but self-interest appeals alone will not get you over the perception hurdle. You may not find a solution to your specific need in textbooks that teach how to design communications tactics. You must be able to create innovative delivery systems and then follow the principles of persuasive communication theory to send your messages in creative ways that command attention.

The diversity of tactics available is limited only by the imagination. Nevertheless, there are abundant numbers of books, articles and other references that identify a variety of the standard communications tools and their appropriate uses. We refer you to a broad range of easily available resources (some of which are identified in this chapter's references and additional readings) that suggest dozens of tactics and instructions on their preparation and use.

Because of the vast resources which give specific direction on preparing and using communications tools, it is not our purpose here to review specific tactics. Rather, it is more important to provide a process to assist communications professionals in determining how to select the tactics most appropriate for a specific public, purpose and message.

Most popular introductory textbooks in communication segment tools and tactics into written, spoken and visual categories. But today's communications professionals focused on key publics and messages recognize that, in the radically changed communication environment, such divisions are artificial. Most effective tactics combine at least two, and often all three, of those senses. Further, that type of categorization puts undue emphasis on the medium or channel, with less thought of the purpose, the target audience and the message itself. Such categorization may be partially responsible for communication practice that is excessively tactic-driven rather than strategic.

Figure 8.6
Hierarchy of strategies, channels and tactics

STRATEGIC APPROACH	CHANNEL	TACTICS
PAID MEDIA	• Instagram (segmented and moderately interactive media)	• Sponsored influencer content • Photo ads • Video ads • Carousel ads • Stories ads • Explore ads
EARNED MEDIA	• "New York Times" (mass-produced mass media)	• Press conference • Media pitch • News release • Backgrounders • Fact sheets • Photos • Videos
SHARED MEDIA	• Instagram (segmented and moderately interactive media)	• Stories • Reels • Carousel posts • Photo posts • Video posts • Strategic hashtags • User-generated content posts
OWNED MEDIA	• Organization's website (segmented and moderately interactive media)	• Web page copy • Photos • Videos • Podcasts • White papers • Chatbots • Email list • SEO subscription form
INTERPERSONAL COMMUNICATION	• In-person meeting (highly personal and interactive communication)	• Talking points • Printed materials • Slide deck

For this reason, using the level of personalization and degree of interactivity approach applied earlier to channels is equally effective for tactics. Tactics inherit many of their characteristics from the channels that are used to disseminate them. Think of how DNA enables parents to pass certain traits on to their children. These inherited genetic traits create a family resemblance among members of the same family. Inheritance works in a similar way between channels and tactics. Tactics used within highly personal communications channels will naturally be more personalized and interactive than tactics used within mass-produced mass media channels. But not all tactics available within a specific channel will have the same level of personalization and interactivity. There will be some variety. For example, Instagram, a social media communications channel, offers users a variety of different tactics to communicate with followers, each with different levels of personalization and interactivity. Figure 8.7 shows how some of these tactical options on Instagram differ in their levels of personalization and interactivity. Because tactics are the communications vehicles that are ultimately experienced by your key publics, you should determine the combination of tactics within each channel that will ensure the desired levels of personalization and interactivity you envisioned when creating your strategies.

Other considerations in selecting tactics

Although tactic selection should depend primarily on the public and the best way to reach them to accomplish your purpose, the content of the message will also be a determinant. For example, detailed messages with lots of information usually require a printed or online channel and tactic that allows a receiver the luxury of revisiting or studying the content. Similarly, broadcast messages must typically be simple and highly memorable because they cannot be reviewed at will unless they are also posted on the internet as videos or podcasts. In both of these cases, the content and length or complexity of the message are factors in media selection.

You should also remember that combinations of tactics are often preferable to tactics used individually or in isolation. If you determine that a critical company policy statement included in a press kit may not be fully appreciated by key opinion leaders unless you use a more personally interactive tactic, mail it to them separately with a handwritten note from an organizational executive or some other influential indicating key points that may specifically interest them. If you think your key investors need more personal attention regarding the latest stock jump, email them a copy of the news clipping with an FYI corner notation from the president of the company. There are a number of ways to "personalize" existing mass and segmented media messages.

On the other hand, some personal and interactive messages may be made mass through media coverage, editorial comments or online posting. However, use care when deciding whether to turn a personal message into a mass message. It may not only dilute the appeal, but it may alienate those originally touched by the personal message.

Additionally, combining tactics stimulates greater care in assuring they are integrated to support and enhance each other. Using nametags at a staged event can be planned to strategically support other tactics. You might color code the tags to identify separate key publics and prepare separate packets of supporting materials to be distributed based on name tag color. All tactics should be developed to magnify the effect of other tactics. They should be timed to support and enhance each other. The whole of the tactics supporting any strategy should be greater than the sum of the parts. They are like pieces to a puzzle that must interlock for the complete picture to appear.

Summary

Carefully planned strategies and tactics will ensure not only that your messages reach your target publics but also that they motivate a desired action or behavior. Strategies determine which communications channels are most appropriate to

Figure 8.7
Levels of personalization and interactivity in tactics

STRATEGIC APPROACH	CHANNEL	TACTICS	PERSONAL-IZATION	INTERACTIVITY
SHARED MEDIA	• Instagram (segmented and moderately interactive media)	• Stories	• Disappears after 24 hours • Appears in Stories feed • @mentions	• Interact in real-time with followers • Interactive stickers (polls, quizzes and emoji sliders) • #hashtags • Links (swipe ups)
		• Reels	• Easy to create • Appears in Explore feed • @mentions	• Shopping integration button • Up to 30 hashtags • Interactive stickers (polls, quizzes and emoji sliders) • #hashtags • Likes, comments, saves and shares
		• Carousel posts with captions	• @mentions	• Swipe to the next slide • #hashtags • Likes, comments, saves and shares
		• Photo posts with captions	• @mentions	• #hashtags • Likes, comments, saves and shares
		• Video posts with captions	• @mentions	• #hashtags • Likes, comments, saves and shares

reach key publics. Tactics detail the creative tools designed to convey your messages and solicit action from your key publics. They are the specific tasks to be implemented in a campaign.

Because many practitioners often find themselves choosing and implementing the same strategies and tactics over and over, it is important to remember the need for creativity. Additionally, channels and tactics are best chosen by how much interactivity and personalization is required by the strategy. Don't fall into the trap identified in the quote at the beginning of the chapter that reminds us, "Tactics without strategy is the noise before defeat." Strategic communication requires creative thinking and implementation, particularly in the planning of strategies and tactics.

Application case

ASD - Rockin' the spectrum
from Jake's House and Edelman

CORE PROBLEM

Jake's House, a small Canadian nonprofit organization focused on helping families affected by autism, needed to fundraise during the COVID-19 pandemic. Not only did the pandemic make raising money more difficult for Jake's House, but Jake's House was also competing for funding against other autism-support organizations, as well as many other types of charities.

BACKGROUND RESEARCH

Jake's House is based in Ontario, Canada, and seeks "to provide meaningful support to families living with autism across Canada." This includes fostering a diverse community where everyone has a place, encouraging people to be aware, accepting and inclusive, and empowering people to reach their potential. According to the Public Health Agency of Canada, one in every 66 children has autism spectrum disorder (ASD). Popular media depictions perpetuate a misperception that people on the spectrum don't want to interact with other people. However, research shows that people on the spectrum are four times more likely to feel isolated and lonely. Even though people with autism have limitations, they have diverse talents including musical ability.

GOAL

Raise funds for Jake's House and provide an inspirational rallying point for the Canadian autism community.

OBJECTIVES
- Secure 8 to 10 million earned media impressions by the end of the campaign.
- Achieve $1 million in donations by the end of the campaign.
- Increase volunteers for Jake's House by 15% by the end of the campaign.

KEY PUBLIC

Gen X, or those born between 1965-1980, represents a significant slice of the population in Canada. One in four Canadians are Gen Xs and they can afford to donate money to charitable organizations. Many have annual household incomes exceeding $100,000. Almost 20% of Canadian Gen Xs make between $150,000 and $200,000 a year. They are highly educated. Members of Gen X are likely to be college graduates. They also use a variety of media channels. Most own a smartphone or tablet. They also watch traditional TV and listen to the radio. Gen X has been called the "MTV Generation," indicating an interest in music and music videos.

BIG IDEA

Form a band named ASD (i.e., autism spectrum disorder) comprised of autistic performers who will play cover versions of famous pop songs. The publicity generated by the ASD band will give "those who have difficulty with self-expression the chance to show the world what they are truly capable of, on their own terms."

Self-interests: community, family, music.
Opinion leaders: government officials, famous musicians.
Channels: mobile apps, websites, television, radio.
Primary messages:
- Individuals with autism do not shun the spotlight.
- Those on the spectrum can accomplish amazing things.
- Donate to Jake's House to help individuals with autism do amazing things.

Assume you have been asked by Jake's House and Edelman to choose the communications channels, develop the strategies and identify the tactics needed to execute the campaign. Use the information provided in this case and principles from this chapter to complete the following tasks regarding communications channels, strategies and tactics.

1. Make a list of the potential communications channels that:
   - Your key public or its influencers find relevant and trustworthy.
   - Are best suited to delivering the messages intended for the key public or its influencers.
   - Will result in enough repeat exposure that your key public will believe and remember the message.
2. Use the personalization and interactivity grid (Figure 8.3) to categorize the channels you identified in the previous task. Does your list of channels have enough personalization to persuade and motivate your key public? Does your list of channels give you enough reach to meet the criteria set in the objectives? Refine your list of channels based on this analysis.
3. Use the PESO model to categorize the channels you identified and refined in the previous two tasks. Which channels are paid, earned, shared or owned. How much control do you have over each of these channels? What are the pros and cons of the level of control you have over each channel? What impact does your level of control have on the key public's trust of those channels? Refine your list of channels based this analysis.
4. Now that you have thought through your list of potential communications channels, write one informational strategy for the key public that follows the strategy formula described in Figure 8.1.
5. Next, write one motivational strategy for the key public that follows the strategy formula described in Figure 8.1.
6. Choose one of your strategies and brainstorm a list of four or five tactics that could be used to accomplish the strategy. As you come up with ideas for tactics, be sure to keep in mind the communications channel you will be using to deploy those tactics, the target public you are communicating with who will be consuming and engaging with those tactics and the message you are trying to send (including the big idea) that will be embedded within those tactics. Which tactics have the desired levels of personalization and interactivity within each channel?

References and additional readings

Allergy Face website. (2013). www.zyrtec.com/passion/beauty.

Barnhart, B. (2021, March 26). Everything you need to know about social media algorithms. *SproutSocial*. Retrieved from https://sproutsocial.com/insights/social-media-algorithms/

Broom, G. & Sha, B. L. (2012). *Cutlip and Center's Effective Public Relations* (11th ed.). Englewood Cliffs, NJ: Prentice-Hall, Inc.

Brubaker, P. J. & Wilson, C. (2018). Let's give them something to talk about: Global brands' use of visual content to drive engagement and build relationships. *Public Relations Review, 44*(3), 342-352.

Clio Health. (2014). Clio Healthcare 2013 winners. Retrieved from www.cliohealthcare.com/winners_media2013/public_relations

Crul, S. (2022, August 25). The fragmentation of social media. *Freedom Lab*. Retrieved from https://www.freedomlab.com/posts/the-fragmentation-of-social-media

Dietrich, G. (2020, September 8). What is the PESO model? *SpinSucks*. Retrieved from https://spinsucks.com/communication/peso-model-breakdown/

Dietrich, G. (2014). *Spin Sucks: Communication and Reputation Management in the Digital Age*. Indianapolis, IN: Que Publishing.

Edelman Worldwide. (2022). 2022 Edelman Trust Barometer. Retrieved from https://www.edelman.com/sites/g/files/aatuss191/files/2022-01/2022%20Edelman%20Trust%20Barometer%20FINAL_Jan25.pdf

Edelman Worldwide. (n.d.). The ASD band: Jake's House. Retrieved from https://www.edelman.com/work/jakes-house-asd-band

Freberg, K. (2022). *Social Media for Strategic Communication: Creative Strategies and Research-Based Applications* (2nd ed.). Thousand Oaks, CA: Sage.

Hainsworth, B. E. & Wilson, L. J. (1992). Strategic program planning. *Public Relations Review, 18*(1), 9–15.

Hallahan, K. (2001). Strategic media planning: Toward an integrated public relations media model. In R.L. Heath (Ed.), *Handbook of Public Relations* (pp. 461-470). Thousand Oaks, CA: Sage.

Handley, A. & Chapman, C. C. (2012). *Content Rules: How to Create Killer Blogs, Podcasts, Videos, Ebooks, Webinars (and more) that Engage Customers and Ignite Your Business*. Hoboken, NJ: John Wiley and Sons.

Hendrix, J. A., Hayes, D. C. & Kumar, P. D. (2012). *Public Relations Cases* (9th ed.). Boston, MA: Wadsworth Cengage Learning.

Howard, C. & Mathews, W. (2000). *On Deadline: Managing Media Relations* (3rd ed.). Prospect Heights, IL: Waveland Press.

Jake's House. (n.d.). About Jake's House. Retrieved from https://www.jakeshouse.ca/about/

Kelleher, T. (2021). *Public Relations* (2nd ed.). New York, NY: Oxford University Press.

Luttrell, R. M. & Capizzo, L. W. (2019). *Public Relations Campaigns: An Integrated Approach*. Thousand Oaks, CA: Sage.

Macnamara, J., Lwin, M., Adi, A. & Zerfass, A. (2016). 'PESO' media strategy shifts to 'SOEP': Opportunities and ethical dilemmas. *Public Relations Review*, 42(3), 377-385.

McLachlan, S. & Newberry, C. (2021). 22 benefits of social media for business. *Hootsuite Blog*. Retrieved from https://blog.hootsuite.com/social-media-for-business/

Moroney, G. (2019). *PRIMER: Introduction to PR planning*. International Association for the Measurement and Evaluation of Communication. Retrieved from https://amecorg.com/wp-content/uploads/2019/11/AMEC-PRIMER-planning-guide-MM2019.pdf

Newsom, D., Turk J. V. & Kruckeberg, D. (2012). *This Is PR: The Realities of Public Relations* (11th ed.). Belmont, CA: Wadsworth Publishing Company.

PRSA.org (2014). A case of allergy face: Zyrtec helps beauty bloom. Retrieved from http://apps.prsa.org/SearchResults/download/6BW-1402A09/0/A_Case_of_ALLERGY_FACE_ZYRTEC_Helps_Beauty_Bloom_f

PRWeek. (2014). PRWeek awards 2014. http://awards.prweekus.com/winners/2014.

Xie, Q., Neill, M. S. & Schauster, E. (2018). Paid, earned, shared and owned media from the perspective of advertising and public relations agencies: Comparing China and the United States. *International Journal of Strategic Communication*, 12(2), 160-179.

Scott, D. M. (2013). *The New Rules of Marketing & PR*. Hoboken, NJ: Wiley and Sons.

Sommerfeldt, E. J., Yang, A. & Taylor, M. (2019). Public relations channel "repertoires": Exploring patterns of channel use in practice. *Public Relations Review*, 45(4), 101796.

Supa, D. W. & Zoch, L. M. (2021). *Strategic Media Relations in the Age of Information: An Evidence-Based Approach*. New York, NY: Oxford University Press.

Tam, L., Mehta, A. & Goodlich, H. (2021). Towards greater integration in media planning: Decision-making insights from public relations practitioners. *Journal of Marketing Communications*, DOI: 10.1080/13527266.2021.1986740

The Holmes Report. (2021). Jake's House: ASD – Rockin' the Spectrum. *The Sabre Awards*. Retrieved from http://WARC.com

Wilcox, D. L., Cameron, G. T. & Reber, B. H. (2014). *Public Relations: Strategies and Tactics* (11th ed.). Upper Saddle River, NJ: Pearson Education.

Wilson, L. J. (1997). *Strategic Program Planning for Effective Public Relations Campaigns* (2nd ed.). Dubuque, IA: Kendall/Hunt.

Wilson, L. J. (1995). *Strategic Program Planning for Effective Public Relations Campaigns*. Dubuque, IA: Kendall/Hunt.

Zyrtec YouTube channel. (2013). www.youtube.com/user/zyrtec.

CHAPTER 9
SOCIAL AND DIGITAL MEDIA

"A brand is no longer what we tell the consumer it is — it is what consumers tell each other it is."

—SCOTT COOK
FOUNDER OF INTUIT

LEARNING IMPERATIVES

- Understand how social and digital media help build and maintain brands.

- Know how to use paid and organic media to effectively engage with publics.

- Understand the role of content marketing in shaping issues and brand perceptions.

- Be able to choose the best mix of social media, digital media and content marketing for your organization.

- Know how to craft content that both informs and motivates behavior.

191

© RoBird/Shutterstock.com

While you slept last night people searched 2.5 billion times on Google, posted 714 million times on Facebook, uploaded 28 million images on Instagram and swiped 462 million times looking for love on Tinder. Social and digital media have completely changed the way we live!

Social media

Social and digital media have changed the way we get our news, interact, shop, and express ourselves. More than two-thirds of the world's nearly 8 billion people have smart phones and 5.2 billion are connected to the internet. An estimated 4.5 billion people use **social media**.

⣿ SOCIAL MEDIA

A collective of online communications channels that enables users to create and share content and participate in community-based input, interaction and collaboration.

Although social media has often been guilty of proliferation of misinformation and even disinformation, it is also true that, now, the ease with which we access data and information has made it more difficult for people to lie, for police and criminals to get away with bad behavior, and for businesses to offer poor service. Social and digital media have created new levels of transparency in our society not previously experienced, leading to the emergence of a "callout culture" that continues to grow.

The stories of people getting caught in their lies are everywhere and sometimes quite humorous. One girl posted a picture of herself hiking on the Lake Okahumpka Park trail with the caption, "Nature is the ultimate healer to all our problems #naturelovers." Her sister posted a picture of the photoshoot that was staged right in the girl's backyard. In another case, Kennedy Jones posted on Twitter, "I just got a DM from @Sethrogen and it just says 'fart.'" Actor/comedian Seth Rogen responded the same day, "No you didn't." A guy named Rob posted, "Ran the 5k in 10 mins. training is going good..." to which someone quickly responded, "The world record is 12 minutes."

On a more serious note is the curious case of George Santos. The recently elected U.S. representative admitted to fabricating his entire resume. He falsely claimed to have worked for Goldman Sachs, graduated from Baruch College, owned New York real estate and started the animal charity Friends of Pets United. He even claimed to be a "proud American Jew" and a descendant of Holocaust survivors. Turns out he isn't Jewish, only "Jew-ish." As Rabbi Hirsch mockingly said, "I never said I was from Scotland, only Scott-ish. I never said I read a lot of books in college, only that I was book-ish." After the false claims were discovered, the congressman says he "got away" with lies before and was surprised to get caught this time.

"Whether you've had a bad flight, less than desirable service at a restaurant or simply an underwhelming experience with a new product, there is hope, says Peter Suciu, a "Forbes" contributor. "We live in the era of 'callout culture,' where individuals can quickly voice their displeasure publicly in a way that simply didn't exist in the past...

Social media has allowed everyone to have a voice, and in this callout culture there is the chance that news of very bad service can spread quickly. Companies now face a serious backlash, and this includes corporate giants as well as small businesses."

The incentive to act professionally has never been higher. A recent study by "WhoIsHostingThis.com" noted that it can take dozens of glowing reviews to reverse the damage from a single scathing complaint, especially if that complaint goes viral. Social media channels are now used more often than email or websites to reach brands. Even the term "customer service," typically associated with a company's response to a complaint, is being replaced with "customer care," defined as proactively meeting customers' needs.

The use of social media channels by both consumers and brands to exchange information, learn about experiences, resolve issues and proactively meet needs is one of many trends emerging from our modern digital culture.

While the world emerged in 2022 blinking in the daylight after two years spent indoors and online, the habits and relationships they built remain. Still, the number of engaged social media users grew 10% year-on-year with nearly 230 million new users coming online in 2022. Despite the increase in users, the amount of time people spend online seems to have plateaued. So what's changing? Figure 9.1 identifies the trends that are changing how we must think about and use social media.

 Figure 9.1
Social media trends

Game on. People all over the world are spending more time on game consoles, which have become "media hubs" with users accessing live TV and on-demand services. In-game advertising is a multibillion dollar industry. Organizations should connect and engage with publics in thoughtful and authentic ways. Use gaming to have some fun with your publics!

Social agility required. The lightning-speed changes in social media require a constant review of strategies and platforms to ensure alignment with your organization's mission, objectives, publics and messages. Pay attention to changing platform content policies and communities, and look for opportunities on new platforms to gain a "first-mover" advantage connecting with key publics.

24/7 social experience. With business and customers spanning nearly every time zone, speed and responsiveness must be key performance indicators. The focus on "customer care" means users expect immediate response 24/7 and are loyal to those brands that provide it. Dedicate resources to a 24/7 service structure and meet your publics where they are – across a wide variety of social platforms.

Time online has peaked. With less time to spare, media fatigue, and subscription churn it is increasingly difficult to capture attention. Make every engagement count. Track issues, engagement and reviews, and genuinely listen to users. Make engagement personal with human-led personal responses.

Community is key. People are gravitating to online communities that reflect them. Communities are receptive to brands and organizations that act authentically and contribute constructively. Look for communities to engage with using different channels and nuanced messaging that matches the platform and the community's needs.

Adapted from ICUC Social's 2023 Social Media Trends Report.

Social media is so pervasive in our lives that it will naturally be part of most company, government and nonprofit campaigns. As we discussed in Chapter 8, however, you should still think strategically about whether or not social media is appropriate for your campaign. If you determine that social media should be in the mix of channels that will form your strategy, the next step is to determine how you will use social media to inform, persuade and motivate behavior among your key publics so that you ultimately accomplish your campaign goals and objectives. Our goal here is to help you leverage social media in your campaigns to connect with key publics by learning how to choose the best platforms, create great content, disseminate news, hijack current events and use social media as a listening tool, all to accomplish objectives and get a solid return on your social media investment.

Choosing the best platforms

Several classes could be dedicated to choosing the best social media platforms for a campaign. There are close to 200 different social platforms running today. To simplify this process, take a look at Figure 9.2. This figure focuses on eight of the largest and most prominent platforms, comparing a wealth of comparable data mined from multiple sources to better understand the strengths and weaknesses of the different platforms.This is the kind of information you will need before choosing any platform to reach and connect with your publics.

Avery Horzewski, a successful marcom consultant, provides six tips for choosing the right social media platform for your business.

1. ***Start with your audience.*** While Facebook has the most active users, if your key public hangs out on Snapchat, that's where you need to be.
2. ***Consider your company.*** Your channel selection should be influenced by your products, services, brand personality and type of business. Consider how visual your brand is. Some channels have broad appeal; others are more niche.
3. ***Research your competitors and others in your industry.*** Analyze your competitors. What platforms are they using and how engaged are their publics on each channel?
4. ***Align with your overall social media marketing goals.*** Why are you on social in the first place? If you're interested in sharing content and engaging with your audience, TikTok or Instagram may be good options. If your primary goal is news dissemination or customer support, Twitter and Facebook could be better choices.
5. ***Understand the different platforms and their uses.*** Twitter is great for interaction and trending topics while LinkedIn lends itself to more professional exchanges and company information. Some are highly visual and support videos well. Some offer disappearing content.
6. ***Keep in mind your available resources.*** Using social media requires a commitment. Horzewski says, "You need to tend it, nurture it, give to it what you'd like to see come back to you." Limit your channels according to the resources you have to tend them.

Let's look at a campaign where you want to communicate in a highly visual way with teenage girls. Pew Research Center data confirms that a large percentage of adult women use Facebook, but so do men. On the other hand, the data show that

Figure 9.2
Comparing social media platforms

Social platform	Number of active users	Largest user groups	% U.S. adults using platform	% U.S. adults income $75K+	% U.S. adults college graduates	Average time per day	Typical content	Cost per click
Facebook	2.91 billion	25-34 (30%) 18-24 (22%)	women 77% men 61%	75%	73%	33 minutes	Photos & links Information Live video	$
Youtube	2.6 billion	25-34 (21%) 35-44 (17%)	women 80% men 82%	90%	89%	30 minutes	How-tos Webinars Explainers	$$
Instagram	2 billion	18-24 (31%) 25-34 (30%)	women 44% men 36%	47%	49%	29 minutes	Inspiration & Adventure Questions/ polls	$$
Tik Tok	1.8 billion	10-19 (33%) 20-29 (30%)	women 24% men 17%	20%	19%	89 minutes	Entertainment Humor Challenges	$
LinkedIn	810 million	25-34 (60%) 18-24 (22%)	women 26% men 31%	50%	51%	8 minutes	Long-form content Core values	$$$
Pinterest	431 million	25-34 (36%) 18-24 (22%)	women 46% men 16%	40%	37%	14 minutes	Recipes Creative ideas How-tos	$$
Snap Chat	319 million	18-24 (39%) 25-34 (23%)	women 28% men 22%	28%	23%	25 minutes	Silly Feel-good Trends	$
Twitter	211 million	35-44 (28%) 25-34 (27%)	women 22% men 25%	34%	33%	31 minutes	News Discussion Humor	$$

more women use Pinterest, Instagram and Snapchat than men, an indication that these platforms may be more appealing to your key public. Then again, are teenagers' social media habits the same as adults? You may want to choose a more segmented, teen-friendly social media platform such as TikTok. Which platform will be the best option?

First, you might look at how many teenagers use these platforms (Figure 9.3). User data show that TikTok has the youngest user mix with nearly two-thirds of its users being under 30 years old. Next is Snapchat followed by Instagram.

Now, let's look at gender. More women use all three platforms than men. Now consider the tools these platforms offer. We want to communicate in a highly visual way. Instagram is the most developed for visual content followed by TikTok then Snapchat. What type of information are we sending? Is it serious? Funny? Detailed? Assuming our message is humorous and short, we might choose to create a series of short videos. This being the case, TikTok would probably be a good fit, but may not be the only choice.

Figure 9.3
Changes in social media use among teens

% of U.S. teens who say they ever use any of the following apps or sites

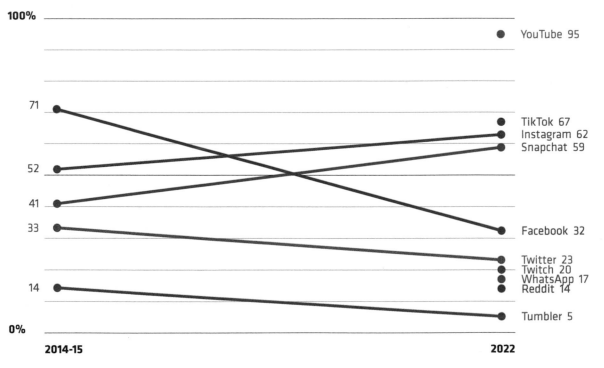

Note: Teens refer to those ages 13 to 17. Those who did not give an answer are not shown. The 2014-15 survey did not ask about YouTube, WhatsApp, Twitch and Reddit. TikTok debuted globally in 2018.

© 2022 Pew Research Center

If you were trying to reach males age 50+ with information about prostate screenings, what channel would you choose? How about pitching couture clothing to middle-aged women? Understanding the demographics of each platform (as in Figure 9.2) as well as the tools they provide can help you narrow the selection. Most platforms provide basic demographic information to advertisers and many publish it on their websites. Gather data to identify key demographics like age, gender, income, education, ethnicity, and language so you know who is using the platforms you are considering.

Next, determine how people are using them. Are they sharing stories, posting pictures, seeking news and information? What is their level of engagement? How often do they visit? How long do they stay? Do they post or comment? Take another quick look at Figure 9.2. The king of engagement is TikTok. Active users spend an average of 89 minutes a day. The next closest is Facebook at 33 minutes followed by Twitter at 31 minutes and YouTube at 30 minutes.

But don't just blindly choose TikTok as your platform of choice. Tap into each platform's published analytics to find out more about the demographic segment you're trying to reach. Then determine how much engagement you really need to effectively communicate your messages.

Now evaluate how well-suited a platform is to your purpose. Determine the activities at which each platform excels and what services it provides. Then match up the platforms with the needs of your key publics and messages.

Finally, consider the platform's potential to grow. Being an early adopter or "first-mover" can be a unique opportunity for branding and visibility. It helps you stay relevant in a fast-changing communications and marketing environment and builds trust with influencers and opinion leaders by connecting with them early before a platform gets too crowded.

The first step to early adoption is to engage with a new platform. You need to understand its nuances before you can determine how to use it. Starbucks was an early adopter of Pinterest. But the brand did little to direct its followers, and its **pinboard** became a target for negative responses.

Honda, on the other hand, picked up quickly that Pinterest provided an opportunity for collaboration. "It was a brilliant pivot, and one that would shape the future of marketing on Pinterest," writes Rosie Scott, a digital content strategist and avid blogger. "Honda launched a campaign called Pintermission, promising $500 to five top pinners to take a break from their pinning habit by taking a spin in a new Honda."

Take the time to begin personally using a new site before deciding if it's a good platform for your organization's engagement. Once you decide to engage, quickly seek out the influencers.

PINBOARD
Pages on Pinterest where users can save individual pins organized by a central topic or theme.

Creating great content

Social media content must be fresh, concise, visually interesting and highly shareable. The news media have been in the business of telling shareable stories for hundreds of years. News stories hook readers by focusing on story angles that emphasize timeliness, impact, proximity, conflict, unusualness and prominence. You can apply the same principle to social media content.

Hook your readers by creating content that is relevant and timely. You can't talk about "yesterday's game." Yesterday may as well have been last year.

TIPS FROM THE PROS

Making your social media work harder

Adam Durfee, PRNews Social Media Innovator of the Year and global social media director for Boncom International, a multinational agency focused on nonprofit and cause-based work, tips you off on how to use social media to amplify your message.

The rise of digital media has caused many to view it as a "brave new world" completely unlike anything we have experienced before in communications. But my work in this area has led me to realize that the basic principles of public relations and marketing communication still apply. The following two tips are prime examples.

Treat social media posts like any other media "pitches." Social media feeds work a lot like internet news feeds with algorithms as the editors. Have a message you want to pitch? Make sure it has a hook or it won't make it into your feed.

Time and time again I've worked with organizations trying to promote a product on social media without an interesting hook. If you approached a news organization that way, they'd tell you to "buy an ad," the same response any major social platform would give to fluffy, generic content. Start instead by asking yourself, "What's the story I'm telling?" "What's going to get social media scrollers to stop and look at what I've got?"

Reprinted by permission of The Utah Division of Forestry, Fire and State Lands.

I was recently on a team to design fire prevention messaging for social media. Instead of creating bland posts about dowsing campfires and being careful with fireworks, we created a rapper, "DJ Extinguish," and turned him into a TikTok star. We baked fire prevention messaging into the raps. We even choreographed a dance called the "Designated Dowser" that went viral. A single video from DJ Extinguish was seen by more people than all the previous prevention posts in an entire year. It might be hard to spice up messages about fire prevention, but you can change how they're delivered (400K followers).

Explore the boundaries of different platforms. So many people think of social media as a series of posts, stories, reels,etc. Putting your clients and campaigns in that type of restricted thinking can severely limit your ability to cut through the noise.

Try thinking about social media platforms as a tool kit. Here's an example. A state health department was trying to get more people to sign up for suicide prevention training. The training system they were using was not only expensive but also difficult for most people to access.

We recommended the department try something totally different. What if a social media platform could actually be used as the training platform? A tool like Instagram could be cheaper, easier for everyone to use, and scalable — adding as many people and as much content as needed.

The suicide prevention Instagram account @LiveOnUtah was converted into an online classroom. PowerPoint slides became Carousel posts. Lecture notes became captions. Student questions were posted as comments where "professors" could respond for all to see. The suicide prevention Instagram account trained more than 125,000 people in its first 30 days. The reach of the account increased by more than 4 million. What could you use a social media platform to accomplish?

Contributed by Adam Durfee. © Kendall Hunt Publishing Company.

Make your content shareable by including a strong self-interest appeal. This appeal could be funny, informative, tragic, celebratory or draw on any number of other emotions. The key to making content shareable is to provide something no one else has. People share things that demonstrate their personalities, show what they're interested in and, perhaps more than anything else, elevate their standing among their peers.

In social media, sentence length should be short and varied. Ideas must be communicated crisply. Visuals that may have been an afterthought in the past must be a forethought in today's media environment. Every blog post pretty much needs a picture — and the picture will largely determine how much attention the post gets. Social media posts with videos drive engagement. And videos on website landing pages increase conversion rates.

Disseminating news

TikTok insists it's an entertainment app, not social media. But more and more Americans are getting their news from TikTok, according to a new Pew Research Center survey. The percentage of people getting news from TikTok has tripled since 2020. About 10% of all U.S. adults now regularly get news on the app. For adults under 30, that jumps to 26%.

The truth is the news goes where the people are. It's not surprising that TikTok is becoming a source of news for millions. "Traditional" media have almost all migrated to social platforms and are also 24/7. Using social media to disseminate news about your company or cause has been a common practice for more than a decade. It works because of its immediacy, control and broad reach. A post can be made very quickly and immediately becomes available to the world. Organizations can control the content (within the platform's guidelines). They can draft it, edit it, stage it and film it before the world sees it. The reach for social posts, as we have already seen, can be tremendous.

Essentially, social and digital media have become an integral part of an organization's entire media relations function. A good practice is to choose a platform for your organization to regularly release news. Then archive on your website in an online "newsroom" any news released on social media as well as through traditional print and broadcast media. All of these media relations efforts should be occurring simultaneously. Today, Twitter is one of the most used platforms for releasing breaking news. Live tweets and real-time updates are used to track developing situations. Facebook Live is another popular way to release breaking news and timely interviews.

MINI CASE

Can United get away with breaking guitars?
Dave Carroll and United Airlines

Country music singer and songwriter Dave Carroll was stunned to see baggage handlers for United Airlines tossing his band's instruments while unloading their plane in Chicago. His band, Sons of Maxwell, was on their way from Canada to Nebraska for a weeklong concert tour. Carroll says that a woman sitting behind them, who didn't know they were musicians, yelled, "My God, they're throwing guitars out there." Mike, the bass player, looked out the window in time to see his bass guitar being heaved without regard by a baggage handler. Carroll's $3,500 Taylor guitar had already been tossed to the tarmac. Appeals for help from the flight attendant were referred to the gate agent who referred them to another agent, who referred them to a United employee who said, "But hun, that's why we make you sign the waiver."

   The airline had insisted the band check their instruments, but had not given them a damage waiver. Carroll's prized Taylor guitar had been severely damaged, costing him $1200 to repair. He spent nine months appealing to the airline to pay for the repairs to his guitar, speaking with United employees in Canada, India, Chicago and New York. When United finally denied Carroll's claim and said the issue was closed, the band leader decided to take matters into his own hands.

© Matthew Jacques/Shutterstock.com

CORE CHALLENGE

The core challenge was to persuade United Airlines to cover the cost of repairs to Dave Carroll's guitar that had been damaged as a result of the airline's baggage policy and negligence in baggage handling.

DAVE CARROLL'S STRATEGY

"It occurred to me that I had been fighting a losing battle all this time and that fighting over this at all was a waste of time," Carroll said. "The system is designed to frustrate affected customers into giving up their claims and United is very good at it. But I realized that as a songwriter and traveling musician I wasn't without options." Carroll decided to leverage his musical talents and the power of social media to rally others to his cause.

In his final reply to United, Carroll told the airline he would be writing three songs about his United experience. He also said he planned to make videos for these songs and post them on his website and on YouTube. Viewers could vote on which they liked best. His objective was to get 1 million YouTube views within a year. The airline's response was a sarcastic, "Good luck with that!"

RESULTS

- Carroll reached his objective of 1 million views in just four days. United eventually attempted to compensate Carroll, but he refused the offer, suggesting the money be given to someone else whose luggage had been damaged.
- The first YouTube video received 3.2 million views and 14,000 comments within 10 days of its release. To date, Carroll's music videos have been watched more than 25 million times.
- In the end, the videos cost Carroll about $150. Conversely, the bad publicity severely damaged United's reputation and contributed to a 10% drop in stock price – costing United shareholders an estimated $180 million.
- Because United failed to respond publicly even after the videos were posted, the airline's story was never told. Conversely, Carroll's story was picked up and shared with an estimated 100 million people through social media and traditional media, including CNN, "The Wall Street Journal," BBC, CBS "This Morning" and many other news outlets.

Hijacking current events

A common media strategy to market a brand using a viral news story is **newsjacking**. This strategy is frequently adopted by major brands to help them trend and expand their brand reach. In rare cases, the brand can become the center of the news story.

David Meerman Scott popularized the term newsjacking in 2012 when he released his book, "Newsjacking: How to Inject Your Ideas into a Breaking News Story and Generate Tons of Media Coverage." The basic idea is to find ways to make your organization part of a trending story that people are already talking about. This approach requires constant scanning of news, popular culture and conversations on social media. It also means that organizations need to be flexible enough to respond to abrupt changes in the news cycle or shifts in popular culture.

After a legal battle with Irish fast-food chain Supermac's, McDonald's lost its exclusive "Big Mac" trademark. While the fast-food giant could still keep using the name Big Mac for its sandwich in Europe, the

NEWSJACKING

Injecting your brand or organization into the conversation on a trending news story.

ruling noted that any other company could also use the term Big Mac on its menus and in its marketing.

Fast food competitor Burger King took full advantage of the situation by launching a handful of marketing content discussing its own Big Mac-like products. Burger King released European menus that promoted its own "Big Mac-ish" sandwiches and offered a limited-time, flame-grilled Big Mac that it claimed was bigger and tastier than the McDonald's menu item.

MoonPie, a company that has been making prepackaged marshmallow dessert sandwiches since 1917, adopted a full newsjacking strategy in 2017, coupled with a savage Twitter persona, to stand out in the escalating retail food wars. They also wanted to appeal to a younger target market. Throughout the year @moonpie tweeted about annual events including New Year's Eve, the Super Bowl, Mardi Gras, Pi Day, St. Patrick's Day, April Fool's Day and Mother's Day, with minimal success.

However, MoonPie struck gold on Aug. 21, 2017, when Hostess Snacks' Twitter account attempted to newsjack one of the biggest news stories of the year — the Great American Solar Eclipse. People traveled from all over the country to be in the 60-70 mile wide "path of totality," where the moon completely covered the disc of the sun and caused it to go dark. To join the conversation, @Hostess Snacks posted a picture of a cupcake eclipsing the sun tweeting that Hostess had "declared Golden CupCakes the official snack cake of the eclipse." @MoonPie simply tweeted, "Lol." The snarky response went viral. Patrick Wells of Tombras Group, the agency that manages the MoonPie Twitter account, explained his approach to "Forbes," "We posted it because it felt like something you'd honestly say back to someone saying something ridiculous to you." To date, the Tweet has generated 1,368 comments, 158,700 retweets and 435,700 likes. At the height of the Tweet's virality, 300 new people followed the account each day. This one timely tweet generated 1.1 billion media impressions in news outlets like "People," "USA Today," "Time," "Forbes" and "Business Insider." It also drove a 17% sales increase from social media alone, and September 2017 was the best sales month to date in the company's 100-year history.

The 2017 newsjacking strategy was so successful for MoonPie that the company has continued this light-hearted approach to marketing. When the U.S. shot down the Chinese spy balloon and several other unidentified flying objects in February 2023, @moonpie released an official statement welcoming the aliens and inviting them to satisfy their earthly cravings with delicious MoonPies!

Social media listening tools

One of the advantages of social media is the opportunity to receive immediate feedback. This allows organizations to monitor what is being said about them. Dell computers, for example, receives more than 25,000 mentions per day. The company uses various listening tools and filters to separate what they deem as important messages from background noise. Dell has been pretty successful at finding the messages that actually matter. These are messages from influential Twitter users with thousands of followers, stories posted on top tech blogs and forums, and urgent customer requests.

Similarly, Southwest Airlines is a very active brand on social media. The low-cost airline is a leader in customer service and social media interaction. They scored No. 1 in customer satisfaction in the J.D. Power 2022 North America Airline Satisfaction Study and have 2.1 million Twitter followers.

When Ryan, a 32-year-old consultant and frequent flyer, was stranded like thousands of others because of the weather. He tried unsuccessfully to make a reservation online and then phoned the reservation center, only to get a busy signal. So, he tweeted, "Why is your reservation number busy? Had a flight canceled today and can't seem to get through to reschedule. Ridic." Southwest's social media team responded within two minutes. Social media listening can quickly tell you when you have a problem or weakness in your system.

However, sometimes the situation is insurmountable. The combination of a brutal winter storm and massive system failures at Southwest Airlines in December 2022 led to 15,000 flight cancellations (10 times more than any other carrier) leaving 2 million passengers stranded over the Christmas holiday. On Dec. 28, 2022, the hashtag #southweststolechristmas was trending on Twitter as people shared their horror stories.

Weeks after the company's initial response during the crisis, Southwest's Chief Administration and Communications Officer Linda Rutherford acknowledged the company's failure. "Learning from failure is one of the greatest lessons in life. Some of the greatest comebacks in history are rooted in taking a hard look in the mirror, taking accountability, and doing what's required to not repeat your failures of the past."

Since the airline's meltdown, the company has begun testing new resource management systems and looking at ways to shore up its ability to communicate with passengers. We'll see if the airline can maintain its No.1 customer satisfaction ranking in 2023 and 2024.

In contrast, the social media team at Netflix is very good at what they do. Tech writer Alina Gorbatch says, "That's proven by the fact that their social media following keeps growing – Netflix U.S. alone has almost 6 million followers on Twitter. That is the whole population of Colorado!"

She continues,

> "They know key target audience factors: millennial; used to having friends that exist only online; crave attention; do research before purchasing; value peers' opinions more than that of movie stars; live for humor, self-irony, and sarcasm. And Netflix's social media marketing team keeps all of that in mind – they post hilarious tweets, re-tweet opinions of users with only a couple of followers, and work with relevant influencers."

Netflix acts as every internet user's best friend. The company explained at the Shorty Awards, "When we aren't posting, we're listening, looking for the new trends igniting the entertainment world."

Through social listening, Netflix learned that many binge-watchers were falling asleep. Netflix saw this as an opportunity to show that they listen, they care, and they are creative. In response, they invented Netflix Socks – smart socks that detect when the user is dozing off, send a signal to the user's TV and pause the show. This way, no one wakes up to a screen of spoilers and confusion. The product was cheered, went viral, got tons of coverage and even won a Shorty Award for creative use of technology (Gorbatch 2022).

Social media listening can quickly tell you when you have a problem or weakness in your system. It can also point out opportunities that may have gone unnoticed.

ROI (RETURN ON INVESTMENT)

Profit earned on an investment divided by the cost of that investment.

KPI (KEY PERFORMANCE INDICATOR)

An important measure tied to a campaign or social media objective and used to evaluate its success.

REACH

The total number of people who see your content.

ENGAGEMENT

An umbrella term for actions that reflect and measure audience interaction with your content.

CONVERSION

When a user completes a desired action, usually a purchase.

Return on social media investment

Many people think social media is free media. Nothing could be further from the truth. Managing and succeeding in social media takes time, people and technology — all of which are limited resources with associated costs. It takes time to listen. It takes people to generate the massive amounts of necessary content. It takes technology to analyze the results and adjust your strategy. And increasingly it means spending money to put your content in front of the publics you want to see it. Is it worth it?

As we will discuss in Chapter 12, measurement is crucial in evaluating whether or not we have reached objectives. Social media largely falls into the outtake objective category (key publics' response to messages). But to determine if social media strategies are truly worth the expenditure, we should focus on one of our measurement tools: **return on investment (ROI)**.

Joy Elena, CEO of Sleepenvie, a high-end mattress and pillow retailer that has had success selling its products on social media, told "AdWeek," "If you have 1 million followers and they aren't making actual purchases, then you should revisit your strategy. Businesses need to identify performance indicators that are most important to them and track those indicators." Commonly referred to as **key performance indicators (KPIs)**, these metrics focus on digital and social media outcomes and outtakes like **reach**, **engagement**, **conversions** and customer loyalty. The most commonly used metrics are shown in Figure 9.4.

As you consider different measures to evaluate your social media success, make sure you tie your measures to the objectives you've already established. Measuring the impact of your social media efforts requires upfront planning. You will need several tools to accurately determine engagement and how far user's actions take them. You may want to start with a resource like the Social Media Measurement Framework, which was created by the International Association for the Measurement and Evaluation of Communication (AMEC), to identify potential KPIs across a variety of outcomes, including exposure, engagement, preference, impact and advocacy. Posting content for and interacting with key publics on social media isn't worth much if it doesn't lead them to action that accomplishes your goals and objectives.

Figure 9.4
Most common metrics used to measure social media ROI

% of respondents

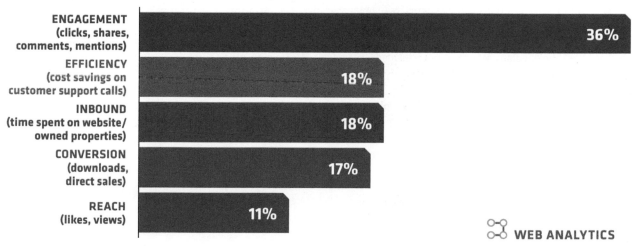

ENGAGEMENT (clicks, shares, comments, mentions) 36%
EFFICIENCY (cost savings on customer support calls) 18%
INBOUND (time spent on website/owned properties) 18%
CONVERSION (downloads, direct sales) 17%
REACH (likes, views) 11%

Source: Altimeter, "The 2021 State of Digital Content," May 14, 2021

"Sprout Social" writer Rebekah Carter identified the following KPIs to track conversions from social media content: sales revenue, lead conversion rate and non-revenue conversions. Some KPIs can be determined using social media data that you can access through the analytics portal of your social media accounts. However, many of the most valuable KPIs track users' behavior as they move from your social media channels to and through your website. Gathering data of this sort requires the use of **web analytics**.

According to Usability.gov, "Web analytics is the collection, reporting, and analysis of website data." This data is collected through a **tracking pixel** or code that is embedded in a website's HTML. The tracking pixel transfers the data to a web analytics platform like Google Analytics, where it can be mined for insights about your website visitors' behaviors.

Some other terms you may encounter as you work with social media channels are CPM, CPC and CPA. **CPM** stands for cost per "mille," or thousand, the amount of money you spend to generate 1,000 impressions of your message. **CPC** stands for cost per click or the amount of money it costs you to get someone to click on your web or social media content. **CPA** stands for the cost per action or the amount of money it costs for a customer conversion, such as getting a person to buy a product or share their contact information with you.

We are seeing the rise of better social media measurement tools that don't just track clicks and likes, but rather look at real measures of engagement in the form of discussion, shares across multiple platforms/channels and actions taken. Christina Newberry of measurement firm Hootsuite, recommends steps to determine the ROI of your social media (see Figure 9.5). Remember that measuring ROI on social media isn't primarily designed to see if your organization and campaign objectives are met. It is designed to determine if the expenditure on social media strategies is worth its contribution to those objectives.

WEB ANALYTICS
The measurement, collection, analysis and reporting of internet data for the purpose of understanding and optimizing web usage.

TRACKING PIXEL
A snippet of code embedded in a website's HTML that captures and tracks user data.

CPM (COST PER MILLE OR THOUSAND)
The cost of generating 1,000 impressions of your content.

CPC (COST PER CLICK)
The cost of getting a person to click on your content.

CPA (COST PER ACTION)
The cost of converting a website or social media user into a customer.

Figure 9.5
Determining ROI of social media strategies

Step 1: Calculate how much you spend on social media. Your social media costs might include:
- The cost of tools and platforms for managing social.
- The budget allocated to social ad spends.
- Content creation: In-house and external content creation costs, including working with creators and/or freelancers.
- The ongoing costs for your social media team (salaries, training, etc.).
- Agencies and consultants, if you use them.

Step 2: Define clear social objectives that connect to overall business goals. Clear social media objectives help define how social actions align with business and departmental goals. Think about various ways your social media investment might create value, like:
- Business conversions (such as lead generation, newsletter signups or sales).
- Brand awareness or sentiment.
- Customer experience and loyalty.
- Employee trust and job satisfaction.
- Partner and supplier confidence.
- Security and risk mitigation.

Step 3: Track metrics that align with your objectives. All social media metrics can tell you something about whether you're achieving objectives and meeting your goals. Metrics you can track to prove ROI include:
- Reach.
- Audience engagement.
- Site traffic.
- Leads generated.
- Sign-ups and conversions.
- Revenue generated.

Step 4: Create an ROI report that shows the impact of social. Once you've got your data, share the results with the right stakeholders to show how social media marketing affects your organization's bottom line. Here are some ways to make your report stand out:
- Use a template.
- Use plain language (avoid jargon and insider acronyms).
- Tie results back to the relevant business objectives.
- Use KPIs to track short-term progress.
- Articulate limitations and be clear about what you can (and can't) measure.

Source: C. Newberry (2022). Hootsuite

Paid digital

Paid digital refers to external marketing efforts that involve a paid placement or boosted social content. With rising inflation and a global economic slowdown, companies need to be more careful than ever about how they spend advertising and marketing dollars. Figure 9.6 identifies a number of trends to consider.

 Figure 9.6
A few digital marketing trends

TikTok is big. The platform generated $4.6 billion in revenue in 2021 and now has over 1.8 billion monthly active users. It is focusing on usability for businesses and improving targeting options for advertising which will make it an even better brand platform.

"Creator economy" is growing. Platforms are investing in quality content creation by providing incentives to content creators (employees, customers, subject matter experts) to provide engaging content. Platforms like TikTok, YouTube and Twitch are searching for creators that have a voice and a fan base.

Video, video, video. Video has great power to inform and connect, and 86% of businesses use it as a marketing tool. Used for everything from explaining to training, YouTube, LinkedIn and Instagram are the top three channels used for video campaigns.

Use content to drive connections. Look for ways to use content to make connections with and build communities. People want to buy from companies with values that align with their own. The right content can demonstrate an organization's values in meaningful ways.

Redefine creator/brand partnerships. There's sooooo much content out there, and some is not aligned with the right influencer or targeted at the right public. Creators want to grow and expand, and are looking for brand partnerships that align with their content. Brand-audience fit is important, as are brand values and purpose, ease of collaboration and whether they actively use the product or service.

Signal-based marketing. There is a shift from technical-based marketing to anticipation marketing where customer "signals" tell you what they want. Algorithms match signals to anticipate needs and wants allowing for more personalization on platforms like Google, Facebook and other social channels.

Increase in martech spending. Martech spending in the U.S. passed $20 billion in 2022, primarily from companies investing in marketing technology (martech software) to create, execute, manage and measure the performance of content, campaigns and experiences. It is also used to streamline customer journeys and implement omnichannel marketing campaigns.

Metaverse to become real. Growth of the metaverse has been slower than expected, but experts believe it is about to become real as brands plot their strategy for this new era of immersive virtual communication. "Nike recently announced that they are going to allow people to design their own trainers, and sell those or wear them in the metaverse."

Adapted from C. O'Brien (2022), Digital Marketing Institute.

Figure 9.7
Digital advertising spending worldwide from 2021 to 2026

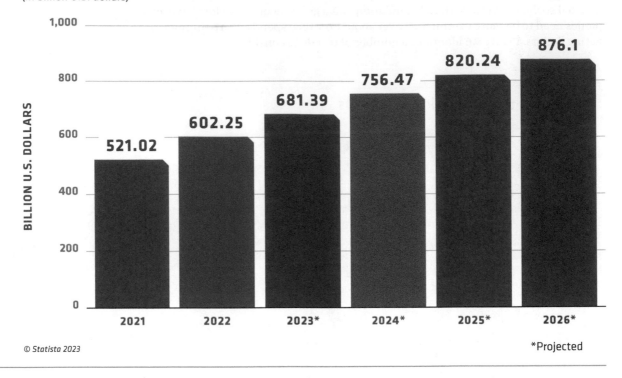

(in billion U.S. dollars)

© Statista 2023

*Projected

According to Clodagh O'Brien of the Digital Marketing Institute,

> "As customers become more discerning about the products and services they buy, there's also a global cost of living crisis that brands will need to plan for in 2023. That means it's more important for brands to be transparent and think about their messaging and research or tweak their strategy in the coming year. It also means that marketers need to know the trends coming down the line so they can plan and take advantage of any new developments."

Worldwide spending in digital advertising has grown exponentially and is expected to reach nearly $900 billion in 2026 (see Figure 9.7). Paid media is an essential component of revenue growth and brand awareness for online businesses. The five basic types of paid digital media are: paid search, native advertising, display advertising, paid social and influencer marketing.

Paid search
Paid search advertising is a digital marketing strategy that allows companies/organizations to pay to have links to their websites show up higher on relevant search engine results pages. The goal is to drive traffic to a specific site.

Google is by far the biggest player in the search sphere. Google Ads operates under a **pay per click (PPC)** model. That means marketers target a specific keyword on Google and make bids on the keyword — competing with others also targeting the keyword. The bids you make are "maximum bids" or the maximum you're willing to pay for an ad. For example, if your maximum bid is $4 and Google determines that your cost per click is $2, then you get that ad placement. If they determine that it's more than $4, you do not get the ad placement. Alternatively, you can set a maximum daily budget for your ad. You'll never spend more than a specific amount for that ad per day, helping you get a better sense of how much you should budget for your digital ad campaign.

When a user searches the keyword, sees the ad and clicks on it, the marketer pays a small fee for that click (thus PPC). The idea is that the more users click on an advertisement, the more likely they will help accomplish the advertisement's purpose (e.g., become a lead, make a purchase).

Search ads play a critical role capturing the attention of people searching for a specific topic or product. They are particularly effective when used to increase a company's customer base or when an organization wants to become a thought leader on a given subject.

PPC (PAY PER CLICK)
Paying for social media advertising based on each time a user clicks on ad content.

Native advertising

This type of digital ad is designed to mimic the look, feel and function of the platform it appears on. It is meant to not look like an ad, but to look like editorial content. While most native advertising is found on social media, it can appear in many places and in many forms. Some interesting uses of native ads that "blend in" are: Spotify playlists, Instagram and Snapchat story filters, social in-feed ads, TikTok videos and sponsored articles or posts.

Native advertising is meant to mirror the appearance of regular content on an app or website and thus not appear as an ad at first glance. There are some critiques of native ads as "tricking" users into thinking they are engaging with non-advertising content. However, most native advertising distributes high-quality content in engaging formats.

Let's say you run a candy company that uses milk from dairy farms in your area. You could partner with an online publisher to create "advertorial" content. This is essentially a paid placement for editorial content you control. Your content could highlight local dairy farmers and their impact on the community. This article would then be published with the disclosure that the content is sponsored or promoted by your company. While it is still a paid ad, customers will appreciate your company's authenticity if the content is engaging, insightful and educational.

Native advertising doesn't always have to come in the form of a content post. Music player giant Spotify can create custom playlists based on a company's services, products or themes, and use Spotify's user data to recommend specific playlists based on listening history. A great example of this is Netflix and Spotify teaming up to promote the show "Stranger Things." Users could enable

© Daniel Constante/Shutterstock.com

a "Stranger Thing" mode that assigned them to a playlist based on a character. Not only did this promote the show through background art design and logos, but it resonated with listeners since the playlist tracks mimicked their own listening interests.

Native advertising has a 40x higher click-through rate than classic display ads and 53% of consumers look at native ads more often than classic display ads. This form of promoted content allows marketing communication teams to create high value, enjoyable experiences for target publics. Native ads blend in, are considered relevant and are growing in popularity. The biggest downside to native advertising is the amount of work that typically goes into producing these ads.

Display advertising

When most people think of online advertising, display advertising usually comes to mind. These are the banner ads, pop-ups and promotional image tiles that appear on websites, apps and social media platforms across the web.

Businesses work with platforms like Google Display Network and Facebook's Audience Network to create display ads and target relevant customers. The targeting capabilities of these tools are rather impressive. However, display ads tend to have little impact on your business. Display ads can help drive brand awareness, but not much else. They have an incredibly low average click-through rate of 0.35% and can come off as intrusive and annoying to customers. Most people ignore display ads or even download ad blockers to avoid them completely.

Paid social advertising

Social media marketing is one of the best ways to interact with potential customers online. Seventy-two percent of adults in the U.S. use at least one social media site. With so many social media users, you can leverage customer data to create highly targeted ads for your publics. You also have the option of producing ads in a variety of formats that make sense for your business—photo ads, video ads, story ads, retargeting ads and promoted posts.

It often costs relatively little to promote social media posts and increase their reach beyond what the algorithms typically serve up. By boosting or promoting an important post, story or video, it will appear in the news feeds of more people. It's not cost effective to boost every post, but boosting a select few each month might be a good way to increase your company's exposure.

For social advertising, Facebook's specific audience-targeting ability is unlike any other platform. You can target micro audiences, customers who have done business with your competitors and retarget your previous customers. Facebook has the most diverse user demographics and gives you the greatest control.

However, as more businesses have realized the effectiveness of Facebook ads, the cost of those ads has gone up. Other platforms are becoming increasingly competitive— eating away Facebook's share of social ad dollars.

Twitter's platform is a powerful tool for organic reach with customers. You can run Twitter ads, but it may be difficult for brick-and-mortar companies to realize any worthwhile results. LinkedIn is an excellent channel for creating business-to-business (B2B) ads. You have the benefit of targeting ads based on criteria like job title and job industry. Keep in mind that LinkedIn is a professional community, so only consider running ads there if it aligns with your business model.

YouTube video ads typically have high engagement rates with customers. The downside is that video content is costly to produce. YouTube can also be quite pricey in comparison to other types of digital advertising. Pinterest offers a great advertising option for connecting with a predominantly female audience. However, the platform is best suited for e-commerce businesses looking to sell items online. Snapchat and TikTok users are typically between ages 18–24, making them good channels for reaching younger audiences.

Regardless of the platform mix you choose, it is a best practice to run A/B ad tests. Create at least two versions of an ad and test them out before allocating your entire ad budget. You will be surprised by what you learn from A/B testing. This will help you maximize the return on your advertising dollars.

Influencer marketing

Influencer marketing involves a brand collaborating with an online influencer to market one of its products or services. The field has blossomed into a $16.4 billion business. And companies are seeing strong returns. Businesses are making an average of $5.2 ROI for every $1 spent on influencer marketing.

An early example of influencer marketing involved YouTube celebrity PewDiePie. He teamed up with the makers of a horror film set in the catacombs under Paris, creating a series of videos in which he underwent challenges in the catacombs. Werner Geyser, an influencer marketing expert, says, "It was pitch-perfect content for PewDiePie's 111 million subscribers and received nearly double the views as the movie's trailer."

Geyser explains:

> Influencers, unlike celebrities, can be anywhere. They can be anyone. What makes them influential is their large followings on the web and social media. An influencer can be a popular fashion photographer on Instagram, or a well-read cybersecurity blogger who tweets, or a respected marketing executive on LinkedIn. Within any industry, there are influential people — you just have to find them. Some will have hundreds of thousands (if not millions) of followers. But many will seem more like ordinary people. They may only have 10,000 followers, less in some cases. Yet, they will have developed a reputation for being the experts in their field.

Influencer marketing means compensating the influencer for content they create and share with others. Compensation can be as little as free products, flights or hotel stays, but more often involves a paid contract to produce and share a specified amount of content. The best approach is to treat influencer marketing like a long-term collaboration, avoiding dictating what you'd like the influencer to do, rather guiding them and providing real feedback as they work with your organization. The other key is not to expect immediate results. Influencer marketing is a long-term strategy to build awareness and credibility.

"Carefully consider your approach to influencer marketing," says Geyser. He advises doing research before crafting a strategy, plan and budget. He suggests finding the right influencers "organically" by subscribing to a platform or working through an agency. He stresses the need to be patient and personal in your relationships with influencers.

Choosing the right influencer is critical. Make sure their followers are real and that engagement with them is substantive. Spend time to understand the influener's "brand" and make sure it aligns with your company's identity and goals.

Content marketing

Content marketing is the process of planning, creating, distributing, sharing and publishing content for the purpose of selling products or services via channels like social media, blogs, websites, podcasts, apps and print publications. Some of the best types of content to share are videos, infographics, consumer tools, research articles and other editorial content. Content marketing fits into the owned and shared categories of the PESO model.

Content marketing establishes expertise, promotes brand awareness and keeps your business top of mind when it's time for customers to buy what you sell. The

© TierneyMJ/Shutterstock.com

ultimate goal is to reach your target publics to increase brand awareness, engagement, loyalty and sales or some other action. Content marketing is all about laying the groundwork, building a strong base of trust and support for a company or organization to flourish.

As we learned in Chapter 1, trust is our most important asset. Without it companies will not survive, politicians will ultimately fail and social organizations will flounder.

Creating winning marketing content

Good writers know to avoid clichés "like the plague." If you're not reading something fresh, you tend to stop reading altogether. To be useful, marketing content must offer the reader, viewer or user something they don't already have.

There are literally hundreds of best tips for digital marketing content creation out there. However, we felt that Hubspot writer Janet Aronica took a fresh approach with her "6 Tips for Creating Content That Spreads Naturally." Here's a brief summary of those tips.

1. **Don't try something new.** Examine your analytics and see what's generating the most views, shares and leads and create content that replicates that success.
2. **Surprise people.** Create marketing content that evokes a strong emotional reaction so your audience feels compelled to share it.
3. **Nail your headline.** It must be "attention-grabbing and intriguing." She stresses that subject lines and headlines must show the content will be useful, ultra-specific, unique and urgent.

4. **Show don't tell.** Visuals like photos, videos and graphics increase engagement and shares. A strong infographic can tell your story better than a thousand words and a good video captures attention and results in conversions.

5. **Enable your blog to market your content.** Use your blog space to improve the presentation of your content and offer "further recommendations" to earn the attention and loyalty of new visitors.

6. **Don't forget about SEO.** Use keyword research. Optimize and update your marketing content and it will surface more frequently on search engine results.

Another creative approach is to develop useful consumer tools. Mortgage banks offer free online mortgage calculators that enable consumers to quickly calculate mortgage payments under several different scenarios. The right tools can entice users to spend time with you. Mortgage banks capture email leads when users log in to use these tools.

Finally, consider adding visuals to your email marketing. One of the many reason's Warby Parker stands out from other online glasses retailers is its fun and eye-catching (no pun intended) email marketing campaigns. In one recent series of emails, Warby Parker welcomes summer vacation with its bright crystal-themed eyewear. The calls to action in the email are easy to spot, the colors are bright and fun, and the company's social media accounts are clearly presented.

Investing in owned channels

Building a number of owned channels can be one of the best ways to engage with publics. Investing in websites, email lists, **SMS** (text) marketing, blog content and podcasts can all yield strong results. Some of these channels, such as email and SMS marketing, can yield almost immediate results. The best way to build email and SMS lists is through social media campaigns and website pop-ups. To encourage enrollment, offer incentives for customers to sign up and then deliver exclusive content and deals to reward those who give you their email address and phone number.

SMS marketing is one of the fastest growing areas of marketing. Figure 9.8 compares email to SMS marketing open rates, click through rates and conversion rates. With such high click through and conversion rates, it's easy to see why companies are investing in SMS. The biggest challenge with SMS marketing is convincing people to share their phone numbers and to opt in for marketing content. SMS marketing also costs more than using emails and requires a third-party app to manage permissions and deliver messages.

Investing in robust web content, podcasts, YouTube channels and other owned content can also pay long-term dividends. Marriott International, the world's largest hospitality company, has invested heavily in owned content to reach the "next

SMS (SHORT MESSAGE/ MESSAGING SERVICE) Sending short text messages from one cell phone to another or from a computer to a cell phone.

Figure 9.8
Email vs. SMS marketing

	EMAIL MARKETING	SMS MARKETING
OPEN RATES	11%–15%	95%–99%
CLICK THROUGH RATES	1%–3%	30%–40%
CONVERSION RATES	.09%–1.5%	20%–30%

Source: Chatitive

generation of travelers." The company built a content studio, created TV shows, published a number of blogs, produced short films and launched its own travel network.

"We have a very intimate relationship with our customers," says David Beebe, Marriott vice president of global creative and content marketing. "They sleep with us, after all. It's sort of a joke, but it's true."

Marriott's success story relies on the fact that they managed to build a great culture of storytelling, using stories to build relationships and make people care. Beebe explains, "Content marketing is like a first date. If you only talk about yourself, there won't be a second one." We invite you to learn more about Marriott's success in the Application Case at the end of this chapter.

Summary

Social and digital media have completely changed the way we live. They have changed the way we get news, interact with each other, shop and work. Despite some being 20 years old, social media channels continue to evolve and new channels emerge. TikTok is the fastest growing social media channel. It boasts 1.8 billion active users, nearly as many as Instagram. The use of designed visuals, photos and videos continues to rise. Highly visual content is most effective at capturing attention and garnering engagement.

Paid digital media is a huge industry at nearly $700 billion worldwide. While paid search and social media advertising account for the lion's share, native advertising is the fastest growing segment. Influencer marketing also remains popular and continues to grow.

The goal of content marketing is to increase brand awareness, engagement and loyalty. It is a successful way to lay the groundwork and build a strong base of support and trust for a company. Many companies and organizations have seen their investment in owned content pay off through enhanced loyalty, higher sales and increased involvement.

Application case

How to become a successful media company
from Marriott International

In 1927, J. Willard Marriott opened a nine-stool root beer stand that grew into the Hot Shoppes restaurant chain and later into Marriott International, the world's largest hospitality company. Today the company has 30 brands with 8,000 properties in 131 countries and territories.

Bill Marriott, chairman of the board and son of the founder, says the company's strategy has always been to "take care of our people and they will take care of our guests." He added, "My father lived by the motto, 'success is never final.' We've always been a change maker. We're always looking over the hill for the next opportunity."

CORE OPPORTUNITY

How can Marriott connect with the next generation of hotel guests?

BACKGROUND

The company began its storytelling journey more than 10 years ago with the launch of a blog called "Marriott On the Move," written by Bill Marriott. His first response to writing a blog was, "Why the heck would anyone want to read a blog from me?" But execs convinced him that he was the best person to tell the company's story.

With the blog's success, the company delved deeper, much deeper into owned content. In 2013 and 2014, Marriott hired several marketing execs and storytellers from the Walt Disney Company and in 2015 added media veterans from CBS and "Variety."

The company recognized that younger travelers spent a lot of time online, that they were looking for fun, creative content and that they could be just as loyal to brands as their parents.

CREATING OWNED CONTENT

By 2015 Marriott had created a successful TV show, "The Navigator Live;" a short film, "The Two Bellmen;" an online travel magazine; and had even ventured into virtual reality with "Oculus Rift." According to Marina Mouka, a writer for "Medium," "The projects generated immediate success, from high engagement metrics to millions in direct revenue and even content licensing deals."

The company continued to produce short films including sequels to "The Two Bellmen" and "French Kiss," set at a Marriott hotel in Paris. They also built a global content studio called "M Live" with nine screens, showing everything from the social media campaigns of Marriott's different brands to real-time booking information and Marriott's editorial calendar.

Charley Gallay / Stringer / Getty Images Entertainment / Getty Images

SUCCESS

Since it was released, "French Kiss" has been viewed over 6 million times on YouTube. Perhaps more impressively, a bookings promotion related to the film also drove $500,000 in revenue for the hotel.

"We did not get this far by saying, 'I want to build a media company,'" says David Beebe, vice president of global creative and content marketing. "First and foremost, [the goal] is to engage consumers. Get them to associate with our brands, build lifetime value with them. Content's a great way to do that."

The company's media success came from "scaling content, then building a community around that content, and driving commerce," Beebe explains. This combination is the key to reaching millennials who are increasingly seeking more intimate connections and experiences when they travel.

In May 2022, Marriott announced the launch of its own travel media network powered by Yahoo. The Marriott Media Network allows the company to further leverage its content and offer brand advertisers exposure to high-intent travelers. The network will tap into the more than 164 million members in Marriott Bonvoy, the company's award-winning travel program, and leverage owned channels including display, mobile, video, email and digital out-of-home (in-room television and digital screens).

Assume you are a member of Marriott's content creation team. The company has been successful at reaching millennials. But what about Gen Z travelers? Do some research and suggest two or three types of owned content you think Marriott should create to engage with Gen Z. Explain what makes this content different from content created for millennials.

References and additional readings

Ahmad, I. (2018, March 6). The state of video marketing in 2018 [Infographic]. *Social Media Today*. Retrieved from https://www.socialmediatoday.com/news/the-state-of-video-marketing-in-2018-infographic/518339/

AMEC. (2023). Measurement and Evaluation Resources. *International Association for the Measurement and Evaluation of Communication*. Retrieved from https://amecorg.com/

Armistead, D. (2009, July 21). Examining 'United breaks guitars' – lessons learned the hard way. Retrieved from http://socialwebstrategies.com/2009/07/21/examining-united-breaks-guitars-lessons-learned-the-hard-way/

Aronica, J. (2022, October 10). 6 tips for creating content that spreads naturally. Retrieved from https://blog.hubspot.com/blog/tabid/6307/bid/33906/6-tips-for-creating-content-that-spreads-naturally.aspx

Barnhart, B. (2022, March 2). Social media demographics to inform your brand's strategy in 2022. *Sprout Social*. Retrieved from https://sproutsocial.com/insights/new-social-media-demographics/#facebook-demographics

Battisby, A. (2021, October 21). 9 ideas for social media videos. *Digital Marketing Institute*. Retrieved from https://digitalmarketinginstitute.com/blog/9-ideas-for-social-media-videos

Beer, J. (2017). Meet the agency that turned MoonPie into Twitter's funniest snack cake. *Fast Company*. Retrieved from https://www.fastcompany.com/40510696/meet-the-agency-that-turned-moonpie-into-twitters-funniest-snack-cake

Bertam, M. (2022, January 19). What is newsjacking: 5 examples that get it right. *Search Engine Journal*. Retrieved from https://www.searchenginejournal.com/newsjacking-examples/476182/#close

Block, J. (2020, April 1). Bill Marriott talks about his new book, "Success Is Never Final, and The Deal That Slipped Away." *Small Business Journal*. Retrieved from https://thesbjournal.com/featured/bill-marriott-talks-about-his-new-book-success-is-never-final-and-the-deal-that-slipped-away/

Boachie, P. (2018, August 21). Top 5 KPIs social media marketers need to track and improve. *AdWeek*. Retrieved from https://www.adweek.com/digital/top-5-kpis-social-media- marketers-need-to-track-and-improve/

Bump, P. (2021, December 14). 8 recent examples of newsjacking in action. Retrieved from https://blog.hubspot.com/marketing/newsjacking-examples

Carroll, D. (2008). United breaks guitars: Story. Retrieved from http://www.davecarroll-music.com/music/ubg/story/

Carter, R. (2018, January 16). The ultimate list of social media KPIs to leverage business growth. *Sprout Social*. Retrieved from https://sproutsocial.com/insights/social-media-kpis/

Cavello, M. (2022, December 14). 140 must-know social media statistics for 2023. *G2*. Retrieved from https://www.g2.com/articles/social-media-statistics

Champion, J. (2022, July 26). 20 Content marketing examples that stand out in 2022. Retrieved from https://blog.hubspot.com/marketing/marketing-examples-online-resources

Chen, J. (2021, September 2). Choosing the right social media channels for your business. *Sprout Social*. Retrieved from: https://sproutsocial.com/insights/social-media-channels/

Dean, B. (2021, October 10). Social media usage & growth statistics: How many people use social media in 2022? *Backlinko*. Retrieved from: https://backlinko.com/social-media-users

Evans, M. (2012, February 13). Broken guitar leads to startup consumer gripe site. Retrieved from http://www.theglobeandmail.com/report-on-business/small-busi- ness/starting-out/broken-guitar-leads-to-startup-consumer-gripe-site/article4171528/

Facebook. (2023, February. 25). @SamsungUS. Retrieved from https://www.facebook.com/SamsungUS

Farbeen, F. (2019, February 4). Burger King pokes fun at McD's for losing Big Mac trademark. *Marketing-Interactive*. Retrieved from https://www.marketing-interactive.com/burger-king-pokes-fun-at-mcds-for-losing-big-mac-trademark/

Forbes. (2022). What Are 4 Areas of SEO? Beginners Guide to Understanding SEO. Retrieved from https://books.forbes.com/blog/what-4-areas-of-seo-beginners-guide-seo/?device=c&network=x&keyword=&creative=&matchtype=&utm_channel_source=google+ads&utm_id=17427129337&utm_medium=cpc&device=c&utm_term=&utm_content=&placement=&matchtype=&adposition=&network=x&target=&utm_campaign=Leads-Performance+Max-JM&gclid=Cj0KCQiAo-yfBhD_ARIsANr56g53AaVbQ3sBEOLIS2-jN-uJFIxDqnWeF3fe5oJXUfokeAUGq4SJHJwaAgzlEALw_wcB

Gencher, N. (2023, January 20). 4 consumer trends to watch in 2023. *GroundTruth*. Retrieved from: https://www.groundtruth.com/insight/consumer-trends-to-watch/

Geyser, W. (2023, January 20). What is influencer marketing? — The ultimate guide for 2023. *Influencer Marketing Hub*. Retrieved from https://influencermarketinghub.com/influencer-marketing/

Gilbertson, D. (2014, January 8). Airline passengers increasingly vent on social media sites about travel woes. *USA Today*. Retrieved from http://www.usatoday.com/story/travel/flights/2014/01/08/frustrated-fliers-turn-to-twitter/4368629/

Gomez, R. (2022, December 4). How 3 top brands provide social media customer service and support. *Sprout Social*. Retrieved from https://sproutsocial.com/insights/social-media-customer-service/

Gorbatch, A. (2022, February 25). 4 inspiring social listening examples from brands doing it right. *Jeff Bullas*. Retrieved from https://www.jeffbullas.com/social-listening-examples/

Grush, L. (2017, August 21). Solar eclipse 2017: What you need to know. *The Verge*. Retrieved from https://www.theverge.com/2017/8/7/16025284/total-solar-eclipse-2017-date- time-lunar-map-glasses-path

GWI (n.d.). Connecting the dots: Discover the trends that'll dominate 2023. Retrieved from: https://www.gwi.com/connecting-the-dots

Horzewski, A. (n.d.). 6 tips for choosing the right social media platform for your business. *Aventi Group*. Retrieved from https://aventigroup.com/blog/6-tips-for-choosing-the-right-social-media-platform-for-your-business/

Howarth, J. (2023, January 6). 6 key public relations trends in 2023. *Exploding Topics*. Retrieved from: https://explodingtopics.com/blog/public-relations-trends

Howarth, J. (2022, December 6). 9 key consumer behavior trends (2023-2026). *Exploding Topics*. Retrieved from: https://explodingtopics.com/blog/consumer-behavior

Huffington Post. (2009, August 24). 'United breaks guitars': Did it really cost the airline $180 million? Retrieved from http://www.huffingtonpost.com/2009/07/24/united-breaks-guitars-did_n_244357.html

ICUC Social. (2022). 2023 social media trends. Retrieved from https://icuc.s3.ca-central-1.amazonaws.com/2023+Social+Media+Trends+Report.pdf

Iqbal, M. (2023, January 31). Twitter revenue and usage statistics (2023). *Business of Apps*. Retrieved from https://www.businessofapps.com/data/twitter-statistics/

J.D. Power. (2022, May 11). North American airline passenger satisfaction declines: Here's why that's good news, says J.D. Power. News release. Retrieved from https://www.jdpower.com/business/press-releases/2022-north-america-airline-satisfaction-study

Jones, K. (2021, June 29). How social media helps SEO [final answer]. *Search Engine Journal*. Retrieved from https://www.searchenginejournal.com/social-media-seo/196185/#close

Kim, E. K. (2017, July 19). The Great American Eclipse is coming: How to catch the best views. *Today*. Retrieved from https://www.today.com/money/great-american-solar-eclipse-2017-travel-tips-best-views-t113965

Kneen, B. (n.d.). CPM, CPC, and CPA pricing for online media. Retrieved from https://written.com/blog/51/cpm-cpc-cpa-pricing-online-media

Lebedeva, A. (2016, July 10). PESO model: Implement and measure the four media types. *Spin Sucks*. Retrieved from: https://spinsucks.com/communication/implement-measure-peso-model/

Lebow, S. (2021, June 14). The top metrics content executives use for measuring performance. *Insider Intelligence*. Retrieved from https://www.insiderintelligence.com/content/top-metrics-content-executives-use-measuring-performance

Marriott International (2022, May 16). Marriott International introduces travel media network, powered by Yahoo. *News Center*. Retrieved by https://news.marriott.com/news/2022/05/16/marriott-international-introduces-travel-media-network-powered-by-yahoo

MasterClass. (2022, February 10). Native advertising definition: 5 examples of native advertising. Retrieved from https://www.masterclass.com/articles/native-advertising

Media Update (2022, July 20). The role of social media platforms in news dissemination [Infographic]. *Search Engine Journal*. Retrieved from https://www.searchenginejournal.com/social-media-seo/196185/#close

Meta. (2021, January 27). Reporting the news live on Facebook. *Meta Journalism Project*. Retrieved from https://www.facebook.com/journalismproject/tools/video/facebook-live-for-newsrooms

Michigan Tech. (n.d.). Five ways to improve your site's ranking (SEO). Retrieved from https://www.mtu.edu/umc/services/websites/seo/

Morris, S. (2018, May 15). Tech 101: What is a tracking pixel? Retrieved from https://skillcrush.com/2012/07/19/tracking-pixel/

Morris, T. (n.d.). The world wide ebb: How social media, and the internet as a whole, reached a tipping point. *GWI*. Retrieved from: https://www.gwi.com/connecting-the-dots/world-wide-ebb

Mouka, M. (2019, February 9). Marriott International: Becoming a media company. *Medium*. Retrieved from: https://medium.com/entrepreneurial-journalism/marriott-international-becoming-a-media-company-d3569a886b35

Newberry, C. (2022, January 4). How to prove and improve your social media ROI (free calculator). *Hootsuite*. Retrieved from https://www.jeffbullas.com/social-listening-examples/

O'Brien, C. (2022, December 5). What are the top digital marketing trends for 2023? *Digital Marketing Institute*. Retrieved from https://digitalmarketinginstitute.com/blog/what-are-the-top-digital-marketing-trends-for-2023

OneUpWeb. (2020, July 10). What is the PESO model for marketing? Retrieved from: https://www.oneupweb.com/blog/the-blurred-lines-of-paid-owned-and-earned-media/

Pereira, J. (2023, February 16). 25+ SMS marketing statistics for 2023: Stats, facts, & trends. *StartupBonsai*. Retrieved from https://startupbonsai.com/sms-marketing-statistics/

Pew Research Center. (2022, August 8). Teens, social media and technology 2022. Retrieved from https://www.pewresearch.org/internet/2022/08/10/teens-social-media-and-technology-2022/pj_2022-08-10_teens-and-tech_0-01a/

Pew Research Center. (2021, April 7). Social media fact sheet. Retrieved from https://www.pewresearch.org/internet/fact-sheet/social-media/

Reuters. (2019, January 15). McDonald's loses 'Big Mac' trademark case to Irish chain Supermac's. Retrieved from https://www.reuters.com/article/us-mcdonald-s-corp-trademark-supermacs/mcdonalds-loses-big-mac-trademark-case-to-irish-chain-supermacs-idUSKCN1P92JA

Rockcontent. (2021, August 13). Check out our native advertising examples and tips for implementation. *Rockcontent*. Retrieved from https://rockcontent.com/blog/native-advertising-examples/

Roseman, E. (2012, May 18). Dave Carroll is still having problems with airlines. *The Star*. Retrieved from http://www.thestar.com/business/2012/05/18/dave_carroll_is_still_having_problems_with_airlines_roseman.html

Ruby, D. (2023, January 5). YouTube statistics (2023) — Trending facts & figures shared. *Demand Sage*. Retrieved from https://www.demandsage.com/youtube-stats/#:~:text=YouTube%20has%20more%20than%202.6,via%20its%20Website%20and%20Apps.

Rutherford, L. (2023, February 9). Southwest's chief administration and communications officer on December disruption. *PR Daily*. Retrieved from https://www.prdaily.com/southwests-chief-administration-communications-officer-on-december-disruption/

Sato, M. (2022, October 24). TikTok is increasingly becoming a news source. *The Verge*. Retrieved from https://www.theverge.com/2022/10/24/23420679/tiktok-pew-study-us-adult-news-comsumption-survey-facebook-twitter

Scott, D. M. (2012). Newsjacking: How to Inject Your Ideas into a Breaking News Story and Generate Tons of Media Coverage. Hoboken, NJ: John Wiley & Sons, Inc.

Scott, R. (2014, March 6) Case studies showing how early adopters benefit from new social media platforms. *Smart Insights*. Retrieved from http://www.smartinsights.com/socialmedia-marketing/social-media-governance/case-studies-early-adopter-social-mediaplatforms

Search Engine Land. (n.d.). What Is SEO / search engine optimization? Retrieved from https://searchengineland.com/guide/what-is-seo

Smith, B. & Pelham, S. (2018). Responding while the record button is always on: Flying high and low with United Airlines corporate culture and stakeholder empowerment. *Arthur W. Page Society*. Retrieved from https://page.org/study_competitions/2018-case-study-competition

Sparrer, C. (2021, July 6). Paid, earned, shared and owned media: Making PESO work for you. *Forbes*. Retrieved from: https://www.forbes.com/sites/forbescommunicationscouncil/2021/07/06/paid-earned-shared-and-owned-media-making-peso-work-for-you/?sh=31de8315c38e

Spin Sucks. (n.d.). Do More with the PESO model. Retrieved from: https://spinsucks.com/

Statista. (2023). Digital advertising spending worldwide from 2021 to 2026. Retrieved from https://www.statista.com/statistics/237974/online-advertising-spending-worldwide/

Stieb, M. (2023, February 24). The talented Mr. Santos: Here's every single lie told by George Santos. *Intelligencer*. Retrieved from https://nymag.com/intelligencer/2023/02/the-everything-guide-to-george-santoss-lies.html

Tran, T. (2020, September 17). A beginner's guide to using Google Ads (previously Google Adwords). *Hootsuite*. Retrieved from https://blog.hootsuite.com/google-ads/#:~:text=Ads%20work%20exactly.-,How%20Google%20Ads%20work,to%20pay%20for%20an%20ad.

Traphagen, M. (2018, August 14). Why author reputation matters more than ever for search. *Search Engine Journal*. Retrieved from https://www.searchenginejournal.com/why-author-reputation-matters-for-search/262799/

Turner, K. D. (2022, February 8). 100+ new LinkedIn features for 2022 & into 2023! Retrieved from https://www.linkedin.com/pulse/new-linkedin-features-2022-kevin-d-turner/

Twitter. (2023, February 26) @SouthwestAir. Retrieved from https://twitter.com/SouthwestAir

Van Grove, J. (2009, July 15). United breaks guitars surpasses 3 million views in 10 days. Retrieved from http://mashable.com/2009/07/15/united-breaks-guitars/

Vanek Smith, S. (2022, December 29). Southwest Airlines' #epicfail takes social media by storm. *NPR*. Retrieved from https://www.npr.org/2022/12/29/1145996040/southwests-meltdown-social-media

Wagner, K. (2018, August 8). 'Stories' was Instagram's smartest move yet: Can it become Facebook's next big business? *Vox*. Retrieved from https://www.vox.com/2018/8/8/17641256/instagram-stories-kevin-systrom-facebook-snapchat

Wasserman, T. (2013, May 11). KPI: What is a key performance indicator? *Mashable*. Retrieved from: http://mashable.com/2013/05/11/kpi-definition/

Wigmore, I. (2014, July). Part of the personal computing glossary: Social media. *WhatIs*. Retrieved from http://whatis.techtarget.com/definition/social-media

Yelp. (n.d.) 4 types of digital advertising to grow your business. Retrieved from https://business.yelp.com/advertise/types-of-digital-advertising/#:~:text=The%20four%20main%20types%20of,%2C%20native%2C%20and%20display%20advertising.

Yeung, K. (2013, May 5). LinkedIn is 10 years old today: Here's the story of how it changed the way we work. *The Next Web*. Retrieved from http://thenextweb.com/insider/2013/05/05/linkedin-10-years-social-network/

Zen Media. (n.d.). The future of public relations: 14 PR trends for 2023. Retrieved from: https://zenmedia.com/blog/pr-trends-shaping-the-industry/

Zettasphere. (n.d.) Mind boggling stats for 1 second of internet activity. Retrieved from: https://www.zettasphere.com/mind-boggling-stats-for-1-second-of-internet-activity/

CHAPTER 10
CALENDARING AND BUDGETING

*"Do not squander time, for that is
the stuff that life is made of."*

—BENJAMIN FRANKLIN
**AMERICAN INVENTOR,
JOURNALIST AND STATESMAN**

LEARNING IMPERATIVES

- Learn a strategic planning approach to calendars
  and budgets.

- Understand the importance of calendaring interactivity
  among tactics and publics.

- Learn the value of creativity in the calendaring and
  budgeting processes.

I n all relationships, timing is everything. Whether responding to a crisis or pursuing an opportunity, timing plays a crucial role in strategic communications.

The next step in the Strategic Communications Matrix — calendaring tactics and budgeting for their cost — requires specific detail. It is important to remember that a calendar and a budget are not just strategic planning tools. As we see in the next chapter, they are also important tools to manage the implementation of a plan. They must be considered carefully so that timing and cost are addressed within the overall framework of the organization's goals as well as the plan's objectives. They require meticulous attention to detail. If timing is off, your plan may fail. If you have not budgeted precisely, you will have cost overruns that may have long-term consequences.

Planning for implementation must be meticulous to ensure communication with stakeholders and key publics is strategic — designed to accomplish your objectives in support of the organization's mission. Nevertheless, in today's fluid communication environment we must be flexible, able to adjust and change directions at a moment's notice based on a continual flow of research, information and data.

Electronic tools for calendaring and budgeting abound. One of the best for a calendar is a Gantt chart (see Figure 10.1) that allows you to view the schedule for each public by day, week or month. Budgeting programs should perform calculations automatically to ensure accuracy. If you use an Excel or Google spreadsheet, make sure you check your formulas.

As shown in the Matrix Applied in this chapter, both the calendar and budget should detail tactics by public and strategy. Then your client or manager can quickly determine what tactics will target a specific public and how much each will cost. It also makes you more aware of the cost of information and persuasion efforts among each of your key publics. And it enables you to be conversant in the interactive scheduling of the campaign by public. It provides an easy "line-item veto" when your client or manager wants to eliminate a public or strategy for any reason. It is a simple matter to delete that section of your plan and subtract the cost from the total.

STRATEGIC COMMUNICATIONS MATRIX

ACTION PLANNING

6. CALENDAR AND BUDGET

Calendar Organized by public and strategy showing when each tactic begins and ends. A Gantt chart is recommended. It helps show the work required as well as the flow of the campaign.

Budget Organized by public and strategy estimating the cost of each tactic. The budget indicates where costs will be offset by donations or sponsorships. Subtotals are provided for each strategy and public.

Calendaring

Never forget that a calendar is strategic. When you calendar a plan, you are not just picking dates; you are **scheduling** and sequencing tactics. Scheduling involves finding the premier moment for an event to be held, a story to be pitched, social media content to be shared or promoted or an ad campaign to be launched. Timing is critical to success.

    Sequencing is focused on determining the optimal ordering of tactics over time, or which tactics should be used before, after or at the same time as other tactics. The sequencing of a campaign should take into account the cognitive and behavioral milestones a key public must pass through to accomplish all of a campaign's objectives. For example, tactics focused on generating awareness should come before tactics that seek to motivate action. It may be helpful to think about your campaign in phases or stages that correspond with your outcome objectives (e.g., an awareness phase followed by an attitude phase followed by a behavior phase).

    A few important guidelines can help make sure your calendaring is effective in accomplishing your campaign objectives.

SCHEDULING
Finding the premier moment in time for a tactic to be used.

SEQUENCING
Determining the optimal ordering of tactics over time.

Figure 10.1
What is a Gantt chart?

A Gantt chart is a horizontal chart (usually a bar chart) developed as a production control tool in 1917 by Henry L. Gantt, an American engineer and social scientist. Frequently used in project management, a Gantt chart provides a graphical illustration of a schedule that helps to plan, coordinate and track specific tasks in a project. You can schedule a one-time tactic (X) or an ongoing tactic (X--X). Gantt charts may be simple versions created on graph paper or more complex automated versions created using project management applications such as Microsoft Project, Excel or Google Sheets. Dozens of other software packages are also available to help build effective Gantt charts.

SIMPLE GANTT CHART

Calendar: Campaign to increase blood donations

Start date: 7/1/2024	July				August				September			
Weeks	1–7	8–14	15–21	22–28	29–5	6–12	13–19	20–26	27–2	3–9	10–16	17–23	24–30
Public: *Denver area adults, ages 18-55*													
Strategy 1: *Convince residents through local mass media that donating blood is safe and needed.*													
Tactic: *Run radio PSAs*			X	▬	▬	▬	▬	▬	▬	▬	▬	▬	X
Tactic: *Letter-to-the-editor writing campaign*						X	▬	▬	X				
Tactic: *Interviews on local drive-time radio talk shows*										X	▬	▬	X
Tactic: *Blood Services spokesperson training*										X			

TIPS FROM THE PROS

What peak movie and TV season can teach you about PR

Lisa Arledge Powell, president and co-founder of MediaSource, a story-centric communications agency based in Columbus, Ohio, tips you off on how to use timing and placement to your advantage like a seasoned Hollywood executive.

Are you a sucker for a good holiday movie? Does Netflix always seem to know exactly when you need a new show? You're not alone, and it's because Hollywood is excellent at knowing how to push your buttons.

As a PR pro, your goal is to drive great results for your company or client. So what does that have to do with movies and TV shows?

A massive amount of planning goes into each film and television show, and these principles can be applied to your work as well. Just because your team isn't planning the launch of the newest blockbuster doesn't mean you can't learn from the approach of everyone from production companies to creators of cheesy holiday shows.

Here are some cues you can take from Hollywood if you're looking to make a big splash.

Maximize impact with great timing. For the film and television industry, timing is everything. Big-budget blockbuster? Definitely a summer release. The new prestige TV show? Sunday night is the spot.

Every media release is planned to maximize its desired impact, which depends on the goals of the production. For film studios, a potential award-winner should be released late in the year, when movies are much more likely to garner awards buzz. For streaming services like Netflix, Hulu or HBO Max, the holiday season is the time to push out loads of content because people have plenty of time to sit and watch.

Hollywood is excellent at planning its launches and you should be too. If you have a piece of content or a PR campaign ready to go, you'll need to plan for its best possible release. This begins, as always, with strategy. By establishing your goals early – like a studio decides between a summer blockbuster or a winter awards contender – you'll be better equipped to find the right news hook, season or even day for your own announcement.

With great timing, you can set yourself up for great success.

Drive anticipation and create a buzz. Not getting the best response to your press releases and marketing materials? Have you considered getting an earlier start for extra impact?

Movies, TV shows, albums and more don't just appear out of thin air and start garnering attention. Trailers, promo photos and other prelaunch content appear far before the final product makes its way to your television or local theater.

Take the latest biopic from 2022, Elvis. The movie premiered in late June, but its first trailer was released all the way back in February. All that anticipation has resulted in countless think pieces, trailer reviews and conversations about the film's evolution since the start of its publicity.

Whether your team is publicizing an event, a product or a broad subject, keep in mind the power of a campaign. Try to think in steps: creating a prelaunch buzz, maintaining interest and capitalizing on the big moment, whatever that may be.

Find the best home for your content. Even the best content needs a good home, and Hollywood production companies and streaming services are (usually) excellent at finding a great fit for their content. It's not just about releasing blockbusters in the summer or feel-good Oscar bait in the winter.

Take 2021's big Disney+ release of the animated movie, Encanto, for example. The streaming giant had been receiving pushback for months for bypassing a theater premiere and pushing new content straight to their streaming platform ahead of the release of this movie. So, Disney decided to offer a 30-day exclusive theater window for the movie before offering it for streaming on Disney+. This effort drove early viewers of the movie to the theaters, who had been struggling to garner audiences since the COVID-19 pandemic, while also giving the movie the top spot on the company's own streaming platform.

How can you emulate Hollywood? Remember the importance of your content's ultimate home. While timing and capturing impact are important, sometimes a good fit can be even more crucial. If you think you can earn your client better results by skipping your news hook or waiting until after a holiday to secure a great publication, it can be worth it to emphasize fit over timing.

And if all else fails, finding a place where your content will be front and center (like the Disney+ streaming platform) could be the difference between a smash hit and a big disappointment.

Contributed by Lisa Arledge Powell. © Kendall Hunt Publishing Company.

Interactivity is key. The sequencing of tactics should be such that you magnify, reinforce and build on other tactics within publics and across publics. Schedule the grade-school poster contest to conclude in time to use the winning posters in your efforts to solicit sponsorships from local businesses. Time your social media communication to peak when publics are getting messages in more formal earned media channels.

Check for conflicts seasonally and within communities. It is difficult to compete with traditional events and efforts. The annual Oktoberfest is probably not the time to schedule the launch of the hospital's new alcoholic rehab wing.

Build on tradition and other regularly scheduled events. While you need to avoid conflicting events, building upon related traditions can leverage awareness and motivation. The beginning of a new school year might be a great time to launch an effort to change a habit or routine. Perhaps when the kids go off to school is the best time for the local library to start a parent readers' circle.

Always provide enough lead time for production and other arrangements. Plan for collateral material to be complete far in advance of the time it is needed. Make all reservations and invitations to key participants well in advance of the event. Doing so will leave time to reprint or rebook, if needed. Major conferences reserve venues years in advance. Most campaigns cannot be pulled off overnight.

Plan backward from the implementation date. If the launch is in July, when should the media pieces be prepared and placed to support the launch? Is the media element a promotion or a follow-up? When should collateral material be completed to be available at the launch? When should your social media conversations start to build anticipation? When should invitations be printed and sent to ensure people have time to schedule it and RSVP?

A planning calendar for a proposed plan simply schedules the date each tactic will be used. Implementation task lists, explained in the next chapter, will help you make timely preparation for each tactic.

MATRIX APPLIED

Calendar

This calendar maps out a four-month American Dental Association (ADA) campaign to decrease the incidence of tooth decay among elementary school children by motivating them to practice good dental hygiene. (The strategies and tactics shown are illustrative. An actual campaign of this type would require more tactics to accomplish message delivery and motivate behavior.)

Item	Month: Sept				Oct				Nov				Dec			
Week:	1	2	3	4	1	2	3	4	1	2	3	4	1	2	3	4
Key Public: *Students*																
Strategy: *Motivate brushing/flossing through classroom activities*																
Tactics: Chart to mark daily brushing					X	—	—	—	—	—	—	—	—	—	—	X
Tactics: Disposables for those who didn't brush/floss					X	—	—	—	—	—	—	—	—	—	—	X
Tactics: Interactive tablet app with activities for kids					X	—	—	—	—	—	—	—	—	—	—	X
Tactics: Mr. Tooth erasers						X				X				X		
Strategy: *Motivate through class lessons on dental hygiene*																
Tactics: Video on how to brush/floss					X											
Tactics: Learning activity on hygiene		X														
Key Public: *Parents*																
Strategy: *Promote through PTA*																
Tactics: PTA Facebook social plug-ins			X				X				X				X	
Tactics: Brochure at parent/teacher conferences					X	—	X									
Tactics: Mailer on cumulative costs of dental work		X														
Strategy: *Remind through take-home collateral*																
Tactics: Brush/floss kit sent home					X											
Tactics: "I'm a good brusher" stickers							X				X				X	
Key Public: *Teachers*																
Strategy: *Motivate by providing classroom resources*																
Tactics: Lesson plans on website	X	—	—	—	—	—	—	—	—	—	—	—	—	—	—	X
Tactics: Learning activity ideas	X	—	—	—	—	—	—	—	—	—	—	—	—	—	—	X
Tactics: Classroom brushing chart	X	—	—	—	—	—	—	—	—	—	—	—	—	—	—	X
Tactics: YouTube videos	X	—	—	—	—	—	—	—	—	—	—	—	—	—	—	X
Strategy: *Motivate through ADA appeal*																
Tactics: Dimensional mailer asking cooperation	X															
Tactics: Magnet with website for campaign resources/FAQs	X															
Tactics: Online survey to measure participation		X												X		
Tactics: Resource website	X	—	—	—	—	—	—	—	—	—	—	—	—	—	—	X

Budgeting

The budget should be considered strategically as well. The issue should not only be total cost, but also who will pay and how. Highly creative plans find solutions to budgetary limitations, many of which result in greater creativity and persuasive power. Recruiting volunteers to do work that would have been a budgetary item results not only in lower cost but also in greater support and advocacy from opinion leaders in a community. Building **partnerships** between organizations — whether

PARTNERSHIP

A mutually beneficial short- or long-term cooperative relationship to reach common goals.

TIPS FROM THE PROS

Spending your money strategically

Judith T. Phair, APR, Fellow PRSA, president of PhairAdvantage Communications, former vice president of communications for the Graduate Management Admission Council and former PRSA president, tips you off on budgeting so your first-rate public relations programs don't end up as exercises in "what might have been."

Effective budgeting is one of the most strategic things you can do to advance your department and organization – and your career. To be valued as a trusted adviser and counselor, a public relations professional needs to know the business side of the client or organization. Carefully building, justifying, maintaining and monitoring a budget is a critical part of strategic planning. A well-constructed budget provides a built-in method for setting expectations and evaluating results. Here are some things to keep in mind when crafting a financial scenario that will truly show return on investment and set the stage for gaining funding for future projects.

Know the organization's business plan. Understand the relationship of your work to key elements of the business. What are the top priorities, including financial priorities?

Budget strategically. Think about why dollars will be spent, as well as how. Justify each expenditure with measurable results.

Budget realistically. Match the budget to expectations. If the organization doesn't have the resources to meet its expectations, show what would be required as well as what can be done within existing boundaries. Offer alternative scenarios, along with a strategic analysis of what the return on investment would be with greater expenditures.

Consider both direct and indirect costs. Staff labor is not "free," nor is the use of equipment, office space and the like.

Measure the return on investment. Remember, also, that the return does not need to be monetary to provide real value. If you invest in a program to create the climate for an effective fundraising campaign or to boost public support for (or against) legislation, that ultimately contributes to the organization's bottom line.

business-to-business (B2B) or corporate-to-nonprofit — often strengthens the credibility of the appeal. Combining with other actors in a cooperative cost-sharing effort provides a unity of action that is more persuasive and far-reaching than acting unilaterally.

Even requesting small contributions from target publics (e.g., $2 admission to an event with the proceeds donated to a relevant local charity) can be effective. Making something free doesn't always make it appealing. In fact, many people consider that something free may not be worth their time. Among certain publics, you are more likely to get attention and participation if there is some monetary investment — even if only small.

MINI CASE

Charitable giving made easy with Giving Machines
Latter-day Saint Charities and Boncom

Latter-day Saint Charities, a largely volunteer humanitarian organization that sponsors relief and development projects in 195 countries and territories around the world, noticed that there was a year-over-year increase in the amount of charitable giving by individuals but that global humanitarian needs were still significant. Millions of children were still suffering from malnutrition. And millions of people were still living without clean water. Latter-day Saint Charities works independently and in cooperation with other charitable organizations and governments.

CORE OPPORTUNITY
Boncom was tasked by Latter-day Saint Charities to offer an easy way for people to give back during the holiday season.

BONCOM'S LATTER-DAY SAINT CHARITIES STRATEGY
In 2017, Boncom created and launched a concept to bring giving to city streets in an unexpected way: Giving Machines. Giving Machines look like regular vending machines, but instead of being stocked with soda and candy, they offer patrons an opportunity to purchase shoes, meals, first aid kits—even chickens and sheep—that are donated through local and global charities to people in need around the globe.

The Giving Machine concept was developed using the behavior change principles of gamification and social proof. The Giving Machines were intended to be a fun and desirable way for people to give and feel the collective impact of their donation. A key part of the strategy was to make the Giving Machines available during the holiday season when many people are focused on charity, service and gift giving.

In the campaign's first year, three Giving Machines located in Salt Lake City, Utah, raised over $550,000 during the holidays. In its second year, Boncom placed 14 Giving Machines in five U.S. cities, but with a new wrinkle—the machines were officially launched on Giving Tuesday, a global holiday on the Tuesday after Thanksgiving to celebrate and encourage generosity. In New York, the Giving Tuesday launch was included in the Lincoln Center's annual community Winter's Eve celebration. In other cities, the smaller Giving Tuesday kick-off events featured ribbon-cutting ceremonies with representatives from participating charities and members of the local communities. After just one month, Giving Machine donations more than tripled from the previous year, resulting in $2.3 million raised.

Courtesy of BonCom.

Now in its sixth year, the campaign has placed Giving Machines in a variety of cities around the globe. With the global expansion, Boncom has adopted a strategy of location-specific timing. At each of the locations—including Manila; London; New York City; Las Vegas; Laie, Hawaii; Denver; and Salt Lake City—launch events are timed to coincide with relevant holiday dates. In New York City, the launch happened on Giving Tuesday; in Manila, the launch occurred at the start of a big shopping week. Events in Salt Lake City, Utah; Gilbert, Arizona; and London were timed right after the Thanksgiving holiday, when people were just starting to think about Christmas.

RESULTS

- Each event brought in significant local media coverage and even more social awareness and served as the launch for each location. From the 10 location launches to the end of December, earned media coverage reached over 9.2 million people. Social media reached an estimated global audience of more than 90 million people.
- The Giving Machines earned a Public Relations Society of America Silver Anvil in the public service category, the highest industry honor in the country.
- The American Advertising Federation recognized the Giving Machines with a 2018 national Silver ADDY in the public service category, a 2019 Silver ADDY for branding elements, and a 2020 Gold ADDY in the corporate social responsibility ambient media category.
- Most importantly, the Giving Machines have raised significant funds for charity in each of the six years of the campaign. In 2022, more than $5.8 million was raised for more than 40 local and global charities.

MATRIX APPLIED

Budget

The school district and ADA are collaborating to improve adolescent dental hygiene. (See Matrix Applied Calendar.) This budget does not include the ADA's portion of the campaign; it is for the school district's costs only. The district has 10 elementary schools, a total of 200 teachers and 3,500 children.

		Detail
Key Public: *Students*		
Strategy: *Motivate brushing/flossing through classroom activities*		
Tactics:	Chart to mark daily brushing	Download from ADA website
	Disposables for those who didn't brush/floss	Local dentists provide
	Interactive tablet app with activities for kids	Download from ADA website
	Mr. Tooth erasers	20% discount from national supplier
Strategy: *Motivate through class lessons on dental hygiene*		
Tactics:	Video on how to brush/floss	Download from ADA YouTube channel
	Learning activity on dental hygiene	Download from ADA website
Key Public: *Parents*		
Strategy: *Promote through PTA*		
Tactics:	PTA Facebook social plug-ins	Embedded on website/blog
	Brochure at parent/teacher conferences	Provided by ADA
	Mailer on cumulative costs of dental work	Design, printing and mailing
Strategy: *Remind through take-home collateral*		
Tactics:	Brush/floss kit sent home	Local dentists subsidize 50%
	"I'm a good brusher" stickers	Provided monthly by ADA/3 months
Key Public: *Teachers*		
Strategy: *Motivate by providing classroom resources*		
Tactics:	Lesson plans on website	Download from ADA website
	Learning activity ideas	Download from ADA website
	Classroom brushing chart	Download from ADA website
	YouTube videos	Stream from ADA YouTube channel
Strategy: *Motivate through ADA appeal*		
Tactics:	Dimensional mailer asking cooperation	ADA designs, district prints and mails
	Magnet with website for campaign resources/FAQs	ADA provides
	Online survey to measure participation	Sent by ADA
	Resource website	Maintained by ADA

	Quantity	Per item cost	Total projected	Sponsored credit	Actual projected
			$0.00	$0.00	$0.00	$0.00
	3,500	$0.25	$875.00	$875.00	$0.00
		$0.00	$0.00	$0.00	$0.00
	10,500	$0.10	$1,050.00	$210.00	$840.00
Strategy subtotal			*$1,925.00*	*$1,085.00*	*$840.00*
		$0.00	$0.00	$0.00	$0.00
		$0.00	$0.00	$0.00	$0.00
Strategy subtotal			*$0.00*	*$0.00*	*$0.00*
Public subtotal			$1,925.00	$1,085.00	$840.00
		$0.00	$0.00	$0.00	$0.00
	2,500	$0.00	$0.00	$0.00	$0.00
	7,000	$0.76	$5,320.00	$0.00	$5,320.00
Strategy subtotal			*$5,320.00*	*$0.00*	*$5,320.00*
	3,500	$1.50	$5,250.00	$2,625.00	$2,625.00
	10,500	$0.00	$0.00	$0.00	$0.00
Strategy subtotal			*$5,250.00*	*$2,625.00*	*$2,625.00*
Public subtotal			$10,570.00	$2,625.00	$7,945.00
		$0.00	$0.00	$0.00	$0.00
		$0.00	$0.00	$0.00	$0.00
		$0.00	$0.00	$0.00	$0.00
		$0.00	$0.00	$0.00	$0.00
Strategy subtotal			*$0.00*	*$0.00*	*$0.00*
	200	$0.50	$100.00	$0.00	$100.00
	200	$0.00	$0.00	$0.00	$0.00
		$0.00	$0.00	$0.00	$0.00
		$0.00	$0.00	$0.00	$0.00
Strategy subtotal			*$100.00*	*$0.00*	*$100.00*
Public subtotal			$100.00	$0.00	$100.00
Campaign total			$12,595.00	$3,710.00	$8,885.00

Your budget should have eight columns. This format is easy to set up in a spreadsheet. The first column identifies the public and strategy. The second column identifies the tactics that fall under each strategy. The third column provides a little detail about each tactic (e.g., 40-page, full-color brochure; two-minute YouTube video; custom-designed iPhone cases). The fourth column gives the quantity needed. The fifth column provides the cost per unit. The sixth column is the total projected cost for that budget item. The seventh column identifies the sponsored credit (i.e., how much of the given tactic will be donated). The eighth column provides the actual projected cost of each tactic (i.e., number of units times per item cost, minus sponsored credit equals actual projected cost). Each column is important. They show the scope and cost of each tactic as well as external support in terms of discounts and sponsorships. It is crucial for clients or supervisors to know how much your creativity and partnerships have saved.

This format breaks the cost of your campaign down by public, strategy and tactic. You can quickly see where your resources have been allocated. It is important to know what it will cost to reach a particular public or to see quickly that one strategy is going to cost more than the rest of the campaign. Good budgeting makes it relatively easy to do a mental cost-benefit analysis to determine if each expenditure is worth the gain. The strategic planning process is dynamic. Proper budgeting will help you identify potential areas of concern. It should also help you to identify areas where greater creativity might be needed to do things differently and for a lower cost. Executives expect this kind of analysis.

Nevertheless, don't automatically reject a public because of cost. Be creative in finding ways to do what you have planned in more frugal ways, like using volunteers or collaborating with other organizations to share costs. Also, don't forget to seek out sponsorships. Strategic partnerships and sponsorships can foster win-win relationships and in many ways buy you influence you couldn't afford and/or acquire on your own.

Summary

Strategic planning does not end at tactics. Your approach to calendaring and budgeting must also be strategic. Tactics should be timed to gain maximum benefit from other tactics in the plan and from external events and annual community calendars. Strategic budgeting allows you to creatively manage cost while leveraging other relationships. The calendar and budget should be just as much a part of your strategic and creative planning as are the other elements of the plan.

Application case

PEEPS® are back

from the PEEPS® Brand and Coyne Public Relations

For 70 years, PEEPS marshmallow chicks and bunnies have been a staple of Easter celebrations. However, Just Born Quality Confections, the company that makes

MINI CASE

Krispy Kreme Doughnuts gives graduates their "Senior Moment" during pandemic

Krispy Kreme Doughnuts and FleishmanHillard

Like every business around the world in 2020, Krispy Kreme was figuring out how to market to customers during the COVID-19 pandemic. Research showed that living with the realities of the pandemic (quarantines, stay-at-home orders, cancellations and rapidly rising transmission statistics and deaths) was making people feel sad and isolated. The one thing that Krispy Kreme had to offer during these challenging times was "joy and smiles."

   FleishmanHillard's social media listening and news media analysis found that people were desperate to celebrate major life events and were willing to adapt in creative ways to make these celebrations possible. However, FleishmanHillard observed that there wasn't much conversation about how to help high school and college seniors celebrate their upcoming graduation since traditional ceremonies had been canceled. The best that anyone had come up with was virtual commencements featuring celebrity speeches. But close analysis of the social media conversation showed that what graduating seniors wanted the most was a way to celebrate this major life accomplishment with their friends.

© Ben Gingell/Shutterstock.com

CORE OPPORTUNITY

Krispy Kreme needed to create a way for high school and college seniors to celebrate their graduation with friends in a COVID-safe way that was true to its mission and the passion its customers have for Krispy Kreme Doughnuts.

FLEISHMANHILLARD'S KRISPY KREME STRATEGY

Krispy Kreme created a special "Graduate Dozen" ($15 value), which featured a mix of iced and filled doughnuts decorated with the number "2" and glazed doughnuts that had a natural "0" (i.e., doughnut hole) to honor the class of 2020. At the start of what the doughnut chain dubbed "Senior Week" (May 18-24), any high school or college senior could go to the drive through of their local Krispy Kreme wearing their cap and gown, a Class of 2020 shirt or a letterman jacket and get a free Graduate Dozen.

The Silver Anvil entry for this campaign described this approach as focused on creativity and timing: "Because Krispy Kreme does not buy any television, radio or out-of-home advertising, the brand puts a premium on creativity and timeliness of PR and PR-led strategies that can generate widespread earned media coverage and social media engagement." In particular, the campaign scheduled its Senior Week during the peak of the high school and college graduation season when news and social media attention would be focused on graduation-related stories.

RESULTS

The Graduate Dozen campaign was so successful that Krispy Kreme won a PRSA Silver Anvil Award of Excellence. And the company repeated the Graduate Dozen campaign in 2021 and 2022.

- The 2020 Graduate Dozen campaign resulted in a 36% increase in same store sales compared to the same week in 2019.
- The 2020 campaign was a trend on Twitter and became the number one search on Google.
- The 2020 campaign also generated 2,300 placements and 613 million viewers/impressions in one week.
- The 2020 campaign yielded a low CPM for paid social media ads of $1.19, a decrease of 66% compared to the average paid social media CPM for the same year.

PEEPS, had to shut down production and distribution in 2020 because of the COVID-19 pandemic. As a result, the company wasn't able to sell PEEPS for Halloween, Christmas or Valentine's Day.

CORE PROBLEM

After a nine-month hiatus, Just Born Quality Confections was ready to relaunch PEEPS for Easter 2021. The relaunch was scheduled to start in January and Easter in 2021 was on April 4, giving the company only three months to let people know that PEEPS were back.

BACKGROUND RESEARCH

A national survey found that people wanted to celebrate bigger and better for Easter 2021. In addition, the pandemic inspired people to create new home-centered traditions for their Easter celebrations from baking treats at home to playing holiday games with family members.

OBJECTIVES

- Increase awareness for PEEPS® during a shorter Easter season from January-April ahead of the 2021 Easter holiday.
- Increase sales of PEEPS® by 5% compared to 2020.

PAID MEDIA

The campaign used the following paid tactics.

- Social media advertising using Just Born's social channels.

EARNED MEDIA

The campaign used the following tactics to garner coverage in consumer food, lifestyle, parenting and traditional news media outlets.

- "PEEPS® Are Back" news release
- News release announcing PEEPS' partnership with Pepsi
- News release announcing PEEPS' partnership with Kelloggs (Kellogg's PEEPS® Cereal)
- News release announcing PEEPS' partnership with Crocs
- News release announcing PEEPS' partnership with HipDot makeup
- News release announcing PEEPS' partnership with Pez
- News release announcing PEEPS' partnership with Build-A-Bear
- News release announcing PEEPS' partnership with 7-11
- Video MAT Feature (compilation of DIY recipes with partner Duncan Hines)
- April Fools Product Announcement (joke partnership with Green Giant to create a cauliflower-flavored PEEPS® bunny)

SHARED MEDIA

The campaign used the following tactics on Facebook, Instagram and Twitter.

- "PEEPS® Are Back" social announcement
- Instagram Live series featuring crafting and baking influencers who shared how they make PEEPS®-inspired Easter treats
- Organic posts highlighting PEEPS' brand partnerships
- Organic posts featuring unique recipes that combine PEEPS with other brands' products, such as Duncan Hines and Rice Krispies®

Assume you have been hired by Coyne PR to create a strategic calendar for the "PEEPS® Are Back" campaign. Use the information provided in this case and principles from this chapter to complete the following tasks regarding calendaring.

1. What is the optimal release time for each of the "PEEPS® Are Back" campaign tactics? When will you get the most bang for your buck? Check for conflicts seasonally and within communities. Don't compete with traditional events. Build on tradition and other regularly scheduled events. Find ways to insert your messages into conversations that you already know will be happening (and that relate to your campaign). Describe your ideas for how to schedule tactics to take advantage of timing.

2. Consider the potential for interactivity and synergy among the "PEEPS® Are Back" campaign tactics to drive anticipation and create a buzz. Is there a way to create phases or steps in the deployment of the campaign tactics that create a build, a buzz or a natural progression of desired communication outcomes? Describe your ideas for how to sequence the tactics to create interactivity and synergy.

3. Create a strategic campaign calendar for the "PEEPS® Are Back" tactics in Gantt chart format. You can use Excel or Google Sheets to create your Gantt chart.

References and additional readings

Coyne PR. (n.d.). Peeps. Retrieved from https://www.coynepr.com/brand/peeps/

Gantt.com. (2012, June 20). What is a Gantt chart? Retrieved from www.Gantt.com Griffin, C. (2017, April 19).

GivingTuesday. (n.d.). About GivingTuesday. Retrieved from https://www.givingtuesday.org/about/

How to build accurate PR agency project budgets. Retrieved from www.mediabullseye.com/2017/04how-to-build-accurate-pr-agency-project-budgets/

Just Born Quality Confections. (2021, Feb. 03). They're back! PEEPS® make a triumphant return to shelves this Easter. Cision: PR Newswire. Retrieved from https://www.prnewswire.com/news-releases/theyre-back-peeps-make-a-triumphant-return-to-shelves-this-easter-301221015.html

Krispy Kreme. (2022). Krispy Kreme® celebrates class of 2022 with free senior day dozen for high school and college seniors wearing class swag on May 25. Retrieved from https://investors.krispykreme.com/news-releases/news-release-details/krispy-kremer-celebrates-class-2022-free-senior-day-dozen-high

Krispy Kreme. (2021). Krispy Kreme® brings back free 'Graduate Dozen' for high school and college seniors on May 13. Retrieved from https://investors.krispykreme.com/news-releases/news-release-details/krispy-kremer-brings-back-free-graduate-dozen-high-school-and

Krispy Kreme. (2020). KRISPY KREME® to celebrate Class of 2020 with 'Graduate Dozen' available one week only and FREE for all high school and college seniors on May 19. Business Wire. Retrieved from https://www.businesswire.com/news/home/20200512005465/en/KRISPY-KREME%C2%AE-to-Celebrate-Class-of-2020-with-%E2%80%98Graduate-Dozen%E2%80%99-Available-One-Week-Only-and-FREE-for-All-High-School-and-College-Seniors-on-May-19

Krispy Kreme & FleishmanHillard. (2020a). Krispy Kreme Doughnuts gives graduates their "Senior Moment" during pandemic. Retrieved from https://www.prsa.org/conferences-and-awards/awards/search-silver-anvil-case-studies

Krispy Kreme & FleishmanHillard. (2020b). Krispy Kreme Doughnuts gives graduates their "Senior Moment" during pandemic. Retrieved from https://www.warc.com/

Latter-day Saint Charities. (n.d.). About us. Retrieved from https://www.latterdaysaintcharities.org/about-us?lang=eng

Moroney, G. (2019). *PRIMER: Introduction to PR Planning*. International Association for the Measurement and Evaluation of Communication. Retrieved from https://amecorg.com/wp-content/uploads/2019/11/AMEC-PRIMER-planning-guide-MM2019.pdf

PEEPS [@PEEPSBRAND]. (n.d.). Instagram. Retrieved from https://www.instagram.com/peepsbrand/

PEEPS [@PEEPSBRAND]. (n.d.). Twitter. Retrieved from https://twitter.com/peepsbrand

PEEPS [@PEEPSBRAND]. (n.d.). Facebook. Retrieved from https://www.facebook.com/PeepsBrand/

PEEPS & Coyne Public Relations. (2021). PEEPS® makes a triumphant return to shelves for Easter. Retrieved from https://www.prsa.org/conferences-and-awards/awards/search-silver-anvil-case-studies

Tam, L., Mehta, A. & Goodlich, H. (2021). Towards greater integration in media planning: Decision-making insights from public relations practitioners. *Journal of Marketing Communications*, DOI: 10.1080/13527266.2021.1986740

The Church of Jesus Christ of Latter-day Saints, Thatcher+Co. & Boncom. (2019). Micro donations meeting local and global needs — One vending machine at a time. Retrieved from https://www.prsa.org/conferences-and-awards/awards/search-silver-anvil-case-studies

CHAPTER 11

IMPLEMENTATION AND COMMUNICATIONS MANAGEMENT

*"Ideas are easy.
Implementation is hard."*

—GUY KAWASAKI
AMERICAN MARKETING SPECIALIST,
AUTHOR AND VENTURE CAPITALIST

LEARNING IMPERATIVES

- Learn how to make the transition from planning to executing.

- Learn how to use calendars and task lists to manage the production and implementation of tactics.

- Understand how to use budgets to manage the production and implementation of tactics.

- Understand how to use strategy briefs to develop tactics with effective secondary messages.

- Understand the importance of quality control, measurement and flexibility in the process of implementation.

The third step of the RACE model is communication. The steps of the Strategic Communications Matrix described in the preceding chapters have taught you how to create a communications plan. But carrying out the plan — actually communicating with publics — can be more difficult than you might have expected when you crafted your plan.

For example, digital agency Grow developed a campaign for footwear and apparel brand adidas to celebrate the brand's 30th anniversary sponsoring the Boston

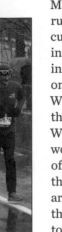

Marathon®. The campaign's big idea was to treat every runner in the April 2018 race like a legend. The execution of this idea required the Grow team to capture individual footage of 30,000 runners, edit that footage into personalized highlight films and publish the films on a campaign-branded website 24 hours after the race. Without a doubt, this was a creative idea. But imagine that you are tasked with turning this idea into reality. Where would you start? What would you do next? How would you pull this off? These questions get to the core of implementation. They highlight the need to think through the personnel, technology and resources that are needed; the deadlines that must be met; the tasks that must be accomplished; and the obstacles that have to be overcome to bring a campaign to life.

The Grow team relied heavily on technology to capture and edit the videos. A customized software program combined the unique RFID data from each runner's bib with video footage captured by an on-site film crew. However, Murphy's Law — anything that can go wrong will go wrong — is a potent force to deal with when implementing a campaign. Unexpectedly, the film crew members weren't able to determine where they could place their cameras until the morning of the race. This development made it difficult to sync the camera footage with the RFID data. Fortunately, the team had tested the technology at other races before the marathon and knew how to deal with the situation. Unanticipated weather conditions also made the film crew's task difficult. Race day was windy, rainy and cold, posing a challenge to runners and the film crew. Drew Ungvarsky, CEO and executive creative director of Grow, said, "Unexpectedly, the greatest challenge was also the greatest payoff." The weather serendipitously helped the runners connect with the campaign message, "Here to Create Legend," as they watched themselves on their personal highlight reels persevering through the rain and the wind.

The adidas campaign, which resulted in 100,000 video views with a 95% completion rate within two days of the marathon, illustrates two important considerations about implementation. First, execution of a plan requires translating big ideas into bite-sized tasks that when completed properly bring the ideas to life. Second, you don't have control over everything. It's impossible to anticipate every contingency; however, you need to have enough flexibility to accomplish your objectives while rolling with the punches. The majority of campaigns that fail do so because they had poor execution, not because they had bad strategy.

This chapter will explain the essential tools for managing the implementation of a plan: campaign calendars and implementation task lists, a budget to track actual costs, strategy briefs and a quality control checklist. The calendars and task lists keep all strategies and tactics for each public coordinated and on schedule. The budget keeps you on track financially. Strategy briefs help you check that the messages in your tactics are targeted to the right public and accomplish what your analysis and plan say they need to accomplish to reach the goal. And the quality control checklist ensures that tactics are error-free.

STRATEGIC COMMUNICATIONS MATRIX

COMMUNICATION

7. IMPLEMENTATION

Project Management
A list of tasks required to implement each tactic. Use the tactics in the calendar to track all activities required in the campaign. Use the budget to help manage actual costs against estimates.

Tactic Creation
Use strategy briefs to align tactics with strategies. Develop secondary messages to give credibility to the primary messages embedded in each tactic. Facts, testimonials, examples and stories provide the ethos, pathos and logos of persuasion.

Quality Control
Best practices that guide creators and editors in producing quality content. Check to ensure tactics support strategies and objectives.

Nevertheless, remember that you should complete every step of the planning — through evaluation criteria and tools — before you implement the plan. Once you have completed the plan, check its logic by laddering back through the steps of the matrix from the end to the beginning. Make sure the tactics are appropriate for the strategies. Verify that the strategies will enable you to reach your key publics. Ensure that the primary and secondary messages will inform or persuade your key publics effectively and allow you to accomplish your objectives. Check to see that the big idea is infused throughout your entire campaign. And, finally, confirm that all aspects of your plan are firmly rooted in your research and insights. Once you have completed and verified your plan, use the tools described in this chapter as your implementation road map.

Managing by calendar

To manage a project well, you must be able to visualize the outcome in your head. You must be able to see how an effort comes together to communicate messages to an individual public and across all your publics. The Gantt chart format recommended in the previous chapter for the calendar helps you see the timing and sequencing of tactics by public throughout the entire timeframe of the project or campaign. You can manage (or delegate management) by public if needed. The same format allows you to identify a selected timeframe — for example, the first week of June — and consider every tactic being implemented among all publics within that time frame. It provides a holistic view of every tactic integrating across all publics; it displays the whole picture of the campaign among all publics for that timeframe. As a management tool, it helps you keep all the balls in the air because you visualize the entirety of events, but it still allows you to narrow your focus to one public as needed.

Managing by task list

As mentioned in Chapter 10, implementation task lists contain detail for each tactic in the proposed plan. The added detail breaks down individual tactics into actionable tasks. You can apply the same calendaring concepts you used to create the campaign calendar to identify the tasks and preparation needed for each tactic in your plan (see Matrix Applied: Implementation task list). In essence, this approach allows you

MATRIX APPLIED

Implementation task list

This implementation task list outlines the individual tasks needed to produce a video for an American Dental Association (ADA) campaign to decrease the incidence of tooth decay among elementary school children by motivating them to practice good dental hygiene. (The tasks shown are illustrative. An actual video of this type would require more detailed tasks to effectively guide its production.)

			Month:	August						
Key Public: *Students*		**Assigned to:** *Jennifer*	**Days:**	26	27	28	29	30	31	1
Strategy: *Motivate through class lessons on dental hygiene*										
Tactic: Video on how to brush/floss										
Tasks:	Brainstorm video ideas			X						
	Finalize video strategy brief								X	
	Create storyboard									
	Create shot list									
	Secure actors and location									
	Film									
	Edit									
	Supervisor approval									
	Post									

to create a detailed roadmap for each tactic that can help you avoid mistakes and delays. It may also reveal hidden pitfalls that could derail your efforts.

Use the Gantt chart format to map out the production of each tactic. This format allows you to see the number of tasks and the amount of time needed to complete each one. Use the campaign calendar to determine the delivery deadline for the tactic. Next, identify the tasks needed to complete the tactic. Then, work backward from the delivery deadline to schedule task completion dates. Once you know when each task must be completed, you can assign tasks and deadlines to the appropriate members of your implementation team. You can also assign a different team member or supervisor to approve each task. The implementation task list will help you keep everyone on track. You can use project management software, like Asana, Basecamp or Zoho Projects, to create and manage task lists that keep everyone on your team up-to-date and on the same page.

	September				October
	2 3 4 5 6 7 8	9 10 11 12 13 14 15	16 17 18 19 20 21 22	23 24 25 26 27 28 29	30 1 2 3 4 5 6
	X				
	X				
		X-----------X			
			X-----------X		
				X-----------X	
					X
					X

Managing by budget

Not only do you need to keep track of the timeline of the campaign and the timing of the tasks involved in creating individual tactics, but you also need to monitor expenses so the project doesn't go over budget. During the action planning phase, you created the campaign budget using projected costs. Projected costs are your best estimates of what the actual costs will be during implementation. However, when you start to implement your campaign, you will incur costs to produce and disseminate your tactics that may be different than what you projected. Prices tend to fluctuate causing your estimated costs to be higher or lower than the actual costs. Other factors can also affect your budget projections. For example, there may be unanticipated changes in sponsorship deals that could increase or decrease your financial ability to produce a tactic.

You can easily convert your eight-column budget document from a planning tool to a project management tool by adding a ninth column to record actual costs. Adding this column will make it easy to compare actual costs against the projected costs for the entire campaign or for specific publics, strategies or tactics. Moira Alexander, a project management expert, author and commentator, explains that budgets should be revisited, reviewed and reforecasted often. She said, "Your chances of keeping a project on track with frequent budget review are far greater than if you forecast once and forget about it."

Tactic creation

The process of developing communications tactics must employ creativity and innovation. The Strategic Communications Matrix provides the analytical framework necessary to channel creativity in the planning process. Shifting from the analytical

TIPS FROM THE PROS

Plan–but be ready to pivot. . . together

Marcus Hardy, an account director at strategic communications firm Intrepid and formerly of agencies and Fortune 500 companies all over the world, tips you off about how sometimes tactical execution must pivot.

Many probably still remember the classic "Friends" episode, "The One with the Cop."

In it, Ross purchases a new couch and recruits Rachel and Chandler (the two friends least inclined to manual labor) to help him heft it up multiple flights of stairs in an NYC walkup building. Ross is ready for the challenge, and has even diagrammed the process ahead of time.

But, as soon as the team reaches the point of execution, chaos ensues. Diagramming aside, the couch is far too big. Chandler is painfully hung out over a banister on the first turn. Rachel is doing the best she can at the rear with no way to see in front of her. As the trio rounds the first turn, Ross frustratedly, obnoxiously and repeatedly orders his friends to "PIVOT!" in a way that earns him a well-deserved "shut up, shut up, shut up!" from Chandler.

Sometimes our well-laid strategic communications plans run into similar trouble. Whether it's a fickle client, a CEO who decides to get overly hands-on, a story that winds up being a dud with the media or a social tactic that is rendered ineffective by an algorithm change, we must master the art of the mid-executional pivot. Here are four things I've embraced in my career to manage these pivots.

Prose isn't precious, but messaging is. Writing is the bread-and-butter of the communications industry, and few things are more gut wrenching than someone important parachuting in at the last minute and insisting on edits. This is where the strategy briefs taught in this textbook come in handy yet again. They help you focus on the message(s) and purpose of a given tactic clearly.

Sometimes the exact structure of a sentence doesn't matter as much as the message and intent being kept, and it's usually faster to quickly placate a stakeholder versus dying on the hill of every bit of copy. So, let the CEO meddle with the verbiage far too late in the game if they insist. Just make sure you defend the key message(s) you laid out in your brief so that the tactic stays true to the strategy.

Don't invite unforced pivots and speed bumps. Coming from someone who is typo-prone, believe me when I say you'll make errors in your work. This is a part of why we work in teams and why quality control is crucial. Embrace the controls and manage up if they seem to slow things down — because there are few feelings worse than being done with an executional step, and then being forced to pivot as you scramble to hit the "edit" button or to issue a correction.

Generally, it's inadvisable to send out anything externally or even to a client that hasn't been read by another human, and ideally read aloud to check for tone in addition to grammar and factual accuracy. Also, hyperlinks — always check and ideally shorten all your links!

Use flexible project tools and embrace transparency. If there is anything I hope your generation of communicators achieves, it is the death of things like email-based "versioning" on documents and the dreaded "action items" list nobody winds up reading post-meeting. I once had a news announcement that made it to version 34 before it was approved — unreal! When a pivot happens in the field, you often don't have time for this type of back-and-forth, asymmetric communication.

Push your teams and organizations to embrace project management tools such as Trello, Microsoft Planner and Notion to keep everyone on the same page and every task on-deadline and in the open for all to see. Additionally, use Office 365, Google Documents, Canva or similar cloud-based content creation tools to remove territoriality in editing, speed approvals and move faster.

Bonus tech tip: Get handy with Excel, particularly with formulas and pivot tables. If all else fails, organizing and breaking down complex information in a spreadsheet might be ugly, but it almost always works.

"Simple is smart." This is the catchphrase of one of my first clients, NYC-based branding firm Siegel+Gale. There is nothing wrong with having a few complex tactics in a campaign, but having a multiplicity of simple, easily adaptable tactics (and simple, sharp messaging) is often a saving grace when pivots come.

Ross tries to return his couch to the store at the end of the episode after having sawed it in half to try to get it to go up the stairs. Fortunately, if you're set up well with what you'll learn in this chapter, you won't have to cut your campaign apart when the inevitable pivot comes.

mind to the creative often causes us to lose strategic focus. So it is also necessary to channel creativity at the tactical level. Otherwise, the creator may lose focus on the public, purpose and message.

Strategy briefs

The secret to maintaining focus in the creative process at the tactical level is to employ an analytical tool used to design the content of a tactic before actually producing it. **Strategy briefs** have been devised for this purpose to supplement and extend the strategic planning process. Take a minute to study Figure 11.1. Strategy briefs are simple outlines uniquely tailored to the development of a specific tactic. They ask questions and contain categories of information for the strategic planner to complete before beginning work on the specific tool or tactic. They ensure that tactics will be consistent with the overall plan and that all important details are included in the copy or visuals. Similar to an outline used to organize and detail a paper or presentation, the strategy brief is an analytical piece that joins the public, purpose and message in a logical, persuasive fashion.

Each strategy brief begins by identifying the key public, which must be one of the publics identified in the campaign plan and the public for which the strategy supported by the specific tactic was designed. If your strategy brief begins by identifying a public who is not in your strategic plan, then you need to reevaluate. Either you neglected an important public in your plan, or you're wasting time and money on an unnecessary tactic. The strategy brief also states the desired action and identifies the key public's self-interest as part of the appeal.

The brief then gets specific in terms of details. Keeping in mind the public and purpose identified at the top, it asks, what are the primary and secondary messages that the key public needs to receive to understand and perform the desired action? These become the copy for your tactic and, in effect, the first draft of the communications tool.

The primary messages are pulled from those you previously designed in step five of the matrix for the particular public you are targeting with this tactic. For each of the primary messages you need to communicate in this tactic, you will need to develop **secondary messages**. As shown in the Matrix Applied below and in Figure 11.1, secondary messages are related to specific primary messages. This is the reason secondary messages are represented by bullet points that are nested under each primary message. Secondary messages contain the meat, or evidence, that validate the information provided or the claims made in the primary messages. There are usually far more secondary messages than primary messages. However, the format of the tactic will also influence the number and type of secondary messages you will need. For example, a news release will need more secondary messages than a billboard. The secondary messages contain all the facts, statistics, case studies, anecdotes, testimonials and other details that support the primary messages. Another way to think about secondary messages is that they provide the ethos, pathos and logos needed to either inform or persuade your public.

You should develop your secondary messages with the key public you are trying to reach and the objective you are trying to accomplish in mind. Remember that strong motivational messages always tap into a public's self-interests. Never forget that people don't do what you want them to just because you ask them to do it. They must first become informed and then motivated. Richard Wirthlin, a world-renowned

STRATEGY BRIEF
An analytical tool that infuses strategic planning into the creation of effective tactics.

SECONDARY MESSAGES
Bulleted details that include facts, testimonials, examples and all other information or persuasive arguments that support a public's primary message.

Figure 11.1
Strategy brief – news release

Key public (brief profile including motivating self-interests):

Secondary publics (if any):

Action desired from public(s):

News release's tie to campaign big idea:

Media contacts and email addresses:

News hook:

Proposed headline:

Proposed lead:

SEO terms (key words or phrases):

Primary messages (two-three short statements, similar to sound bites)
Secondary messages (bulleted supporting data, facts, examples, stories, testimonials, etc.)
   1. Primary:
      Secondary:
      •
      •
      •
   2. Primary:
   Secondary:
      •
      •
      •
   3. Primary:
   Secondary:
      •
      •
      •

Opinion leaders and how they will be used (testimonials, quotes, etc.):

Photos/charts/graphics (if any):

Where and when distributed:

Additional uses after publication:

Timeline/deadline:

Tip: Use the strategy brief for an email news pitch to send your news release to targeted reporters, bloggers, etc.

MATRIX APPLIED

Strategy brief

As part of its campaign to address the recent outbreak of bubonic plague in rural areas, the Arizona State Department of Health developed a strategy to raise awareness among outdoor recreationalists of the risk of plague in certain areas through targeted recreational venues. One of the tactics identified to implement this strategy is a flyer that will be distributed by park rangers and venue employees at fee stations, information booths and park shops and restaurants.

Strategy brief – flyer

Key public (brief profile including motivating self-interests): Outdoor recreationalists. This public includes all those who participate in outdoor recreation in Arizona's rural areas. Most commonly at risk are middle- to upper-class men ages 20 to 45. Most in this group tend to feel invulnerable to risk. They are typically informed about bubonic plague and plague prevention but may be unaware of the current outbreak. Self-interests include enjoying nature, outdoor fun, health and safety.

Action desired from public(s): Outdoor enthusiasts need to be aware of the recent plague outbreak and practice smart plague prevention.

Flyer's tie to campaign big idea: The flyer should prominently feature the campaign hashtag (#AZfightsplague), logos and graphics.

Primary message (usually one short primary message, similar to a sound bite).

Secondary messages (bulleted supporting data, facts, examples, stories, testimonials, etc.)
1. Primary: You can have many more seasons of outdoor fun by practicing smart plague prevention.
   Secondary:
   - The plague has been found in rodents living in rural areas of the state.
   - To stay healthy and safe, always use insect repellent containing DEET applied to both skin and clothing when outdoors.
   - Stay away from debris and other areas where rodents may hide. Never touch or handle wild animals or rodents.
   - Wear protective clothing as appropriate.
   - Tell your friends about the outbreak and encourage them to prevent the spread of the plague.
   - Go to www.AZfightsplague.org or follow us @AZfightsplague on Instagram or TikTok for more information.

Opinion leaders and how they will be used (testimonials, quotes, etc.): Park rangers and venue employees at fee stations, information booths and park shops and restaurants will distribute the flyers. They can answer any questions visitors may have.

Color palette: Black and white.

Art: Map showing areas where bubonic plague has been detected.

Size(s) of flyer: 8.5 x 5.5 (half page).

Location(s) of flyer: National parks, national monuments and state parks fee stations, information booths, park shops and restaurants.

Print quantity: High-quality photocopies on laser printer paper.

Method and timing of distribution: Campaign staff will print and distribute the flyers by the end of March to ensure availability prior to the spring season.

Additional uses after distribution: The flyer will be available to download as a PDF from the campaign website as part of the #AZfightsplague toolkit.

Timeline/deadline: Flyers need to be printed and distributed by the end of the month.

market researcher and founder of Wirthlin Worldwide, advised communicators to "persuade through reason and motivate through emotion." In order to do so, your messages must contain rational information (logos), be delivered by someone the key public trusts (ethos) and contain an emotional appeal (pathos) to a public's self-interest.

Your primary and secondary messages should be stated specifically enough in the strategy brief that another member of your campaign team, your firm or your department in an organization can edit and produce the communications tool without much other information. The messages contain each piece of information necessary to inform the public and motivate them to act. That means, for example, that you must be specific and accurate about dates and times of events you are publicizing, provide contact information for individuals to request more information and include statistics when supporting logical arguments.

After identifying the primary and secondary messages to be used in this product or tactic, the strategy brief requires you to list opinion leaders and how they are used either as part of the messages or in distributing the tactic. For example, in a brochure on personal hygiene for low-income parents, you might use testimonials or information from a recognized health care provider. You may also ask nurses at free clinics to distribute the brochure. Both methods use third-party influentials or opinion leaders to strengthen the appeal.

Make sure to include specific details in your strategy brief. When the brain is in the analytical mode, you can determine exactly what information must be included to accomplish your purpose. But when the brain shifts to the creative mode, you may fail to include critical information in the process of creating great copy. You must channel your creativity by knowing the public, purpose and message, and then you must check the resultant creation against the strategy brief that your analytical mind created for effectiveness.

The most frequently omitted detail in primary and secondary messages (or copy) is the information that provides a way for the public to do what you have asked them to do. Nothing is more frustrating to people than to be persuaded to act but not be given the information necessary to do so. Provide a phone number to call, a website to get more information or specific instructions on what to do.

Next, the strategy brief details your distribution plan. If it is a media product, designate each specific media channel (television or radio station, newspaper or blog) that will receive the tactic. Indicate the delivery method and if any follow-up is required. If it is a brochure or flyer, indicate how it will be distributed. If it is your own blog post, tell how you will direct other social media traffic to your post.

Appendix B contains strategy briefs for several different tactics. These include tools like a news release, website, special event, infographic and video. Each strategy brief has been appropriately altered to request the specific information needed for that kind of tactic. Although the strategy briefs provided in this text cover a wide range of communications tools, you can create your own brief for any tool you wish to use. Before designing your own strategy briefs, make sure you understand each communications tool or product well enough to custom design your own briefs. Remember that the strategy brief is an analytical tool used to guide the development of creative products that will support your strategic plan. Each must contain the specific detail that you determined was necessary to inform, persuade and motivate the public to action.

The use of strategy briefs will save you time and frustration in the development of your tactics. You should spend more time developing your strategy briefs than creating the actual tactics. You will find that, if you plan your strategy briefs carefully and

TIPS FROM THE PROS

How to make your messages sing

Quin Monson, founding partner at Y2 Analytics (a research and analysis firm serving corporate, nonprofit, government and political clients) and professor of political science at Brigham Young University tips you off about the importance of message design and testing.

To change attitudes and behaviors, your communication must repeat the same messages over and over. Effective message testing provides crucial intelligence to help you choose the most effective messages to sell your product or elect your candidate.

Follow these three steps to ensure your messages are persuasive and stay aligned with research findings.

Start with a broad list of possible messages. Use the following sources to generate your list:
- Expert knowledge (from the client or others).
- Previous research (from other candidates or products).
- Focus groups or in-depth interviews (especially helpful when the product or issue is new).
- Professional research (including opponent and competitor research).

Translate themes into brief messages, like sound bites. This is a challenging task that requires solid communication skills. Unlike typical survey questions that should be neutral, your messages should present the information as statements of fact. Avoid false information and be careful with negative messages. While incendiary statements may be true, you may want to avoid messages that could be deeply embarrassing or strike the wrong tone. If the public won't use the information, don't waste money on it.

Here are examples of two message statements that really sang in a survey about a proposed law to legalize medical marijuana:

- The proposed law makes it legal to buy 100 marijuana joints every two weeks and to have as many as 200 marijuana joints in public with no limit to the amount of marijuana allowed in homes.
- Under this proposal, marijuana could be sold in our neighborhood shopping malls, and as close as 300 feet from our homes and only 600 feet from our schools, parks and playgrounds.

Always test your messages. To ensure you don't step in something nasty or waste money on an ineffective message, you must test your messages before using them. Typically, this is done with a survey. But be wary of relying solely on what survey respondents tell you is the best or most persuasive message. Self-reported motivations for attitudes and behavior can be unreliable. Instead, use the change in the attitude or behavior after the messages are shared to assess their effectiveness.

The following are other ways to test your messages.

- Use focus groups before fielding a survey with your message statements to verify the language and message is understood as intended. After the strongest performing messages are translated into advertising, ask questions about how images, physical characteristics of actors, tone of the delivery, music and other features affect how the message resonates.
- Pretest messages with individuals who fit your profile. You can do this informally and quickly if focus groups are too expensive.
- Run an A / B test on social media to measure message effectiveness. This is another good way to test messages before spending all your budget.

Contributed by J. Quin Monson. © Kendall Hunt Publishing Company.

completely, your communications tools will always be on target and will take less time and money to create.

Once a communications product (tactic) is completed, you can use the strategy brief to succinctly explain your product's purpose and use. It will demonstrate the quality of your planning and the strategic thought behind the development of each tactic. It also shows your client or manager that the product was the result of systematic planning and thought. Executives will be more assured of the wisdom of committing resources to production when products have been designed to achieve the purpose identified in your campaign to reach goals and objectives already established.

Quality control

Communicators cannot afford to make mistakes in the production and dissemination of their tactics. Relatively simple mistakes like typos and grammatical errors can damage your professional reputation and distract publics from your message. Bigger mistakes like factual errors, cultural insensitivity or bad messaging can turn your campaign into a crisis. To avoid making mistakes that might derail your strategic

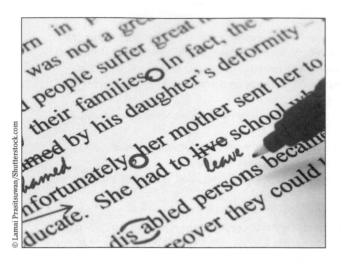

plan, you need to create an approval process for tactics before they are disseminated. This means someone (or multiple people) other than the person who produced the tactic should review it before it's made available for public consumption. It's much better to catch mistakes before flyers are printed, emails are sent, websites are published or social media content is posted. As a popular proverb states, "Measure twice, cut once."

Steve Goldstein, a writer for "PRNews," explains that all writers have their blind spots: the grammar, style and usage mistakes they make consistently, sometimes without being aware of them — like using "lead" when you mean "led;" misusing "their," "there" and "they're;" mixing up "effect" and "affect;" or using "it's" when you should use "its." He recommends developing your own quality control checklist to proof your work before it is published or sent to others for approval. The checklist should remind you to pay attention to common mistakes, such as typos and AP style, but it should also remind you to watch out for the specific mistakes you tend to make. You should add items to this list as you become aware of blind spots in your writing. You can also add items to the list to aid you in fact checking your work. For example, the following questions can help you avoid costly errors.

- Are names of people and organizations spelled correctly?
- Did you use the correct title for a company spokesperson?
- Did you use the correct dates and times?
- Are your quotes or summaries of quotes accurate?
- Are the quotes attributed to the right people?
- Did you use the correct data or statistics to back up a persuasive argument?

Another blind spot that can keep you from producing effective tactics is the curse of knowledge. According to authors Chip and Dan Heath, knowledge becomes a curse when the person communicating an idea can't remember what it was like not to know or understand the idea in the first place. This makes it difficult to communicate with publics who don't know what you know because you assume people know things they really don't know. Daniel Pinker, a linguist at Harvard University, has written and lectured on the curse of knowledge. He explains, "It simply doesn't occur to the writer that readers haven't learned their jargon, don't seem to know the intermediate steps that seem to them to be too obvious to mention, and can't visualize a scene currently in the writer's mind's eye. And so the writer doesn't bother to explain the jargon, or spell out the logic, or supply the concrete details — even when writing for professional peers." One way to beat the curse of knowledge is to have colleagues review your work and identify areas where you are making assumptions that need more clarity or detail. Another way to beat the curse of knowledge is to copy test your tactics with members of your target publics to see whether your messages enlighten or confuse them.

A different tool you can use to gauge the quality of a tactic is the strategy brief that should have guided its creation. Strategy briefs outline the publics, purpose and messages for each tactic. If the tactic was created by following the strategy described

MINI CASE

Commercial satellite imagery combats Russian disinformation
Maxar Technologies

Maxar describes itself as a space technology and intelligence company. They design and manufacture satellites and spacecraft components that enable internet connectivity, television service and radio reception on Earth. Their high-resolution imaging satellites provide the images used by a variety of map-based navigation services. Not surprisingly, Maxar partners with the U.S. government in providing geospatial intelligence for the country's national security efforts.

Several months before the Russian military invaded Ukraine, Maxar began releasing satellite imagery to the media showing the buildup of troops and equipment along the Ukrainian border. At the time, Russian officials were denying any plans to invade, insisting that they were instead conducting routine military exercises. Shortly before the invasion, Russian officials said they were moving troops and equipment away from the border.

CORE OPPORTUNITY
Maxar's satellite constellation was monitoring Russia's military operations on the Ukrainian border and was in a position to share images of what was actually happening on the ground with the rest of the world, demonstrating its commitment to sharing for the social good.

Satellite image © Maxar Technologies.

MAXAR'S STRATEGY

Prior to the buildup of Russian forces on Ukraine's border, Maxar had developed an image-sharing service that it called the News Bureau. Through the company's News Bureau initiative, Maxar made much of its imagery available to news organizations around the world to support global transparency and combat the spread of disinformation. However, the tempo and frequency of the News Bureau's interaction with news media accelerated in 2022 due to the situation in Ukraine.

Maxar had been monitoring the evolving situation in the region since Russia invaded Crimea, Ukraine, in 2014. Activity picked up again in early 2021 and accelerated in late 2021 as more Russian troops and equipment were deployed near the Ukrainian border. Maxar shared imagery of those troop movements with the news media to combat Russia's disinformation about what was happening.

The BBC ran a story on Feb. 17, 2022, that mentioned Maxar by name and used satellite images of a field hospital, a pontoon bridge, an artillery training and an airstrip full of attack helicopters to make the case that "widescale Russian military activity persists close to Ukraine's borders, despite recent Russian claims of de-escalation and withdrawal."

Similarly, soon after the invasion began, Maxar satellites collected images on Feb. 28, 2022, of a large, 40-mile Russian convoy making its way toward Kyiv at the same time that the Russians were publicly insisting that they were pulling their forces back from the border.

As the war unfolded, Maxar continued to provide satellite images to its news organization partners to document the reality and magnitude of the conflict, including evidence of potential war crimes and human rights violations committed by the Russian military in Ukraine. For example, in Mariupol, the city theater had become a main bomb shelter for civilians. It was housing more than 1,000 people. As one of Maxar's News Bureau analysts who spoke Russian was looking at images of the area, he noticed that the word "children" had been painted in large, white Russian letters–both in the front and back of the theater so it could be seen from the sky and signal to the Russians that this was not a military target.

The Associated Press reported that the theater was bombed days later. When Maxar satellites collected new images of the location the word "children" was still visible on the ground. News reporting out of Mariupol said that more than 600 people were killed in the attack and Maxar images of the aftermath of the attack were included in the coverage.

RESULTS

- Between February 2022 through January 2023, the Maxar satellite constellation collected more than 5.1 million square kilometers of high-resolution satellite images over Ukraine.
- The Maxar News Bureau produced and released more than 500 images to the news media. More than 400 reporters joined Maxar's distribution list.
- More than 60,000 mentions of Maxar appeared across broadcast and online news and blogs.
- As interest in the company increased during this time, the number of unique visitors to the company's website increased by more than 2,200%.
- Maxar posted its News Bureau images on Maxar social media channels and saw an increased number of followers and increased engagement. Followers of Maxar's Twitter account increased 74% during 2022.

in the strategy brief, you can have confidence that it will have the intended effect when it is distributed to its intended audience. However, if the tactic is "off strategy," meaning it isn't tied to the strategy brief, it's not likely to be effective and should be revised before it is used in the campaign. You, or those who have project oversight, can compare finalized strategy briefs with drafts of tactics to ensure they target the right public, appeal to the right self-interest, accomplish the right objectives and communicate the right messages. You can also use strategy briefs to keep assigned content creators on task by ensuring that the distribution information on the brief reflects deadlines and milestones on the implementation task lists and campaign calendar.

Ongoing monitoring and feedback

The implementation management tools described in this chapter — the campaign calendar, implementation task lists, the nine-column budget, the strategy briefs and the quality control checklist — are the maps you use to keep your implementation efforts on track. While these tools provide structure, accountability and deadlines, implementation also requires flexibility to adapt to changing circumstances and unanticipated responses. Prussian military strategist Helmuth von Moltke described the need for flexibility this way, "No strategy survives first contact with the enemy."

When you plan the evaluation (the final step in the Strategic Communications Matrix), you will plan for measurement throughout the implementation phase. These measurements provide checkpoints for your progress toward reaching the objectives and goal. But what if your measurements reveal that you are not on track?

The implementation management tools give you the flexibility to make adjustments as the plan unfolds. Changes in the timing of production or distribution of tactics can be addressed in the calendar and task lists. Sometimes monitoring will reveal a need to make fundamental changes to your plan. Adjustments to tactics could include tweaks to messages or changes in distribution channels. These changes should be reflected in the strategy briefs and will flow naturally into the tactics as they are created. Adjustments to the strategy might require you to go back to your planning documents to rework and refine your plan to get back on track. The necessary alteration may be as simple as adding or changing a single tactic or as grand as revamping an entire public.

Summary

The campaign calendar is a planning tool that becomes a management tool once you have begun the actual implementation of your communications plan. Use it to manage your efforts for each public as well as to manage the whole campaign from a macro perspective. Implementation task lists break tactics down into their component tasks and allow you to track them to completion. Strategy briefs are used to create and confirm that communications tactics are consistent with your overall strategy. Self-generated quality control checklists remind you of the common grammar, style and usage mistakes you personally tend to make and should check before mass producing or distributing your tactics. Coupled with ongoing monitoring and feedback, these management tools allow for flexibility and adjustment to keep the plan on track.

Exercises

1. Select any of the plans you have prepared for the Application Cases in other chapters of this book. Identify a tactic from that plan and create an implementation task list for it. Identify all of the tasks that would need to have been completed to produce and distribute the tactic. Be as thorough as possible. Create a Gantt chart that shows the order in which the tasks would need to have been completed. Identify deadlines for each task.

2. Create a strategy brief for the tactic you selected to complete exercise one. Use the appropriate strategy brief template in Appendix B or create your own following the general guideline of the strategy brief templates. When you get to the messaging section of the strategy brief, develop secondary messages that support your primary messages. Think through the logistical details of creating the tactic. What kind of visuals or design elements will it need? How will it be distributed? What is the timeline for creating it?

3. Create your own personal quality control checklist. Include common errors in grammar, spelling, usage and style. Identify areas where you know you are weak. Talk with others who are familiar with your work to help you identify any blind spots you might not be aware of.

4. Review a few of your past attempts to communicate information with another person. You could look at personal emails and social media posts or communications tactics you made for class or a client. Consider who you were communicating with and try to see past your own assumptions. Did you fall victim to the curse of knowledge?

References and additional readings

adidas. (2018) Here to create legend website. Retrieved from http://www.heretocreatelegend.adidas.com

adidas. (2018, April 5). adidas introduces 'Here to Create Legend' 2018 Boston Marathon® campaign featuring 30K personal highlight videos delivered to 30K runners within hours. [Press Release]. Retrieved from https://news.adidas.com/us/Latest-News/adidas-introduces--here-to-create-legend--2018-boston-marathon--campaign--featuring-30k-personal-hig/s/118fc950-53c9-406c-98ff-34881adb6f0f

Alexander, M. (2017, Aug. 18). Project management: 5 tips for managing your project budget. Retrieved from https://www.cio.com/article/2406862/project-management/project-management-project-management-4-ways-to-manage-your-budget.html

Gardner, F. (2022, February 17). Ukraine: Satellite images show Russian military activity. *BBC*. Retrieved from https://www.bbc.com/news/world-europe-60421378

Goldstein, S. (2016, May 19). A quality control checklist for all your writing. Retrieved from https://www.prnewsonline.com/a-quality-control-checklist-for-all-your-writing/

Grow website. (2018). Retrieved from https://thisisgrow.com/work/here-to-create-legend

Guillodo, L. (n.d.). Quote #25: No strategy survives first contact with the enemy. *Arthur D. Little Digital Problem Solving*. Retrieved from http://www.digitalproblemsolving. com/quote/no-strategy-survives-first-contact-with-the-enemy

Heath, C. & Heath, D. (2008). *Made to Stick: Why Some Ideas Survive and Others Die*. New York: Random House, Inc.

Hinnant, L., Stepanenko, V., El Deeb, S. & Tilna, E. (2022, Dec. 22). Russia scrubs Mariupol's Ukraine identity, builds on death. *Associated Press*. Retreived from https:// apnews.com/article/russia-ukraine-war-erasing-mariupol-499dceae43ed77f2ebfe75 0ea99b9ad9

Maxar. (n.d.). Retrieved from https://www.maxar.com/

News Bureau. (n.d.). *Maxar*. Retrieved from https://www.maxar.com/news-bureau

Richards, K. (2018, April 19). adidas created personalized videos for 30,000 Boston Marathon runners in 24 hours: Brand worked with agency Grow to pull off the feat. *Ad Week*. Retrieved from https://www.adweek.com/brand-marketing/adidas-created-personalized-videos-for-30000-boston-marathon-runners-in-24-hours/

Sheffer, G. & Fernandez, M. (Hosts). (2022, September 26). Battling misinformation using satellite imagery with Maxar VP of Communications Fernando Vivanco [Audio podcast episode]. In *The Crux of the Story*. Retrieved from https://heptagon-dodecahedron-cdbg.squarespace.com/season-5/fernando-vivanco

Strobel, W. P. & Gordon, M. R. (2022, January 4). Russia's military buildup near Ukraine is an open secret. *The Wall Street Journal*. Retrieved from https://www.wsj.com/ articles/russias-military-buildup-near-ukraine-is-an-open-secret-11641292202?st=g wi0uo2jsd5d6ey&reflink=desktopwebshare_permalink

Sleek, S. (2015). The curse of knowledge: Pinker describes a key cause of bad writing. [Blog post]. Retrieved from https://www.psychologicalscience.org/observer/the-curse-ofknowledge-pinker-describes-a-key-cause-of-bad-writing

CHAPTER 12

COMMUNICATIONS MEASUREMENT AND EVALUATION

*"One accurate measurement
is worth a thousand
expert opinions."*

—GRACE HOPPER
COMPUTER SCIENTIST AND
UNITED STATES NAVY REAR ADMIRAL

LEARNING IMPERATIVES

- Understand the importance of measurement and evaluation in demonstrating results.

- Understand how to plan measurement and evaluation based on what you are trying to accomplish.

- Understand how to determine evaluation criteria and the appropriate measurement tools.

O ver two decades ago, surveys among public relations professionals found that they generally "lacked confidence to promote evaluation methods to employers and clients" (Watson, 2001). Lack of knowledge, lack of standards, lack of budget and lack of interest in measurement and evaluation seemed to be the primary reasons practitioners did not propose or conduct evaluation research (Macnamara, 2015).

Since then, the communications industry has responded to these challenges. An international coalition of industry associations issued the Barcelona Declaration of Measurement Principles. The latest version of these seven basic principles is shown in Figure 12.1. The Institute for Public Relations created a Measurement Commission and an online repository of measurement and evaluation resources. And the International Association for Measurement and Evaluation of Communication (AMEC) launched an "Interactive Evaluation Framework" to help communicators "prove the value of communication in an age of accountability."

However, research continues to show that "communication measurement practices are still in a nascent stage" (Zerfass, Verčič, & Volk, 2017) with most communicators measuring media and channels but neglecting to measure the impact of communication on organizations and publics.

At the same time, measurement has become the watch word and "results, results, results" the mantra of executives. Instead of viewing an organization's communication as a kind of mystical intangible — intangible methods, intangible effects and intangible results — we must measure everything in our effort to build strong relationships with key publics and contribute to our organization's success. This is the crucial step that will finally make us strategic.

We must be focused on what we are trying to accomplish, who we need to reach to achieve it, what messages will motivate them and how best to send those messages so they pay attention and act. Executives demand hard data measuring our results in each one of those key elements to success. They use data to evaluate success and to drive decision-making. As W. Edwards Demming, a business management scholar and consultant, once said, "In God we trust. All others must bring data."

Organizations — commercial, governmental and nonprofit — are managed to produce results and to accomplish their missions. Each function of the organization must be able to demonstrate its contribution to the accomplishment of the mission. The ability to prove results is critical not only for the organization but also for the employees doing the work. There is little reward to working daily in efforts that you cannot be sure are making a contribution.

Measurement and evaluation models

MEASUREMENT
What can be observed or counted in a campaign.

Measurement and evaluation of a communications campaign consists of two separate but related activities. The first activity is communications measurement. The Institute for Public Relations describes **measurement** as "what can be observed and counted of a public relations program or campaign." In the same way that you use a ruler to measure the length of a physical object, you use communications measurement tools to collect data about the reach, engagement and performance of your communications.

Figure 12.1
Barcelona Principles 3.0

1. Setting goals is an absolute prerequisite to communications planning, measurement and evaluation.
2. Measurement and evaluation should identify outputs, outcomes and potential impact.
3. Outcomes and impact should be identified for stakeholders, society and the organization.
4. Communication measurement and evaluation should include both qualitative and quantitative analysis.
5. Advertising Value Equivalents (AVEs) are not the value of communication.
6. Holistic communication measurement and evaluation includes all relevant online and offline channels.
7. Communication measurement and evaluation are rooted in integrity and transparency to drive learning and insights.

Source: International Association for the Measurement and Evaluation of Communication

The second activity is **evaluation**. According to the Institute for Public Relations, communications evaluation compares the measurements you have taken against "desired public relations objective[s] and the extent to which activities contributed value to the organization." Comparison against some standard or criterion is at the heart of evaluation. For example, in a 100-meter sprint, runners' times to complete the race are measured by a stopwatch in seconds and milliseconds. The criterion for winning the race is to have the fastest time. So, the winner is determined by comparing the recorded times of the individual racers. Once the winner is declared, race commentators usually compare the winning runner's time against the world record for that race to evaluate the winning runner's performance in a historical context.

The communication literature contains several models of evaluation. They basically all evaluate success along three standards. The first is success that justifies the budget expenditure. The second is effectiveness of the program. The third is whether objectives were met. While these standards are all worthwhile gauges of success, put yourself in the position of a CEO. What are they looking for? In a word, results.

Results may mean meeting the objectives, they may mean success that justifies the budget expenditure or they may mean effectively carrying out a program. But what we should focus on as our organization's marketing, public relations and social media communications specialists is setting objectives that are measured in terms of results. We also need to justify budget expenditures in terms of results and determine program effectiveness in terms of results.

AMEC developed an Integrated Evaluation Framework to help communicators implement the Barcelona Principles and demonstrate effectiveness. The framework outlines four levels of measurement that align with the four types of objectives we discussed in Chapter 5: outputs, outtakes, outcomes and impacts. When used in combination, they paint a complete picture of program effectiveness.

 EVALUATION
Comparison of measurement data against a standard or criterion.

- **Outputs:** Whether our tactics succeeded in delivering the right motivational messages to the right publics.

© create jobs 51/Shutterstock.com

- ***Outtakes:*** What those publics did with our messages when they received them.
- ***Outcomes:*** What effect our messages had on key publics.
- ***Impacts:*** The results that were achieved by the campaign.

The first two measurement levels — outputs and outtakes — are particularly useful as tactical monitoring tools during campaign implementation. In Chapter 5, we suggested that you wait until this last step of the planning process to create output and outtake objectives. Now that you know what the tactics of your campaign will be, identifying which outputs and outtakes you want to measure is fairly straightforward. Keep in mind that while outputs and outtakes usually are not sufficient to demonstrate program effectiveness on their own, they can help you make critical adjustments to your plan during implementation so you can ultimately achieve your outcome and impact objectives. They can also help you make the case that your tactics and messages led to the outcomes and impacts your campaign was designed to achieve.

The Mini Case in this chapter demonstrates how outputs, outtakes, outcomes and impacts can be laddered using AMEC's Integrated Evaluation Framework to show the effectiveness of your campaign across all four levels of measurement. In a similar way that the Awareness-Interest-Desire-Action (AIDA) funnel is used in marketing, AMEC's evaluation framework can help you map out and track the journey of your key publics from their initial encounter with your tactics (outputs), through their engagement or interaction with those tactics (outtakes), to the cognitive, emotional or behavioral changes that result from engagement with those tactics (outcomes), to the publics' changes in thoughts, feelings, opinions, beliefs or behaviors (impacts).

Simply stated, outputs are measurements of a communications plan's tactics. Output measurements typically include the number of tactics distributed, events held or materials produced, as well as reach, share of voice, mentions, tone of coverage and message inclusion on social or earned media channels (e.g., media impressions).

Outtakes are measurements of message reception. They measure whether your messages made it through the selective perception and retention filters of target publics. Measuring outtakes allows communicators to determine the effectiveness of their tactics in breaking through the media clutter and capturing attention. Some outtakes are relatively easy to measure because they focus on the engagement (e.g., views, clicks, shares and downloads) of your key publics with digital messages. However, outtakes can also include non-digital takeaways for key publics (e.g., message recall, awareness, understanding and retention) that may be more difficult to measure, but more valuable to know.

Both outputs and outtakes are necessary precursors to the next two measurement categories — outcomes and impacts. Both of these measurement categories are used to determine the results of a campaign on publics and organizations. Outcomes measure the effect of messages on key publics. The Institute for Public Relations describes outcomes as "more macro and often more perceptual in nature." In other words, outcomes try to measure if our communications efforts had an effect on the way members of our key public think, feel, believe or behave. While influencing behavior is the ultimate goal of strategic communications, often changes in awareness, beliefs, values and attitudes are necessary precursors to changing or reinforcing desired behaviors.

Impacts measure the effect of a communications campaign on core business objectives. This type of evaluation is used to figure out the extent to which

TIPS FROM THE PROS

Telling your measurement story

Emily Peet, director of research & analytics at EvolveMKD tips you off on communicating measurement results with your clients and colleagues.

As researchers and communicators, it's our role to measure the results of our communications efforts for our clients or colleagues. But data and results without effective storytelling are meaningless to non-researchers. As important as measuring our results is our responsibility to translate those results in a way that arms decision makers with the information they need to make smart strategic decisions and drive continuous improvement over time.
Here are three things to consider when choosing how to share results with your audience.

Put yourself in the decision maker's shoes. Your role is to give them the information they need to act on the results. Try to anticipate how they will use results, what questions they might ask and what's in it for them. Understand that not all executives are data-savvy, so you'll need to consider what context they'll need to make sense of the numbers.

So what?! A good report should answer the question "why does this matter" and provide recommendations and next steps, especially along the lines of "what worked," "what did not work" and "what we could improve on in the future."

Everyone loves a good story. Talking about data at length can be a quick way to lose the interest of your audience. Try framing your results as a story, starting with outputs and moving to impact in a way that reads something like:

"Our objective was to move the needle on this outcome, X to Y. To accomplish this, we undertook the following communications activities (outputs), which reached this many people among our target audience (outtakes). As a result our target audience changed in this way (outcomes) and we are closer to realizing Z business objective (impact)."

© Emily Peet. Reprinted by permisison.

communications efforts had a positive impact on performance indicators that are important to the overall organization. These indicators may include reputation, relationships, sales or donations. These measurement categories are particularly important because evaluation that does not measure end results simply cannot stand the test of today's organizational managers. And communications professionals who cannot demonstrate that their efforts produce the desired outcomes within acceptable expenditures are themselves expendable.

Evaluation is actually relatively easy if it is planned from the beginning of a campaign using the Strategic Communications Matrix. Good evaluation owes a lot to good objectives. If the objectives are written as outputs, outtakes or outcomes that must be accomplished to reach the goal, then the evaluation will be results-oriented. Two steps must be considered in evaluating any plan. First, by what criteria should we judge success (or what are the benchmark metrics that we will evaluate against)? Second, what are the best tools to collect the measurements that will allow us to evaluate success?

STRATEGIC COMMUNICATIONS MATRIX

EVALUATION

8. EVALUATION CRITERIA AND MEASUREMENT TOOLS

Evaluation Criteria
Specific and measurable results taken from each of the objectives. Focus on outputs, outtakes, outcomes and impacts.

Measurement Tools
The methodologies needed to gather the data for the evaluation criteria. These tools must be included in the objectives and in the calendar and budget.

Evaluation criteria

EVALUATION CRITERIA
Metrics or standards set to measure success.

MEASUREMENT TOOL
Method used to gather data needed to assess whether evaluation criteria were met.

It is particularly important in this era of "big data" to set clear objectives that outline the metrics that will guide our measurement efforts and that will define the **evaluation criteria** by which we will gauge our success. One of the best ways to make sense of the never-ending sea of data that surrounds us is to clearly define success in terms of specific, measurable objectives so it becomes clear what data is relevant for measurement and evaluation. This approach will enable you to "measure what matters," a mantra of Katie Delahaye Paine, a public relations measurement and evaluation expert, consultant and author.

Evaluation criteria are automatically determined when objectives are set. Objectives are designed to provide direction to planning and to identify the results that define success. Clients and managers will judge success by the criteria (objectives) you have set. In this step of your plan, restate your objectives in terms of success, and designate an appropriate **measurement tool** to measure each one, including a date for the measurement to be made. For example, if one of your objectives is to increase name recognition of your client from 30% to 80%, the metric for success would be written, "Achieve 80% name recognition of the client's name among key publics by June 30, 2024, as measured by an online survey."

The successful achievement of all campaign objectives should result in the accomplishment of the goal, which may or may not be directly measurable. If you have followed the communications matrix, accomplishing the overall goal will signify to management that you have achieved success in all three standards identified above. You can justify the expenditure because you reached your goal within the proposed budget. You demonstrate effectiveness because your strategies and tactics combined to accomplish the goal. And, you met the campaign objectives, which resulted in the accomplishment of the goal.

Make sure to establish meaningful criteria of success. The communications industry has published a variety of resources to help you understand and choose appropriate evaluation criteria. For example, the Institute for Public Relations publishes definitions of metrics and methods in its online "Dictionary of Public Relations Measurement and Research." The Paine Publishing website aggregates resources on measurement standards and best practices. Also, AMEC's social media-specific evaluation framework guides communicators through measurement criteria needed to evaluate every stage of the marketing funnel. This integrated approach to measurement is becoming increasingly common as communicators use a combination of paid, earned, shared and owned media tactics to reach publics.

In addition to evaluating program results (i.e., outcomes and impacts), you should look at the effectiveness of different parts of your plan, including how well strategies and tactics performed (i.e., outtakes). Always keep in mind that message exposure doesn't mean message receipt. Remember that behavior is the ultimate measure.

You should also evaluate your own performance: your professionalism, creativity and ability to direct or implement a communications effort (i.e., outputs). You can add evaluation factors that specifically address your success and effectiveness in community relations, media relations or some other skill area. While media placement is not a measure of whether a public received and acted upon a message, it is still a factor to be evaluated within the context of effective strategies and tactics.

Only through honest self-evaluation will you improve your skills. What did you do well? What could you have done better? Where do you need more training or experience? These are primarily internal measures and do not usually become part of the formal campaign put together using the Strategic Communications Matrix. But they are, nonetheless, important. Converting your objectives to evaluation criteria is your primary evaluation of results. Additional criteria that address your team's specific capability and expertise are highly useful secondary criteria to measure your effectiveness and improve your performance.

Measurement tools

Each objective must be converted to an evaluation criterion or metric, and each criterion must be measurable by a measurement tool. Measurement tools are essentially research, or data gathering, tools. They are the same kinds of methodologies used in the research stage of the matrix, but they focus on collecting data related to the activities of your communications campaign. They include website data, social media data, search data, content analysis of news coverage, surveys of key publics, and behavioral data, such as sales volume, vote counts, dollars raised or saved, and legislative bills passed or failed. As stated in the Barcelona Principles, the rules of research apply in measurement and evaluation. Sound methodology will not only give you credibility but also reliable and valid data on which to base future efforts.

Typically, evaluation measurements require a benchmark measurement before the program begins, during the program or both. Without adequate planning for the evaluation process, the benchmarks are often not taken before the campaign starts, resulting in no data for comparison. Unless you know where you started, you cannot determine how far you've come.

Although measurement tools are essentially the same as research methods, many research organizations have specialized in measurement and evaluation services. It would be wise to access the websites and newsletters on evaluation and measurement produced by specialty firms like Paine Publishing or Cision. While

MINI CASE

Global Development Bank:
Connecting communications to climate change

from EvolveMKD and Rockland Dutton Research & Consulting

The Global Development Bank (GDB) is an international organization whose mission is to create a prosperous, equitable and sustainable world while maintaining its mission to eradicate poverty. To achieve this, the GDB funds projects in developing nations across a multitude of sectors including climate change, education, food security, trade and agriculture.

MEASUREMENT AND EVALUATION PROBLEM

The GDB needed a way to measure and evaluate the impact of its communications activities to support the bank's mission and performance, particularly among certain initiatives such as climate change where the intended outcomes and impact are difficult to quantify.

MEASUREMENT AND EVALUATION SOLUTION

The GDB developed a framework to establish a consistent communications measurement and evaluation practice across the organization. The figure below visualizes the construct of the framework starting at the bottom, laddering communications outputs that drive outtakes, that create changes in understanding, trust, leadership and advocacy (outcomes) among target audiences. Ultimately, the outcomes enable the delivery of the communication goals that support the Global Development Bank's mission (impacts).

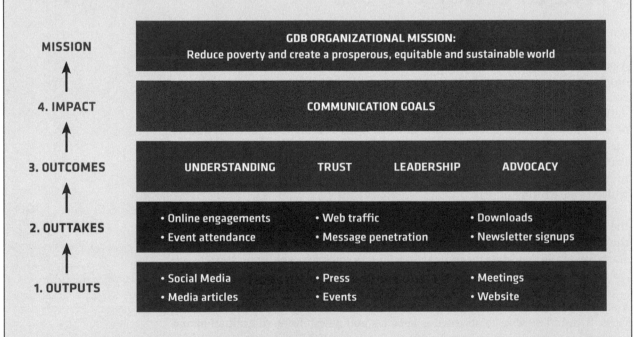

MISSION	**GDB ORGANIZATIONAL MISSION:** Reduce poverty and create a prosperous, equitable and sustainable world			
4. IMPACT	**COMMUNICATION GOALS**			
3. OUTCOMES	UNDERSTANDING	TRUST	LEADERSHIP	ADVOCACY
2. OUTTAKES	• Online engagements • Event attendance	• Web traffic • Message penetration		• Downloads • Newsletter signups
1. OUTPUTS	• Social Media • Media articles	• Press • Events		• Meetings • Website

The framework identified four specific elements where communicators could set objectives for their upcoming climate change campaign in South Asian countries.

Outputs were defined as communications activities ranging from social media campaigns, events and articles in the media, to high-level meetings with foreign policy leaders and lobbying/activism.

Outtakes were defined as online engagements, event attendance, web traffic, key message penetration, downloads of GDB research and more. Examples of specific outtake objectives included:
- Securing a 40% share of voice from the bank on climate change issues in South Asian media by year end.
- Having 25% of those who visit the climate change website represent South Asian countries by year end.
- Increasing social media engagements by South Asian policy makers by 10% by year end.

Outcomes measures were established to measure audience changes in four overarching areas.
- Understanding: The target audience understands or is aware of how the GDB contributes to reducing the effect of climate change in the area.
- Trust: The target audience views the GDB as a trusted partner who will do what is right for the region.
- Leadership: The target audience sees the GDB as a leader on the issue of climate change.
- Advocacy: Top policy makers' actions are influenced by the GDB in support of the projects being undertaken.

The Global Development Bank used their existing survey deployed in all the countries in which they work to measure the change in policy makers' opinions as a result of communications outputs.

Impact measures were derived from the organizational mission, which is ultimately too broad to attribute to communications alone. Instead, the GDB established a series of communication goals that were specific to the climate change campaign, while laddering up to the broad organizational priorities. Goals included:
- Securing political support for the GDB's climate change initiatives.
- Influencing policy designed to mitigate damage to natural resources.
- Establishing the GDB as a leader in research and policy on the issue of climate change.

RESULTS

The objective of the climate change campaign was to influence policy makers in South Asia to support the bank's project to reduce ocean plastics in the region. To accomplish this, the GDB organized several meetings with key policy makers, ran a social media campaign, and secured top-tier media coverage, reaching 15 policy makers and over 300,000 civilians. As a result, 95% of policy makers surveyed said that they plan to support the GDB's ocean plastic project both publicly and financially.

evaluation tools for some objectives may be obvious, others may require complicated formulas that would, for example, combine measures of sales, media placements and social media referrals in some kind of sliding scale that measures the effect of communications, marketing and customer engagement on product sales.

Clearly articulated measurement tools must include the source of information and how it will be obtained. Include all necessary tasks when describing the evaluation tool for each criterion. Use the example in this chapter's Matrix Applied as a guide to construct measurement tools that show results against previously established benchmarks.

Adding measurement tools to calendars and budgets

The evaluation process necessitates reviewing your calendar and budget to ensure that all measurement tools are scheduled and costs estimated. You can designate a separate section of the calendar and budget to specifically address the planned

MATRIX APPLIED

Evaluation criteria and measurement tools

A regional banking institution's research shows that while the public perceives it is financially strong, well-managed and safe, brand loyalty even in the financial industry is dependent upon perceptions of the quality of customer service and the involvement of the organization in its local communities. The bank implemented a campaign highlighting community relations efforts and improved customer service. It had four objectives, each of which became an evaluation criterion to measure success.

Objective one: Improve the bank's overall customer service ratings from 4.8 on a seven-point scale to 5.8 within six months (21% increase).
Evaluation criterion (outcome)
Customer service ratings are 5.8 or higher on June 1, 2024 (six months after the campaign begins).
Measurement tool
Use the bank's automated email survey system to measure customer satisfaction ratings two weeks before and two weeks after June 1, 2024, and take the aggregate score. As an additional step, monitor monthly customer satisfaction scores to gauge the progress during the campaign.

Objective two: Improve the public perception of the bank as customer service-oriented from 40% using that descriptor to 60% using that descriptor within one year (50% increase).
Evaluation criterion (outcome)
Sixty percent of customers will feel the bank is customer service-oriented on January 1, 2025 (one year after the campaign begins).
Measurement tool
Replicate the values perception survey upon which the campaign was built in June 2024 to measure progress toward the objective and the first week of January 2025 to determine if the objective was met.

Objective three: Raise awareness of the bank's local contributions to the community to 60% within six months.
Evaluation criterion (outcome)
Sixty percent of residents will know about at least one of the bank's contributions to the community on June 1, 2024.
Measurement tool
Add an unaided recall question to the values perception survey upon which the campaign was built. Determine progress toward the objective with the interim survey in June 2024 and a final survey the first week of January 2025.

Objective four: Maintain a 94% customer retention rate during 2024 and a 95% retention rate for the four years after that (through 2028).
Evaluation criterion (outcome)
The bank loses less than 6% of its current customers in 2024 and less than 5% of its customer base each year from 2025 through 2028.
Measurement tool
Use the bank's customer records to determine what percent of current customers remain each year. The number of customers on the first day of January each year will serve as the benchmark.

measurement. A wiser choice might be to include measurement as part of the planned strategies and tactics for each public. Only with this kind of planning can you ensure that appropriate benchmark research is done in the beginning and throughout the campaign to compare with evaluation research. It also enables you to incorporate appropriate measurement and evaluation in the detailed planning for tactics. For example, if you need to measure the number of attendees at events or traffic to a blog, you will build into the tactic a method for tracking those numbers. Trying to guesstimate such figures later only causes your evaluation to be inadequate and your claim to success suspect. Finally, including the measurement tools in the calendar and budget for each public ensures that funding is available for this critical function.

Summary

Communications and marketing professionals cannot expect to be taken seriously unless they positively demonstrate the results of their efforts. Measuring the effectiveness of communications efforts can be a straightforward process if you use the Strategic Communications Matrix. The matrix focuses your efforts to set objectives that are the outcomes which will combine to reach the overall goal. Evaluation of the objectives should be as strategic a function as any part of the process. Objectives become the evaluation criteria or metrics and must meet the highest standards of measurement. Effective planning will also include determining how to evaluate the effectiveness of specific strategies and tactics as well as your own performance.

Tools for measuring success are basically the same as the methodologies used in research. Nevertheless, many professional research firms now specialize in evaluative research and can design specific tools for your needs. Make sure to include the measurement tools needed in the calendar and budget for each public so this critical process is not overlooked.

Application case

Alaska Airlines Next-Level Care
from Alaska Airlines with C+C and Mekanism

CORE OPPORTUNITY
The COVID-19 pandemic took a heavy toll on the airline industry. According to the U.S. Government Accountability Office, there were 96% fewer passengers flying in April 2020 than the previous year. This meant that airlines like Alaska had to ease traveler's fears about contracting COVID-19 on airplanes if they wanted to keep their customers in the air.

BACKGROUND RESEARCH
Research found that 74% of Americans were nervous about flying and that 92% of employers had canceled or postponed business travel. However, government,

TIPS FROM THE PROS

Measurement beyond impressions

Alessandra Simkin, Erin Graves, Shalon (Roth) Kerr and Andrea Roley, seasoned healthcare communication pros, tip you off on how to make measurement more impressive than just impressions.

The most effective public relations pros agree measurement is more than impressions, and yet clients and leadership keep requesting those numbers anyway. How can you show stakeholders that taking PR measurement beyond impressions helps to better celebrate success – while also providing greater insight into opportunities for improvement? Below are five steps that we recommend to help make measurement frameworks more impressive than mere impressions.

Define your client(s). By "client," we mean anyone who matters to you. Who do you need to dazzle? Who is your immediate client – and who are their clients? Your immediate clients should be obvious, but you might need to dig a little to discover who they're trying to impress. Maybe it's their boss, for instance. There are always main clients if you're on the agency side of the business, and oftentimes marketing colleagues if you're in-house. They could also be sales teams, C-level executives or board members who influence the role of public relations at an organization's macro level.

Determine what your client wants out of their metrics. Clients have different business challenges and opportunities, but what they want is never to merely secure social media impressions. Whether they want to find new ways to build global consumer brands in the United States; ensure that patients, news media and investors understand the findings of an important clinical program; or challenge public perceptions about a complicated societal issue, we have to learn why clients want to use public relations to solve the challenges they face. By digging into the client's business challenges and asking specific questions at the outset, we can help them think more about baseline measurements that will make measuring at the end of the program much stronger and more helpful.

Ensure your plan addresses your client's challenges, and then measure it. It's obvious that counting campaign impressions doesn't help clients show their bosses how public relations helps achieve the organization's goals. So the question becomes: What metrics will demonstrate the value of public relations? In one trend we've seen, clients are looking for PR programs that support sales goals. When assembling a plan, think about metrics that will show the client how PR addresses their actual business challenges, and how you will collect baseline and post-campaign data.

Sell it. Plans that directly address business challenges have helped us avoid being asked to include ad-equivalency metrics in our recap decks. If you still get that question anyway, explain your rationale for including those additional metrics. Educate your client about other metrics to consider, such as tonality and share of voice. Be clear about metrics that will be more challenging to capture and explain proxies that could be used instead.

Celebrate your measurements. When you define your client(s) in the first step, also take time to consider how you may need to present measurement data differently for each client's particular needs. For example, a communications client may be interested in the volume of media coverage and message pull-through (maybe even impressions). And while a marketing client will be more interested in lead-generation indicators, a sales client will want to know if customers noticed. In addition to celebrating what worked, some clients may want to understand what didn't work and why. Think of ways to create productive dialogues around information and how to improve recommendations for the next time.

Ultimately, to make your PR measurements more impressive than impressions, take time at the beginning to map out who asked for support and why. Use our step-by-step approach to identify metrics that matter, manage expectations and find proxies for metrics that are trickier to track.

© Alessandra Simkin, Erin Graves, Shalon (Roth) Kerr and Andrea Roley. Reprinted by permission. The original, unabridged version of this article is available on PRsay, PRSA's blog at http://prsay.prsa.org/2019/10/11/5-steps-to-make-your-pr-measurement-more-impressive-than-just-impressions/.

academic and industry research found a significantly low risk for contracting COVID-19 from the air on an airplane, especially when all of the passengers wore masks.

COMMUNICATION GOAL AND OBJECTIVES
To educate the public on travel safety and help guests feel comfortable flying again.

Objective 1: Earn national recognition as the safest U.S. carrier to fly.

Objective 2: Place the Next-Level Care program and policies in 250 national media stories, 100 trade stories and 1,500 stories in key markets, and garner at least 2.5 billion impressions from program launch through the end of the year.

Objective 3: Drive positive brand awareness and understanding of airline safety with a content package on Alaska's owned channels garnering at least 35,000 views.

STRATEGIES AND TACTICS
- Press event for the launch of Next-Level Care: An initiative of 100 measures that Alaska Airlines was taking "to enhance the safety and well-being of guests."
- Blog post on Alaska Airlines' website "debunking myths and outlining how air travels through the cabin."
- Animated graphic about how cabin air is cleaned on Alaska Airline's social media and in-flight video screens.
- B-roll for new media about Alaska Airlines president traveling to Hawaii (which had a 14-day quarantine for people without a negative COVID-19 test) and going through COVID testing and preclearance processes.
- "Safety Dance" ad that highlights Alaska Airlines efforts to keep travelers safe during the pandemic. The actors in the ad were all Alaska Airlines employees. This story was pitched to national media.

Assume you have been hired by Alaska Airlines to measure and evaluate their strategic communications campaign. Use the information provided in this case and principles from this chapter to complete the following tasks regarding measurement and evaluation.

1. Identify the evaluation criteria in each objective.

2. Determine what type of measurement will be needed for each objective: output, outtake, outcome or impact.

3. Identify the appropriate evaluation tool needed to measure each of the objectives.

4. Create a measurement and evaluation plan that describes how you would use each tool to collect the data needed to determine whether or not the evaluation criteria were met, not met or exceeded.

5. Compare your measurement and evaluation plan with the strategies and tactics used in the campaign. Does your measurement and evaluation plan allow you to assess the effectiveness of the strategies and tactics in achieving campaign success? What works well? What might be missing from the measurement and evaluation plan?

References and additional readings

Alaska Airlines. (n.d.a). Next-Level Care. Retrieved from https://www.alaskaair.com/content/advisories/coronavirus

Alaska Airlines. (n.d.b). Alaska Airlines introduces Next-Level Care. Retrieved from https://www.youtube.com/watch?v=jt3jwKe8gIk

Alaska Airlines, C+C & Mekanism. (2021). Next-Level Care. Retrieved from https://www.prsa.org/conferences-and-awards/awards/search-silver-anvil-case-studies

International Association for the Measurement and Evaluation of Communications. (n.d.). Barcelona Principles 3.0. Retrieved from https://amecorg.com/barcelona-principles-3-0-translations/

International Association for the Measurement and Evaluation of Communications. (n.d.). A taxonomy of evaluation towards standards. Retrieved from https://amecorg.com/amecframework/home/supporting-material/taxonomy/

International Association for the Measurement and Evaluation of Communications. (n.d.). Interactive Evaluation Framework. Retrieved from http://amecorg.com

IPR Measurement Commission. (n.d.). Institute for Public Relations. Retrieved from https://instituteforpr.org/ipr-measurement-commission/

Lindenmann, W. K. & Likely, F. (2002). Guidelines for measuring the effectiveness of PR programs and activities. Institute for Public Relations. Retrieved from https://www.instituteforpr.org/wp-content/uploads/2002_MeasuringPrograms.pdf

Macnamara, J.R. (2015). Breaking the measurement and evaluation deadlock: A new approach and model. *Journal of Communication Management*, 19(4), 371-387.

Macnamara, J.R. (2018). A review of new evaluation models for strategic communication: Progress and gaps. *International Journal of Strategic Communication*, 12(2), 180-195.

Michaelson, D. & Stacks, D. W. (2017). *A Professional and Practitioner's Guide to Public Relations Research, Measurement, and Evaluation.* New York: Business Expert Press.

Paine, K. D. (2011). *Measure What Matters.* Hoboken, NJ: John Wiley and Sons.

Stacks, D. W. & Bowen, S. A. (2013). *Dictionary of Public Relations Measurement and Research* (3rd ed.). Institute for Public Relations. Retrieved from https://www.instituteforpr.org/wp-content/uploads/Dictionary-of-Public-Relations-Measurement-and-Research-3rd-Edition.pdf

The Measurement Standard. (2014). The newsletter of public relations and social media measurement from Salience Insight. Retrieved from http://kdpaine.blogs.com/themeasurementstandard/

U.S. Government Accountability Office. (2021, Oct 21). COVID-19 pandemic: Observations on the ongoing recovery of the aviation industry. Retrieved from https://www.gao.gov/products/gao-22-104429

Watson, T. (2001). Integrating planning and evaluation: Evaluating the public relations practice and public relations programs. In R. L. Heath (ed.), *Handbook of Public Relations* (pp. 259-268). Thousand Oaks, CA: Sage Publications, Inc.

Weiner, M. (2021). PR Technology, *Data and Insights: Igniting a Positive Return on Your Communications Investment.* Kogan Page: NY, New York.

Zerfass, A., Verčič, D., & Volk, S.C. (2017). Communication evaluation and measurement: skills, practices and utilization in European organizations. *Corporate Communications: An International Journal,* 22(1), 2-18.

CHAPTER 13

PRESENTATIONS

"The ability to present is probably the number one skill lacking today. If you can't present well, you're not going to move up in the company."

—CINDY PETERSON
FOUNDER OF PRESENTATIONS FOR RESULTS,
A COACHING AND CONSULTING FIRM

LEARNING IMPERATIVES

- Understand how to create and give a presentation that achieves positive results.

- Understand that a presentation does more than sell an idea – it convinces the client of your ability to implement that idea.

N early all of today's practitioners would admit to losing a client to someone else, not with a better idea or plan, but simply with a better presentation. Most decisions, whether to fund an in-house corporate campaign or to outsource work, are based more on a presentation than on substance. In fact, more often than firms would care to admit, agencies are selected based on their presentation and then asked to implement not their own proposal, but someone else's idea. This reality has led to firms actually copyrighting their proposals to prevent ideas from being taken without compensation. The problem is, you can't copyright ideas — only the tangible or recorded expression of them. So shady business people simply find another way to "express" your idea.

Why would an executive like someone's idea but not choose them to implement it? The simple answer: presentation. You cannot view a presentation as simply giving the substance of your idea or proposal. A presentation is a visual and personal demonstration of your capability, personality, capacity and creativity. It must inspire confidence and create chemistry between you and a potential client or executive.

Following a strategic communications approach

© Rawpixel.com/Shutterstock.com

The reality of today's business environment is that few executives have the time or patience to read lengthy reports or proposals. Hopefully someone on the project team will read the entire proposal or communications plan, but that cannot be guaranteed. The only two probable points of exposure to your plans, campaigns or ideas are the executive summary and the client presentation. If these are engaging and to the point, an executive might take the time to look deeper into your plan. If not, you will lose their attention and support.

The key to the success of both an executive summary and a presentation is the strategic communications approach. Your goal is to grab the audience's attention and convince them to not just adopt your proposal, but to let you implement it. With that goal in mind and specific objectives to support it, analyze the public(s) to be addressed, your relationship with them and their motivating self-interests. Then design your executive summary and presentation to deliver those messages and lead your audience — perhaps only one key decision maker — to the conclusions you want them to reach. Remember you aren't just selling your idea; you are selling your creativity and ability to implement that idea better than anyone else. You must appeal directly to the presentation participants' self-interests, creating a personal connection or chemistry and inspiring confidence in you. Weaving in the influence of opinion leaders may also be useful.

Selecting the appropriate type of presentation

One of the strategic decisions you will need to make is choosing the type of presentation you're going to give. You should base this decision on what you know about the audience and what they expect from the presentation. For instance, is the audience

TIPS FROM THE PROS

Overcoming presentation anxiety

Lenny Laskowski, president of LJL Seminars, international professional speaker and author of the best-selling book, "10 Days to More Confident Public Speaking," tips you off on how to keep those nerves in check.

The majority of speaking anxiety comes from nervousness. I employ a variety of physical and mental techniques to calm nerves.

PHYSICAL TECHNIQUES

Take a brisk walk before you speak. Physical activity will loosen up your entire body and get your blood circulating. If you are speaking in a large hotel, as I often do, take a walk around the hotel and burn off some nervous energy. Just don't get lost and keep an eye on the time.

Loosen up your arms and hands. While sitting in your seat before you speak, dangle your arms at your sides – letting blood flow to the tips of your fingers. When blood flow is directed away from your skin, fingers and toes, you often feel a tingling sensation, and your skin may begin to look pale and feel cold. Dangling your arms and hands reestablishes blood flow; you will start to feel better and more relaxed. Also while sitting, turn your wrists and shake your fingers to force the blood to flow to your hands and fingers.

Don't sit with your legs crossed. Stand up well in advance of being introduced and walk around so the blood flows in your legs. This will also prevent leg cramping when you first stand. Scrunch your toes. But be careful not to scrunch so tightly that you get a cramp.

Loosen up your facial muscles. Wiggle your jaw back and forth gently. Yawn (politely, of course). Use deep-breathing exercises.

MENTAL TECHNIQUES

Prepare and rehearse. This is the single-most important thing you can do.

Visualize success. Think "success" using visualization techniques. Visualize the audience applauding you when you are done.

Be natural but enthusiastic.

Be personal. Be conversational, and include some personal stories during your speech.

Focus on your message, not on your nervousness.

looking for a motivational message or deep dive into your research findings? Is the audience expecting you and your team to present for the entire time? Or do they want to have a conversation as the presentation unfolds? In addition, you will need to consider the situation. Is this a formal or informal occasion? How many people will be in the audience? How will the meeting room be set up? What type of technology will be available? The more you learn about the audience and the situation, the more you can make an informed choice about the type of presentation that will help you accomplish your goals and objectives.

There are four types of presentations that strategic communicators are commonly asked to give. Each is described in detail below to help you decide which one is the best fit for your needs.

> ***"TED-like" presentation.*** You are probably familiar with technology, entertainment and design or TED Talks. These are short talks given in front of large audiences at the annual TED conference. They rely heavily on attention-grabbing visuals and engaging storytelling to get people excited about an idea. This type of presentation can be used in a business setting where little interaction with the audience is expected but audience members need inspiration or motivation. According to Carmine Gallo, a senior contributor at "Forbes," you can create your own TED-like presentation by using "entertaining, humorous and insightful stories," avoiding bullet points, combining attractive pictures with text, showing video clips and surprising your audience. A well-known example of using the element of surprise was Bill Gates releasing mosquitoes on stage during his TED Talk about malaria in developing countries. Gallo also suggests rehearsing your presentation until you can present it as smoothly as an actual TED Talk speaker.
>
> ***Persuasive presentation.*** This is the standard type of presentation in a business setting. It's usually accompanied by slides that present information in categories, use visuals to make information easily digestible and rely on text to make important arguments. The IESE Business School shared the following structure for a persuasive presentation:
>
> - Grab the audience's attention.
> - Tell your audience in one sentence what the presentation is about.
> - Outline the main points of your argument.
> - Support each of your main points by highlighting the benefits, not the features.
> - Summarize your argument in one sentence and give the audience a call to action.
>
> After putting together a draft of your presentation, you can follow the advice shared by author Dorie Clark in a "Harvard Business Review" article to make sure it's actually going to be persuasive. She suggested asking six questions about your persuasive strategy.
>
> - What problem are you solving?
> - Why is solving this problem important now?
> - How have you verified your idea?
> - How can you simplify and clarify the information you are presenting?

- Have you incorporated any stories or examples in addition to facts and figures?
- Have you included a call to action?

Research presentation. Research presentations are data heavy and provide detailed information about research findings. Often, they use data visualization strategies to help the audience quickly understand complex data. Usually these take the form of charts and graphs. Also, they logically connect the findings to actionable insights and recommendations. Research presentations can be shared with and understood by people who were not at the presentation without much additional explanation. Nancy Duarte, an author and expert on persuasive presentations, coined a term for this type of presentation: slidedocs, or "visual documents developed in presentation software that are intended to be read and referenced instead of projected." You can find more information about how to create effective slidedocs for your research presentations at www.duarte.com/slidedocs/.

Pitch deck. A pitch deck usually consists of a limited number of slides that are framed around a big idea. The slides rely on visuals to capture the audience's attention and communicate information quickly. Pitch decks are used to sell new ideas to management or clients. Alejandro Cremades, a "Forbes" contributor, identified three important aspects of this type of presentation. First, the pitch must be clear and simple. Second, it must be compelling. And third, it must be easy to act on. Aaron Lee, co-founder of Leneys, an online fashion brand, wrote an article that explores pitch deck best practices from well-known companies like Facebook and Airbnb. Some of his observations include hooking your audience with a powerful introduction, using solid numbers to sell your idea and tailoring analogies to your audience to help them understand your idea. Author Guy Kawasaki suggests using the 10/20/30 rule when creating pitch decks. Simply stated, the rule is have no more than 10 slides, give your presentation in 20 minutes or less, and, if you need text, use a 30-point font.

Respecting your audience

Knowing that your audience has little time, you must get to the key points and solutions quickly to capture and retain interest. You must show the logic and the creativity that make the proposal workable. Give just enough detail to sell the plan but not so much as to lose the interest of the target audience. A few details, carefully inserted, will help add credibility. Always include the cost in terms of time and resources (money). Remember that an executive decision maker typically has only three questions that matter:

© Rawpixel.com/Shutterstock.com

- Is this the best solution or plan (i.e., is there really a need, and will it work)?
- How much will it cost?
- Is this the right team to accomplish it?

To convince an executive to spend time and money on your plan, you must address the core of the challenge or opportunity, as well as the macro-level logic, creativity and appropriateness of the solution proposed. Your big idea may be in the form of branding, identification with a key societal issue, a change in the logo or slogan, a new focus on community relations or a number of other overarching ideas. Just remember that executives usually have a broad, holistic view of problems, opportunities and programs. Their vision encompasses the whole organization, not just your part of it. They want to see the grand solution and creative integration of that solution across organizational functions and publics. They also want to know if it is the most cost-effective approach to the situation and why they should support the plan. Remember, for them to internalize your plan, you must first capture their attention and make them want to work with you.

Presenting your plan

A presentation of your solution or plan is a multisensory version of an executive summary. A presentation is not a speech. You can't just stand up and talk. By its nature, a presentation is visual. The visual elements can add emotion and help create impressions of consistency, dependability and competency about the team. They must be very carefully considered and developed to support your approach, not detract from it.

No matter how much time you have to make your presentation, you must capture the attention of your audience in the first few seconds. Establish the need and the broad solution immediately. Then sketch in the details as time and interest permit. Make sure to show creative work — slogans, logos, visual tactics — to engage and excite the target audience, but don't continue describing details after interest in them wanes. Get back quickly to the rationale for selecting this plan and the cost of doing so. Also address the cost of not embracing your solution. Then end on a positive note and with the only wise course of action: hiring you.

Here are some general principles for presentation success.

Immediately capture attention and hold it. If attention wanes, do something to engage the audience.

Keep the end result in mind at all times. The goal is to gain approval and selection of your plan and your team by the decision makers. Everything you do and say in the presentation must be focused on that goal.

Establish a relationship. Try to bond with the key decision maker whether they are a client or an executive in your organization. Inspire confidence.

Keep it short, concise and to the point. Long presentations will lose the audience. Set a time limit for each discussion point in the presentation and stick to it. Keep the presentation moving and the ideas flowing. If you sense your audience is losing interest, shift your style to liven up the presentation or, better yet, move on.

Use logical and customized organization. Use a research-based, analytical approach to problem-solving that the client will understand. Focus on opportunities and solutions. Customize the presentation to meet the self-interests and needs of the target audience. A sample organization for a campaign presentation is found in Figure 14.1, but remember to tailor the format to your specific audience. Use examples relevant to the target audience's experience. And keep it visual and memorable.

Be prepared. Organize well. Use appealing visual aids. Rehearse thoroughly. An audience can always tell when someone is unprepared. Further, your ability to improvise when unexpected problems arise (such as your software not being compatible with the provided technical equipment) is directly related to how well prepared you are. Don't expect to be able to ad-lib in an emergency if you haven't thoroughly prepared and practiced.

Figure 14.1
Sample organization of a campaign presentation

1. Capture attention.

2. Introduce yourself and review the agenda.

3. Review the opportunities and problems, demonstrating understanding of the potential client's position through research.

4. Present your unique approach for solving the problem.

5. State the objectives and publics/messages necessary to accomplish them.

6. Show some of the creative work. Planning typically has no visual appeal and must be accompanied by creative work to sell your solution.

7. Overview the budget using simple graphics.

8. Provide the rationale for implementing the plan, as well as the inherent difficulties and the cost of not accepting your proposal.

9. Summarize the campaign and ask for the contract or business.

Using technology

In today's high-tech environment, expectations for professionalism are high. Presentation software abounds. You should know the different programs, along with their features and capabilities, and not be tied to any one program. Use the program that best meets the needs of the presentation. Become proficient with many programs. Remember that you will be selected based on the quality and impressiveness of the presentation. You can't just have good ideas; you have to be able to present those ideas in a creative, innovative way.

Remember also that high-tech presentations have their pitfalls. Computer-designed and driven presentations are absolutely requisite, but when the technology fails, for whatever reason, the failure reflects on the presenter. While a great presentation can demonstrate the creativity, capability and innovativeness of a team, a poor presentation can ruin any chance of success.

Technical difficulties are unacceptable. If you are using technology of any kind in a presentation, make sure you know the equipment or computer programs, how to operate them and how to quickly troubleshoot problems. Author and presentation guru Jim Harvey identified five common technology fails you can plan in advance to avoid.

> ***The presenter can't connect a computer or device to the projection system.*** In general, this means you need to bring a selection of adapters (e.g., DVI, HDMI, and FireWire) that will allow you to connect to a variety of ports. Make sure that the adapters work with the ports on your computer or device. Also, you should verify that the operating system on your computer or device and the presentation software you plan to use are compatible with the technology at the venue.
>
> ***Video or other multimedia files don't work.*** There is nothing worse than setting up a video clip during a presentation and then not being able to show it. If you plan on using video or multimedia files, make sure they work in your software's presentation mode before getting up in front of your audience. Also, understand how your computer or device operates when connected to a projector. There may be settings you have to adjust for it to properly display video through a projection system. If you plan on showing video clips that are hosted on the internet, you will need to ensure that you have access to Wi-Fi or cellular data in the presentation room.
>
> ***Audio files don't make any sound.*** If you plan on using audio during your presentation, you need to check that the presentation system you will be using has speakers. If it doesn't you should rethink your approach or request that speakers be added to the room configuration. Also, make sure that you bring the proper audio cables to connect your computer or device to the sound system. It can help to do a sound check of your computer before the presentation to ensure that the sound card is functioning properly.
>
> ***Presentation slides look different.*** Sometimes you won't have the option of using your computer or device to give your presentation. You may have to transfer your presentation file to a computer that is already hooked up to the presentation system. This can wreak havoc on your presentation format because the new computer won't have access to the same source files you used to create it. This means fonts will be changed, images won't look as crisp and links to embedded video and audio files can be lost. To avoid this problem, you will need to transfer all of the source files to the new computer along with the presentation file.
>
> ***Your password protected screensaver comes on during the presentation.*** Avoid this embarrassing problem by turning off your screensaver before giving the presentation. Also, make sure you turn off any programs or apps that may want to notify you about new updates, messages or emails while you are presenting.

Recognize also that technology tends to reduce and sometimes eliminate the personal connection between the presenter and the client or executive. The presenter must be conscious of the relationship and work to maintain the personal connection. When possible, use a remote or have someone advance your slides. Using a remote will allow you to move freely about the room, cutting the invisible tether that keeps so many people tied to a podium or laptop. By moving around, using hand gestures and pointing out significant information or visuals on the screen, you can help your audience engage not only with the presentation but also with you.

The presentation is an opportunity to interact with the client or executive and begin to build trust. Technology should support but never drive a presentation. Presentations should always be driven by purpose and content. In today's business climate, a good presentation is your key to opening the door. A bad presentation means your ideas may never see the light of day, or you may sit by and watch as some other team executes them.

Summary

Presentations are the most significant channels used to communicate almost every public relations or marketing plan. No matter how revealing the research, no matter how creative and ingenious the strategic plan, no change will occur unless you effectively communicate the plan or solution to the decision makers. You must also demonstrate the criticality of their expending resources on this plan or solution and convince them that you are the person or team to pull it off. As with all communication, your target audience must first be persuaded to pay attention to the message and then be persuaded to act on the content. Persuading decision makers to use your solutions requires the same two-step process. You must gain their attention and then their approval.

In our fast-paced world, presentations are the key to getting decision makers to pay attention to and more deeply examine a proposal. They should be approached with the same care and analysis used in your planning.

Exercises

1. Select any of the plans you have prepared for the Application Cases in other chapters of this book and create a short presentation that would engage a decision maker and cause them to listen to your ideas. Follow the steps in Figure 14.1, and make sure you have an attention-getting tactic at the beginning of the presentation.

2. Visit other classes within which presentations are being given. Do your own analysis of their effectiveness. Which presentation types were used? What techniques worked well and why? What did not work, and what would you have done differently?

3. Create a chart that analyzes the features, benefits and negative aspects of a variety of presentation software programs. Analyze what they do well and where they fall short, and describe the kind of plan they are most appropriate to present.

References and additional readings

Boylan, B. (2001). *What's Your Point?: The 3-step Method for Making Effective Presentations.* Avon, MA: Adams Media Corporation.

Clark, D. (2016, Oct. 11). A checklist for more persuasive presentations. *Harvard Business Review.* Retrieved from https://hbr.org/2016/10/a-checklist-for-more-persuasive-presentations

Cremades, A. (2018, March 2). How to create a pitch deck. *Forbes.* Retrieved from https://www.forbes.com/sites/alejandrocremades/2018/03/02/how-to-create-a-pitch-deck/

Daum, K. (2013). 5 tips for giving really amazing presentations. Retrieved from www.inc.com/kevin-daum/5-tips-for-giving-really-amazing-presentations.html

Duarte, N. (n.d.). Slidedocs. Retrieved from https://www.duarte.com/slidedocs/

Gallo, C. (2017, April 23). The difference between TED Talks and 'TED-like' presentations. *Forbes.* Retrieved from https://www.forbes.com/sites/carminegallo/2017/04/23/thedifference-between-ted-talks-and-ted-like-presentations

Harvey, J. (2016, Aug. 2). 5 most common tech problems for presenters ... and how to avoid them. Retrieved form https://www.presentation-guru.com/the-5-most-commontechnical-problems-for-presenters-and-how-to-avoid-them/

IESE Business School. (2015, Feb. 23). How to deliver persuasive presentations. *Forbes.* Retrieved from https://www.forbes.com/sites/iese/2015/02/23/how-to-deliver-persuasive-presentations/#6e6c4d4c6935

Kawasaki, G. (2015, March 5). The only 10 slides you need in your pitch. Retrieved from https://guykawasaki.com/the-only-10-slides-you-need-in-your-pitch/

Lee, A. (n.d.). 30 legendary startup pitch decks and what you can learn from them. Retrieved from https://piktochart.com/blog/startup-pitch-decks-what-you-canlearn/

Leech, T. (2004). *How to Prepare, Stage, and Deliver Winning Presentations.* New York: AMACOM.

Skills You Need. (n.d.). Deciding the presentation method. Retrieved from https://www.skillsyouneed.com/present/presentation-method.html

Young Entrepreneur Council. (2013). 13 tips for giving a killer presentation. *Huffington Post Small Business.* Retrieved from www.huffingtonpost.com

CHAPTER 14

ETHICS, PROFESSIONALISM AND DIVERSITY

"A little integrity is better than any career."

—RALPH WALDO EMERSON
AMERICAN POET

LEARNING IMPERATIVES

- Understand that your career success depends upon the quality of your ethical and professional behavior.

- Understand the values and ethical standards upon which to base decisions and behavior.

- Be cognizant of professional codes of ethics and resolve to abide by them.

- Understand the characteristics of professionalism and begin to develop behaviors consistent with those characteristics.

- Appreciate the contributions of diverse individuals and adopt an attitude of acceptance.

ETHICS
Personal and professional value systems and standards that underlie decisions and behavior.

As you begin to read this chapter, many of you are thinking, "Really? Do I need to read more junk about **ethics**?"

But before you answer, ask yourself:

- Do I care that my behavior could cost thousands of people — myself included — to lose hundreds of millions of dollars saved for retirement?
- Do I care that my actions not only caused me but also many others to lose their jobs because my company went out of business?
- Do I care that nobody will hire me because of my poor reputation?
- Do I care that I might lose everything and end up in prison?

These are only a few of the documented consequences suffered many times over in the past few years by real business and communications professionals — people just like you — who didn't give much thought to ethics. You may think that you would never do anything that is drastically unethical or unprofessional. They didn't think so, either. Their road to professional and personal disaster began with a tiny step — a small, seemingly insignificant breach of ethics or **professionalism**.

It is unfortunate that even with increased emphasis on and discussion regarding professional ethics in the last couple of decades, we seem to have had a greater number of high profile incidents rather than fewer. Studies show a continual decline in ethical behavior.

PROFESSIONALISM
Characteristics and behavior befitting a professional.

In 2016, Wells Fargo announced that its employees created millions of fake accounts without customers' knowledge.

Advocacy is a critical function in a free market economy and a free society. Without advocacy, people are unaware of the full range of choices available to them from consumer products to political opinions. Because some organizations have abused the public trust by using manipulative communication and marketing practices and sometimes even deceit, communicators today are often labeled "flacks" or "spin doctors," implying the less than trustworthy practices of advocating questionable causes and twisting the truth. Because of past abuses perpetrated by a few, almost all organizations, corporations and institutions continue to face an uphill battle to gain the trust of their publics.

In his book, "The Cheating Culture: Why More Americans Are Doing Wrong to Get Ahead," David Callahan presents dozens of examples of people who attained great professional success only to take devastating falls because their success came at the expense of their integrity. He demonstrates how our business culture, and even American culture, condones cheating — a little fudging on your tax return, failure to return the excess change you get at the grocery store or lying on a resume. He argues that our culture is breeding dishonesty and ethical breaches as necessary and acceptable to achieve success. That is until the perpetrators crash and burn. Callahan asserts:

> Human beings are not simply creatures of their economic and legal environment. We don't decide whether to cut corners based only on a rational calculus about potential gains and losses. We filter these decisions through our value systems. And while more of us will do wrong in a system where cheating

is normalized or necessary for survival or hugely profitable, some of us will insist on acting with integrity even if doing so runs counter to our [short-term] self-interest.

A shifting landscape

Contributing to the decline in ethical behavior is the shifting landscape of communications media. Mistrust of media is at an all-time high with "fake news" becoming all too common — even now used in social media to sucker people into clicking on purely marketing ploys. Misinformation and deception are reasons the latest trust studies show high levels of mistrust of owned and social media and neutral trust of traditional media. Some communications professionals still do not understand the disastrous consequences for our profession of corrupting the societal channels of communication. If the major channels of information dissemination in our society are not trusted, how can we possibly expect our messages will be trusted?

© Volodymyr Nikitenko/Shutterstock.com

Pay for play

One of the driving factors of this ethical quagmire is the meteoric rise of social media. Social media channels like Facebook, Instagram, LinkedIn, Twitter and YouTube expect you to pay to reach your target audiences. And other media channels have followed suit. While traditional advertising is easy to identify, paid placement options aren't just for traditional advertising. A number of media channels, including traditional news media channels, have developed paid marketing products that are meant to look like the editorial content that regularly appears on those channels. OBI Creative identifies four types of paid content in the "earned media" sphere.

- Affiliate programs: Paying bloggers and others to promote your product or service to their loyal followers.
- Brand ambassadors: Buying access to audiences of bloggers, celebrities or influencers — paying to transfer the trust their audiences have in them to your brand, product or service.
- Sponsored content: Paying to run content (created by you or by the blogger, celebrity or influencer) on their media.
- Native advertising: Paying for placement like advertorials of products that is consistent with the content around it and connects with the audience.

According to Stephanie Zercher of Marsden Marketing, **pay for play**,

> [are] not such dirty words any longer. In a time with fewer journalists and a need for content driven by the digital world, the lines between traditional PR (in which you earned coverage by pitching your company's story to reporters) and marketing (in which you generally pay to reach your audience) hasn't just blurred. It's been erased and replaced by a new paradigm — a hybrid that calls

PAY FOR PLAY
Compensating media for content placement, product reviews, editorial mentions or other promotion.

on PR's ability to shape content for paid opportunities that often look a lot like what a journalist would typically produce.

The crux of the ethical issue is whether the audience knows the coverage or placement is being compensated. That knowledge, or lack thereof, determines if the public is being manipulated. As explained by Darcy Silvers in "PR Fuel,"

> The Public Relations Society of America (PRSA) Code of Ethics promotes transparency in communications. Its code states that ethical practitioners must "encourage disclosure of any exchange of value that influences how those they represent are covered." The Society of Professional Journalists' Code of Ethics encourages its members to act independently. It states that journalists must "refuse gifts, favors, fees, free travel and special treatment... [to avoid compromising] journalistic integrity."

Traditionally, pay for play meant things like compensating a broadcaster for an on-air mention or endorsement, or buying advertising in a magazine or even a weekly community newspaper to get articles or news stories accepted. With the rise of social media, the issue of disclosure came to the forefront, particularly with blogs. Bloggers wanted compensation to review and endorse products or ideas. That's how they make money to support their work. Pay for play with bloggers became so prevalent that the Federal Trade Commission (FTC) established guidelines governing it. In fact, the FTC considers pay for play without disclosure deceptive advertising. According to Tom Biro of Rusty George Creative,

> The challenge isn't even so much that certain organizations and individuals want to be paid to cover things. It's that many, many influencers are absolutely pretending that it's not the case [that they are being compensated] so that their readers, listeners, or viewers take their word for it.

This is where the ethical mandate of disclosure becomes critically important. The issue isn't so much that we employ tactics of pay for play; the issue is whether we are doing so in a manipulative or deceptive way. If the latter, we are violating the very trust upon which our relationships with our key publics depend.

Disinformation

Another deceptive communication practice that thrives on the internet and social media is disinformation. Disinformation has also seeped into news media coverage despite long-held journalistic ethics of accuracy, independence, accountability and transparency. Disinformation is false, misleading or biased information that someone deliberately shares to deceive, mislead or confuse others. Here's a simpler way to say it: Disinformation is manipulative lies or half truths. Sharing or amplifying disinformation runs contrary to the principles of honesty, transparency, fairness and respect that serve as the basis for all of the professional associations' codes of ethics found in Appendix C.

Sadly, despite its obvious violation of ethical principles and its potential for harm, disinformation has become an epidemic, resulting in distrust of media channels, sources of information and societal institutions. Disinformation has become such a major societal problem that a 2022 study by the Institute for Public Relations found that Americans now rank disinformation near the top of the list of their concerns, along with health care costs, the economy, homelessness and crime. The same study showed that people are increasingly turning away from media channels to people close to them who they trust for accurate, truthful information: family, friends, coworkers and "people like me."

According to a 2021 report from the Aspen Institute's Commission on Information Disorder, what makes disinformation particularly dangerous is its ability to spread rapidly because it is sensational. The result is "a cascading effect of misinformed people sharing falsities" that can have real-life consequences – sometimes even life or death consequences – for people who believe the information or are the targets of it.

This situation calls for professional communicators to lead the way in adhering to standards of honest and truthful communication. Blake D. Lewis III, APR, Fellow PRSA, explained that being honest and truthful starts with what we share in our own personal spheres of communication, including on social media and in our interpersonal interactions. Additionally, he said we have a responsibility to take a stand against disinformation in our professional roles:

> The rapid rise of misinformation and disinformation demands that communications professionals go beyond offering counsel and take a strong, consistent stance against the untruthful messages that some members of the public call "spin." When audiences question a message's validity, it increases the likelihood that all messages will be questioned.

Ethics

The ethics and behavior of organizations and individuals have come to the forefront in terms of the expectations of an organization's stakeholders. According to Wilcox, Cameron and Reber (2014):

> Ethics refers to the value system by which a person determines what is right or wrong, fair or unfair, just or unjust. It is expressed through moral behavior in specific situations. An individual's conduct is measured not only against his or her own conscience but also against some norm of acceptability that has been societally, professionally, or organizationally determined.

As the statement implies, ethical decisions are made at several different levels. At the highest level, every society has an implied ethical standard. American culture has some basic societal values — like honesty, integrity, fairness and equity — that are still considered universal, values we should not lightly abandon. Nevertheless, societal standards of ethics often deteriorate to become the equivalent of legal standards.

ETHICAL CODES
Written and formalized standards of behavior used as guidelines for decision-making.

TRANSPARENCY
Disclosing truthful information about an organization that holds the organization accountable and helps publics make decisions.

AUTHENTICITY
Aligning an organization's behavior and communication with core values that are important to its key publics.

With trust at a premium now in our society, the second level of ethical standard-setting is in organizations that have formulated their own **ethical codes** based on core corporate or organizational values. The goal is to guide employees to comply in programs, procedures and practices. To be credible, the values and codes must permeate the organization's communication practices.

At the third level, communications and marketing professionals may choose to subscribe to professional codes of behavior like those provided by the American Marketing Association, the American Advertising Federation, the Public Relations Society of America or other similar professional organizations (see Appendix C: Professional Codes of Ethics). Finally, underlying each of these ethical levels are personal standards of behavior based on individual value systems.

Organizational ethics

For 15 years, the Arthur W. Page Society has conducted research with chief communication officers (CCOs) about what organizations need to do to survive in a rapidly changing and unpredictable business environment. Their first major report in 2007, "The Authentic Enterprise," showed that publics' demands for **transparency** resulted in **authenticity** becoming "the coin of the realm for successful corporations and for those who lead them." Authentic organizations openly align their internal and external behavior and communication with a set of core values that are societally accepted and important to their key publics. In other words, organizations actually are who they say they are and, as a result, they become trustworthy.

Sadly, the demand for transparency mirrors the disintegration of public trust in all societal institutions over many years. It also coincides with the increased availability of broadband internet, as well as the proliferation of mobile devices and social media apps that enable instantaneous communication and expose organizations to constant public scrutiny.

Brad Rawlins, a leading scholar on transparency, explained that transparency goes beyond the simple disclosure of information. Transparency requires organizations to act ethically. Rawlins says organizations must be willing to disclose all legally releasable information to the public, whether it paints the organization in a positive or negative light. Next, they must share information that may affect their publics, giving publics the opportunity to make informed decisions. Similarly, the PRSA Code of Ethics explains that disclosure of information should be done with the intent of "[building] trust with the public by revealing all information needed for responsible decision making."

Finally, Rawlins says organizations must show they are holding themselves accountable for their actions, policies and practices. The focus on meeting publics' information needs and organizational accountability is what differentiates transparency from disclosure. While these aspects of transparency may be painful for organizations to comply with at times, Rawlins asserts that they ultimately can make the organization better:

> Transparency will expose an organization's weaknesses, and areas that need improvement. Hiding these does not make them go away. Positive feedback that everything is okay, when it isn't, only reinforces the debilitating behavior. Sure, transparency might make an organization feel uncomfortable, but it will also motivate it to improve.

Not surprisingly, research shows that when organizations are more transparent they are also more trusted.

The Edelman Trust Barometer has demonstrated the impact of organizational ethics on trust. Reporting on the Trust Barometer's 2020 results, Antoine Harary, president of Edelman Intelligence, said,

> After tracking 40 global companies over the past year through our Edelman Trust Management framework we've learned that ethical drivers such as integrity, dependability and purpose drive close to 76% of the trust capital of business. . . . Trust is undeniably linked to doing what is right. The battle for trust will be fought on the field of ethical behavior.

While ethical communication with our publics is of primary importance, customer service has become the face of most organizations. And it seems to be the area most difficult to manage. Outsourcing customer service, even offshoring it to other nations, has become the punchline of jokes about high-tech and credit-card customer service. In many industries, customer service lines are typically staffed by hourly employees, some making not much more than minimum wage. The result is a low level of competence and high turnover as employees seek for better jobs with better pay and advancement potential. But what could be more important in establishing trust than quality customer service? The example set by Nordstrom is widely known. Stories abound of the upscale retail clothing giant allowing customers to return virtually any item — even items obviously not purchased in their stores! On industry trust scales, Nordstrom always ranks at the top.

Codes of ethics and professional standards

Because our effectiveness as professionals is directly dependent upon whether or not we are trusted, professional ethical standards are critical to the strength of our profession. (See examples in Appendix C.) But professional ethical codes are not without problems. By their nature, such codes tend to establish the basest acceptable behavior, bordering on legality rather than morality. Over time, such standards tend to reduce the overall level of ethical practice to that minimally acceptable expectation. To quote James E. Faust in an address given to law students in 2003:

> There is a great risk of justifying what we do individually and professionally on the basis of what is "legal" rather than what is "right." ... The philosophy that what is "legal" is also "right" will rob us of what is highest and best in our nature. What conduct is actually "legal" is, in many instances, way below the standards of a civilized society. ... If [we] accept what is legal as [our] standard of personal or professional conduct, [we] will rob [ourselves] of that which is truly noble in [our] personal dignity and worth.

Further, it is usually quite difficult for a professional organization to enforce a code of ethics. Much has been written about ethical codes and their problems. Nevertheless, professionally it is deemed important for organizations to establish ethical codes for their members. Such codes are viewed as crucial for maintaining professional status, respect and legitimacy. They are also guidelines to entry-level professionals seeking to establish their own ethical standards based on a personal

MINI CASE

Deception by one of the world's largest automakers causes $30 billion loss

Volkswagen

Volkswagen, a German automobile manufacturer, had a large and dependable market for its diesel-engine cars in Europe. But sales were not as good in the United States. In 2006, Volkswagen executives planned to increase U.S. market share by developing more fuel-efficient diesel engines.

CORE PROBLEM
Volkswagen engineers discovered the new diesel engine couldn't meet strict U.S. emissions standards.

VOLKSWAGEN'S STRATEGY
Volkswagen executives decided to cheat rather than fix the problem. The automaker installed sophisticated software, later called a "defeat device," that could detect when a car was undergoing an emissions test and temporarily increase its engine's pollution controls so it would pass. Two years later, Volkswagen launched a marketing campaign that promoted its diesel-powered cars as environmentally friendly alternatives to its competitors' hybrid cars.

In May 2014, West Virginia University researchers published the results of a study funded by the International Council on Clean Transportation that reported emissions testing results from Volkswagen's "TDI" diesel engine in two different models: the 2011 Jetta and the 2012 Passat. The researchers wanted to know whether emissions results from lab tests would be different than emissions levels under normal driving conditions. Their study revealed that when they drove the cars on the road, nitrogen oxide emissions were nearly 40 times greater than the legal level permitted in the U.S. This discovery led the California Air Resources board to investigate the German automaker.

During the investigation, Volkswagen officials gave investigators false and misleading information. Volkswagen also issued a recall on all 500,000 U.S. diesels, explaining a software upgrade would fix the emissions issue. However, the upgrade didn't make much of a difference, which caused investigators to become more skeptical and dig deeper.

As the investigation unfolded, Volkswagen employees destroyed thousands of documents that contained incriminating evidence about the defeat device. But the company couldn't hide the truth forever. On September 3, 2015, Volkswagen executives admitted to the California Air Resources Board and the Environmental Protection Agency that its cars were equipped with a defeat device. On September 19, the EPA's formal violation notice to Volkswagen went public. It was estimated that as many as 11 million cars across the globe were affected, including the Audi, Porsche and Lamborghini brands.

The day after the announcement, Volkswagen's stock price dropped 17.1%, the equivalent of losing $15 billion in market value in one day of trading. Volkswagen dealers and customers in the U.S. reported feeling betrayed by the company as car values plummeted by 13%.

VOLKSWAGEN'S CRISIS RESPONSE
On September 19, executives of Volkswagen Group of America instructed its dealerships to stop selling its remaining inventory of 2015 TDI diesel vehicles. The following day, Volkswagen CEO Martin Winterkorn made a public apology and explained that he had ordered an internal investigation. The next day, Michael Horn, the highest-ranking Volkswagen executive in North America, apologized to an audience in Brooklyn, New York, who were there to celebrate

the launch of the 2016 Passat. He admitted that Volkswagen had "totally screwed up" and promised that the company would "make things right" with all its stakeholders. A day later, Winterkorn released a video apology promising that Volkswagen would be transparent, repair the damage caused by the scandal and regain the publics' trust.

On September 22, a German newspaper reported that Volkswagen planned to fire Winterkorn and replace him with Matthias Mueller, who was running the Porsche brand at the time. Volkswagen spokespeople denied the claim, but the next day, Winterkorn resigned. In his parting statement, he denied knowing about or participating in the defeat device scandal. He insisted that a small group of renegade engineers within the company were at fault. The day after Winterkorn's resignation, Mueller was named the new CEO. Later that week, Volkswagen announced it would replace software on the 11 million affected vehicles at a cost of approximately $6.5 billion,

In November, Volkswagen offered its U.S. customers two $500 gift cards in an attempt to pacify their anger about the scandal and their frustration that the company hadn't announced a plan to fix their cars. However, even though Volkswagen planned to recall cars in Europe, it did not offer its European customers any compensation based on the justification that its behavior wasn't illegal under European regulations. Later that month, Horn apologized to attendees at the Los Angeles Auto Show and promised that the company would soon unveil its plans to fix the affected cars.

RESULTS

The U.S. Department of Justice filed a complaint against Volkswagen for alleged violations of the Clean Air Act. A year later, Volkswagen agreed to plead guilty to three felony counts and pay $4.3 billion in criminal and civil penalties. Six executives and employees were indicted. Also, the U.S. Federal Trade Commission (FTC) sued Volkswagen for deceiving consumers with its advertising. A settlement reached required Volkswagen to pay $10 billion to owners of affected vehicles. This was the largest false advertising case in FTC history. Eventually, Volkswagen Group of America announced that the owners of cars with TDI diesel engines would either receive a vehicle buyback or a fix to bring their vehicles to meet emissions standards at a cost of $14.73 billion. Estimates put the cost of the global scandal at $30 billion.

© MDart10/Shutterstock.com

value system. Most professional codes of ethics incorporate stated values that include truth, honesty, fairness, good taste and decency. Basing behavior on these values will always provide a solid foundation of personal ethics for any communications professional.

Personal ethics and decision-making

Our personal ethics are based on our system of values and beliefs. According to Davis Young, you cannot be forced to lose your values; they are only lost if you choose to relinquish them. As was discussed in the chapter on persuasion, values and beliefs are the building blocks for attitudes that direct behavior. Although a very personal determination, our values and ethics are heavily influenced by our culture and background. In American culture, truth, freedom, independence, equity and personal rights are highly valued and contribute to the formulation of most of our value systems and resultant ethical standards. But another important influence on our value systems is our personal and societal definition of success.

In the late 1980s, Amitai Etzioni, having just completed a book on ethics, prepared to teach the subject to students at Harvard Business School. After a semester of effort, he lamented that he had been unable to convince classes full of MBA candidates that "... there is more to life than money, power, fame and self-interest." Etzioni's experience is disconcerting but not surprising. The situation is no better today. Our society has put such an emphasis on money, power and fame as measures of success that these factors have become the decision-making criteria for generations of professionals. Yet those same professionals, at the ends of their careers (and usually in commencement speeches to graduating college students), regret not having spent enough time with family or serving the community. Our analysis of key publics' self-interests should lead us to the conclusion that money, power and fame are usually secondary motivators when placed next to important life issues.

Perhaps our personal definitions of success and the pressure to reach the perceived societal definition of success have caused us to neglect those things in life that really matter. Those definitions necessarily affect our ethical standards and decisions. It would, therefore, seem important to take another look at our measure of personal success, and reestablish basic values to shape moral and ethical behavior. Ralph Waldo Emerson's definition of success (Figure 14.1) may be a viable starting point.

Figure 14.1
An enduring definition of success

"To laugh often and love much; to win the respect of intelligent persons and the affection of children; to earn the approbation of honest citizens and to endure the betrayal of false friends; to appreciate beauty; to find the best in others; to give of one's self; to leave the world a bit better, whether by a healthy child, a garden patch, or a redeemed social condition; to have played and laughed with enthusiasm and sung with exultation; to know that even one life has breathed easier because you have lived, this is to have succeeded."

— **RALPH WALDO EMERSON, 1803–1882**

Consistent with contemporary measures of success, most decisions to behave unethically seem to be based primarily on financial and power considerations. Most professionals find the temptation to behave unethically becomes overwhelming only when money is the decision factor. The more there is to gain or lose financially, the greater the temptation to behave contrary to what the individual and organization know to be ethical. When your ability to support and feed your family and keep a roof over your head is threatened, you become more open to an unethical alternative. And increasingly, the more chance there is to gain monetarily or to progress to more elevated positions of power and prestige, the more likely some people are to throw ethics and professionalism to the wind — and personal integrity with it.

According to Stephen Carter, a Yale University law professor, acting with integrity is comprised of three steps: discerning what is right and what is wrong, acting on the basis of that assessment and openly expressing that your actions are based on your own personal understanding of what is right and wrong.

Now is the time, as you prepare to launch your career, to make the commitment to act with integrity in everything you do. Just like you believe none of the disasters mentioned at the beginning of this chapter will ever plague your career, so did each of the many people who ended up in prison or in the unemployment line. Choose now to act with integrity. Thomas Friedman, author of *The World is Flat*, says that globalization and technology have made us **hyperconnected**. People can easily find out where you live, how old you are, how much your house is worth, what you watched, what you bought and on and on. In other words, you can't hide from the decisions you make.

Choose now to understand the ethical standards of public relations and marketing and to follow them assiduously. Choose now to maintain a professional reputation that causes people to want to be associated with you, to want to work with you and to feel confident about hiring you.

Once you have compromised, you can expect the demand for compromise to continue. Even changing jobs doesn't necessarily free you. Whatever reputation you establish will follow you to at least some degree for the rest of your professional life. In the communications profession where personal credibility and trustworthiness is an imperative, reputation can mean the difference between success and failure. All professional codes and standards aside, ethics come down to our personal decisions of appropriate behavior. The six simple rules in Figure 14.2 may help you to protect yourself against situations which will compromise your ethics and your professionalism.

Yet most industries have been slow to learn. They say they understand the importance of customer service but haven't been able to resolve issues with the age-old system of entry-level, minimum-wage employees. They add layers of supervision and management, building their customer service around a hierarchical reporting structure rather than focusing on building a trust-based relationship with crucial publics.

A case in point is media giant Comcast. Their customer service difficulties have become legend with the YouTube video of a serviceman napping on a customer's couch while on hold with the Comcast service line. In a more recent case, a Comcast customer called to

✂ HYPERCONNECTED
When people are connected to organizations and society through multiple channels such as email, phone, social media and instant messaging.

Figure 14.2
Six rules for ethical decision-making

1. ***Make your ethical decisions now.*** Examine your value system, and define your personal and professional ethics now, before you are in a situation where you are pressured to succumb. Examine current case studies of ethical dilemmas and make decisions about what your own conduct will be. It is much easier to stick to ethical decisions you have already made based on personal and professional values than it is to make those decisions in the face of pressure and financial need.

2. ***Develop empathy.*** Treat others as you would expect to be treated. Don't judge others too harshly and lend a helping hand. You may be fortunate not to have faced their dilemmas, but it may only be a matter of time. A little empathy and compassion go a long way and increase the chance of receiving compassion and assistance when you need it.

3. ***Take the time to think things through.*** Don't be railroaded or rushed into making decisions. When you are pressured to make a quick decision about something and you feel uncertain or confused, take your time. Chances are that if you feel rushed when making an ethical decision, you are being railroaded into doing something unethical and unwise, something you would not do if you had more time to think it through.

4. ***Call a "spade" a "spade."*** Lying, cheating and stealing by any other names are still lying, cheating and stealing. In today's complex business environment, we have an incredible ability to sanitize issues and rationalize behavior by using less poignant terms like "white lies" or "half-truths" or "omission" or "creative storytelling." But deception of any kind is lying; winning by anything but honest and ethical means is cheating; and appropriating anything that does not rightfully belong to you or your employer is stealing. Applying the terms that most people agree are prohibited by both personal and professional standards will help you make ethical decisions in complex or confusing situations.

5. ***Recognize that every action and decision has an ethical component.*** Ethical dilemmas seldom emerge suddenly. They are the culmination of several seemingly innocuous decisions and actions leading to the point of ethical crisis. Every decision you make has an ethical component even if it is not immediately obvious. Make sure to review the ethical ramifications of actions and decisions along the way. Project where a given decision will lead. Doing so will help you avoid many ethical crises that might otherwise "sneak up" on you.

6. ***Establish a freedom fund.*** Start today to save some money from each paycheck you receive. Establish a separate savings account and habitually contribute to your freedom fund. Much unethical behavior is a result of feeling you simply cannot afford to behave otherwise. You have financial obligations in life, and losing your job may mean you will lose your car or your home or that you won't be able to feed your family. If you are asked to do something that violates your personal or a professional code of ethics, you should first try to reason or negotiate not to do it. If you are unable to convince your employer, a freedom fund allows you to quit a job rather than compromise standards and jeopardize your professional reputation. Initially, plan to accumulate the equivalent of three-to-six months net salary in your freedom fund. As you are promoted to higher professional levels, raise the balance to a year or more of net income. A freedom fund is designed to pay the bills until you find another job. The greater your professional stature, the longer you should expect to look before finding an acceptable position. Plan accordingly, and never withdraw money from your freedom fund for anything else. If you do, it won't be there when you need it. In today's environment, it is almost certain that you will need to rely on your freedom fund to preserve your ethical standards.

get an improper $35 charge reversed. Five phone calls and nine different customer service representatives later, the customer was being billed for hundreds of dollars more, and the charge was still not reversed. Finally, after threats to publicize the company's incompetence, the corporate public relations department intervened to resolve the issue.

Customers armed with social and new media tools can wield a lot of power. The "United breaks guitars" case discussed in Chapter 9 is a prime example. The airline's customer service failure cost the company millions of dollars.

Many large and fast-growing organizations, like Comcast, find it difficult to manage customer service for tens of millions of customers. But it is crucial that this frontline communication function is structured and managed effectively. A company may allocate huge budgets for public relations to build trust with its key publics, but all that will be for naught if trust is not maintained at other touch points. Quality, respectful customer service is one of the foundations of trust required in today's marketplace.

Characteristics of professionalism

Professional reputation is one of the few enduring possessions. Businesses may come and go. Circumstances may, at times, cause difficulties in your career. Your professional success is dependent upon your building a good reputation; it is a critical element of professionalism.

Obviously, ethical behavior is one of the most important attributes of a solid professional. But it is not the only attribute. In fact, lists of characteristics and attributes necessary for professional survival abound. Four key categories of attributes deserve attention.

© Monkey Business Images/Shutterstock.com

Personal and professional development

A professional should never stop learning. Take advantage of formal and informal means of education, and follow these tips to help you build a sound reputation and a successful career.

- Strengthen your skills and keep up with changes and innovations, particularly in the areas of technology and social media.
- Read profusely both in and out of the field. One of the reasons behind the broad liberal arts curriculum in communication programs is the need for communicators and business professionals to be familiar with other areas of knowledge. The skills needed to communicate come from the communication curriculum. Background in and content of what you will be communicating comes from other fields of study.
- Obtain membership in at least one professional association, and actively pursue the educational opportunities offered therein.

- Read the news, blogs and professional journals. Read the important new books that everyone is reading. Read national and international publications that broaden your knowledge of current events and world information. You will be interacting with people in personal, professional and social situations. It is imperative that you be able to converse about current events, new discoveries, important studies and research, politics, sports, entertainment and other topics. Thoroughly knowing your profession will not only impress the decision makers you work with but also help you keep your job.
- Learn from your colleagues and fellow professionals. Be actively involved in professional organizations that provide networking opportunities. Be willing to serve in those organizations and diligently do good work. Call professionals you meet to gain information and advice and be available to mentor. Send them appropriate notes of congratulations, thanks and encouragement. Send out lots of holiday greetings. Keep your network vital and alive by developing relationships that demonstrate your care and respect for others.
- Finally, don't be afraid to ask questions. Have confidence in yourself, your knowledge and your ability, but remain humble and teachable. Overconfidence often masks incompetence. Don't be afraid to admit you have more to learn.

Work habits and job performance

Know your own strengths and weaknesses, and own up to your mistakes. Otherwise, you'll never overcome your challenges. Prioritize tasks, allocate time and work within constraints. Don't be concerned with the number of hours worked, but with the results and successes. Be goal-oriented, not just task-oriented. Pay attention to details, and always deliver work on time. Work hard and be absolutely dependable.

Do not undermine your coworkers. Work with people, not against them. Do not make enemies in the workplace by failing to be a supportive team member. If you want to be promoted, do your job well and then help do the job of the person you would like to replace. Help that person whenever possible. When people are promoted, they often have a hand in selecting a replacement. Make yourself the obvious choice.

Personal conduct

Always act in a professional manner, and dress professionally. Always be on time. Be aware of what goes on around you. Observe procedures and power structures (formal and informal) and work within them. Always be ethical, and never allow yourself to be persuaded to compromise your personal standards. The respect of others is directly proportional to your respect for yourself and your respect for them. Work toward a balance in your life. Don't live to work or you'll be too stressed to maintain other vital relationships in life. If all you have in life is your job, you might be good at what you do, but you'll be very dull. Cultivate other interests and relationships. Be a generous contributor and serve in your community.

PROFESSIONAL COURTESY
Exhibiting good manners by being thoughtful and considerate of others.

Human relations

Courtesy is fast becoming a lost art in our culture. A few years ago, Ann Landers provided a concise perspective of **professional courtesy** in one of her columns:

TIPS FROM THE PROS

How to preserve your reputation

Anthony D'Angelo, APR, Fellow PRSA, is the director of the master's program in communications management and the financial and investor communications emphasis at Syracuse University's Newhouse School of Public Communications. He is the former co-chair of the Commission on Public Relations Education and former national chair of PRSA. After a decades-long career in corporate and agency strategic communication, he tips you off on how to safeguard your reputation.

Trust is the sine qua non — absolute necessity — of the public relations profession, and reputation its stock in trade. Ethics and professionalism, therefore, are not optional. Without those attributes reflected in consistent behavior, a public relations professional will certainly fail. Here are the implications if you're pursuing a public relations career.

Trust and credibility are hard won and easily lost. No organization can exist without trust from the publics, internal and external, on which its survival depends. Trust and credibility are earned, daily, by people and organizations whose words and actions are in harmony. The video matches the audio, the product matches the claim, the delivery matches the promise, every time. In an increasingly cynical and disillusioned world, organizations that operate according to an ethical code and strive to live according to stated values have the best shot at succeeding. It's hard to do, and every person and organization makes mistakes. Still, public relations and message strategies not grounded in ethical behavior will undoubtedly implode. Without trust, they're just noise. Audiences are too sophisticated and perceptive to be duped.

It's not enough to have good intentions. The marketplace does not reward those who merely intend to behave ethically. Ethical action is expected and required. PR professionals must, therefore, know what they stand for personally, as well as on behalf of the organizations they represent. They must also always behave that way — even in environments that have different rules than they are used to, such as in crisis situations or in foreign countries. Fortunately, you don't have to make up your own professional code; you can study the PRSA Code of Ethics and similar industry guideposts to learn the foundational principles of our profession. They will help you navigate very complex, contentious issues that you will inevitably encounter in your career.

Professionalism is an extension or expression of an ethical foundation. Indeed, treating others with civility, courtesy and respect is not "nice to do," it is professionally imperative. Recognize that you teach people how to treat you through your behavior, as do organizations. If you supply courtesy and respect in your public relationships, you will find it returned. The same holds true for inconsiderate behavior, rudeness and animosity. Furthermore, there is a direct relationship, too often overlooked, between courtesy and credibility. The high road to a satisfying career is demanding, but the people you meet there are inspiring and helpful.

Warren Buffet was wrong, at least when he said, "It takes 20 years to build a reputation and five minutes to ruin it." Thanks to social media, it takes less than five minutes. Stay vigilant.

When you get right down to it, good manners are nothing more than being thoughtful and considerate of others. They are the principal lubricant of the human machinery we use when we interact with others.

Be personable and likeable. Learn to work well with people, treating them as equals. Work with and respect administrative assistants, secretaries and other staffers. They can help you succeed or cause you to fail. Develop relationships that win loyalty and dedication. Know people's names (and the proper spelling) and use them. Be a mentor to newcomers.

Keep a sense of humor and of perspective. Don't hold grudges and stay out of office politics for at least the first year in any company. It will take that long to figure out the informal power and communications structure. Never allow yourself to believe the job couldn't be done without you. Remember that cooperative effort is the key to success. Always be grateful and show that gratitude openly and often. Give others credit freely for their contributions.

Embracing diversity

 **DIVERSITY**
Appreciating differences in culture, gender, race, background, lifestyles and experience, allowing them to strengthen us rather than divide us.

In today's world, both ethics and professionalism demand that we embrace **diversity**. Because issues of diversity in our society have come to the fore, detractors may scorn their importance. More damaging, though, are those who have taken up the cause because it is trendy, rather than because it is morally right and a critically important part of the essence of our humanity.

Often, we wrongly equate diversity with equal employment opportunity and hiring quotas, failing to recognize that diversity celebrates the differences in all people, uniting them for better solutions and a brighter future. Harnessing diversity in our organizations and communities means creating an environment in which all individuals, regardless of difference, can work toward reaching their personal potential while serving the common good. Diversity does not focus just on race or gender. It addresses the contributions all individuals have to make because of their differences, not in spite of them. The following quote is often attributed to Nelson Mandela, but it was actually written by "The New York Times" bestselling author, Marianne Williamson and quoted by Mandela. She wrote in her book "A Return to Love:"

> Our deepest fear is not that we are inadequate. Our deepest fear is that we are powerful beyond measure. It is our light, not our darkness, that most frightens us. We ask ourselves, who am I to be brilliant, gorgeous, talented and fabulous? Actually, who are you not to be? You are a child of God. Your playing small doesn't serve the world. There's nothing enlightened about shrinking so that other people won't feel insecure around you. We were born to make manifest the glory of God that is within us. It's not just in some of us; it's in everyone. And as we let our own light shine, we unconsciously give other people permission to do the same. As we are liberated from our own fear, our presence automatically liberates others.

Diversity demands we examine privilege in our lives and accept the responsibility that comes with that privilege. It requires that we set aside "tolerance" in preference of acceptance and inclusion. It requires that we not identify one right way, one mainstream to which all others must conform, but that we recognize myriad viable paths to a solution. It means we must set aside ethnocentrism and learn to appreciate the variety of our world and its inhabitants.

In the workplace, issues of diversity become even more critical. In today's environment, employers seek not only trained and skilled individuals; they are looking for versatility, flexibility and skill in operating in diverse environments. They require not only job skills, but skills in communication and human relations. Preparing for the workforce, especially as a communicator, means preparing for work in diverse environments with individuals who are different in many ways, among them culture, race, gender, religion, sexual orientation, physical ability, age, national origin and socioeconomic status. Figure 14.3 is an example of how one professional association, PRSA, defines diversity and inclusion and talks about their importance to the communications industry.

The following are some guidelines to developing characteristics to embrace diversity.

> ***Understand yourself and your history.*** The first step to embracing diversity is to understand yourself and the part played in your life by culture. Culture largely determines behavior. When we accept something as correct, right or proper, we have usually made a cultural judgment. Understand also the privileges and opportunities you have been afforded that have contributed to the person you are now. Recognize that with those privileges come responsibilities and own up to those responsibilities. Also identify situations in which you were disadvantaged and how they have contributed to who you are. Rather than feeling self-pity, use those circumstances to develop empathy for others. We have all experienced both privilege and disadvantage to some degree. Reaching out to join cooperatively in the elimination of disadvantages of any kind is a positive way to deal with our own disadvantages.
>
> ***Shed the guilt and stop the blame.*** One of the biggest barriers to embracing diversity is guilt. Guilt is manifested in defensive postures. "It's not my fault," is heard all too often when we deal with issues of diversity. Learn to recognize a statement of fact without feeling blamed. It is a fact that certain groups in our society have been disadvantaged in ways that have been difficult to overcome. Supporting their efforts is not an admission of guilt. It is an attempt to prevent further pain and suffering by helping overcome disadvantages, regardless of their cause. On the other hand, do not become engaged in blaming behaviors. It does no good to blame people and drive them into a defensive posture. Blame and guilt are divisive, not unifying or productive.
>
> ***Minimize ethnocentrism.*** Although ethnocentrism is typically manifested between national cultures, it is present within nations as well. Ethnocentrism, or identifying our own particular culture and circumstance as the ideal to which all others should strive, is like wearing blinders. Different doesn't mean wrong or less effective. It just means different. Just as there is not only one right answer in creatively solving problems, there is not just one "right" culture. Appreciate your own culture but recognize it is not better — just different — than other cultures.

Avoid stereotypes. Stereotyping is sometimes a useful tool in understanding publics, but when we talk about diversity it is almost always harmful. Don't assume stereotypical characteristics about people with whom you have not worked or become acquainted. Also avoid the tendency to classify people as valuable members of a team just because of their membership in a particular group that may be a target public. Their value as a skilled communicator transcends the traits that classify them. All trained communicators should be able to marshal the resources and research to target any public.

Appreciate different ways of doing things. Learn not only that there is more than one right answer or way to accomplish something but also that different ways of doing something may have advantages not evident at first glance. Appreciate that using different approaches may enhance the creativity of the whole team. And, recognize that sometimes a different approach has a contribution to make that standard methods could not. Western medicine is a typical example of ethnocentrism and stereotyping that has hindered the widespread use of less traumatic treatments that work. Eastern-trained healers who work with the nervous system, the body's electrical impulses and pressure points have been successful time and time again at curing ailments Western medicine pronounced incurable.

Recognize professionalism and ability. Stereotypes often prevent us from recognizing the skills and competence of individuals. Professional communications and marketing skills are not genetic. If we begin to look at colleagues as fellow professionals instead of classifying them by their differences, we will find we have more in common than we thought.

Learn to develop relationships with individuals. Begin to see people as individuals: living, breathing and pursuing a quality of life similar to that which you pursue. Friendships begin when people take the time to get to know one another as human beings. Ask questions if you are uncertain how to behave. Whereas "Blacks" used to be appropriate terminology, many now refer to themselves as African-Americans. Many Native Americans prefer to be addressed by tribal affiliation. Hispanics include Puerto Ricans, Cubans, Mexicans and Mexican-Americans, to name only a few. Ask people how they define themselves and then show respect for the individual by adopting that definition in your interactions with them. It is the same personal respect you would wish to be accorded.

© EDHAR/Shutterstock.com

In the marketing, communications and advertising professions, more often than not, we work in teams. Seldom is a solution developed or implemented by one person in isolation from others. Learning to harness diversity means learning to let differences work for you, allowing diversity to enhance solutions and performance. In today's world, those who excel professionally will be those who have learned to appreciate and embrace diversity.

Figure 14.3
PRSA's statement on diversity and inclusion

Diversity and inclusion are integral to the evolution and growth of PRSA and the public relations industry.

The most obvious contexts of diversity include race, ethnicity, religion, age, ability, sexual orientation, gender, gender identity, country of origin, culture and diversity of thought. However, in a rapidly changing society, diversity continues to evolve and can include class, socioeconomic status, life experiences, learning and working styles, and personality types and intellectual traditions and perspectives, in addition to cultural, political, religious and other beliefs.

These defining attributes impact how we approach our work, connect with others and move through the world.

Inclusion, according to the Society for Human Resource Management (SHRM), is defined as "the achievement of a work environment in which all individuals are treated fairly and respectfully, have equal access to opportunities and resources, and can contribute fully to the organization's success."

Inclusion is not just about having that "seat at the table" but is about ensuring everyone's voice is heard and fully considered. Diversity and inclusion are proactive behaviors.

Respecting, embracing, celebrating and validating those behaviors are integral to PRSA's DNA. Diversity and inclusion are vital to the success of our profession, our members and the communities in which we live and work. It is essential and is our responsibility as members of PRSA to carry this forward.

Source: PRSA Do-I Chapter Toolkit

Summary

It is only logical to conclude our examination of strategic communications planning with a discussion of professionalism and ethical practice. Without these elements, no communications effort will succeed over the long term. Successful communication is based on trust, and trust is built by exhibiting professional and ethical behavior. Ethics are based on individual and group value systems (ethical codes) governing acceptable behavior. Value systems must place a premium not only on ethical behavior but also on diversity. True professionals exhibit a sincere commitment to an environment in which all may reach their potential while contributing to the overall goals.

Exercises

1. Do some thinking about your own personal value system and how it will drive your ethical choices in the professional world. Develop your own definition of success and identify the ethical standards it implies.

2. Look up the codes of ethics in Appendix C and decide which one best exemplifies your approach to the profession.

3. Read one of PRSA's Ethical Standards Advisories (ESA) at https://www.prsa.org/about/ethics. Take notes about how you would apply the guidelines in the advisory to similar situations you may encounter in your professional life.

4. Read one of the latest winning case studies from the Arthur W. Page Student Case Study Competition (https://page.org/study_competitions). Evaluate how well the organization featured in the case study followed one of the Codes of Ethics in Appendix C. You may want to focus on the Arthur W. Page Principles. Write a brief report about your findings that explain what the organization did well and where it can improve.

5. Open a savings account designated as your freedom fund.

6. Complete the Arthur W. Page Center's training modules about public relations ethics and diversity. https://pagecentertraining.psu.edu/

7. Initiate a serious discussion with one or two friends about diversity. Explore your similarities and your differences. Speak honestly about how you have been advantaged as well as disadvantaged.

8. Review PRSA's Voices4Everyone website (https://voices4everyone.prsa.org/) to learn more about disinformation, diversity and inclusion, civility and civic engagement. Use the website's resources to develop a plan that will help you detect and avoid spreading disinformation in your personal life and on behalf of the organizations you will work for.

9. Watch one of PRSA's Diversity Dialogue videos at https://www.prsa.org/diverse-dialogues. Or review AAF's diversity, equity and inclusion videos at https://vimeo.com/showcase/7628309. Write a one-page report on what you learned about diversity.

References and additional readings

Arthur W. Page Society. (2012). Building belief: A new model for activating corporate character and authentic advocacy. Retrieved from https://knowledge.page.org/wp-content/uploads/2019/02/Full_Report.pdf

Arthur W. Page Society. (2007). The authentic enterprise. Retrieved from https://knowledge.page.org/wp-content/uploads/2019/02/Download_Report.pdf

Auger, G. A. (2014). Trust me, trust me not: An experimental analysis of the effect of transparency on organizations. *Journal of Public Relations Research*, 26(4), 325-343.

Biro, T. (2017, November 17). Pay-for-play is everywhere: The lines between paid and organic are blurry and getting blurrier. *PR Week*. Retrieved from https://www.prweek.com/article/1450565/pay-for-play-everywhere

Callahan, D. (2004). *The Cheating Culture: Why More Americans Are Doing Wrong to Get Ahead*. Orlando, FL: Harcourt, Inc.

Carter, S. L. (1997). *Integrity*. New York: HarperPerennial.

Department of Justice. (2017, Jan. 11). Volkswagen AG agrees to plead guilty and pay $4.3 billion in criminal and civil penalties; Six Volkswagen executives and employees are indicted in connection with conspiracy to cheat U.S. emissions tests. [Press Release]. Retrieved from https://www.justice.gov/opa/pr/volkswagen-ag-agrees-plead-guiltyand- pay-43-billion-criminal-and-civil-penalties-six

Edelman. (2020). 2020 Edelman Trust Barometer reveals growing sense of inequality is undermining trust in institutions. Retrieved from https://www.edelman.com/news-awards/2020-edelman-trust-barometer

Etzioni, A. (1989). Money, power and fame. *Newsweek*, 18 September, 10.

Ewing, J. (2017, March 16). Engineering a deception: What led to Volkswagen's diesel scandal. Retrieved from https://www.nytimes.com/interactive/2017/business/volkswagen- diesel-emissions-timeline.html

Faust, J. E. (2003, February 28). Be healers. [Address given to the J. Reuben Clark Law School at Brigham Young University]. Provo, UT.

Federal Trade Commission. (n.d.). Disclosures 101 for social media influencers. Retrieved from https://www.ftc.gov/business-guidance/resources/disclosures-101-social-media-influencers ww

Friedman, T. L. (2007). *The World is Flat* (3.0). New York: Farrar, Straus and Giroux.

Gates, G., Ewing, J., Russell, K. & Watkins, D. (2017, March 16). How Volkswagen's 'defeat devices' worked. Retrieved from https://www.nytimes.com/interactive/2015/business/ international/vw-diesel-emissions-scandal-explained.html

Hakim, D. (2016, Feb. 26). VW's crisis strategy: Forward, reverse, U-turn. Retrieved from https://www.nytimes.com/2016/02/28/business/international/vws-crisis-strategyforward-reverse-u-turn.html

Howard, C. M. & Mathews, W. K. (2013). *On Deadline: Managing Media Relations* (5th ed.). Long Grove, IL.: Waveland Press.

Institute for Public Relations. (2022). Third annual disinformation in society report. Retrieved from https://instituteforpr.org/2022-disinformation-report/

Jordans, F. & Pylas, P. (2015, Sept. 21). Volkswagen rocked by US emissions scandal as stock price falls. Retrieved from https://www.csmonitor.com/World/Europe/2015/0921/Volkswagen-rocked-by-US-emissions-scandal-as-stock-price-falls

LeBeau, P. (2015, Oct. 7). Volkswagen dealer: Biggest fraud I have ever seen. Retrieved from https://www.cnbc.com/2015/10/07/vw-dealers-customers-feel-betrayed-by-emissions-cheating-scandal.html

Lewis III, B. D. (2020). The consequences of misinformation. *PRSay*. Retrieved from http://prsay.prsa.org/2021/03/19/the-consequences-of-misinformation/

Li, Z. C., Tao, W. & Wu, L. (2020). The price of good friendships: Examining the roles of relationship norms and perceived controllability in service failure encounters. *International Journal of Business Communication*, DOI:10.1177/2329488420907119

Lienert, P. & Cremer, A. (2015, Nov. 9). Volkswagen moves to appease angry customers, workers. Retrieved from https://www.reuters.com/article/us-volkswagen-emissions/volkswagen-moves-to-appease-angry-customers-workers-idUSKCN-0SY1UO2015111 0#C9uTjqR7OU2PdOgW.97

Mota, J. (2015, Sept. 21). Volkswagen's apology on TDI scandal by President and CEO Michael Horn [Video]. Retrieved from https://www.youtube.com/watch?v=dyiTwCu-CRqg

NPR. (2015, Sept. 21). Volkswagen stock plummets as CEO apologizes for emissions cheat. Retrieved from https://www.npr.org/sections/thetwo-way/2015/09/21/442174444/volkswagen-stock-plummets-as-ceo-apologizes-for-emissions-cheat

OBI Creative. (2018, April 19). PR worth paying for. Retrieved from https://www.obicreative.com/paid-pr/

PRSA. (n.d.). Pay for play. *BEPS Position Papers*. Retrieved from https://www.prsa.org/about/ethics

Silvers, D. (n.d.). Pay-for-play PR — Is the gamble worth it? *PR Fuel*. Retrieved from https://www.ereleases.com/pr-fuel/pay-for-play-pr-gamble/

Rawlins, B. (2008). Give the emperor a mirror: Toward developing a stakeholder measurement of organizational transparency. *Journal of Public Relations Research*, 21(1), 71-99.

Riley, C. (2017, Sept. 29). Volkswagen's diesel scandal costs hit $30 billion. Retrieved from https://money.cnn.com/2017/09/29/investing/volkswagen-diesel-cost-30-billion/index.html

Tannen, D. (1994). Gender games. *People*. 10 October, 71–74.

The Aspen Institute. (2021, November). Commission on Information Disorder final report. Retrieved from https://www.aspeninstitute.org/publications/commission-on-information-disorder-final-report/

Volkswagen Group (2015, Sept. 22). Video statement Prof. Dr. Martin Winterkorn. [Video]. Retrieved from https://www.youtube.com/watch?v=wMPX98_H0ak

Washkuch, F. (2016, Oct. 6). How Volkswagen's emission crisis unfolded. Retrieved from https://www.prweek.com/article/1365154/volkswagens-emissions-crisis-unfolded

Wilcox, D. L., Cameron, G. T. & Reber, B. H. (2014). *Public Relations: Strategies and Tactics* (11th ed.). Upper Saddle River, NJ; Pearson Education.

Young, D. (1987, November 8–11). Confronting the ethical issues that confront you. [Address given at the 40th Annual PRSA National Conference]. Los Angeles.

Zercher, S. (2017, March 28). Pay for play: Where paid PR and marketing join forces for good. Retrieved from https://www.marsdenmarketing.com/blog/pay-for-play-where-pr-and-marketing-join-forces-for-good

APPENDIX A

TIPS FROM THE PROS

APPENDIX B

STRATEGY BRIEFS

Strategy brief – backgrounder/brief history

Key public (brief profile including motivating self-interests):

Secondary publics (if any):

Action desired from public(s):

Focus on an event, organization or issue:

Backgrounder's tie to campaign big idea:

Proposed title:

Primary messages (two-three short statements, similar to sound bites)
Secondary messages (bulleted supporting data, facts, examples, stories, testimonials, etc.)

1. Primary:
   Secondary:
   -
   -
   -

2. Primary:
   Secondary:
   -
   -
   -

3. Primary:
   Secondary:
   -
   -
   -

Opinion leaders and how they will be used (testimonials, quotes, etc.):

Photos/charts/graphics (if any):

Where and when distributed:

Additional uses after distribution:

Timeline/deadline:

Strategy brief — billboard/poster

Key public (brief profile including motivating self-interests):

Secondary publics (if any):

Action desired from public(s):

Billboard/poster's tie to campaign big idea:

Primary message (usually one short primary message, similar to a sound bite)
Secondary messages (bulleted supporting data, facts, examples, stories, testimonials, etc.)

1. Primary:
   Secondary:
   -
   -
   -

Opinion leaders and how they will be used (testimonials, quotes, etc.):

Color palette:

Art:

Size(s) of billboard/poster:

Location(s) of billboard/poster:

Print quantity and offset printing spot colors (if applicable):

Method and timing of distribution:

Additional uses after distribution:

Timeline/deadline:

Tip: Use this strategy brief to create a wireframe before designing your billboard/poster.

Strategy brief — blog post/feature story

Key public (brief profile including motivating self-interests):

Secondary publics (if any):

Action desired from public(s):

Blog post/feature story's tie to campaign big idea:

Tone:

News hook:

Proposed headline:

Proposed lead:

Proposed nutgraf:

Proposed background:

Proposed conclusion:

Embedded links to internal and external sites:

SEO terms (key words or phrases) and tags:

Primary messages (In a feature story, these are categories of information you will present in the body of the feature story. Use your primary messages as subheads — usually two-six categories.)

Secondary messages (In a feature story, these are the quotations, data, facts, examples, or anecdotes that develop the body of the story under each primary category.)

1. Primary:
   Secondary:
   -
   -
   -

2. Primary:
   Secondary:
   -
   -
   -

3. Primary:
   Secondary:
   -
   -
   -

Opinion leaders and how they will be used (testimonials, quotes, etc.):

Photos/graphics/art:

Distribution contact (publication, editor's name, email and phone):

Distribution once published:

Additional uses after publication:

Timeline/deadline:

Tip: If you are managing a blog, you should do a strategy brief for every blog post, and you must also create and maintain an editorial calendar.

Strategy brief — brochure

Key public (brief profile including motivating self-interests):

Secondary publics (if any):

Action desired from public(s):

Brochure's tie to campaign big idea:

Primary messages (In a brochure, these are categories of information you will present on each panel of the brochure. Use your primary messages as headlines or subheads for each panel — usually two-six panels.)

Secondary messages (In a brochure, these are the quotations, data, facts, examples, or anecdotes that you will feature on each panel of your brochure.)

1. Primary:
   Secondary:
   -
   -
   -
2. Primary:
   Secondary:
   -
   -
   -
3. Primary:
   Secondary:
   -
   -
   -

Opinion leaders and how they will be used (testimonials, quotes, etc.):

Color palette:

Cover title and cover copy:

Cover photos/graphics (if any):

Internal photos/graphics:

Brochure size, paper (weight, finish):

Print quantity and offset printing spot colors (if applicable):

Where and when distributed:

Additional uses after distribution:

Timeline/deadline:

Strategy brief – direct mail piece

Key public (brief profile including motivating self-interests):

Secondary publics (if any):

Action desired from public(s):

Direct mail piece's tie to campaign big idea:

Tone:

Proposed p.s.:

Primary messages (two-three short statements, similar to sound bites)
Secondary messages (bulleted supporting data, facts, examples, stories, testimonials, etc.)

1. Primary:
   Secondary:
   -
   -
   -

2. Primary:
   Secondary:
   -
   -
   -

3. Primary:
   Secondary:
   -
   -
   -

Opinion leaders and how they will be used (testimonials, quotes, etc.):

Color palette:

Cover title and cover copy:

Cover photos/graphics (if any):

Internal photos/graphics:

Print quantity and offset printing spot colors (if applicable):

Mailer size and paper (weight, finish, etc.):

Postage:

Source of mailing list:

Where and when distributed:

Additional uses after distribution:

Timeline/deadline:

Strategy brief – email news pitch

Publication:

Reporter/editor being pitched:

Email contact:

Related stories published by reporter:

Reporter/beat assignments:

Story being pitched:

Story's tie to campaign big idea:

News hook (that would interest the reporter):

Proposed email subject line:

Resources/assets you can offer:
1. Interviews:
2. Research/data:
3. Images:
4. B-roll:

Primary message (one-three short statements, similar to sound bites)
Secondary messages (bulleted supporting data, facts, examples, stories, testimonials, etc.)

1. Primary:
   Secondary:
   -
   -
   -
2. Primary:
   Secondary:
   -
   -
   -
3. Primary:
   Secondary:
   -
   -
   -

Photos/charts/graphics:

Timing of pitch:

Planned follow-up with media:

Timeline/deadline:

Tip: Reporters typically will not open attachments.

Strategy brief — fact sheet

Key public (brief profile including motivating self-interests):

Secondary publics (if any):

Action desired from public(s):

Fact sheet's tie to campaign big idea:

SEO terms (key words or phrases):

Primary messages (two-three short statements, similar to sound bites)
Secondary messages (bulleted supporting data, facts, examples, stories, testimonials, etc.)

1. Primary:
   Secondary:
   -
   -
   -

2. Primary:
   Secondary:
   -
   -
   -

3. Primary:
   Secondary:
   -
   -
   -

Opinion leaders and how they will be used (testimonials, quotes, etc.):

Color palette:

Graphics/charts (if any):

Finished size:

Where and when distributed:

Additional uses after distribution:

Timeline/deadline:

Strategy brief – infographic

Key public (brief profile including motivating self-interests):

Secondary publics (if any):

Action desired from public(s):

Infographic's tie to campaign big idea:

Primary messages (In an infographic, these are categories of information used as subheads — usually two-six categories.)

Secondary messages (In an infographic, these are the hard data or facts that fit under each primary category. Use vector elements such as avatars, ideograms, ribbons and speech bubbles to convey information quickly.)

1. Primary:
   Secondary:
   -
   -
   -

2. Primary:
   Secondary:
   -
   -
   -

3. Primary:
   Secondary:
   -
   -
   -

Graphs and charts to be used (for comparison use column and bar charts; for transition use line or area charts; for composition use pie or waterfall charts):

Other images or icons to be used (photos, avatars, ideograms, illustrations, ribbons, speech bubbles and word clouds):

Color palette:

Fonts:

Where posted/distributed:

Additional uses after distribution:

Timeline/deadline:

Strategy brief – letter to the editor

Key public (brief profile including motivating self-interests):

Secondary publics (if any):

Action desired from public(s):

News reference (previous story and publishing date):

Letter to the editor's tie to campaign big idea:

Primary messages (two-three short statements, similar to sound bites)
Secondary messages (bulleted supporting data, facts, examples, stories, testimonials, etc.)

1. Primary:
    Secondary:
    -
    -
    -

2. Primary:
    Secondary:
    -
    -
    -

3. Primary:
    Secondary:
    -
    -
    -

Opinion leaders and how they will be used (testimonials, quotes, etc.):

Length (newspaper's suggested word count):

Distribution contact (publication, editor's name, email and phone):

Distribution once published:

Additional uses after publication:

Timeline/deadline:

Tip: Use a typical letter format complete with your signature, title, city, state and contact information.

Strategy brief – media advisory

Key public (brief profile including motivating self-interests):

Secondary publics (if any):

Action desired from public(s):

Media advisory's tie to campaign big idea:

Media contact and email address:

Proposed email subject line:

Proposed headline:

Key information (use these categories as subheads in your advisory):

    Who:
    What:
    When:
    Where:
    Why:
    How:

Opinion leaders and how they will be used (testimonials, quotes, etc.):

Photos/charts/graphics:

When and where distributed:

Planned follow-up with media:

Timeline/deadline:

Strategy brief — media kit/online newsroom

Key public (brief profile including motivating self-interests):

Secondary publics (if any):

Action desired from public(s):

Media kit's tie to campaign big idea:

Media contacts and email addresses:

Proposed content (fact sheet, executive bios, infographics, videos, backgrounders, photos, etc.) and how it appeals to the key public's self-interests. Each communications piece should have its own strategy brief.
  1.
  2.
  3.
  4.
  5.

Opinion leaders and how they will be used (testimonials, quotes, etc.):

Proposed packaging (location on web, folder, box, envelope, etc.):

Color palette:

Packaging graphics (logo, photo, etc.):

Method and timing of distribution (digital, sent with story, handed out at event, etc.):

Print quantity (if applicable):

Specific media to receive kit:

Proposed follow-up with media (if any):

Timeline/deadline:

Tip: Today's media environment requires most organizations to maintain at least a basic online newsroom presence.

Strategy brief – news release

Key public (brief profile including motivating self-interests):

Secondary publics (if any):

Action desired from public(s):

News release's tie to campaign big idea:

Media contacts and email addresses:

News hook:

Proposed headline:

Proposed lead:

SEO terms (key words or phrases):

Primary messages (two-three short statements, similar to sound bites)
Secondary messages (bulleted supporting data, facts, examples, stories, testimonials, etc.)

1. Primary:
   Secondary:
   -
   -
   -

2. Primary:
   Secondary:
   -
   -
   -

3. Primary:
   Secondary:
   -
   -
   -

Opinion leaders and how they will be used (testimonials, quotes, etc.):

Photos/charts/graphics (if any):

Where and when distributed:

Additional uses after publication:

Timeline/deadline:

Tip: Use the strategy brief for an email news pitch to send your news release to targeted reporters, bloggers, etc.

Strategy brief – newsletter

Key public (brief profile including motivating self-interests):

Secondary publics (if any):

Action desired from public(s):

Newsletter's tie to campaign big idea:

Overall tone:

Masthead text and graphics:

Lead story:

Lead story graphics:

Regular features or sections—special columns, reports and letters—and how they appeal to the key public's self-interests. Each feature and story should have its own strategy brief.
1.
2.
3.
4.

Other stories or articles (each should have its own strategy brief):

Color palette:

Photos/graphics:

Opinion leaders and how they will be used (testimonials, quotes, etc.):

Finished size, number of pages and paper (weight, finish, etc.):

Print quantity and offset printing spot colors (if applicable):

Where and when distributed:

Additional uses after distribution:

Timeline/deadline:

Editorial calendar:

Strategy brief – op-ed piece

Key public (brief profile including motivating self-interests):

Secondary publics (if any):

Action desired from public(s):

Op-ed's tie to campaign big idea:

Position to be taken in the op-ed:

Tone:

Proposed headline:

Proposed lead:

Primary messages (In an op-ed, these are the main arguments that support your position.)

Secondary messages (In an op-ed these are the quotations, data, facts, examples, or anecdotes that support your main arguments.)

1. Primary:
   Secondary:
   -
   -
   -
2. Primary:
   Secondary:
   -
   -
   -
3. Primary:
   Secondary:
   -
   -
   -

Opinion leaders and how they will be used (testimonials, quotes, etc.):

Distribution contact (publication, editor's name, email, and phone):

Distribution once published:

Additional uses after publication:

Timeline/deadline:

Strategy brief – print ad

Key public (brief profile including motivating self-interests):

Secondary publics (if any):

Action desired from public(s):

Print ad's tie to campaign big idea:

Tone:

Slogan or tagline (if any):

Primary messages (two-three short statements, similar to sound bites)
Secondary messages (bulleted supporting data, facts, examples, stories,
testimonials, etc.)

1. Primary:
   Secondary:
   -
   -
   -
2. Primary:
   Secondary:
   -
   -
   -
3. Primary:
   Secondary:
   -
   -
   -

Opinion leaders and how they will be used (testimonials, quotes, etc.):

Color palette:

Photos/graphics:

Ad size, format and resolution:

Ad placement (publications):

Additional uses after publication:

Timeline/deadline:

Strategy brief – radio ad or PSA

Key public (brief profile including motivating self-interests):

Secondary publics (if any):

Action desired from public(s):

Radio ad's tie to campaign big idea:

Tone:

Format (jingle, single voice, dialogue, etc.):

Length (10 seconds, 15 seconds, 30 seconds, 60 seconds, etc.):

Slogan or tagline (if any):

Primary messages (two-three short statements, similar to sound bites)
Secondary messages (bulleted supporting data, facts, examples, stories, testimonials, etc.):

1. Primary:
   Secondary:
   -
   -
   -

2. Primary:
   Secondary:
   -
   -
   -

3. Primary:
   Secondary:
   -
   -
   -

Opinion leaders and how they will be used (testimonials, quotes, etc.):

Title:

Proposed voice actors:

Sound effects:

Music:

Permissions:

Production quantity:

Where and when distributed:

Additional uses after airing:

Timeline/deadline:

Strategy brief – social media posts (Facebook, Instagram, LinkedIn, Twitter)

Key public (brief profile including motivating self-interests):

Secondary publics (if any):

Action desired from public(s):

Social media posts' tie to campaign big idea:

Photo or graphics (if applicable):

Hashtags and/or text links (if applicable):

SEO terms (key words or phrases):

First five posts (include primary/secondary message elements; may not include all elements below):

1. Message:
    Art/video:
    Links:
    Hashtags:
    @ tags:

2. Message:
    Art/video:
    Links:
    Hashtags:
    @ tags:

3. Message:
    Art/video:
    Links:
    Hashtags:
    @ tags:

4. Message:
    Art/video:
    Links:
    Hashtags:
    @ tags:

5. Message:
    Art/video:
    Links:
    Hashtags:
    @ tags:

Analytics to monitor posts:

Editorial calendar:

Strategy brief – special event

Key public (brief profile including motivating self-interests):

Secondary publics (if any):

Action desired from public(s):

Tentative event date/deadline:

Event location:

Event theme (should tie to overall big idea):

Slogan or tagline (if any):

Primary messages (two-three short statements, similar to sound bites)
Secondary messages (bulleted supporting data, facts, examples, stories, testimonials, etc.)

1. Primary:
   Secondary:
   -
   -
   -

2. Primary:
   Secondary:
   -
   -
   -

3. Primary:
   Secondary:
   -
   -
   -

Opinion leaders and how they will be used (testimonials, quotes, etc.):

Desired atmosphere/tone:

Key visual elements:

Interactive activities (if any):

Collateral pieces (print, multimedia, web, etc.) — each will need individual strategy briefs:

Takeaways (gifts, mementos, swag, etc.):

Special guests:

Targeted media to invite:

Planned promotion:

Tip: Always use a detailed checklist and calendar when planning and executing a special event.

Strategy brief – speech

Key public (brief profile including motivating self-interests):

Secondary publics (if any):

Action desired from public(s):

Speech's tie to campaign big idea:

Proposed title:

Speaker:

Venue:

Length:

Audience (the key public may be broader than the physical audience of the speech):

Opening attention-getting device (humor, story, statistics, etc.):

Primary messages (two-three main ideas or points in the speech)
Secondary messages (bulleted supporting data, facts, examples, stories, testimonials, etc.):

1. Primary:
   Secondary:
   -
   -
   -
2. Primary:
   Secondary:
   -
   -
   -
3. Primary:
   Secondary:
   -
   -
   -

Opinion leaders and how they will be used (testimonials, quotes, etc.):

Visuals and/or video to be used (if any):

Conclusion:

Speech publication or distribution:

Additional uses after delivery:

Timeline/deadline:

Strategy brief – video

Key public (brief profile including motivating self-interests):

Secondary publics (if any):

Action desired from public(s):

Video's tie to campaign big idea:

Slogan or tagline (if any):

Proposed title:

Tone:

Hook:

Format (jingle, voice-over, situation, etc.):

Length (30 seconds, 60 seconds, up to three minutes maximum):

Primary messages (two-three short statements, similar to sound bites)
Secondary messages (bulleted supporting data, facts, examples, stories, testimonials, etc.)

1. Primary:
   Secondary:
   -
   -
   -

2. Primary:
   Secondary:
   -
   -
   -

3. Primary:
   Secondary:
   -
   -
   -

Opinion leaders and how they will be used (testimonials, quotes, etc.):

Proposed actors:

Location(s):

Props/equipment needed:

Photos/graphics:

B-roll:

Sound effects:

Music:

Permissions:

Where and when distributed:

SEO description for posting:

Additional uses after posting:

Timeline/deadline:

Tip: Always create a storyboard and shot list before you begin shooting video.

Strategy brief – website

Key publics (brief profiles including motivating self-interests of each key public):

Secondary publics (if any):

Action desired from publics:

Website's tie to campaign big idea:

Tone:

URL:

SEO terms (key words or phrases):

Primary messages for the home page (two-three short statements, similar to sound bites):
  1. Primary message:
  2. Primary message:
  3. Primary message:

Primary navigation categories and subcategories (indicate how they appeal to the key publics' self-interests):

  1.
      a.
      b.
      c.
  2.
      a.
      b.
      c.
  3.
      a.
      b.
      c.
  4.
      a.
      b.
      c.

Opinion leaders and how they will be used (testimonials, quotes, etc.):

Visual design elements (logos, pictures and illustrations):

Color palette:

Fonts:

Interactive elements:

Promotion to drive traffic to URL:

Social media links:

Timeline/deadline:

APPENDIX C
PROFESSIONAL CODES OF ETHICS

Following are brief summaries of the principles and values in the ethical codes for several professional communications and research associations. URLs are provided to access the full code for each of the associations.

American Marketing Association (AMA) — Statement of ethics

Adopted by members of the AMA in 2008. URL: https://myama.my.site.com/s/article/AMA-Statement-of-Ethics .

Ethical norms
1. Do no harm.
2. Foster trust in the marketing system.
3. Embrace ethical values:
   - Honesty
   - Responsibility
   - Fairness
   - Respect
   - Transparency
   - Citizenship

The Arthur Page Society — The Page principles

URL: https://page.org/site/the-page-principles

Seven proven principles

1. Tell the truth.
2. Prove it with action.
3. Listen to the stakeholders.
4. Manage for tomorrow.
5. Conduct public relations as if the whole enterprise depends on it.
6. Realize an enterprise's true character is expressed by its people.
7. Remain calm, patient and good-humored.

Association for Institutional Research (AIR) — Statement of ethical principles

Approved by the AIR Board of Directors September 13, 2019. URL: https://www.airweb.org/ir-data-professional-overview/statement-of-ethical-principles.

Act with integrity

- Recognize the consequences of institutional research.
- Acknowledge the rights of individuals whose information is used.
- Protect privacy and maintain confidentiality.
- Be responsible data stewards.
- Provide accurate and contextualized information.
- Deliver appropriate information and analyses.
- Be fair and transparent.
- Avoid conflicts of interest and disclose them when unavoidable.
- Strive to make research accessible.
- Share knowledge of the institutional research field.
- Value lifelong learning and the enhancement of the field.
- Draw on and contribute to relevant and emerging scholarship and developing trends.
- Be committed to serving as educators and role models on the ethical use of data.

Global Alliance for Public Relations and Communications Management — Global principles and code of ethics

GA code 2018. URL: https://www.globalalliancepr.org/code-of-ethics.

Principles of professional practice

- Advocacy
- Disclosure
- Honesty
- Integrity
- Expertise
- Loyalty

Institute for Advertising Ethics — Principles and practices for advertising ethics

Adopted 2020. URL: https://www.iaethics.org/principles-and-practices

Principles

1. Share a common objective of truth and high ethical standards.
2. Exercise the highest personal ethics in the creation and dissemination of information.
3. Distinguish advertising, public relations and corporate communications from news and editorial content and entertainment.
4. Disclose all material conditions (e.g., payment or free product) affecting endorsements and the identity of endorsers.
5. Treat consumers fairly.
6. Never compromise consumers' personal privacy or their free choice concerning provision of their information.
7. Follow federal, state and local advertising laws and industry self-regulatory programs.
8. Discuss privately potential ethical concerns and give team members permission to express their ethical concerns.
9. Build trust through transparency and full disclosure.

International Association of Business Communicators (IABC) — Code of ethics for professional communicators

Approved by the International Executive Board May 4, 2016. URL: https://www.iabc.com/About/Purpose/Code-of-Ethics

Ethical principles

1. Be honest.
2. Communicate accurate information.
3. Obey laws and public policies.
4. Protect confidential information.
5. Support the ideals of free speech.
6. Be sensitive to cultural values and beliefs.
7. Give credit to others and cite sources.
8. Do not use confidential information for personal benefit.
9. Do not represent conflicting or competing interests without full disclosure.
10. Do not accept undisclosed gifts or payments.
11. Do not guarantee results beyond ability to deliver.

The International Public Relations Association (IPRA) — Code of conduct

Adopted by the IPRA Board November 5, 2010. The Code consolidates the 1961 Code of Venice, the 1965 Code of Athens and the 2007 Code of Brussels. URL: https://www.ipra.org/member-services/code-of-conduct

Conduct of public relations practitioners

1. Observe the principles of the UN Charter and the Universal Declaration of Human Rights.
2. Act with honesty and integrity.
3. Establish dialogue.
4. Be open and transparent.
5. Avoid and/or disclose any professional conflicts of interest.
6. Honor confidential information.
7. Ensure truth and accuracy.
8. Do not intentionally disseminate false or misleading information.
9. Do not obtain information by deceptive or dishonest means.

10. Do not create or use any organization that actually serves an undisclosed interest.
11. Do not sell copies of documents obtained from public authorities.
12. Do not accept payment from anyone other than the principal.
13. Do not give any inducement to public representatives, the media or other stakeholders.
14. Do not exercise improper influence on public representatives, the media or other stakeholders.
15. Do not intentionally injure the professional reputation of another practitioner.
16. Do not seek to secure another practitioner's client by deceptive means.
17. Follow the rules and confidentiality requirements when employing personnel from public authorities or competitors.
18. Observe this code with respect to fellow IPRA members and public relations practitioners worldwide.

Public Relations Society of America (PRSA) — Code of ethics

URL: https://www.prsa.org/about/ethics/prsa-code-of-ethics

Professional values

- Advocacy
- Honesty
- Expertise
- Independence
- Loyalty
- Fairness

Core principles

- Free flow of information
- Competition
- Disclosure of information
- Safeguarding confidences
- Avoiding/disclosing conflicts of interest
- Enhancing the profession

APPENDIX D
COMPLETE SAMPLE STRATEGIC COMMUNICATIONS PLAN

The State Department of Corrections is planning to construct a new prison in Green Valley, a small farming town 50 miles from an interstate highway. The 7,500 people in the town and 2,500 more in the surrounding area are concerned for the safety of their families and property. The state will face expensive opposition unless attitudes can be changed so that the town is reassured of its safety and welcomes the economic development that will come with the new facility.

BACKGROUND

The external environment: Like the rest of the country, Green Valley is struggling to emerge from the economic downturn that hit this farming community particularly hard. Unemployment and underemployment have been problems, and the construction project, and the staffing and maintenance of a prison in town would be a definite economic boon. Politically, the residents are conservative and supportive of the penal system, but highly publicized incidents of violent crime have them wary of the kinds of people and criminal culture that would be introduced into their community and to their children.

The industry: While the penal system would introduce the seamier side of society to Green Valley, the prison and all the services needed to support the prison would mean several million dollars injected into the area economy annually, and it would mean 750 new jobs with the prison alone, not to mention the jobs that would be added as the town's business community expanded to meet the needs of such a facility. While many of those jobs would be blue collar, hourly positions, a fair percentage would be professional positions in education, health care, management, finance and other professions. Technology, strict regulation and control in this industry renders safety less of an issue than the public may think. That means growth for Green Valley as people move into town to support the new prison, and employment for people in Green Valley who have been without work because of the recent recession.

Competition: The only competition is the publics' perceptions, attitudes and values. Fear for safety and fear for a loss of innocence present opposition. Those can be overcome with accurate information and recognition of the benefits. There is also a potential for legal opposition to a project like this.

Stakeholder research: Green Valley residents are diffused stakeholders. They do not typically interact with the State Department of Corrections, but because the proposal to construct a prison in their town will have a significant impact on their lives, they are more likely to become involved with the department throughout the approval process. The prison proposal will also have an impact on their attitudes about and opinions of the department. Green Valley residents have some power over the elected officials making decisions about the prison through the ballot box and public pressure. They have a legitimate claim on the issue because the prison will be built in their community, which will be left to deal with both the positive and negative impacts. Also, they will feel a sense of urgency for government leaders to address their concerns as deadlines approach for community input and government approvals that move the prison from idea to reality.

The organization: The state prison system keeps a low profile, and has been able to do so because of virtually no incidents threatening public safety in the last couple of decades. The system is efficiently managed, and employees are competent. Its reputation is unsullied.

The service: The service provided by the taxpayer-funded state penal system is necessary. In this conservative area, the justice system is supported, and the concept of prisons is understood and accepted. There is little, if any, opposition to the idea of a prison; there was simply concern that it would be located here. The issue of safety is the primary concern in the minds of citizens, and the exposure of children to the idea of violent crime in society is a close secondary concern. In a small town like this, children and families would see the prison facility daily, a constant reminder of their vulnerability and the criminal element in society.

Promotions: Research shows that other states that have faced this challenge have been most successful when they have invited the community's voice in the process. Providing full information on location, plans, timelines, construction and operation along with inviting public discussion and comment have typically allowed communities to weigh the pros and cons and come to a decision of support. Economic benefits, safety procedures and safety records of other state facilities have all been powerful messages. When communities have a voice in the process, are assured of the safety of their families, recognize the economic benefits and see the meticulous planning for the least disruption of their lives, they tend to be supportive of a prison in their community. A pervasive public information effort, the support of local opinion leaders and community forums have been the most effective tools to engage publics and gain support.

Resources: Opinion leaders will be critical resources in this public information and persuasion campaign, particularly local officials, school administrators and local media. The community's need for economic growth and stability, as well as jobs, can be considered a resource. City hall, the high school and the local recreation center are established community meeting places that can be used for community forums. An online newspaper and a local radio station will also be resources for information dissemination, as well as social media, particularly those also used by local government and police to keep citizens informed.

SWOT analysis:

Strengths	Weaknesses
1. Economic benefits	1. Construction inconvenience
2. Penal system safety record	2. Daily visibility of negative
3. Support of local leaders	element

Opportunities	Threats
1. Jobs	1. Safety
2. Local media and	2. Family values
social media	3. Legal opposition

SITUATION ANALYSIS

The announcement that the state is planning to construct a new prison facility in Green Valley has been met with initial resistance. While residents are generally supportive of the state's penal system, which has an excellent record of safety and competence, they fear the introduction of the criminal element into their peaceful community. Safety has been the overriding concern of residents, overshadowing the economic benefits that would come from the construction and maintenance of this facility. This project would bring in several million dollars annually and 750 jobs to this economically struggling community. It would boost the business and professional communities, improve medical facilities, strengthen funding for education and provide an economic injection that would significantly improve the quality of life for the vast majority of area residents. A solid 80% of residents have expressed concerns over safety, but only 35% could name a potential economic benefit. Fewer than 20% thought the new facility would improve other local services like education and health care. Nearly three-quarters of residents have a favorable opinion of the State Corrections Department, but only one-quarter indicate that they would be fully supportive of a prison in Green Valley. While only 30% are outright opposed to locating the prison here, 45% have significant concerns. Should those concerns not be alleviated, the opposition could potentially mobilize a legal challenge to the project.

The primary challenge seems to be public awareness and education. Other efforts have shown that giving the community a voice in the process and being completely transparent and open about plans and operation have improved community support, especially given the economic benefits. Safety will always be an issue, but the reputation and safety record of the Department of Corrections as well as procedures in place to ensure safety can assure the community that there is low risk associated with housing a prison in the community. Local opinion leaders and local media are well-informed on relevant issues and are supportive. But if opposition can't be converted to support, Green Valley will likely lose the opportunity to improve the standard of living for residents by locating the prison there.

CORE PROBLEM/OPPORTUNITY

Raise public awareness of safety and the benefits of the new prison to gain public support and neutralize opposition so that the Green Valley prison project can go forward without costly delay or legal opposition.

GOAL

To gain public support for the new prison and neutralize opposition to it.

OBJECTIVES

1. Raise awareness of the proposed prison's benefits to the local economy from 35% to 65% within six months, measured by a contracted survey of the community.
2. Raise awareness of the proposed prison's benefits to community services from 20% to 50% within six months and to 75% within 12 months measured by contracted surveys of the community.
3. Generate 6,000 unique visits to the campaign website within six months, measured by digital website analytics.
4. Reduce public concern about safety issues related to the proposed prison from 80% to 50% within six months and to 40% within 12 months, measured by contracted surveys of the community.
5. Increase public support for the proposed prison from 25% who are fully supportive of a prison to 45% who are fully supportive within six months and to 65% within 12 months, measured by contracted surveys of the community.

KEY PUBLICS AND PRIMARY MESSAGES

1. *Town and community leaders.* This public includes Green Valley's elected and public safety officials, as well as leaders of community, religious and educational organizations. These individuals have earned the trust and respect of their community. They are opinion leaders to other publics. They are familiar with the Department of Corrections, understand pros and cons of the prison issue, and are generally supportive of building the prison in Green Valley.

   Self-interests: welfare of Green Valley economy, welfare of Green Valley residents, their professional reputations.

   Opinion leaders: employers, patrons, residents, state and county government officials.

   Channels: personal phone numbers and email addresses, state and county government departments, local newspaper and radio.

   Primary Messages:
   1. The prison will inject millions of dollars into Green Valley's economy every year. It will attract new businesses to the area, enable local businesses to grow and reduce unemployment and underemployment without raising taxes.
   2. Locating the prison in Green Valley will also result in improved health care facilities, additional funding for schools and community infrastructure like parks and roads, and even new housing development.
   3. The safety of the community is a number one priority and has never been compromised in any other prison location in the state.
   4. Your voice and your influence in this process is valued. Participate in our community meetings to let Green Valley residents know what you think about the proposed prison and its benefits to the community.

2. ***Prison neighbors.*** This public includes Green Valley residents who live in a three-mile radius around the planned prison site. Due to the location of the prison on the edge of town, the three-mile radius includes rural farm families whose community roots go back for generations and blue-collar families with young children who are newer to Green Valley. This group is concerned that the construction and operation of the prison will disrupt their daily lives. Many are currently opposed to the prison being built in their backyard. This group is typically conservative and supports law enforcement but is unaware of the proposed prison's safety measures. However, this public would benefit significantly from the influx of funding for education, medical facilities and city infrastructure that would accompany the construction of the prison.

   Self-interests: safety, welfare of their children, economic security, quality of life, community.

   Opinion leaders: family, neighbors, community leaders, town officials.

   Channels: house-to-house information dissemination, opinion leaders, word-of-mouth, local newspaper and radio, and local government digital media.

   Primary Messages:
   1. The construction and operation of the prison will create jobs in Green Valley, giving the community a multimillion dollar economic boost every year.
   2. The operation of the prison will generate funding that will improve Green Valley's education system, health care options and town infrastructure without raising taxes.
   3. The proposed prison site was selected because of the large amount of green space buffering it from the surrounding neighborhoods. The prison construction and operation plan will maximize safety and minimize disruptions.
   4. Your voice in this process is valued. We want to hear your opinions and concerns about the proposed prison. Participate in one of our neighborhood meetings to let us know what's on your mind.

3. ***Prison fence-sitters.*** This public includes working-age adults and their families who live outside the three-mile radius around the proposed prison site. This group includes individuals living in the town and in the surrounding area. Individuals in this group tend to be younger, with a higher proportion between the ages of 20 and 49. Nearly 80% of the individuals in this group are married with an average household size of three people. About 83% are homeowners. Residents in this group have mixed feelings about the new prison. On the one hand, they have significant concerns that the prison will make their community unsafe. However, because many live at a distance from the proposed prison site, these concerns may be easily alleviated. On the other hand, they are open to the new job opportunities, economic growth and improved local services that would result from the construction and operation of the prison. However, most individuals in this group are unaware of the economic benefits of the prison and the positive impact the prison could have on local services like education and health care.

   Self-interests: safety, family, economic security, job growth, community.

   Opinion leaders: family, business owners, community leaders, religious leaders, town officials.

Channels: opinion leaders, community meeting places, local newspaper and radio, local government digital media and social media, and word-of-mouth.

Primary Messages:

1. The construction and operation of the prison will create jobs in Green Valley, giving the community a multimillion dollar economic boost every year.
2. The operation of the prison will generate funding that will improve Green Valley's education system, health care options and town infrastructure without raising your taxes.
3. The State Department of Corrections will be holding community gatherings to share details with you about the location, plans, construction and safety measures of the proposed prison.
4. Your voice in this process is valued. We want to hear what you think about the proposed prison. Participate in one of our community gatherings to let us know what's on your mind.

4. **Local business owners.** Most Green Valley residents work close to home. While a significant number of Green Valley residents are self-employed farmers or work in support of the farming industry, many are employed by local businesses that provide jobs in administrative support, food service, retail sales and transportation. Demographics of this public are diverse with ages ranging from 25 to 65 years. Business owners in Green Valley are hard working entrepreneurs who are committed to their businesses and invested in the success of the community. Many are members of the Green Valley Area Chamber of Commerce and participate in local chapters of community service organizations including Kiwanis and Rotary. This group is cautiously optimistic about the prison because of its potential economic benefits, but it is concerned about the safety of their business investments and the overall safety of the community. Additionally, some local business owners may be concerned about new businesses moving into Green Valley if the prison is built. The influx of new business and workers connected with the prison could change the dynamics of the local economy. But, other local business owners may see the prison as an opportunity to attract new customers and clients, particularly those associated with the prison. Individuals in this group can be opinion leaders for their employees and customers/clients.

Self-interests: economic stability and growth, wellbeing of employees, community development, personal success and achievement.

Opinion leaders: city leaders, Chamber and trade association leaders, industry leaders.

Channels: Chamber of Commerce, community service organizations, local government email and digital channels, opinion leaders, local newspaper and radio.

Primary Messages:

1. The prison will inject millions of dollars into Green Valley's economy every year. It will expand your customer base, enable your business to grow and allow you to hire more workers from the community.

2. The State Department of Corrections will be holding meetings with local business leaders to share details with you about the location, plans, construction and safety measures of the proposed prison, and the infrastructural improvements that will accompany the project.

3. We want to hear what you think about the proposed prison. Participate in one of our local business leader meetings to let us know what's on your mind.

BIG IDEA

The big idea is to take residents on a virtual tour of a reimagined Green Valley five years in the future.

Big idea strategy: The virtual tour will allow Green Valley residents to imagine how their community will benefit from building a prison. The tour will take residents through the proposed prison where they will learn about prison operations and safety measures. It will also take them through the community where they will see how upgraded services, as well as new business and jobs, have improved the quality of life. It will demonstrate the improved school and health care facilities, and upgraded infrastructure (like parks and roads) that the influx of tax dollars will provide. The tours will frame the building of the prison as a "rebirth" story for Green Valley that will appeal to residents and the local media.

Visual representation: A video and stylized map that "imagines" the economic and local service benefits to Green Valley if the prison is built. The map should have a focus on better services closer to home, and include a health care facility, schools, parks, streets and sidewalks in neighborhoods, and other such amenities either missing or in need of upgrade.

Slogan: Imagine Green Valley, www.imagineGreenValley.info, #ImagineGreenValley

STRATEGIES AND TACTICS

1. *Town and community leaders*

    Strategy one: Convince city and community leaders to advocate for building the prison because of the improvements it will bring to the community through interpersonal communication.

    Tactics:

    - In-person visits with town and community leaders to talk to them about the benefits of building the prison in Green Valley.
    - Work with town and community leaders to form a citizen advocacy group that would help disseminate information door-to-door and participate in in-person meetings with residents.
    - Capture statements in writing and on video of these opinion leaders expressing their support for the prison and their confidence that the prison will improve the quality of life in the community.
        - Use these statements on the campaign website www.imagine-GreenValley.info and in the virtual tour.

- Work with town officials to share these opinion leader statements, along with information about upcoming meetings and a link to the campaign website, on their social media platforms.
- Work with Chamber of Commerce, Kiwanis and Rotary club leaders to share these opinion leader statements, along with information about upcoming meetings and a link to the campaign website, on their social media platforms.

2. ***Prison neighbors***

Strategy one: Raise awareness among prison neighbors of the proposed prison's improvements to local services and benefits to the local economy through information dissemination by local opinion leaders and the citizen advocacy group.

Tactics:

- Launch Imagine Green Valley website at www.imagineGreenValley. info, which uses sector opinion leaders and includes:
  - Landing page with an interactive version of the campaign's Imagine Green Valley map.
  - Page about the economic benefits of building the prison.
  - Page about the education benefits of building the prison.
  - Page about the health care benefits of building the prison.
  - Page about the infrastructure benefits of building the prison.
  - Page about the location, plans, timeline, construction and operation of the prison.
  - Page about the safety procedures that will be implemented at the new prison.
  - Page with news about upcoming meetings and events.
  - Page with news coverage about the proposed prison.
  - Moderated community forum that allows residents to make comments and ask questions about the proposed prison and moderators to respond to comments and questions.
  - FAQs.
- In-person visits to each household in the three-mile radius by members of the citizen advocacy group to disseminate pamphlets, answer questions and invite them to a neighborhood meeting held in a local school providing a visual of how schools would benefit.
  - Pamphlet that helps the residents imagine how the prison will improve the local economy providing jobs and increasing funding for needed community services like education, health care and infrastructure.
  - Pamphlet outlining the reasons for the proposed site of the prison, which was chosen because of significant green space separation from the surrounding neighborhoods. The pamphlet will also describe how the construction plan will minimize disruptions and the operation plan will maximize safety.
  - Each pamphlet will direct readers to the campaign website www. imagineGreenValley.info and other social media resources.

Strategy two: Reduce concern among prison neighbors about safety issues related to the proposed prison and assure them their voice is heard through ongoing opinion surveys, in-person meetings and digital resources.

Tactics:

- Hold a series of meetings near the prison site for residents living in the three-mile radius.
  - Use trade show-style informational materials and displays to educate them about the location, plans, timelines, construction, operation and safety procedures of the proposed prison. Information will also include statistics about prisons that were introduced in other communities in the state.
    - Posters
    - Brochures
    - Flyers
    - Maps
    - Videos or cameos from social media sites of town, police/safety services, Chamber and business leaders
  - Virtual tour of Green Valley five years into the future featuring imagined improvements in schools, health care facilities, economic opportunities, infrastructure like parks, roads and sidewalks.
  - Invite public discussion and comment. Allow residents to weigh the pros and cons of the proposed prison.
    - Allow residents to ask questions of the citizen advocacy group members.
    - Capture resident comments through comment cards and online comment submission through the campaign website: www.imagineGreenValley.info.
- Ongoing community opinion surveys measuring level of awareness and understanding of disseminated material and messages (a service-learning project for local high school students).

3. *Prison fence-sitters*

Strategy one: Raise awareness among prison fence-sitters of the proposed prison's improvements to local services and benefits to the local economy through local news media.

Tactics:

- Pitch stories about the benefits of building the prison to local media outlets. Include interview ideas for city and community leaders who are supportive. Story angles include:
  - The Department of Corrections's track record for safety.
  - The economic benefit that prisons have brought to other communities in the state.
  - The impact that building the prison will have on the local economy, unemployment and recession.
  - The types of new businesses that the prison would draw to the area.
  - The number and types of new jobs that would accompany the construction and operation of the prison.

- ○ The impact of building the prison on local health care services.
- ○ The impact of building the prison on local education.
- ○ The impact of building the prison on local infrastructure.
- ○ Invitation for community input at community meetings, through comment cards and through the website.
- Work with members of the citizen advocacy group to pitch and write op-eds for the local paper.
- Work with members of the citizen advocacy group to appear as guests on the local news radio program.
- Invite local media to attend community meetings with residents.

Strategy two: Raise awareness among prison fence-sitters of the proposed prison's improvements to local services and benefits to the local economy through information distributed by community organizations.
  Tactics:
- Work with the local school district to send home flyers to parents of schoolchildren about the benefits of the proposed prison for education in the area, as well as the dates, times and locations of community meetings to be held in Green Valley.
  - ○ Include endorsements from supportive educational leaders on the citizen advocacy group.
  - ○ The flyer will direct readers to the campaign website www.imagineGreenValley.info and other supportive social media.
- Work with local health care providers to disseminate flyers to their patients about the benefits of the proposed prison for health care in the area, as well as the dates, times and locations of community meetings to be held in Green Valley.
  - ○ Include endorsements from supportive health care leaders on the citizen advocacy group.
  - ○ The flyer will direct readers to the campaign website www.imagineGreenValley.info and other supportive social media.
- Work with the local recreation center to disseminate flyers to their patrons about the benefits of the proposed prison for parks, recreation and other infrastructure improvements in the area, as well as the dates, times and locations of community meetings to be held in Green Valley.
  - ○ Include endorsements from supportive community leaders on the citizen advocacy group.
  - ○ The flyer will direct readers to the campaign website www.imagineGreenValley.info and other supportive social media.
- Work with Green Valley religious leaders to disseminate flyers to their congregations about the social service improvements that would come with building the prison, as well as the dates, times and locations of community meetings to be held in Green Valley.
  - ○ Include endorsements from supportive religious leaders on the citizen advocacy group.
  - ○ The flyer will direct readers to the campaign website www.imagineGreenValley.info and other supportive social media.

- Work with Green Valley municipal leaders to disseminate information in town print and digital media about the benefits of the proposed prison for public safety services and infrastructure, as well as the dates, times and locations of community meetings to be held in Green Valley.
  - Include endorsements from supportive municipal leaders on the citizen advocacy group.
  - The flyer will direct readers to the campaign website www.imagineGreenValley.info and other supportive social media.

Strategy three: Reduce concern among prison fence-sitters about safety issues related to the proposed prison and ensure them their voice is heard through ongoing opinion surveys and in-person meetings held in local schools.
  Tactics:
- Hold a series of meetings throughout the Green Valley community for residents who live outside a three-mile radius around the proposed prison site.
  - Use trade show-style informational materials and displays to educate them about the location, plans, timelines, construction, operation and safety procedures of the proposed prison. Information will also include statistics about prisons that were introduced in other communities in the state.
    - Posters
    - Brochures
    - Flyers
    - Maps
    - Videos or cameos from social media sites of city, police/safety services, Chamber and business leaders
  - Virtual tour of Green Valley five years into the future featuring imagined improvements in schools, health care facilities, economic opportunities, infrastructure like parks, roads and sidewalks.
  - Invite public discussion and comment. Allow residents to weigh the pros and cons of the proposed prison.
    - Allow residents to ask questions of the citizen advocacy group members.
    - Capture resident comments through comment cards and online comment submission through the campaign website: www.imagineGreenValley.info.
- Ongoing community opinion surveys measuring level of awareness and understanding of disseminated material and messages (a service-learning project for local high school students).

4. *Local business owners*
Strategy one: Raise awareness among local business owners of the proposed prison's improvements to local services and benefits to the local economy through the Chamber of Commerce and Kiwanis and Rotary clubs.

Tactics:

- Work with the Chamber of Commerce and the Kiwanis and Rotary clubs to disseminate flyers about the benefits of the proposed prison.
  - Include endorsements from supportive business owners and community leaders on the citizen advocacy group.
  - The flyer will direct readers to the campaign website www.imagineGreenValley.info.
- Work with the Chamber of Commerce and the Kiwanis and Rotary clubs to create content for their digital communications channels (websites, emails and social media) about the benefits of the proposed prison for the local economy. The content will direct people to the campaign website www.imagineGreenValley.info.
- Schedule a time to make a presentation to the Chamber of Commerce and Kiwanis and Rotary club members.
  - Use trade show-style informational materials and displays to educate them about the location, plans, timelines, construction, operation and safety procedures of the proposed prison. Information will also include statistics about prisons that were introduced in other communities in the state.
    - Posters
    - Brochures
    - Flyers
    - Maps
    - Videos or cameos from social media sites of city, police/safety services, Chamber and business leaders
    - Provide enough copies of these materials for the business owners to share with their employees
  - Video tour of Green Valley five years into the future featuring imagined improvements in schools, health care facilities, economic opportunities, infrastructure like parks, roads and sidewalks.
  - Invite public discussion and comment. Allow business owners to weigh the pros and cons of the proposed prison.
    - Capture comments through comment cards and online comment submission through the campaign website: www.imagineGreenValley.info.

CALENDAR AND BUDGET

For this sample strategic plan, we have only included a six-month calendar and a budget for one public. A complete strategic plan for this scenario would include a 12-month calendar and a budget for all four publics.

CALENDAR

		Month:	1	2	3	4	5	6
		Week:	1 2 3 4	1 2 3 4	1 2 3 4	1 2 3 4	1 2 3 4	1 2 3 4
Key Public: Prison fence-sitters								
Strategy One: Raise awareness of improvements through local news media								
Tactics:	Pitch stories to local media outlets		X ------	------	------	------	------	------ X
	Op-eds			X ------	------	------	------	------ X
	Local radio guests			X ------	------	------	------	------ X
	Invite media to community meetings				X ------	------	------	------ X
Strategy Two: Raise awareness of improvements through information distributed by community organizations.								
Tactics:	School district flyers		X ------ ------ X					
	Health care provider flyers		X ------ ------ X					
	Recreation center flyers		X ------ ------ X					
	Church congregation flyers		X ------ ------ X					
	Town digital and social media		X ------	------	------	------	------	------ X
Strategy Three: Reduce concern among prison fence-sitters about safety issues related to the proposed prison and ensure them their voice is heard through ongoing opinion surveys and in-person meetings held in local schools.								
Tactics	Community meetings				X ------	------	------	------ X
	Ongoing surveys				X ------	------	------	------ X

BUDGET

		Detail	Quantity	Per item cost	Total projected	Sponsored credit	Actual projected
Key Public: Prison fence-sitters							
Strategy One: Raise awareness of improvements through local news media							
Tactics:	Pitch stories to local media outlets	Emails and phone calls to local journalists		$0.00	$0.00	$0.00	$0.00
	Op-eds	Emails and phone calls to local journalists		$0.00	$0.00	$0.00	$0.00
	Local radio guests	Emails and phone calls to local journalists		$0.00	$0.00	$0.00	$0.00
	Invite media to community meetings	Emails and phone calls to local journalists		$0.00	$0.00	$0.00	$0.00
	Strategy subtotal			$0.00	$0.00	$0.00	$0.00

BUDGET contd.

	Detail	Quantity	Per item cost	Total projected	Sponsored credit	Actual projected
Strategy Two: Raise awareness of improvements through information distributed by community organizations.						
Tactics: School district flyers	Design and printing	8,000	$0.03	$240.00	$0.00	$240.00
Health care provider flyers	Design and printing	4,000	$0.03	$120.00	$0.00	$120.00
Recreation center flyers	Design and printing	6,000	$0.03	$180.00	$0.00	$180.00
Church congregation flyers	Design and printing	8,000	$0.03	$240.00	$0.00	$240.00
Town digital and social media			$0.00	$0.00	$0.00	$0.00
Strategy subtotal				$780.00	$0.00	$780.00
Strategy Three: Reduce concern among prison fence-sitters about safety issues related to the proposed prison and ensure them their voice is heard through ongoing opinion surveys and in-person meetings held in local schools.						
Tactics Community meeting printed materials and displays	Design and printing	Shared by 3 publics	$1,000/3	$333.00	$0.00	$333.00
Community meeting virtual tour	Filming and production	Shared by all publics	$8,400.00/4	$2,100.00	$0.00	$2,100.00
Ongoing survey (participant incentives)	Contracted/ student service-learning	Shared w/prison neighbors	$1,500 x 75%	$1,125.00	$0.00	$1,125.00
Strategy subtotal				$3,558.00	$0.00	$3,558.00
Public total				$4,338.00	$0.00	$4,338.00

EVALUATION CRITERIA AND MEASUREMENT TOOLS

Objective one: Raise awareness of the proposed prison's benefits to the local economy from 35% to 65% within six months (30 percentage point increase).

Criterion (outcome):

Sixty-five percent of Green Valley residents will be able to name at least one economic benefit of building the prison six months after the campaign begins.

Tool:

Ongoing community surveys replicating the portion of the initial survey related to the prison's benefits to the local economy using the six months data set to determine if the objective was met.

Objective two: Raise awareness of the proposed prison's benefits to community services from 20% to 50% within six months (30 percentage point increase) and to 75% within 12 months (55 percentage point increase).

Criterion (outcome):

Fifty percent of Green Valley residents will agree that a new prison facility would improve local services like education and health care six months after the campaign begins and 75% will agree at 12 months.

Tool:

Ongoing community surveys replicating the portion of the initial survey related to the prison's benefits to local services using the six months and 12 months data sets to determine if the objective was met.

Objective three: Generate 6,000 unique visits to the campaign website within six months.

Criterion (outtake):

The campaign website will have had 6,000 unique user visits (presumably one visit for every adult resident in the Green Valley area) six months after the campaign begins.

Tool:

Use Google Analytics to track the number of unique visitors to the campaign website during the first six months of the campaign.

Objective four: Reduce public concern about safety issues related to the proposed prison from 80% to 50% within six months (30 percentage point decrease) and to 40% within 12 months (40 percentage point decrease that is equivalent to a 50% improvement).

Criterion (outcome):

Only 50% of Green Valley residents will still feel concerned over safety issues resulting from the proposed prison six months after the campaign begins and only 40% at 12 months.

Tool:

Ongoing community surveys replicating the portion of the initial survey related to concerns about safety using the six months data set to measure progress toward the objective and the 12 months data set to determine if the objective was met.

Objective five: Increase public support for the proposed prison from 25% who are fully supportive of a prison to 45% who are fully supportive within six months and to 65% within 12 months (40 percentage point increase more than doubling support).

Criterion (impact):

Fifty-five percent of Green Valley will be fully supportive of a prison within six months and 65% will be supportive within one year after the campaign begins.

Tool:

Ongoing community surveys replicating the portion of the initial survey related to support for the prison using the six months data set to measure progress toward the objective and the 12 months data set to determine if the objective was met.

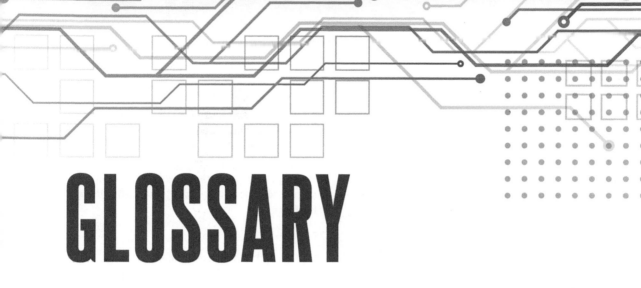

GLOSSARY

A

AMPLIFY
To increase the volume or intensity of something to greatly broaden its reach.

ATTITUDES
Collections of beliefs organized around an issue or event that predispose behavior.

AUTHENTICITY
Aligning an organization's behavior and communication with core values that are important to its key publics.

B

BELIEFS
Inferences we make about ourselves and the world around us.

BENCHMARK
A standard or point of reference against which communications outcomes may be compared or assessed.

BIG IDEA
A creative idea or theme on which a campaign is built.

BIG IDEA STRATEGY
A story hook or archetype.

BRAINSTORMING
A structured group creative exercise to generate as many ideas as possible in a specified amount of time.

C

CHANNEL
The conduit or medium through which messages are sent to a specific public to accomplish a specific purpose.

CONFIDENCE LEVEL
The percentage of certainty that the results of a survey would be the same if replicated with a different sample.

CONTROLLED CHANNELS
You dictate the content, timing and placement or distribution of messages but messages lose credibility.

CONVERSION
When a user completes a desired action, usually a purchase.

CPA (COST PER ACTION)
The cost of converting a website or social media user into a customer.

CPC (COST PER CLICK)
The cost of getting a person to click on your content.

CPM (COST PER MILLE OR THOUSAND)
The cost of generating 1,000 impressions of your content.

CREATIVITY
The process of looking outside ourselves and our routine to discover new ideas and innovative solutions.

CRISIS MANAGEMENT
The process of anticipating and preparing to mediate problems that could affect an organization's environment and success.

D

DEMOGRAPHIC DATA
Information used to segment publics according to tangible characteristics such as age, gender and socioeconomic status.

DIFFUSION OF INNOVATIONS
The process by which a new technology or idea is adopted by a society.

DISINFORMATION
Information that is intentionally inaccurate or misleading.

DIVERSITY
Appreciating differences in culture, gender, race, background, lifestyles and experience, allowing them to strengthen us rather than divide us.

E

EARNED MEDIA
Communications channels owned by a third party who can be persuaded to tell your organization's story using their own resources.

EMOTIONAL APPEAL
Creating a positive or negative feeling leading to a behavioral response (pathos).

ENGAGEMENT
An umbrella term for actions that reflect and measure audience interaction with your content.

ESG PERFORMANCE
How well an organization takes into account social and ecological responsibilities while doing business.

ETHICAL CODES
Written and formalized standards of behavior used as guidelines for decision-making.

ETHICS
Personal and professional value systems and standards that underlie decisions and behavior.

EVALUATION
Comparison of measurement data against a standard or criterion.

EVALUATION CRITERIA
Metrics or standards set to measure success.

EVALUATIVE RESEARCH
Research used to determine the effectiveness of campaign implementation.

EXTERNAL ENVIRONMENT
Economic, political and social developments that occur outside an organization but have an influence on it. The source of opportunities, challenges and risks.

F

FOCUS GROUP RESEARCH
Moderator-led discussions with fewer than 15 participants providing in-depth information on attitudes and behaviors.

FORMAL RESEARCH
Data gathering structured according to accepted rules of research.

FORMATIVE RESEARCH
Research used as a foundation for campaign planning.

FRAME OF REFERENCE
The collective influence of experiences, knowledge, culture and environment that forms our perceptual screen.

FRAMING
Designing a message to influence how an issue or event is perceived.

  # G

GATEKEEPER
A reporter, editor or social media influencer who controls the flow of information that appears on their media channel.

GEN X
Generation born between 1960 and 1980.

GEN Y
Generation born between 1980 and 1999, also called millennials.

GEN Z
Generation born in 2000 and after.

GOAL
The result or desired outcome that solves a problem, takes advantage of an opportunity or meets a challenge.

  # H

HASHTAG
A word or short phrase preceded by a hash (#) used to search for and group together related posts on social media.

HYPERCONNECTED
When people are connected to organizations and society through multiple channels such as email, phone, social media and instant messaging.

 # I

IDEATION
The formation of ideas or concepts.

IMPACT OBJECTIVES
Objectives that focus on the communications campaign's contribution to the organization or society at large.

INFORMAL RESEARCH
Less-structured exploratory information gathering.

INTEGRATED MARKETING COMMUNICATION
The process of unifying communication across channels and publics to achieve an organization's goals.

INTERACTIVITY
The degree to which the channel or tactic provides interaction between the sender of the message and the receiver.

INTERMEDIATE BEHAVIORS
Actions that build relationships with the organization and prepare publics for the ultimate desired behavior.

INTERNAL ENVIRONMENT
Events or conditions inside an organization that influence how it operates. Factors that influence internal environment can be categorized as strengths or weaknesses.

INTERVENING PUBLIC
An influential individual or small group of people used to carry a message to a key public.

ISSUES
Problems or disputes that arise between organizations and publics. Issues can evolve over time changing from emergent to current to crisis to dormant.

ISSUE MANAGEMENT
A long-term approach to identifying and resolving issues before they become problems or crises.

K

KEY PUBLIC
Segmented group of people whose support and cooperation is essential to the long-term survival of an organization or the short-term accomplishment of specific objectives.

KPI (KEY PERFORMANCE INDICATOR)
An important measure tied to a campaign or social media objective and used to evaluate its success.

L

LOGICAL APPEAL
A claim supported by credible evidence (logos).

M

MARGIN OF ERROR
Also known as sampling error, the inherent possible percentage variation of sample data from the whole population.

MEASUREMENT
What can be observed or counted in a campaign.

MEASUREMENT TOOL
Method used to gather data needed to assess whether evaluation criteria were met.

MEDIA RELATIONS
The function of building relationships with reporters, editors and social media influencers so that your information becomes more trusted and relevant.

MENTAL SHORTCUTS
Intuitive decisions that do not rely on conscious cognitive processing.

MISINFORMATION
Information that is unintentionally inaccurate or misleading.

N

NEWSJACKING
Injecting your brand or organization into the conversation on a trending news story.

NONSAMPLING ERROR
Mistakes made in designing and implementing a questionnaire that may include definitional differences, misunderstandings and misrepresentations as well as coding errors and/or problems that negatively influence response rates.

O

OBJECTIVES
Specific, measurable statements of what needs to be accomplished to reach the goal.

OPINION LEADER
A trusted individual to whom one turns for advice because of their greater knowledge or experience regarding a specific topic.

OUTCOME OBJECTIVES
Objectives that focus on the overall effect of a communications campaign on key publics.

OUTPUT OBJECTIVES
Objectives that focus on the dissemination of information and messages to key publics.

OUTTAKE OBJECTIVES
Objectives that focus on key publics' response or reaction to your messages.

OWNED MEDIA
Communications channels that are created and maintained by an organization.

P

PAID MEDIA
Communications channels owned by a third party who is willing to sell time or space.

PARTNERSHIP
A mutually beneficial short- or long-term cooperative relationship to reach common goals.

PAY FOR PLAY
Compensating media for content placement, product reviews, editorial mentions or other promotion.

PERSUASION
Disseminating information to appeal for a change in attitudes, opinions and/or behavior.

PERSUASIVE APPEAL
Appeal to self-interest to enhance persuasion and motivate behavior. Most likely involves ethos, pathos and logos.

PESO MODEL
A categorization of media channels into paid, earned, shared and owned.

PINBOARD
Pages on Pinterest where users can save individual pins organized by a central topic or theme.

PLANNING
The process of using research to chart the step-by-step course to solve a problem, take advantage of an opportunity or meet a challenge.

PPC (PAY PER CLICK)
Paying for social media advertising based on each time a user clicks on ad content.

PRIMARY MESSAGES
Sound-bite statements that encompass what you need the public to do and an appeal to the public's self-interest to act.

PRIMARY RESEARCH
Firsthand information gathered specifically for your current purpose.

PRIMING
Increasing the salience of a public issue through strategically timed media coverage.

PROFESSIONAL COURTESY
Exhibiting good manners by being thoughtful and considerate of others.

PROFESSIONALISM
Characteristics and behavior befitting a professional.

PSYCHOGRAPHIC DATA
Information used to segment publics according to values, attitudes, lifestyles and decision-making processes.

PUBLIC
A specific group of people who share a common interest.

PUBLIC OPINION
What most people in a particular public express about an issue that affects them.

PUBLIC RELATIONS
Strategically managing communication to build relationships and influence behavior.

 Q

QUALITATIVE RESEARCH
Using research methods that provide deeper insight into attitudes and motivations but don't provide statistical significance.

QUANTITATIVE RESEARCH
Using research methods that yield reliable statistical data.

 R

REACH
The total number of people who see your content.

RELATIONSHIP BUILDING
A return to the roots of human communication and persuasion that focuses on personal trust and mutual cooperation.

RESEARCH
Gathering and using information to clarify an issue and solve a problem.

RESEARCH-BASED
When decision-making is rooted in the acquisition, interpretation and application of relevant facts.

ROI (RETURN ON INVESTMENT)
Profit earned on an investment divided by the cost of that investment.

S

SAMPLING ERROR
Measured as margin of error, it indicates the possible percentage variation of the sample data from the whole population.

SCHEDULING
Finding the premier moment in time for a tactic to be used.

SECONDARY MESSAGES
Bulleted details that include facts, testimonials, examples and all other information or persuasive arguments that support a public's primary message.

SECONDARY RESEARCH
Information previously assimilated for other purposes that can be adapted for your needs.

SEGMENTATION
Defining and separating publics by demographics and psychographics to ensure more effective communication.

SELECTIVE EXPOSURE
The function of selecting the communications channels one chooses to pay attention to.

SELECTIVE PERCEPTION
The subconscious function of selecting from the millions of daily stimuli only those messages one chooses to perceive.

SELECTIVE RETENTION
The function of selecting from the stimuli perceived only those messages one chooses to retain.

SELF-INTEREST
The fundamental motivation for an individual's behavior.

SEQUENCING
Determining the optimal ordering of tactics over time.

SHARED MEDIA
Interactive, open access communications channels owned and operated by a media technology company.

SLOGAN
A short, memorable phrase linked to primary messages.

SMS (SHORT MESSAGE/ MESSAGING SERVICE)
Sending short text messages from one cell phone to another or from a computer to a cell phone.

SOCIAL MEDIA
A collective of online communications channels that enables users to create and share content and participate in community-based input, interaction and collaboration.

SOURCE CREDIBILITY
An appeal using an expert or trustworthy source (ethos).

STAKEHOLDER
A broad group of individuals that has a vested interest, or "stake," in an organization.

STRATEGIC COMMUNICATIONS PLANNING
An approach to communications planning that focuses actions on the accomplishment of organizational goals.

STRATEGIC FUNCTION
One that contributes significantly to the accomplishment of an organization's mission and goals.

STRATEGIC MANAGEMENT
The process of evaluating all proposed actions by focusing on organizational goals, usually defined in short-term contributions to the bottom line.

STRATEGIES
Public-specific approaches specifying the channel to send the messages to achieve objectives.

STRATEGY BRIEF
An analytical tool that infuses strategic planning into the creation of effective tactics.

SUBJECTIVE NORMS
Perceived behavioral expectations.

SWOT ANALYSIS
A structured analytical tool set up in a 2-by-2 matrix that examines strengths, weaknesses, opportunities and threats.

 # T

TACTICS
Strategy-specific communications products that carry the message to key publics.

TRACKING PIXEL
A snippet of code embedded in a website's HTML that captures and tracks user data.

TRANSPARENCY
Disclosing truthful information about an organization that holds the organization accountable and helps publics make decisions.

TRIGGERING EVENT
An event that transforms readiness to act into actual behavior.

TRUST
An emotional judgment of one's credibility and performance on issues of importance.

TWO-WAY SYMMETRICAL COMMUNICATION
A dialogue between organizations and publics that maintains mutually beneficial relationships.

 # U

UNCONTROLLED CHANNELS
Someone else dictates the content, placement or timing of messages but messages gain credibility.

 # V

VALUES
Core beliefs or beliefs central to an individual's cognitive system.

VISUAL REPRESENTATION
A physical or digital example of a big idea.

W

WEB ANALYTICS
The measurement, collection, analysis and reporting of internet data for the purpose of understanding and optimizing web usage.

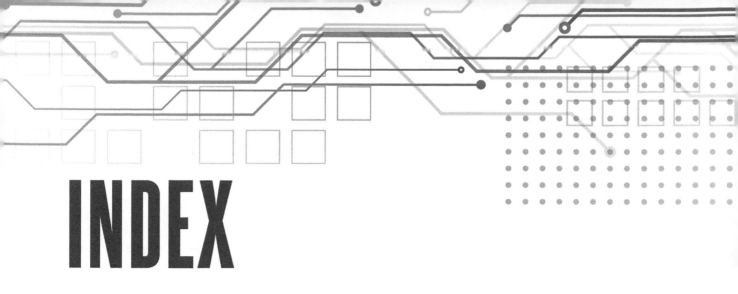

INDEX

S

W

Y

Z